17 75

ECONOMIC ANTHROPOLOGY

Topics and Theories

Monographs in Economic Anthropology, No. 1

Edited by
Sutti Ortiz

UNIVERSITY
PRESS OF
AMERICA

Society for Economic Anthropology

BRESCIA COLLEGE LIBRARY
OWENSBORO, KENTUCKY.
LANHAM • NEW YORK • LONDON

Library of Congress Cataloging in Publication Data
Main entry under title:

Economic anthropology.

(Monographs in economic anthropology; no. 1)
Papers originally presented in the spring of 1981 at
the first conference of the Society for Economic
Anthropology, held at Indiana University, Bloomington.
Includes bibliographies and index.
1. Economic anthropology—Congresses.   I. Ortiz,
Sutti, 1929—   . II. Society for Economic Anthro-
pology (U.S.) III. Series.
GN448.E27   1983   306'.3   83-10296
ISBN 0-8191-3321-3
ISBN 0-8191-3322-1 (pbk.)

Co-published by arrangement with the
Society for Economic Anthropology

Acknowledgements

The papers in this volume were originally presented in the spring of 1981 at the first conference of the Society for Economic Anthropology at Indiana University, Bloomington. The conference was attended by anthropologists, economists and political scientists, many of whom helped bring it into being. But members of the Society are particularly grateful to Professor Harold Schneider, who first conceived of the idea of the Society and brought us together to organize it. Stuart Plattner ensured the swift distribution of papers and, as a chairman, a congenial exchange of ideas. Thayer Scudder, Allan Hoben, Carol Smith, Stephen Gudeman, Sidney Mintz, Frank Cancian, John Bennett, Terrence Hopkins, Richard Salisbury, Gordon Appleby, Peter Hammond, Joyce Riegelhaupt, Peggy Barlett, Hugh Gladwin and Jane Schneider offered many helpful suggestions.

As editor of this book, I owe special thanks to the economists and anthropologists who agreed to explore issues relevant to each theme or approach discussed. The appreciation is shared by the other contributors to the volume, all of whom profited from specific comments about and discussion of the original conference papers. Sara Berry, Caroline Bledsoe, Frank Cancian, Scott Cook, Billie DeWalt, Donald Donham, Robert Drennan, Christina Gladwin, David Grove, Rhoda Halperin, Shinichiro Kurimoto, Henry Rutz, Thayer Scudder, Arnold Strickon and Lillian Trager were the scholars who contributed as commentators at the conference.

We are grateful to the National Science Foundation for having supported the research work of many of the contributors to this volume. The data gathered have served to elaborate the arguments here presented. Furthermore, the Foundation's generous help through Grant # DNS-8217368 has made possible the final preparations for the publication of this conference proceedings. Finally I would like to thank Joyce Martin for her diligence and advice with the problematic details of preparing a manuscript for a press and Sandra Siebenschuh and Diane Russell for their editorial help with some sections of this book.

CONTENTS

CONTENTS

INTRODUCTION

Sutti Ortiz

Scholars search in history for the conception and continuity of intellectual movements as justification for their present separate identities. They look for ancestors and ignore intellectual intermarriages to highlight congruency and purpose. But scholars in economic anthropology cannot hope to find a simple genesis nor an original intellectual community. Our ancestors are still-vivid figures, who only a century ago were beginning to examine the ways in which "primitive" and "backward" people organized their economic life. Their curiosity was inspired by their studies not just in anthropology but also in evolution, history, and economics. Thus the definition of the subject and modes of studying it were, from their very beginnings, shaped not only by the contrasting nature of the information they examined but also by the variety of intellectual links that each had with other disciplines. The subject was at first variously labeled "economic sociology" (Goodfellow, 1939), "primitive economy" (Firth, 1939) and "the economic life of primitive societies" (Herskovits, 1940). Only with the second edition of Herskovits's book did "economic anthropology" become the commonly accepted term.

Given the discipline's mottled origin, it is not surprising that despite its scant history, economic anthropology has redefined itself several times. Each definition has carried with it a certain set of assumptions about research goals, the theoretical centrality of relations and the significant boundaries of the field of inquiry. It thus seemed appropriate to divide the book into parts, four of which reflect major redefinitions of the field. Their sequence, however, does not mirror the intellectual history of the subject matter, a task briefly attempted in this introduction. I hope that by summarizing the limitations, inherent strengths, and controversies about the major schools of thought, this introduction will give the reader a sense of perspective about the field, and place the essays that follow in their historical and intellectual context.

* * *

vii

Initially scholars defined the economy not as a system but as an index of techniques of production, which determine communal surplus, the viability of certain population clusters, the likely types of political organization, the nature of the division of labor, the sizes of units of production, and the likely emergence of intergroup trade. During the thirties and forties, the social and political harnessing of material and natural resources remained the central theme in economic anthropology. For Steward, White, Forde, and other major thinkers of those years, men and societies had to adapt to ecological constraints; and these adaptations shaped the direction of cultural effort and social organization.

This early materialistic definition of economic anthropology has been rejected as simplistic. Scholars writing during the sixties and seventies enunciated a more elaborate, formal and complex homeostatic relation of man to environment. Though ecological and economic anthropology have now become separate fields of inquiry, they shared similar initial frameworks and assumptions; and the findings and theories of each remain central to the other. Indeed, ecological studies are as important to economic anthropology as are those of economists, historians, and archaeologists. Lees in Chapter VIII and Ortiz in the introduction to Part Three stress shared areas of concern and the usefulness of ecological theories in the study of adaptive strategies, the evolution of economic systems and the formulation of planning policies. Nevertheless, the relationship between ecologists and economists remains somewhat ambivalent, as readers will find in Chapter VII.

Initial discussions of technology per se gave way to a concern about how it was used and how it related to social needs. Malinowski, Firth and Goodfellow focused on the behavior of producing and consuming units, explaining and thus making them socially intelligible. Malinowski stressed their social significance; Firth and Goodfellow, on the other hand, considered the problematic nature of activities relating to the provision of goods for material and social welfare. They believed that scarcity, interdependence and uncertainty force producing and consuming units to resolve allocation problems through "rational" processes. Firth and Goodfellow, observing societal solutions to the allocation problem, attempted to reason how production and social constraints affect economic behavior. Part four of this book reviews this approach.

One year after the publication of Firth's and Goodfellow's books, Herskovits published (1940) a more ambitious treatise on the economy of primitive peoples. While recognizing the importance of social factors in defining goals and allocating resources, he felt that the economizing problem could best be studied within the existing frameworks of economic science. This stand encouraged the reexamination of economic principles in the context of nonmarket societies, as well as the explanation of economic events in terms of neoclassical economic theory. Much later LeClair and Schneider (1968, p. 8) were to describe this new phase of economic anthropology almost as though economic theory had been reborn in a cross-cultural setting.

Herskovits's efforts were soon to be challenged by Polanyi, who, mindful of the polemics between marginalists and institutionalists, was skeptical of the universal applicability of formal logical frameworks. He recognized the problematic nature of allocation, but regarded economizing as an empirical problem that may or may not be formalized, depending on the characteristics of the social environment in which economic agents operate. Formal "rational" economizing, he insisted, is only one of many possible organizational principles of an economy. Formal economizing prevails in societies with a considerable division of labor, where arrangements are impersonal and the market system mediates the flow of products and resources. In nonmarket societies, economic activities are best studied as part and parcel of institutional arrangements.

In Part One, contributors discuss the impact of Polanyi's redefinition of economic anthropology. Dalton and Köcke evaluate Polanyi's impact on other scholars, an influence reflected in the discussions about the evolution of marketing systems in Chapters III, IV and V. Neale and Mayhew help us understand the full significance of Polanyi's contribution by linking him to the intellectual tradition of institutional economists. They survey the literature of economists and anthropologists that bears on a joint concern--the sociology of economic activities and the impact of institutions on the evolution of economic systems. One hopes their efforts will encourage more anthropologists to be mindful of the contributions of colleagues in other disciplines.

The substantivist redefinition of economic anthropology, already clearly outlined by 1957, brought forth, as well, a redefinition of the economistic approach to the study of nonmarket systems. Eleven years after the publication of <u>Trade and Market in the Early Empires</u> (Polanyi, et al.), LeClair and Schneider (1968) reviewed the controversy. "The formalist counter-revolution," a section in their book, <u>Economic Anthropology</u>, included a number of essays defining the premises of this more structured logical approach. Two essays in the present volume refer to the research of formalist scholars. In Chapter IX, Bennett and Kanel contrast the goals and limitations of formalists with those of substantivists/behaviorists in the analysis of decisions. In Chapter X, Ortiz reviews some of the problems encountered in the attempt to formalize decision models, the various solutions offered and the use of some of these formal models by anthropologists. Formal analysis of macro processes has already been clearly outlined by Schneider in his book <u>Economic Man</u> (1979); the approach retains its intellectual vigor, while profiting from the cautionary debates.

The controversy helped to clarify hidden assumptions, to refocus and redefine the intent of research. However, it also led a growing group of young anthropologists to search for a less contentious approach. They wished both to do justice to the sociological tradition of their anthropology, and to construct hypotheses about systemic relations and economic processes. The sociological explanations of their mentors, rooted in Veblen, Weber, Mauss and Schumpeter, were not helpful to historically (rather than evolutionary) minded anthropologists. Their propositions, while insightful, were not structured enough to satisfy a growing interest in developmental causality. The writings of Nash, Firth, Epstein, Richards, and Belshaw, which were concerned with short-term dynamics, were regarded as not directly relevant.

Godelier was sympathetic to this new goal; in 1965 he suggested that economic anthropology should elucidate, historically, the dynamic laws of precapitalist systems with the aim of outlining sets of possible transformations. However, he regarded rationality as too problematic a concept to use for such analysis. Instead he focused on social, political and technical forces, arguing that maximization and self-gain are not the only causes of a relationship between producers and consumers. Since social, political, and technical forces generate modes of production and distribution, they should serve as the fundamental basis for the analysis of precapitalist systems.

In Part Two of this book Hart traces the relevant intellectual history of Marxism and the incorporation of Marxist ideas via structuralism into economic anthropology. This movement engendered a new approach sufficiently cogent and self-conscious to encourage Clammer (1978) to title his book <u>The New Economic Anthropology</u> despite the fact that, as he himself acknowledges, it does not yet "represent either a 'school' or a solution to what some people insist on seeing as the 'present crisis' in anthropology" (p. 17-18). While questioning the adequacy of the label "Marxist economic anthropology," Hart reviews the contributions of scholars who identify themselves with this tradition and the power of an eclectic approach derived from it. Smith's analysis of development and dependency in Chapter XI illustrates the breakthrough that can be gained through a synthesis of the ideas of Marx, anthropology and economics.

Whatever the fate of the synthesis--and not everyone shares Hart's and Clammer's optimism--this new direction offers some important insights, which other approaches tend to obscure. These include the heterogeneous character of systems and sectors as well as the interdependence of systems; the multifaceted nature of exploitative relations; the economic foundations of political processes; and the conflict of interest in the production process that vitiates the attainment of equilibrium and accounts for the unplanned nature of political and economic development processes. None of these insights is totally neglected by other approaches; indeed, they are discussed in Part One and Chapter XII of this book. But to the Marxists they are fundamental.

In recent years anthropologists have assumed the roles of theoreticians, consultants and agents of development. Their findings and experiences should

not be ignored. Not only have they challenged
existing theoretical assumptions, but they have also
pointed out that we can no longer afford the
complacent position that economic systems are passive
reactants to external agencies or are locked in their
socio-political or cultural matrix. It is for these
reasons that Part Five includes commentaries from
scholars interested in the study of the development
process. Smith's chapter is not only a major
contribution to the study of the transformation of
economic systems; it is also a warning to dependency
theorists that they must pay closer attention to
detailed regional research studies by anthropologists.
Bates urges anthropologists to become more conversant
with some of the issues and frameworks in the
development literature, so we can understand the
implications of some of our basic assumptions--for
example, the assumptions of rationality and
equilibrating relations. Involvement with the
development process has also raised some serious moral
and practical issues. "Development for whom?" is a
question increasingly asked. Bates and Salisbury, in
their respective chapters, urge us to face the moral
question, and provide us with some guidelines to do
so. Salisbury, furthermore, warns us of the hidden
biases in the evaluative tools used by government and
planning agencies. These biases can and must be
corrected.

* * *

A summary overview of the intellectual history of
economic anthropology shows a curious cyclical shift
in epistemologies. At times, we comprehend social
reality through introspection, formalizing the
insights as a set of logical premises. Decision
analysis (Chapter X) is a prototype of this
epistemology. At other times, we gain knowledge
through descriptive models that link units of
production to past and present sociopolitical
realities. Institutional analysis (Part One) is an
example of the second. A third, Marxist epistemology
(Part Two), formalizes this descriptive construct and
poses logical arguments about evolution and
articulation. The first approach focuses on the
allocation problem, the second on production and
circulation, and the third on flows of labor and
value. While decision analysis concentrates on
short-term dynamics, the second and third approaches
are historical. All are able to incorporate the

indeterminance of social events; but while the
individual, rationalistic approach describes that
indeterminance as an uncertainty that affects the
choice of strategies, the institutional and Marxist
approaches describe it as a set of possible
developments.

Theories about and studies of economic systems
differ also in the perspectives used to construct
hypotheses or analyze data. Some focus on producing
units and their allocative or exchanging behavior
(Part Four). Others (Parts One and Two) talk about
the performance of an economy and how it is affected
by the availability of resources to society--to
creative, risk-prone producing units in particular and
to all units of production in general. Proponents of
each of the two perspectives, whatever the labels used
to describe them--micro or macro, individualistic or
organic, individualistic or collectivist--have hardly
been able to communicate with each other. The major
difficulty lies in the problem of aggregation-
disaggregation, discussed in Chapter X and referred to
in the introduction to Part Five. Some theories about
the behavior of economic units assume equilibrating
relations to aggregate data. Macro models at times
assume homogeneity of sectors and overlook the
creative role of individuals in developing adaptive
strategies. The rhetoric about the relative value or
relative truth of the micro and macro perspectives is
monumental in all the social sciences. Unhappily,
anthropologists have often argued the problem
metaphorically, and have therefore missed the chance
to develop a framework for translating the valuable
insights gained from one perspective into assumptions
or propositions to be used as theoretical bases for
the other.

It is hoped that this review of the contributions
and limitations of each approach will encourage a
dialogue and the development of a suitable integrating
framework. Homeostatic, equilibrating systems distort
reality; the categorization of structures into super
and infra strata is too mechanistic and conceptually
cumbersome. Fusfeld (1980) suggests the integration
of relationships into patterns which are associated
with other patterns through logical argument.
Although his suggested framework of pattern models is
not always lucid, his suggestions warrant further
consideration.

Although each approach involves different
perspectives and epistemologies and uses different
assumptions to derive hypotheses, they all analyze the
same information. This shared interest in
noncapitalist economies or noncapitalist sectors of
economic systems makes economic anthropology
indispensable to development economists--indeed, to
any economist concerned with grand theory. We have
provided our colleagues in economics with invaluable
comparative data. But the fundamental raison d'etre
of economic anthropology as a discipline separate from
but related to economics is more fundamental. Our
concern with social reality allows us to elaborate
frameworks of analysis different from those derived
from formal mathematical models. In Chapter IX
Bennett and Kanel contrast the formal economic and
anthropological frameworks, while Chapters I and XII
outline some of the problems caused by over-reliance
on them. Many economists, econometricians and
development planners are aware of these problems.
They sometimes fear that their models may become a
branch of mathematics and logic rather than tools for
an empirical science (Lowe, 1965, p. 5). As a
corrective to the inadequate performance of
overformalized mathematical models, economists have
incorporated social factors as soft, exogenous
variables. Such a solution is not entirely
satisfactory, however, because the selection of
variables remains intuitive. The only guides are
common sense and mathematical properties.

Economic anthropology also has an important
contribution to make to social and cultural
anthropology. Although with Polanyi we all argue that
the economy is embedded in social reality, we must
also agree with Firth, Marx and Bourdieu that the
analysis of social and political institutions remains
superficial if it disregards either obvious or hidden
economic realities. The big men of New Guinea need
pigs, the Nuer need cows, the Tolai need tambu. In
these cases the political realities of the system rest
on the ability of production units to generate the
subsistence, prestige or luxury goods required. To
describe the production of luxuries merely as the
generation of symbolic capital is to tell only half
the story. To express an exchange or a contractual
arrangement over the use of labor or resources purely
as a social relation is to collude with an
intellectual fiction--as is the case, for example,
when one contracting party describes his social

xiv

conditions in honorable terms and, by so doing, fails to fully describe the condition (Bourdieu, 1977, p. 196). The concept of embeddedness contains three images: the relationship of persons through things or commodities, the relationship between persons and commodities and the relationship among commodities through individuals. The second and third images are the subject of economic anthropology; they shed light on the first.

This volume brings together some contrasting approaches to themes and topics in economic anthropology. It does not pretend to summarize the history of the intellectual development of the subject; it can only review some of the more recent researches and lines of argument. I hope that presenting these approaches as contrasting but related movements will highlight the strength of each. To admit to limitations is to recognize the complexity of economic dynamics and the relation of such dynamics to political and social processes. Each approach was developed in response to an instrumental or intellectual need, and each is best understood in its original context. To translate approaches mechanically to other contexts or concerns can lead to serious misrepresentations; to treat them as truth would abort our understanding of reality.

References

BOURDIEU, Pierre. 1977. Outline of a theory of practice. Cambridge Studies in Social Anthropology, No. 16. London: Cambridge University Press.

CLAMMER, John. 1978. The new economic anthropology. London: The Macmillan Press Ltd.

FIRTH, Raymond. 1939. Primitive Polynesian economy. London: George Routledge and Son.

FUSFELD, Daniel B. 1980. The conceptual framework of modern economics. Journal of Economic Issues 14:1-51.

GOODFELLOW, D. M. 1939. Principles of economic sociology. London: George Routledge and Son.

HERSKOVITS, Melville J. 1940. The economic life of primitive peoples. New York: Knopf.

LECLAIR, Edward and Harold K. Schneider, eds. 1968. _Economic anthropology_. New York: Holt, Rinehart & Winston.

LOWE, Adolph. 1965. _On economic knowledge_. New York: Harper & Rowe.

POLANYI, Karl, C. W. Arensberg and H. W. Pearson, eds. 1957. _Trade and market in the early empires_. Glencoe, Ill.: The Free Press.

SCHNEIDER, Harold K. 1974. _Economic man_. New York: The Free Press.

PART ONE

ECONOMY AND SOCIETY

The economy has not always been studied as an independent system with its own inner logic. Adam Smith's invisible hand was social; the values that motivated Veblen's personification of merchants, industrialists and consumers did not correspond to the principles which we are told ensure an equilibrating market; Menger's economic man reasoned to solve his social predicament as well as to protect his profits. In time, however, the need to theorize about the dynamics of production bounded the systems that were outlined. Furthermore, the techniques that eventually were developed to test hypotheses demanded narrower perspectives, innumerable ceteris paribus assumptions and more stringent logical premises. Thus the study of production, distribution and allocation became for some economists a highly specialized field with a language of its own that was used not only to converse with colleagues but also to think about economic premises. With some notable exceptions the mastery of calculus became more important than the mastery of reality and the premises upon which the calculus rested.

Polanyi poignantly alerted anthropologists to the danger of the indiscriminate borrowing of concept and techniques out of context and without regard for the assumptions implied. His clarification of rational action, reasoned economic action and economizing behavior is now welcomed; but at its time it created a controversy that left little room for nonpartisan research amongst economic anthropologists. At the same time, it left the door wide open for others to examine more carefully the institutional context of certain economic arrangements (e.g., money, trade, marketplace exchange) and the significance of certain concepts used by economists. The writings of substantivists, too numerous to mention here, were stimulated by Polanyi's careful warning that one cannot study an economic institution simply by describing it; the total institutional context must also be examined (see Dalton and Köcke's chapter). The significance of concepts used was carefully though polemically examined in the now famous substantivist-formalist controversy, which LeClair and Schneider (1968) summarized in a single volume.

For many other economists the study of economic systems did not float in a mathematical make-believe world of interacting maximizing economic agents nor amongst the organistic models of the early physiocrats and the equilibrating models of their descendants. (See Gudeman, 1980, for an incisive review of this tradition and A. Lowe, 1965, pp. 95-127, for considerations of variants within it.) These economists remained concerned with the study of societies and with the evolution of social systems. They contributed with further developments to the humanistic and behavioral arguments of Veblen, Commons, and Ayres in collaboration with historians and anthropologists. The fruits of these efforts are represented in the writings of American institutional economists and some development economists. In their chapter Neale and Mayhew review the impact of this tradition (see also Bennett and Kanel's chapter and the introduction to the last section of this book) and parallel efforts by some cultural anthropologists writing on economic systems or economic behavior.

Institutional economists were, of course, not the only ones to press for a holistic approach to the study of the economic systems of preindustrial societies. At the turn of the century, in Europe, Karl Bücher was writing on the evolution of economic systems, on the social significance of the division of labor and the transformation of effort into what we call labor. Thurnwald was writing on economic process, stratification and political organization. Many were the social scientists concerned with similar issues but Bücher and Thurnwald stand out as the economists who most influenced Malinowski and held the attention of anthropologists trained by Raymond Firth (see Firth, 1967 and Köcke, 1979 for a review of their contribution and influence). But Weber eventually was singled out as the most influential sociologist to examine the evolution of economic institutions. He was an inspiration to subsequent generations of historians and anthropologists. Thus on both sides of the Atlantic, the study of nonindustrial societies by anthropologists, historians and some economists had a distinct sociological character.

Although it should have been no great revelation to read about the embeddedness of economic institutions, anthropologists obviously needed the reminder by Polanyi (Polanyi, 1957 and Dalton's and

4

Köcke's contribution to this volume). However, Polanyi's message was more than a simple warning. He is still read not just because he talks about embeddedness but because he provided those scholars who wanted to study the interface between economy and society with a clear focus: the study of systems of distribution. By so doing Polanyi redirected us away from narrow tautological functionalist arguments and from Parsonian conceptualizations of societies as functionally interlinked subsystems, to the significance of institutional control of distributive systems and its consequent effect on production. Polanyi was clearly aware of why the study of the market played such a critical role in the writings of classical and neoclassical economists. In turn he made us aware of the significance of the institutional framework in the flow or resources. But unlike Parsons, he had an historian's curiosity. Having profited from Popper's influence he could not turn to historical reconstructions, as some of his predecessors had done. With his own research he urged us to look back in time and to assimilate what we could learn from classical archaeology and history with what we could learn from ethnohistorical and ethnological studies. He provided us not only with a theme to explore but with his own historical analysis of archaic economies. From these endeavors he was able to postulate some general evolutionary trends: external trade preceded internal trade, money and markets; the supply of a medium of exchange and its ability to communicate demand, need and value depended on the existence of certain institutional arrangements; certain modes of distribution implied certain patterns of political structure.

The chapters by Carrasco and Blanton attest to Polanyi's creative influence on the work of ethnohistorians and economic anthropologists working exclusively with archaeological and documentary data. Both these essays examine the concomitant evolution of political and economic systems, taking care to explain the transformation of one system in the context of transformations in the other. But Blanton is not prepared to argue exactly on the same terms as was Polanyi. In fact, he suggests that at least for the Oaxaca area, goods were distributed through a system of marketplaces earlier than Polanyi would have predicted. A changing rhythm of worktime through the advent of double cropping robbed agriculturalists of free time to produce household crafts. This encouraged specialization and exchange (an argument which is, according to Grove's comments, only partially persuasive). Only later, when more important political centers had been developed, did marketplace systems lose their initial independence from administrative control by the polity. Yet in his second hypothesis, he addresses the interconnection between polity and distributive systems, very much as Polanyi had urged us to do. According to Blanton, with the formation of the state, marketplace systems became more elaborate and more firmly under administrative control. But, he continues in this third hypothesis, eventually the polity in this precapitalist system was unable to retain its control on flow of resources; the market system must have developed its own self-regulating mechanisms. During the postclassical period the state could not mobilize as much labor for the construction of public monuments as it had before--in other words, it did not control the market for labor--nor the regional flow of goods. His suggestions, which are more fully documented in his other publications, are derived from parallel suggestions for the transformation of marketing systems, production systems and political systems in China, Peru and Guatemala (as he acknowledges in his references to recent work by Skinner, Smith and Appleby). Neat schemes usually bring out critical response, and some of these criticisms are included in the chapter by Berdan. Nevertheless, neat schemes are stimulating, and Blanton's extensive research will no doubt inspire many more theories--which may be both less ambitious and less resistant to confirmation.

Blanton, in contrast to Pires Ferreira, Barry Cunliffe (1976) and G. R. Wright (1974), has thus moved away from an automatic reinterpretation of Polanyi's hypothesis. This trend is shared by other archaeologists who have analyzed not just the embeddedness of trade but also the benefits received by the trader and the elite that administer it (Earle, 1977). These new efforts are possible because economic anthropologists had introduced location analysis to study marketing systems and their evolution, and because of the sophisticated analytical techniques now available to archaeologists. In recent years statistical analysis, linear programming and mathematical analysis are being used to study distributional patterns and to reconstruct past economic realities (see Earle and Ericson, 1977). It is now possible to reconstruct patterns of distribution within local areas. As Drennan has pointed out in his conference comments on Blanton's essay, new techniques have made us aware that the volume of goods that circulate within a locality is greater than the volume of goods that come from far away. Archaeologists are thus now ready to pay equal attention to redistribution and trade. Their findings will force us to reconsider our historical reconstructions. Quantification has thus given new impetus to archaeological theories.

One hopes that practitioners of this new art will remember Polanyi's admonition to anthropologists and economists who made use of similar approaches without regard for assumptions implied. Gregory Johnson (1976) has already sounded such a warning with respect to the application of regional analysis to archaeological data, as has Plog (1977) with reference to distributional and network analysis. Reidhead (1979) both encouraged and qualified the use of linear programming, and Kohl (1981) repeated previous warnings. To their warnings we should add those of Berdan, who cautions us that it is unwise to extrapolate from descriptions of volume and direction of trade to descriptions of institutional arrangements that ensured and controlled distribution. It is unlikely that the issue of the evolution of distributional systems will be resolved only by archaeologists, but is also certain that they will provide economic anthropologists and economic historians with substantive information about flows in precapitalist systems. The comfortable simple contrast between archaic and market economies, for example, has already been challenged. Blanton makes us aware that volume of resource flow is considerable, and Berdan confirms his suspicion that the state was not always able to control the flow; pochtecas were after all entrepreneurs. We have now new, more precise foci for our research on the interface between polity and economy: the variables that determined the volume and direction of resource flow in Mesoamerica and the impact that a change in flow is likely to have had on the distributive system and the polity that administered it.

References

CUNLIFFE, Barry. 1976. Hill-forts and oppida in Britain. In Problems in economic and social archeology, edited by G. de G. Sieveking,

I. H. Longworth and K. E. Wilson. London: Duckworth & Co.

EARLE, Timothy K. 1977. A reappraisal of redistribution: complex Hawaiian chiefdoms. In Exchange systems in prehistory, edited by Timothy K. Earle and Jonathan E. Erickson. New York: Academic Press.

EARLE, Timothy and Jonathan E. Ericson. 1977. Exchange systems in archeological perspective. In Exchange systems in prehistory. T. K. Earle and J. E. Erickson, eds. New York: Academic Press.

FIRTH, Raymond. 1967. Themes in economic anthropology. London: Tavistock.

GUDEMAN, Stephen F. 1980. Physiocracy: a natural economics. American Ethnologist 7:240-258.

JOHNSON, Gregory. 1977. Aspects of regional analysis in archaeology. In Annual Review of Anthropology 6:479-508.

KÖCKE, Jasper. 1979. Some early German contributions to economic anthropology. In Research in Economic Anthropology, George Dalton, ed. 1:119-169. Greenwich, Conn.: JAI Press.

KOHL, R. L. 1981. Materialist approaches in prehistory. Annual Review of Anthropology 10:89-118.

LECLAIR, Edward E. and Harold K. Schneider. 1968. Economic anthropology. New York: Holt, Reinhart and Winston.

LOWE, Adolphe. 1965. On economic knowledge. New York: Harper and Row.

PIRES-FERREIRA, Jane W. 1975. Formative Mesoamerican exchange networks with special references to the Valley of Oaxaca. Memoirs of the Museum of Anthropology, no. 7, U. of Michigan.

PLOG, Fred. Modeling economic exchange. In Exchange systems in prehistory. T. K. Earle and J. E. Erickson, eds. New York: Academic Press.

POLANYI, K., C. M. Arensberg and H. W. Pearson, eds.
1957. Trade and market in the early empires.
Glencoe, Ill.: The Free Press.

WRIGHT, G. R. 1974. Archaeology and trade.
Addison Wesley Module in Anthropology, no. 49.
Reading, Mass.: Addison Wesley.

I. POLANYI, INSTITUTIONAL ECONOMICS, AND ECONOMIC ANTHROPOLOGY

Walter C. Neale and Anne Mayhew

I. INSTITUTIONAL ECONOMICS

Although European, Polanyi fits into a long tradition within the American economics profession, a tradition usually called "institutional." Essentially this tradition views economies as evolving systems of changing institutions: not only those institutions that might be called "economic," however defined, but all the institutions which affect economic activities. The emphasis has not, as a rule, been on the working of this or that particular institution, but rather upon how a particular institution fits into the system of institutions, upon how the various institutions form an integrated system, and upon how the interacting characteristics of the institutions create stresses and changes in a society. There has, within this broader framework, been a strong tendency to analyze how the working rules of a society and its components, and the associated folkviews, change--particularly as they adapt to changing technologies. The wide range of institutional referents and especially the analysis of institutions as mutually supporting or conflicting underlie the institutional economist's view that his branch of the discipline is significantly more holistic or systemic than the standard, neoclassical branch, which institutional economists regard as "economistic" and hence not amenable to analyses of issues involving structural change. In consequence of their range, institutional economists have been especially interested in economic history, more recently in economic development, and--because its literature presents such a wide variety of cases--in anthropology. And in consequence of the efforts of institutional economists to treat the economic institutions and activities as part of a cultural system, there developed, in earlier years, a strong parallelism with the analysis of structure and function in anthropology, and more recently parallels with the use of the concept of "organizing ideas" and with the view of anthropology as the study of how people "word the world."[1]

11

The earlier institutional economists--the "founding fathers" and their immediate successors--ranged widely indeed, but largely within the boundaries of already industrialized societies. Veblen (1904) and Commons (1923) interpreted early twentieth century American capitalism as a continually changing process emerging from earlier technologies and social processes and ideas and evolving into some other, as yet unknown system--Veblen suggesting that fascism (before such existed) was a likely outcome and Commons suggesting democratic forms of collective action. Ayres (1944, 1952), following Veblen, treated the American economy of the 1930s and '40s as an adaptation to crisis and strain, an adaptation shaped by processes of instrumental valuing. Wesley Mitchell (1913) was the father of modern econometrics, taking the business cycle as his topic, while Copeland (1952) largely started the flow of funds analysis of business activity in order to make quantitative analysis capable of handling all organizations that affect expenditure.[2]

The tradition which these economists established was characterized by an emphasis on descriptive analysis (whether verbal or mathematical) of what is, where it came from, how it works, and how it changes as a consequence of instrumental valuing by participants in the system. They were almost exclusively concerned with modern industrial, capitalist economies. Veblen, and to a lesser extent Ayres, were the only two who made use of anthropological sources, and they did so only for occasional illustration. Polanyi's The Great Transformation (1944), an historical analysis of the evolution of the capitalist system as it integrated modern machine technology into a commercial society, fitted neatly into and became part of the tradition as it had taken shape by the middle 1940s. It was because Polanyi shared the emphasis on process and on instrumental valuing that American institutional economists adopted him into their fold, and that he found their work so congenial.

What Polanyi had set out to argue, both for the scholarly purpose of setting the historical record straight, but also for the more general purpose of illuminating the crisis of the Western World in the twentieth century, was that much of what economists assumed to be part of the natural order was in fact peculiar to a very short period of western history.

In arguing, in The Great Transformation, that the self-regulating market system was a peculiar creation of nineteenth century European civilization, he drew upon the works of anthropologists (especially Bronislaw Malinowski and Richard Thurnwald), in much the same way as Veblen had done earlier.

II.   POLANYI AND ANTHROPOLOGY

Seldom have so few pages (pp. 43-55 and 269-273 of The Great Transformation) had so great an effect upon another discipline and upon interdisciplinary studies. Polanyi presented the "forms of integration"--reciprocity, redistribution, householding, and exchange--in order to answer the question, "If economies other than those of the North Atlantic community in the nineteenth century were not organized as self-regulating markets, how else could they have been organized?" The thirteen pages of Chapter 4, "Societies and Economic Systems," answered the question in logic (the forms of integration) and in substance (brief illustrations from economic history and from anthropology) in order to lay the groundwork for his argument that nineteenth century capitalism was not a socially viable system. These pages, however, attracted the interest of a number of anthropologists. The shift in Polanyi's interest from recent history to the more distant past combined with the interests of several anthropologists and institutional economists to produce Trade and Market in the Early Empires (1957). In this volume, economic anthropology played a larger role (chapters by Arensberg, Chapman, Arnold, Bennett, Neale, and Fusfeld) than it had in Polanyi's earlier work. Following Harris's (1959) review of Trade and Markets, Dalton's replies (1960, 1961, 1963), and then the publication of Dahomey and the Slave Trade (1966) (again, intended as an essay in economic history and comparative economic organization rather than in economic anthropology), the work of Polanyi, his colleagues, his students, and others influenced by him became a focus for work and for dispute in the field of economic anthropology.[3] Thus did anthropologists become involved with Polanyi.

III.   CONTRIBUTIONS OF OTHER INSTITUTIONAL ECONOMISTS

After World War II other institutional economists, whose immediate intellectual roots traced back to Veblen and Ayres or Commons, and some of those

whose evolutionary approach was an immediate
consequence of association with Polanyi, became deeply
involved in economic anthropology. The solutions to
problems of third world economic development, and
understanding of economic change and innovation in
both the third world and in the industrial world,
seemed to require ideas and information that only
anthropologists could supply.

Unfortunately, even as evolutionary economists
became more deeply involved as potential contributors
to--and certainly as borrowers from--economic
anthropology, many anthropologists came to think of
nonstandard economics as being exclusively represented
as a "substantive economics" narrowly defined as the
work of Polanyi and a few of his followers.
"Substantive economics"--a useful enough phrase to
describe much of institutional economics--has been
taken to mean only the work of those who explicitly
used terms developed by Polanyi (forms of integration,
ports of trade, equivalencies). This has meant that a
body of work closely related to economic anthropology
and stemming from the institutional tradition has been
overlooked. It should be better known to scholars in
economic anthropology.

There have been two recent lines of work by
institutional economists that bear upon the interests
of economic anthropologists. One line is work on the
economic organization of tribal and peasant societies,
particularly on how these economies have changed under
the impact of colonial rule, foreign contacts, and new
technologies. Among these studies by institutional
economists[4] are ones of ongoing conflict and
adaptation among peasants, peasant communities,
landlords, and the state (Neale, 1962, 1963, 1967,
1981; Van Roy, 1967, 1971; Rosen, 1966, 1975), of the
effects of culture contact between peasant and tribal
communities (Van Roy, 1967, 1971), and of both the
structure and perceptions of the structure of Indian
village economies (Adams, 1970a, 1970b, 1972). None
of these works argues methodology or issues arising
from the nature or interpretation of theory. Rather,
they are substantive in the sense that they portray a
history, a field study, or a body of literature in
terms of the rules, perceptions, activities, or
responses of the participants in the society studied.
They are "economic" in that they deal with society's
material wherewithal, or in that they deal with the
changing legal and social structures of rights and

powers over material wherewithal and of access to
these rights and powers. They are "sociological" in
that they deal with the effects of social structure
and native ideas about social structure (family,
lineage, loyalty, caste, class, tenurial status).
They are "political" in that they deal with the
effects of power and policy (taxation, monetization,
laws of property and contract, faction, preservation
and extension of position, development programs,
redistribution of rights). They complement, in fact,
the contribution of Salisbury to this volume.

The other line is work on the processes and
effects, political and social as much as economic, of
changing technology and public policy upon the working
rules--and upon the perceptions of cause, effect, and
possibility--in the economic histories of developed
societies. This work is relevant to the interests of
economic anthropologists because it deals with
adaptive and nonadaptive responses of essentially
peasant (Mayhew, 1972) or dependent and oppressed
groups (Street, 1957) to a new technology. These
studies--although each does stand as a contribution to
U.S. history, and does not purport to be a
contribution to theories of change--do bear directly,
by clear implication, upon such current issues in
economic anthropology as cultural perceptions of role,
innovative entrepreneurship, hierarchy, and the
relationship of the "little community" to the "great
tradition" (as, certainly, does Rosen's work, cited
above). Bennett's and Kanel's contribution to this
volume illustrates both of the lines of work
undertaken by institutional economists.

While the works cited are relevant to the
practice and development of economic anthropology, it
should also be understood that the work of
institutional economists owes a great deal to
anthropology. Acquaintance with these studies may
increase appreciation of the importance of
anthropological scholarship to the analysis of
problems not ordinarily classified as anthropological.
Neale's (1962) analysis of the failure of tenurial
reforms under British rule in India relies heavily on
the results of field studies by anthropologists, as
does Rosen's (1966) analysis of the distributive
effects of Indian development efforts. The framework
for Rosen's (1975) comparative account of the problems
of developmental efforts in Southeast Asia is drawn
largely from anthropology. It is difficult to

conceive of Mayhew's (1972) interpretation of farm protest in 19th century America in the absence óf the anthropological literature on role perception and commercialization. Adams's (1981) portrayal of Indian foreign exchange policy as an outgrowth of peasant household attitudes provides an intriguing example of the uses to which studies by anthropologists can be put. Anthropology is also contributing to a new appreciation of the content (Stanfield, 1982) and philosophical understanding (Benton, 1982) of economics. Bennett and Kanel's essay illustrates the contributions of anthropology to the analysis of developed economies.

Notes on Sources Cited

VAN ROY shows how, in the northern Thai peasant economy where widespread use of money and credit and widespread cultivation of an important commercial crop have had long histories, the requirements of the Thai system of multipurpose "entourages" were a barrier to the adoption of new technologies; but also how the earlier development of a system of miang cultivation by hill tribesmen could be adapted to the requirements of the international tea market.

ROSEN's work is closely related to that of Van Roy. Rosen argues that the developmental response of government to the issues and opportunities of economic development in the Philippines, Indonesia, Thailand, and India has been made less effective than it might have been--and must become--because these political systems are permeated with the perceptions, ethics, and obligations of peasant patron-client entourages.

STREET argues that the development and adoption of the mechanical cotton picker was slower than the development and adoption of machines to harvest other important American crops, not only because of inherent physical problems, but also, and as importantly, because the southern social and economic structure emerging from the abolition of the plantation slave economy built in a resistance to mechanization. (Something may be indicated of the subtlety of his analysis, made in the early 1950s, by his prediction that a major consequence of the cotton picker would be greatly increased black attendance at public schools.)

MAYHEW, writing about another century and another part of the U.S., has described how an earlier technological change--the railroad--opened the Midwest to the possibility, and for most farmers, even the necessity, of commercial agriculture; and how this meant that the farmers, because they had to pay for inputs (transportation, land, credit), had to sell their output. It was thus the unambiguous pressures of the commercialization of agriculture consequent upon the spread of the railway network that caused farmers to protest--not falling prices or banking monopolies.

NEALE's work on "the grain heap" (1957) has been widely recognized as part of the substantive tradition, but his studies of Indian land tenure (1962), the conflict between British and Indian notions about property, justice, and public policy (1962, 1963, 1969), as well as his work on independent India's rural development policies (1981) have not been so widely recognized as relevant to economic anthropology. In these works he has tried to explain how government policies (of taxation and property rights in the nineteenth and early twentieth centuries, of democratization and community development since 1950) have been so redirected by villagers' interpretations and reactions that third institutional structures have emerged, third structures intended by neither party.

Notes

[1] For the former phrase we are indebted to Paul J. Bohannan, for the latter to F. G. Bailey; oral communications.

[2] Since Copeland is probably not so widely known as others whom we have mentioned, we suggest Millar (1980) for a brief account of Copeland's work.

[3] The impact of the dispute and the positive legacy of the controversy are reviewed in Dalton's essay in this volume.

[4] We have been selective, making no effort to be comprehensive. Short paragraphs indicating the content of some of the works of the institutional economists cited appear in the appendix.

17

References

ADAMS, John. 1970a. Studies of Indian village economies: a bibliographic essay. Indian Economic and Social History Review 7:109-137.

_____. 1970b. Village economy in traditional India: a simplified model. Human Organization 29:49-58.

_____. 1972. The analysis of Indian rural economy: economics and anthropology. Man in India 70:1-20.

_____. 1981. India's foreign trade and payments since 1965: managing the nation as a peasant household. Pacific Affairs 53:632-642.

AYRES, Clarence E. 1944. The theory of economic progress. Chapel Hill, N.C.: University of North Carolina Press.

_____. 1952. The industrial economy: its technological basis and institutional destiny. Boston: Houghton Mifflin Co.

BENTON, Raymond, Jr. 1982. Economics as a cultural system. Journal of Economic Issues 16:461-471.

COMMONS, John R. 1968 (c1923). Legal foundations of capitalism. Madison/Milwaukee/London: University of Wisconsin Press.

COPELAND, Morris A. 1952. A study of moneyflows in the United States. New York: National Bureau of Economic Research.

DALTON, George. 1960. A note of clarification on economic surplus. American Anthropologist 62:483-490.

_____. 1961. Economic theory and primitive society. American Anthropologist 63:1-25.

_____. 1963. Economic surplus once again. American Anthropologist 65:389-394.

HARRIS, Marvin. 1959. The economy has no surplus. American Anthropologist 61:185-199.

MAYHEW, Anne. 1972. A reappraisal of the causes of farm protest in the U.S., 1870-1900. The Journal of Economic History 32:464-475.

MILLAR, James R. 1980. Institutionalism from a Natural Science point of view: an intellectual profile of Morris A. Copeland. In Institutional economics: contributions to the development of holistic economics, John Adams, ed. Boston/The Hague/London: Martinus Nijhoff Publishing.

MITCHELL, Wesley C. 1913. Business cycles. Berkeley, CA.: University of California Press. The 2nd edition, more easily available, was entitled Business cycles: the problem and its setting. New York: National Bureau of Economic Research, Inc., 1927.

NEALE, Walter C. 1962. Economic change in rural India: land tenure and reform in Uttar Pradesh, 1800-1955. New Haven/London: Yale University Press.

_____. 1963. The Indian peasant, the state, and economic development. Land Economics 38:291-291.

_____. 1969. Land is to rule. In Land control and social structure in Indian history, Robert E. Frykenberg, ed. Madison/Milwaukee/London: University of Wisconsin Press.

_____. 1981. Rural development and politics in India. Pacific Affairs 53:626-631.

POLANYI, Karl. 1944. The great transformation. New York/Toronto: Rinehart and Co., Inc.

_____. 1966. Dahomey and the slave trade. Seattle, WA.: University of Washington Press.

POLANYI, Karl, Conrad M. Arensberg and Harry W. Pearson, eds. 1957. Trade and market in the early empires. Glencoe, Ill.: The Free Press. Reprinted, 1971, as Gateway Edition, Chicago, Ill: Henry Regnery Company.

ROSEN, George. 1966. Democracy and economic change in India. Berkeley/Los Angeles: University of California Press.

_____. 1975. Peasant society in a changing economy: comparative development in Southeast Asia and India. Urbana/Chicago/London: University of Illinois Press.

STANFIELD, J. Ron. 1982. Learning from primitive economies. Journal of Economic Issues 16:471-481.

STREET, James H. 1957. The new revolution in the cotton economy: mechanization and its consequences. Chapel Hill, N.C.: The University of North Carolina Press.

VAN ROY, Edward. 1967. An interpretation of northern Thai peasant economy. The Journal of Asian Studies 36:421-432.

_____. Economic systems of northern Thailand: structure and change. Ithaca, N.Y.: Cornell University Press.

VEBLEN, Thorstein. 1904. The theory of business enterprise. New York: Charles Scribners Sons.

II. THE WORK OF THE POLANYI GROUP: PAST, PRESENT, AND FUTURE

George Dalton and Jasper Köcke

. . . economists have concentrated on studying the market economy, and have left the study of the non-market economy to the anthropologist . . . the economist who studies the non-market economy has to abandon most of what he has learnt, and adopts the techniques of the anthropologist. (W. Arthur Lewis, 1961)

This paper contains four sections and a technical note. The first presents evidence that Polanyi's work is read and used. The second summarizes his main contributions. The third mentions the topics of recent publications by those of us who use Polanyi's theoretical framework. These first three sections are brief and expository. The fourth section describes research in economic anthropology underway but not yet published by the authors of this paper, and explains how this work in process grew out of the past work of the Polanyi group, as well as other work have nothing to do with Polanyi.

I. EVIDENCE THAT POLANYI'S WORK IS READ AND USED

Polanyi wrote and edited five books only the first two of which were published in his lifetime (he died in 1964): The Great Transformation (1944), Trade and Market in the Early Empires (1957), Dahomey and the Slave Trade (1966), Primitive, Archaic, and Modern Economies (1968), and The Livelihood of Man (1977). In 1982 all of Polanyi's books except Dahomey and the Slave Trade are still in print, including the especially important first two, published thirty-eight and twenty-five years ago. We trust this means they are being read. It certainly means they are being bought.

In the 1970s, Polanyi's first four books were translated into several languages. We cite here only the translations we know to exist (there may be others): Trade and Market was translated into Spanish and French; The Great Transformation was translated into German, Japanese, and Italian and will soon be published in French. Dahomey and the Slave Trade and three collections of Polanyi's articles and chapters similar to Primitive, Archaic, and Modern Economies, were translated into Japanese, Hungarian, and Italian.

We know of one book and six articles devoted to assessing Polanyi's work. Allen Morris Sievers' Has Market Capitalism Collapsed? A Critique of Karl Polanyi's New Economics (1949), considers The Great Transformation. We list only articles written by persons who were not Polanyi's students: S. C. Humphreys, "History, economics, and anthropology: the work of Karl Polanyi" (1969); Y. Garlan, "L'oeuvre de Polanyi: la place de l'économie dans les societés anciennes" (1973); a symposium of some seventy printed pages written by a dozen anthropologists and historians in Annales (December 1974) under the title, "L'anthropologie économique et histoire: l'oeuvre de Karl Polanyi," an English translation of which appears in volume 4 of Research in Economic Anthropology (1981). Charles Kindleberger, Professor Emeritus of Economics at M.I.T., chose to write an essay about The Great Transformation for his contribution to the issue of Daedalus (1974) devoted to "Twentieth century masterpieces." In 1980, J. R. Stanfield published an article entitled "The institutional economics of Karl Polanyi." Also L. Congdon wrote "Karl Polanyi in Hungary" (1976).

What has just been said is evidence that Polanyi's work is read. There is also evidence that Polanyi's work is used: several anthropologists, archaeologists, economic historians, and development economists make direct use of Polanyi's concepts (such as "redistribution" and "port of trade") and analytical conclusions (such as "economy embedded in society") to analyze actual economies of time and place. Here is a sample of such empirical application of Polanyi's work: N. Wachtel, "The structure of the Inca state" (1977); R. Hodges, "Ports of trade in early Medieval Europe" (1978); M. Mancall, "The Ch'ing tribute system: an interpretative essay" (1968); P. Wheatley, ". . . From reciprocity to redistribution in ancient Southeast Asia" (1975). Dalton has included four such articles in Research in Economic Anthropology: I. Adelman and C. T. Morris, "Patterns of market expansion in the nineteenth century: a quantitative study" (1978); C. Geertz, "Ports of trade in nineteenth century Bali" (1980); a translation of the seventy page French symposium that appears in Annales (1974) whose English title is "Economic anthropology and history: the work of Karl Polanyi" (vol. 4, 1981); and T. Smith, "Wampum as primitive valuables" (1982).

In sum, Polanyi's work is read and used. All but one of his books are still in print in English. Four of his five books have been translated. His work can now be read in French, German, Spanish, Italian, Japanese, and Hungarian. (There was an early translation of The Great Transformation into Spanish, in the 1950s, and individual articles of his have been translated more widely, into Swedish and Portuguese for example, as well as the languages into which his books have been translated.) There are several articles and a book devoted to assessing his work. The lengthy set of symposium articles that originally appeared in Annales is of special interest because five or more of the contributors of empirical and discussion essays are anthropologists. A number of anthropologists, archaeologists, economists, and historians who are not Polanyi's students--who know him only through his writings--have written at least a dozen articles and chapters employing Polanyi's paradigm.

II. POLANYI'S CONTRIBUTION TO ECONOMIC ANTHROPOLOGY, ECONOMIC ARCHAEOLOGY, AND ECONOMIC HISTORY

Here we can be brief because we have already explained various parts of Polanyi's work repeatedly during the last twenty years (Dalton, 1961, 1968, 1969, 1975; Köcke, 1979). But some preliminary remarks are necessary to point out changes that have occurred in the professional audience interested in economic anthropology, and new contributions to its theory.

Polanyi wrote before Marxian theory began to be used in economic anthropology, before the recent burgeoning of publications on the economic history of what are now third world countries, and before it was understood that the philosophers of science were explaining theoretical issues of importance to economic anthropology.

His work, moreover, was a beginning, not a finished theoretical system. Polanyi got a late start in academic life as a teacher and writer. The Great Transformation (1944) was published when he was 58. He began teaching economic history at Columbia

University in 1947, when he was 61, and had to retire only six years later in 1953, at age 67. Trade and Market (1957) was published when he was 71. Between the publication of Trade and Market and his death seven years later in 1964, he did not undertake fresh research, but rather applied, refined, and extended some of the ideas of Trade and Market in several articles: "The semantics of money uses" (1957); "On the comparative treatment of economic institutions in antiquity with illustrations from Athens, Mycenae, and Alaklakh" (1960); "Ports of trade in early societies" (1963); and "Sortings and 'ounce trade' in the West African slave trade" (1964). It was unfortunate that he did not live long enough to respond in print to criticism of his work.

To understand Polanyi's theoretical system one must first understand the national and international market organization that is a core attribute of capitalist economies, and neoclassical microeconomic theory from Alfred Marshall onward that was invented to analyze the workings of the economy-wide input and output markets integrating capitalist economies. We say this because formalists and Marxists on the one hand, and the Polanyi group on the other, hold totally different positions on whether the similarities between industrial capitalism and the precapitalist economies studied by anthropologists are more important than their differences. The formalists and Marxians say yes, the Polanyi group says no. From this it follows that both formalist and Marxian anthropologists employ theoretical systems originally contrived to analyze nineteenth century industrial capitalism. The Polanyi group, in arguing that the differences between Nuer, Trobriand, and Inca economies on the one hand, and industrial capitalism on the other, are more important than their similarities, concludes that neither microeconomics nor Marxian economics can reveal the most important attributes of economies not integrated by market exchange.

Now to summarize Polanyi's main points: every society of human beings, past and present, may be said to have an economy if we define "economy" as the systematic provisioning of goods; that is, as the arrangements to provide persons and community with goods and services in repetitive fashion. Every society arranges for two kinds of goods and services: those required by people as biological beings (food),

and those required by cohesive social-political groups
or the communities we call bands, lineages, clans,
kingdoms, or nations (for community defense, attack,
religious expression, marriage, etc.). In the
structured provision of these goods and services, all
societies employ natural resources, human labor, and
technology (tools and knowledge). All, or almost all,
also employ one or more practices or institutional
devices, such as local market places, trade with
politically external groups, or some sort of monetary
object. These are the ingredients of Polanyi's
"substantive" definition of "economic," and are
intended to explain exactly what is meant by saying
that every society has an economy of some sort, and to
differentiate this substantitive meaning from the
formal meaning of economic, which means economizing,
or the cost-benefit calculations used to arrive at
profit or utility maximizing solutions that underlie
all microeconomic analyses of household and business
firm decision making in market economies.

In The Great Transformation and its brief
postscript, "Our obsolete market mentality," Polanyi
(1947) argues several themes, only one of which need
concern us here: that the factor input (land, labor,
money) and product output market organization that
came to dominate and integrate nineteenth century
European and American industrial capitalism was
historically and anthropologically unique. All of his
later work follows from this central assertion because
it is devoted to answering two questions: a) why is
formal microeconomic theory inappropriate to analyze
the non-market economies studied by anthropologists
and historians? b) what are the core attributes of
non-market economies, and what conceptual vocabulary
(theory) is needed to explain the organization of
these non-market economies?

To use the conceptual vocabulary of microeconomic
price theory (maximizing, economizing, scarcity,
supply, demand, decision making, etc.) to analyze
non-market economies such as the Trobriand, the Nuer,
or the Inca, is to distort the nature of these
economies in three ways: a) it is to overstate the
similarities and understate the differences between
these economies and industrial capitalism; b) it
prevents one from seeing that what is important and
characteristic in Trobriand, Nuer, or Inca economy
is different from what is important and characteristic
in U.S. or Japanese industrial capitalism;

25

c) specifically, it prevents one from understanding the functioning of external trade and monetary usages in non-market economies, both of which differ essentially from external trade and money in capitalism. Surely the answer to the question, Why don't political anthropologists use the conceptual language of dictatorship and democracy to analyze the stateless political systems of pre-colonial Highland New Guinea? is that the differences between such polities and those of modern America and Russia are more important than their similarities. So too, we believe, their pre-colonial economic systems.

What is certain and should be uncontentious is that all human societies of record have an economy of some sort and that foreign trade, the use of monetary objects, and the use of market places are very widely employed in all sorts of past and present economies. What has been extremely contentious ever since the publication of <u>Trade and Market</u> is the following two assertions made by Polanyi: a) the core attributes of non-market economies are so very different from those of capitalism, that b) a special conceptual vocabulary within a special paradigm--neither formalist nor Marxist--is necessary to understand the structures of non-market economies. Polanyi's shorthand phrase, that in non-market economies, "economy is embedded in society" means the opposite of Marx's economic determinism as well as something which is more important to Polanyi's theory, the absence of economy as a separate sub-system capable of being analyzed apart from Trobriand, Nuer, or Inca kinship and polity: A commonsense way to say the same thing is that all aspects of Trobriand, Nuer, and Inca economy are socially and politically controlled, something that is immediately apparent upon examining, say, the production of staple yams in the Trobriands.

Polanyi's conceptual vocabulary, therefore, is socio-economic because he believed the evidence showed that nothing of economic importance in non-market economies--the production of staple foods, external trade, ceremonial exchange, bridewealth, bloodwealth, obligatory payments to and disbursements by political leaders--existed independently of the political and social institutions and relationships determining what we label "economic" things, activities, and transactions. Reciprocity, redistribution, ports of trade, politically administered trade, special-purpose money, equivalencies, operational devices--are socio-economic terms. (It is a pity it did not occur to Polanyi to illustrate his point with the Soviet Union, a non-market economy where, emphatically, "economy" is embedded in "polity," since the economists who analyze it have been forced to invent a special set of political-economic terms to express this core structural attribute: "command economy," "success indicators," "central planning," "administered prices"; and where we find--as we do in Trobriand economy--foreign trade, money, and market places functioning in a non-capitalist system.)

Finally, there is the empirical application of Polanyi's theoretical scheme to actual economies of time and place. Although he makes it clear that he learned much of importance from the writings of anthropologists--in The Great Transformation, ch. 4 and its appendix, he quotes and refers to Thurnwald, Malinowski, Lowie, Mead, Firth, Goldenweiser, Radcliffe-Brown, Linton, Benedict, Herskovits, Loeb, Mair, Pitt-Rivers, and Lesser--in his empirical essays, Polanyi himself wrote about economies studied by historians and archaeologists rather than those studied by anthropologists. But the contributors to Trade and Market, particularly Arensberg, Neale, and Fusfeld (as well as Polanyi), make it clear that the book's theoretical scheme is designed for economic anthropology as well as economic history. An Oxford economic historian who reviewed the book makes a similar point:

> This book is of outstanding interest. Any anthropologist, and any economic historian whose field of interest lies mainly outside the highly developed societies of the nineteenth and twentieth centuries, will find it challenging and profitable reading. (de Ste. Croix, 1960, p. 510)

III. RECENT RESEARCH

Archaeologists, economic historians, and anthropologists use Polanyi's work on the economic institutions of early kingdom-states to analyze ports of trade, politically administered trade, and redistribution in different parts of the world and at different historical time periods. Some examples of how Polanyi has been used to study trade and redistribution are: Hodges (1978) and Odner (1972) on early Europe; Wheatley (1975) and Geertz (1963) on

Indonesia; Wachtel (1977, Part II, ch. 1) on the Inca; Earle (1977) on Hawaiian chiefdoms. In a paper entitled "The Ch'ing tribute system: an interpretative essay," Mancall (1968) showed how ports of trade in China worked within that variant of politically administered trade that required payments of tribute; this topic is likely to be a promising line of research because of the abundant information on early China and because "tributary relations of alliance" were very common in early states. We should add that there are also formalist archaeologists and formalist economic historians who, in preferring a market interpretation, disagree with their colleagues' usage of Polanyi's concepts, just as is the case in economic anthropology: Torrence (1978), Adams (1975), Hopkins (1973), and Peukert (1978). There are also Marxian interpretations of the economic institutions of early states, such as Claessen and Skalnik (1978) and Mosely (1979) that disagree with Polanyi's approach.

In short, formalist, substantivist and Marxian controversies now also exist among archaeologists and economic historians. But aside from these paradigm disputes and preferences, a great deal of descriptive and analytical work is being published on early foreign trade and the economic organization of early kingdom-states: Heider (1969) on visiting trade institutions; Price (1980) and Kurimoto (1980) on silent trade; Sabloff and Lamberg-Karlovsky (1975) on ancient trade; Murra (1980) on Inca economy and a great deal of work on the economies of kingdoms in precolonial Africa, such as Wilks (1975), Vansina (1973, 1978), and Law (1977, 1978).

Polanyi's work on "special purpose money" has been clarified and improved in the excellent essay by Grierson, "The origins of money." Dalton (1978a) and Smith (1982) show how what they call "primitive valuables" are used as means of reciprocal payment in political and social transactions in aboriginal stateless societies (where reciprocity is the dominant principle of internal organization).

IV. FUTURE WORK

Polanyi left his theoretical system far from complete. For example, he said little or nothing about peasant economies, economic and social change under colonial rule, or post-colonial

development--topics, types of economy, and historical
time periods very much part of economic anthropology.
What he did say about reciprocity, redistribution,
early money usages, and early foreign trade need to be
empirically applied to a much larger number and
greater variety of societies than he himself wrote
about. And so we welcome the recent empirical
applications of Polanyi's theory, for example, by
Hodges (1978), Geertz (19890), and Mancall (1968) on
ports of trade in early Europe, Bali, and China;
Grierson (1980) and Smith (1982) on early money; and
Wheatley (1975), Wachtel (1977), and the several
French contributors to Annales (1974/1981) on
reciprocity and redistribution in Indonesia, Inca, and
elsewhere.

Polanyi neglected to create an important
analytical link in his system; he neglected to show
the necessary connections that exist between "patterns
of integration" (reciprocity, redistribution, and
market exchange), and the specific forms that money
and foreign trade take in societies dominated by each
pattern of integration. For example, he neglected to
show that where reciprocity is the dominant pattern of
integration, as in aboriginal economies in stateless
societies (such as in the Trobriands and Highland New
Guinea), primitive valuables serving as means of
reciprocal exchange or reciprocal payment (Kul
valuables, pigs, pearshells), and as means of
reciprocal external trade (kula, wasi) will also be
employed as the prime forms of money and foreign trade
(Dalton 1978). Polanyi, incidentally, did explain
these connections for capitalism, when showing that
market foreign trade and "general purpose" money were
determined by the domestic dominance of market
exchange. He also showed that politically
administered trade and ports of trade were derivative
expressions of domestic redistribution in early
states. But much remains to be done along these
lines.

The work we are now doing is motivated by more
than our wanting to complete what Polanyi left undone.
The convictions we now hold about what comprises the
subject of economic anthropology, how it relates to
neighboring subjects, and, above all, which specific
topics of research are most important, have been
influenced not just by Polanyi but also by a) what we
have learned from the controversies between
formalists, substantivists, and Marxists; b) what we

have learned from Popper, Kuhn, Rawls, and
Wittgenstein; c) what we have learned from David
Clarke's (1968) showing that the societies studied by
archaeologists and anthropologists can only be grouped
into polythetic sets; and d) what we have learned
from the plethora of recent writings on early economic
history. To explain:

Topics, types of economy, and historical time
periods studied in economic anthropology. It strikes
us as odd that such a basic question as "Exactly which
topics, types of economy, and historical time periods
comprise the subject of economic anthropology?" seems
not to have been answered in the literature. First,
our preferred grouping of types of economy and
historical time periods; then our summary of topics.

Types of Economy and Historical Time Periods
Studied in Economic Anthropology

Aboriginal (pre-colonial) economies in stateless
societies

Aboriginal (pre-colonial) economies in tribal
kingdoms

Peasantries in states, past and present

Economic and social change under colonial rule,
1500-1965

Post-colonial development and modernization

These polythetic groups serve several of our purposes,
only two of which we need to explain here. They point
out that anthropologists study economies as they were
structured (and changed) during different historical
time periods. For example, Murra (1980) describes
Inca economy before the Spanish arrived to smash,
grab, rule, and transform. Geertz (1963) describes
the deep changes caused in Indonesian peasant
economies by Dutch colonial rule. Epstein (1962,
1973) describes the early decades of post-colonial
development and modernization in two villages in
southern India.

Our list also enables us to point out that only
the first set, aboriginal economies in stateless
societies, is, so to speak, the exclusive property of
anthropologists. Only anthropologists (and

30

archaeologists) study the Nuer, Tiv, Yanomamö, North
American Indians, Australian aborigines, societies in
Highland New Guinea--as they were organized before
colonial rule. Each of the other types of economy and
historical time periods listed has counterpart
literatures outside of anthropology; indeed, larger
literatures. For example, the pre-colonial tribal
kingdoms of the Lozi, Azande, and Bunyoro have been
the subjects of ethnographies by distinguished British
anthropologists. But we now have dozens of books and
scores of articles on the economic, political, and
social history of pre-colonial African kingdoms
written by historians--Wilks (1975) on Asante, Law
(1977) on the Yoruba kingdom of Oyo--as well as a new
journal devoted to African Economic History, and
five volumes in the Cambridge History of Africa up
to 1870. In short, what we regard as an integral part
of our present research is to show that, in order for
theory in economic anthropology to be powerfully
persuasive in its explanations (and to be based on
sufficient evidence), we must make important use of
work in other disciplines. Four of the five listings
under "Types of economies and historical time periods
studied in economic anthropology" incorporate work by
non-anthropologists.

There are several sets of topics in economic
anthropology. Some topics relate to the acquisition
of subsistence livelihood and emphasize the uses made
of natural resources, technology, and the organization
of work tasks in the hunting, fishing, gathering,
herding, and agricultural provision of foodstuffs (see
the anthropological studies by Forde (1934),
Malinowski (1935), Lee and DeVore (1968) and the
historical studies by Slicher van Bath (1963).

There is a large literature on what may loosely
be called socio-economic and political-economic
institutions of importance, such as bridewealth and
dowry, ceremonial exchange, "primitive money," and
external trade; also on how market places work in the
societies studied by anthropologists. Here too belong
such topics as the receipts and disbursements by
chiefs and kings in pre-colonial kingdom-states, (for
example, those in Africa). Again, there are
counterpart literatures on some of these topics, such
as economic historians writing on early money
(Grierson, 1978); archaeologists and historians
writing on early external trade (Clark, 1965; Sabloff
and Lamberg-Karlovsky, 1975; Grierson, 1903/1980;

G. DALTON and J. KÖCKE

Van Leur, 1967; Mancall, 1968); an economic geographer
writing an important article on pre-colonial market
places in Africa (Hodder, 1965); and historians
writing on the kinds and amounts of taxes and tributes
received by African kings before colonial rule (Law,
1978). Slavery, of course, is another of those
socio-economic topics of importance to historians
(Finley, 1960, 1980) as well as to anthropologists
(Miers and Kopytoff, 1977).

Another set of topics is the causes and
consequences of deep change in different historical
time periods. Only rarely do anthropologists have
sufficient information to allow them to write about
deep change before colonial rule, one exception is the
influence of the horse on the Plains Indians (Wissler,
1914). By far most of what is written by
anthropologists is on the subject of changes brought
about by European or North American colonial rule
(1500-1965) under headings such as acculturation,
culture contact, applied anthropology, and millenarian
movements. Historians and economists also have
written extensively on this subject. We think there
is much comparative research to be done on the
economic anthropology of colonial impact(s), which
would answer questions such as, How exactly were the
indigenous economies studied by anthropologists made
to change by colonial rule? Why didn't more of what
we now call economic development and cultural
modernization occur under colonial rule? Why, despite
their long fieldwork immersion in the third world,
haven't anthropologists been able to contrive
persuasive theories of colonial change and
post-colonial development? (see Dalton, 1981).
Economists (e.g., Lewis, 1954, 1970; Singer, 1950)
have provided partial answers to these questions.

There is a great deal of work to be done on the
topic of what is now called "development
anthropology." We have some case studies (Epstein,
1962, 1973; Wallman, 1969; Richards, Sturrock, and
Fortt, 1973), symposium volumes (Pitt, 1976; Mathur,
1977), and rather premature attempts at textbooks
(Cochrane, 1971; Long, 1977).

Our future work will also address topics that
relate to the major disputes in the literature of
economic anthropology (the formalist-substantivist-
Marxist controversies), and a dozen other disputes
about the use of concepts: was there "feudalism" in

32

Africa? Are African cultivators to be called "peasants"? Should we use the term "bridewealth" or the term "brideprice"? What exactly is meant by "barter"? What does it mean to say that the economies studied by anthropologists "differ from industrial capitalism only in degree, not in kind"? Or that economic anthropologists should create a "general" or "universal" theory? These words and phrases in quotation marks are really symptoms of unresolved theoretical issues as is the use of several ambiguous concepts such as "surplus," "exploitation," and "primitive money."

Finally, there are what we think of as puzzles in the literature of economic anthropology we would like to try to solve. A few examples: why is it so difficult (why does it take so long) to resolve the differences between formalists, substantivists and Marxists? How does one do so? Why was the potlatch so variously interpreted over so long a period of time? Why, despite the fact that anthropologists began to work in Africa, Latin America, and elsewhere in the third world long before economists began their professional concern with third world development around 1950--why, in 1982, is there still no widely shared anthropological paradigm of development?

CONCLUSION

Even if we date the beginning of Polanyi's economic anthropology with the publication of Trade and Market (1957) rather than the The Great Transformation (1944) it still means twenty-five years of work in print by him, his associates and students, and others who make important use of his work. We see great amounts of work yet to do. These are the questions we are now attempting to answer:

1. What are the boundaries of economic anthropology? What is the full set of topics, types of economy, and historical time periods that comprise the subject?

2. How exactly is the work of economic historians, development economists, and others outside of anthropology to be incorporated into economic anthropology? Why and how must the Polanyi group make important use of outside work?

3. Several profound books on the philosophy of science, linguistic philosophy, and justice are widely thought to have deep implications for all social science. What can we learn from the writings of Popper, Kuhn, Wittgenstein, and Rawls that clarifies--and by so doing, helps to resolve--paradigm disputes between formalists, substantivists, and Marxists in economic anthropology?

4. What are the implications for economic anthropology of David Clarke's (1968) demonstration that human societies can only be grouped into sets having "polythetic" attributes (such as the sets capitalism/communism/underdeveloped)? How can we use this insight to group the societies of interest to economic anthropology into sets that reveal their distinguishing attributes, their similarities, and their differences?

5. What exactly are the similarities and the differences between the theoretical systems of Marx and Polanyi? (See the note which follows this "Conclusion.")

6. Marxian anthropologists very frequently refer to capitalism in their writings on tribal and peasant economies, but <u>not</u> to Soviet or other communist economies. Why not? If the structures of present-day capitalist economies are relevant to Marxian economic anthropology, why aren't the structures of present-day communist economies also relevant; particularly analysis of the rural peasantries of communist economies, and the "surplus" extracted by the government via taxes, the profits of nationalized firms, and the low purchase price the government pays for agricultural commodities it buys for resale? If Marxians call the extraction of such surplus "exploitation" when it occurs under capitalist institutions, why isn't it also exploitation when it occurs under communist institutions?

7. Polanyi said that economies not integrated by market exchange are "embedded in society." What exactly does this mean and what evidence do we have that the statement is true and important for the several sorts of non-market economies studied in economic anthropology?

8. How do we account for and resolve a dozen semantic/conceptual controversies in the literature,

such as bridewealth versus brideprice; are African cultivators to be called peasants; was there feudalism in Africa; how exactly are peasants exploited; what is meant by economic surplus; what is primitive money; why do we call some obligatory payments to central government taxes and others tribute; what exactly do we mean by barter; how does production relate to exchange?

9. Why is there no persuasive anthropological theory of how aboriginal economies changed under colonial rule? Can we contrive one?

10. Why is there no persuasive anthropological theory of post-colonial development? Can we contrive one?

11. How do old studies of "acculturation," "culture contact," "millenarian movements," and "applied anthropology" relate to colonial change and post-colonial development?

A NOTE ON THE POLANYI GROUP AND HISTORICAL MATERIALISM

Economic anthropology is still an "immature" field in Kuhn's (1962) sense, as there does not yet exist a general consensus among its practitioners about the core issues to be raised, the concepts which have the greatest explanatory power, and the deepest analytical conclusions about economy and society to be reached. In short, there is no prevailing paradigm. All three "disciplinary matrices," formalism, substantivism, and Marxism, compete for acceptance.

Although (as Kuhn tells us) it will be effectiveness in use that will eventually decide which theoretical approach will prevail, it is nevertheless useful to clarify the similarities and differences among the three approaches. It appears to us that the differences between formalism and substantivism are much better understood than the differences between followers of Marx and Polanyi. We say this because we repeatedly come across writings by Marxists who seem to claim Polanyi as a member of their family and incorporate his work into historical materialism. For example, in a review of some recent Marxist publications in economic anthropology, Ennew says that:

Polanyi's suggestion that the difference between
pre-capitalist and capitalist societies rests on
the degree of "embeddedness" of the economic in
other institutions, provides both a rationale
and a starting point for a materialist
examination of social forms in which economic
institutions are not as acutely "visible" as
those of capitalism. (Ennew, 1979, p. 108)

About Meillassoux (1960) and Rey and Dupré (1978),
she says: ". . . it is the concept of exchange which
motivates Meillassoux to develop further lines of
inquiry, as it later motivated Dupré and Rey, and the
starting point in each case is not Marx, but Polanyi"
(Ennew, 1979,p. 108). Godelier characterizes
substantivism as ". . . not exactly false but
basically inadequate"--a rather patronizing judgment,
spoken from an enormous height. But he too regards
Polanyi as an ally against the common enemy of
formalism. He says that by denouncing the formalist
definition of economic Karl Polanyi aligned ". . .
himself to a constant theme in the early and later
writings of Marx" (Godelier, 1977, pp. 18, 19). Rey
and Dupré also claim the work of Polanyi and his
associates as an integral part of their historical
materialist approach:

. . . the theory of the history of exchange,
which Bohannan and Dalton as well as Polanyi and
Arensberg are in fact trying to establish must
find its place within a theory of the
reproduction . . . of economic and social
formations and in the articulation of different
social formations. (Rey and Dupré, 1978,
p. 132).

One last example of the same: in discussing the
emphasis placed by Marxists on the ultimately
determining role of the material infrastructure, a
German anthropologist, Riesebrodt, suggests that
substantivism is essentially in agreement with
Marxism. To do so he contrives a remarkable
interpretation of what Polanyi meant by the
"embeddedness" of economy in society: if economy
permeates all parts of society, then economy must
ultimately shape all of society and in some sense is
itself part of the social process of material
reproduction. It seems to Riesebrodt (1973, pp. 79,
81), therefore, that Marx and Polanyi do not represent

rival theories, but rather that substantivism is
contained within historical materialism.

Our purpose is not to point out the glaring
semantic/conceptual ambiguities and misunderstandings
in these examples, but rather to convey our
astonishment at the extent to which several Marxists
claim the work of the Polanyi group as part of their
own paradigm, a claim which we think to be utter
nonsense.

There are, of course, definite similarities
between Marx and Polanyi. Both regarded the
burgeoning of industrial capitalism in nineteenth
century Europe as a unique occurrence in human
history. Marx very clearly separated the capitalist
mode of production from precapitalist modes.
Polanyi's idea of a "great transformation" also
emphasizes the deep differences between industrial
capitalism and the societies which came earlier. His
"substantive" meaning of economic and Marx's "mode of
production" also appear to be similar. In defining
the substantive meaning, Polanyi spoke of ". . . man's
dependence for his living upon nature and his
fellows," and economy as an "instituted process of
interaction between man and his environment." He
characterized "economic elements" as "ecological,
technological, or societal according to whether they
belong primarily to the natural environment, the
mechanical equipment, or the human setting" (Polanyi,
et al., 1957, pp. 243, 248, 249). All this is
obviously similar to Marx's "mode of production," with
its "material forces" and "social relations" of
production (Marx, 1970, pp. 20, 21). But the
conclusions each drew were utterly different. For
Marx, the "mode of production of material life
conditions the general process of social, political,
and intellectual life" in all societies, capitalist
and precapitalist (Marx, 1970, p. 21). But for
Polanyi, Marx's economic determinism is true only for
capitalist society.

> The market mechanism, moreover, created the
> delusion of economic determinism as a general
> law for all human society. Under a market
> economy, of course, this law holds good. . . .
> To attempt to apply economic determinism to all
> human societies is little short of fantastic.
> Nothing is more obvious to the student of social
> anthropology than the variety of institutions

found to be compatible with practically identical instruments of production. (Polanyi, 1947, p. 71)

A further difference between Marx and Polanyi lies in their analysis of future events. Marx predicted that capitalism's chronic and worsening malfunctioning would induce a socialist revolution and then advance through the stage of socialism to an ultimate stage of communism. Indeed, both Marx and Engels (1963, p. 57ff) contended that the meaning of any historical process could only be grasped if the past is interpreted in the light of the future. On this very Marxian attribute, Kolakowski says "Marxism . . . would not be Marxism without its claim to 'scientific knowledge' of the future" (Kolakowski, 1978 III, p. 525). In contrast, Polanyi did no such predicting of the future. His concern in the closing chapters of The Great Transformation (1944) and in "Our obsolete market mentality" (1947) is to argue against iron laws of economic determinism, the laws of Ricardo and Marx.

Capitalism was Marx's main focus of attention--the earlier stages leading to capitalism, how capitalism worked, and what would supersede the breakdown of capitalism. To be sure, in The Great Transformation Polanyi was also concerned with the origins of capitalism, how it functioned in the nineteenth and early twentieth centuries, and its collapse in the nineteen thirties. But even in The Great Transformation (especially chapter 4), he was already concerned with the historical and anthropological uniqueness of capitalism and how differently precapitalist economies were organized. All his later work was, in fact, concerned with these precapitalist economies. His emphasis on the substantive definition of economic is due to his insistence that only this meaning ". . . is capable of yielding the concepts that are required for an investigation of all the empirical economies of the past and present" (Polanyi, et al., 1957, p. 244; our emphasis). From the outset, then, Polanyi included the wealth of ethnographic data available to him. Ever since Hobsbawm's (1964) volume of Marx's notes on precapitalist economic formations, and Krader's (1972) volume of Marx's ethnographic notebooks, we have been aware of the limited range of ethnographic data used by Marx. Here Polanyi had a definite advantage, writing, as he did, some eighty years after Marx, and having access to the work of Malinowski, Thurnwald, and others. Polanyi's use of much more ethnographic data distinguishes his work from Marx's. Another distinction is that Marx's analytical concepts were designed primarily for nineteenth century capitalism.

Marxists today, especially Marxist anthropologists, have to stretch Marx's concepts to accommodate subject matter they were not originally designed for. Marx's own writings are often far from what the several Marxisms today are concerned with. One reason for this multiplication of Marxisms is that from the time of the Third International onwards, Marxism became a rigid cultural and political doctrine in the Soviet-dominated East, but in the West, it was absorbed by numerous groups, some of which initiated thematic innovations that, as Anderson tells us, have also been labeled Marxism:

> The mark of these [thematic innovations] is their radical novelty to the classical legacy of Marxism. They can be defined by the absence of any indication or anticipation of them in the writings of either the young or the old Marx, or the work of his heirs in the Second International. The pertinent criterion here is not the validity of these innovations, or their compatibility with the basic principles of Marxism: it is their originality. (Anderson, 1977, p. 78ff)

But the very originality of these innovations is sometimes so novel that they have little more in common with Marx than the label Marxism and the use of concepts originally employed by Marx in different contexts; so too, the thematic innovations in Marxian economic anthropology (Anderson, 1977). Meillassoux (1975), for example, analyzed the elders' control of access to women among the Guro of West Africa, arguing that women play a central role in each mode of production as bearers of children, who, of course, are future producers: women reproduce producers. And so Meillassoux introduced the notion of biological reproduction into historical materialism, a thematic innovation not to be found in Marx's work. That elders among the Guro control access to women, thus giving them power over junior men, started a lengthy discussion among Marxists about whether or not elders are a class, and whether they exploit juniors. At first Terray (1972, pp. 169, 170) denied that such exploitation by elders of juniors occurred, but later changed his mind (Terray, 1975, pp. 95-96) and agreed with Rey and Dupré (1978) that elders did, indeed, exploit juniors. But then Godelier (1972, p. 274) disagreed that such exploitation took place, because subsistence goods as well as means of production are excluded from social competition in primitive economies, that is, they are accessible to everyone, and so exploitation cannot take place between Guro elders and juniors.

Godelier may be regarded as initiating another thematic innovation in Marxism. He asserted that inequality should not necessarily be viewed as exploitation but rather as an exchange between those in charge of religious or political duties and those who produce goods necessary for livelihood (Godelier 1972, p. 275; 1978, p. 767). Hindess and Hirst (1975, p. 22) then joined in to reject the notion of exploitation in primitive economies because the appropriation of surplus labor in such societies takes the form of communal appropriation where there is no social division of labor between a class of laborers and a class of nonlaborers. But then John Moore, also a Marxist, asserted that exploitation occurred among the Cheyenne of Oklahoma, for a rather remarkable and novel reason:

> The fundamentals of the exploitation of junior women by senior women. . . . are as follows: essentially, the younger women produced more and consumed less than the older women, although all women gradually consumed more and produced less as they got older. (Moore, 1979)

Even about the very basic Marxian concept, "mode of production," we find a similar array (and therefore disarray) of opinion among Marxist anthropologists. When Meillassoux spoke of one mode of production for the self-subsisting agricultural community, Terray (1974) criticized him and suggested the existence of several modes of production (based on different forms of relations of production). At first Meillassoux assented and acknowledged the coexistence of several modes of production in one society (Meillassoux, 1972). But several years later he dismissed the concept of mode of production saying that ". . . this term has no real scientific status in Marx's work" (1975, p. 114). But Terray, who insisted on the simultaneous presence of several modes of production in one society, himself came in for comradely

criticism by a fellow Marxist who pointed out that
Terray failed to establish any relationship between
different modes, and did not explain the shift from
one mode to another (Cooper, 1978, p. 144). Godelier
even more severely criticized Terray's usage of the
concept by saying that from Terray's view ". . . to
the invention of a masculine mode of production
(hunting), which is dominant over a feminine mode of
production (gathering), is just a short step which
certain enthusiastic disciples have already taken"
(Godelier, 1975, p. 25, ft. 13).

Other thematic innovations were also suggested,
such as geographically defined modes of production:
Coquery-Vidrovitch (1975, p. 37) created an "African
mode of production," and Cardoso (1975, p. 1)
"colonial modes of production of the Americas."
Although Godelier criticized such proliferation of
modes of production, he himself talked of "different
modes of production combined in a specific way in a
specific society," when he analyzed Inca society. But
then an equally fervent Marxist, Jonathan Friedman,
(1976, p. 16) entirely dismissed the concept, saying
that ". . . mode of production as a theoretical object
has no explanatory value at all." Finally, Hindess
and Hirst (1975) defined mode of production in such a
rigid fashion that it became sterile.

So too there is disagreement among Marxist
economic anthropologists about the core Marxian
concepts such as: forces of production, relations of
production, surplus, and class. Such disagreement
makes it very difficult to decide what exactly Marxian
economic anthropology is actually saying. In trying
to fill Marx's old concepts and conclusions with new
content important to the subject of economic
anthropology, Marxist anthropologists wind up in utter
disagreement among themselves. It seems that Marxian
economic anthropology shares a name but not a
paradigm. This too distinguishes it from the Polanyi
group, who do, indeed, share a paradigm.

References

ADAMS, R. Mc. 1975. The emerging place of trade in
   civilization studies. In Ancient civilization and
   trade. J. A. Sabloff and C. C. Lamberg-Karlovsky,
   eds. Albuquerque: University of New Mexico Press.

ADELMAN, Irma, and Cynthia Taft Morris. 1978. Patterns of market expansion in the nineteenth century: a quantitative study. In Research in economic anthropology, vol. 1. G. Dalton, ed. Greenwich, CT: JAI Press.

ANDERSON, Perry. 1977. Considerations on western Marxism. London: NLB.

ANNALES. 1974. L'anthropologie economique et histoire: l'ouvre de Karl Polanyi. Annales: Economies, Societés, Civilisations, Decembre.

CARDOSO, C. F. S. 1975. On the colonial modes of production of the Americas. Critique of Anthropology 1(4-5).

CLAESSEN, H. J. M., and Peter Skalnik. 1978. The early state. The Hague: Mouton.

CLARKE, David. 1968. Analytical Archaeology. London: Methuen.

CLARK, G. 1965. Traffic in stone axe and adze blades. The Economic History Review 18:1-28.

COCHRANE, Glynn. 1971. Development anthropology. New York: Oxford University Press.

CONGDON, Lee. 1976. Karl Polanyi in Hungary. Journal of Contemporary History 11:167-183.

COOPER, R. G. 1978. Dynamic tension: symbiosis and contradiction in Hmong social relations. In Relations of production. D. Seddon, ed. London: Frank Cass.

COQUERY-VIDROVITCH, C. 1975. Research on an African mode of production. Critique of Anthropology 1(4-5).

DALTON, George. 1961. Economic theory and primitive society. American Anthropologist 63:1-25.

_____. 1968. Introduction to Primitive, archaic, and modern economies, essays of Karl Polanyi. G. Dalton, ed. New York: Anchor Books.

_____. 1969. Theoretical issues in economic anthropology. Current Anthropology 10:63-102.

_____. 1975. Karl Polanyi's analysis of long-distance trade and his wide paradigm. In Ancient civilization and trade. J. Sabloff and C. C. Lamberg-Karlovsky, eds. Albuquerque: University of New Mexico Press.

_____. 1978. The impact of colonization on aboriginal economies in stateless societies. In Research in economic anthropology vol. 1. G. Dalton, ed. Greenwich, CT: JAI Press.

_____. 1981. The economic anthropology of colonial impact. Paper given at a conference on "Culture, Economy, and Polity in the Colonial Situation," University of Minnesota, May 14-16.

DE STE. CROIX, G. E. M. 1960. Review of trade and market in the early empires. Economic History Review 12:510-511.

EARLE, Timothy K. 1977. A reappraisal of redistribution: complex Hawaiian chiefdoms. In Exchange systems in pre-history. T. K. Earle and J. E. Ericson, eds. New York: Academic Press.

ENNEW, J. 1979. Anthropological views on historical materialism and kinship. Economy and Society 8:99-124.

EPSTEIN, T. Scarlett. 1962. Economic development and social change in South India. Manchester: Manchester University Press.

_____. 1973. South India, yesterday, today, tomorrow. London: MacMillan.

FINLEY, M. I. 1960. Slavery in classical antiquity. Cambridge: Heffer.

_____. 1973. The ancient economy. London: Chatto and Windus.

_____. 1980. Ancient slavery and modern ideology. New York: Viking.

FORDE, C. D. 1934. Habitat, economy, and society. New York: E. P. Dutton and Co., Inc.

FRIEDMAN, J. 1976. Marxist theory and systems of total reproduction. Critique of Anthropology 2(7).

GARLAN, Y. 1973. L'oeuvre de Polanyi: la place de l'économie dans les societés anciennes. La Pensée 171 (October):119-127.

GEERTZ, C. 1963. Agricultural involution. Berkeley: University of California Press.

_____. 1980. Ports of trade in nineteenth century Bali. In Research in economic anthropology, vol. 3. G. Dalton, ed. Greenwich, CT: JAI Press.

GODELIER, M. 1972. Rationality and irrationality in economics. New York: Monthly Review Press.

_____. 1975. Modes of production, kinship, and demographic studies. In Marxist analyses and social anthropology. M. Bloch, ed. New York: Halstead Press.

_____. 1977. Perspectives in Marxist anthropology. London: Cambridge University Press.

_____. 1978. Infrastructure, society, and history. Current Anthropology 19:763-771.

GRIERSON, Philip. 1978. The origins of money. In Research in economic anthropology, vol. 1. G. Dalton, ed. Greenwich, CT: JAI Press.

_____. 1980. The silent trade. Edinburgh: William Green and Sons. Reprinted in Research in economic anthropology vol. 3.

HEIDER, Karl. 1969. Visiting trade institutions. American Anthropologist 71:461-471.

HINDESS, B., and P. Q. Hirst. 1975. Precapitalist modes of production. London: Routledge and Kegan Paul.

HOBSBAWM, E. J. 1964. Precapitalist economic formations. New York: International Publishers.

HODDER, B. W. 1965. Some comments on the origins of traditional markets in Africa south of the Sahara.

Transactions of the Institute of British Geographers, vol. 36.

HODGES, Richard. 1978. Ports of trade in early Medieval Europe. Norwegian Archaeological Review 11:97-101.

HOPKINS, A. G. 1973. An economic history of West Africa. New York: Columbia University Press.

HUMPHREYS, S. C. 1969. History, economics, and anthropology: the work of Karl Polanyi. History and Theory 8:165-212.

KINDLEBERGER, Charles. 1974. Twentieth century masterpieces. Daedalus.

KÖCKE, Jasper. 1979. Some early German contributions to economic anthropology. In Research in economic anthropology, vol. 2. G. Dalton, ed. Greenwich, CT: JAI Press.

KOLAKOWSKI, L. 1978. Main currents in Marxism. 3 volumes. Oxford: Clarendon Press.

KRADER, L. 1972. The ethnological notebooks of Karl Marx. Assen: Van Gorcum.

KUHN, Thomas S. 1962. The structure of scientific revolutions. Chicago: The University of Chicago Press.

KURIMOTO, Shinichiro. 1980. Silent trade in Japan. In Research in economic anthropology, vol. 3. G. Dalton, ed. Greenwich, CT: JAI Press.

LAW, Robin. 1977. The Oyo empire, c. 1606-c. 1836. Oxford: Clarendon Press.

_____. 1978. Slaves, trade, and taxes: the material basis of political power in pre-colonial West Africa. In Research in economic anthropology, vol. 1. G. Dalton, ed. Greenwich, CT: JAI Press.

LEE, R. B., and I. De Vore, eds. 1968. Man the hunter. Chicago: Aldine.

LEWIS, W. Arthur. 1954. Economic development with unlimited supplies of labour. The Manchester school. May 1954.

_____. 1970. Tropical development, 1880-1913. Evanston: Northwestern University Press.

LONG, Norman. 1977. An introduction to the sociology of rural development. London: Tavistock.

MALINOWSKI, B. 1935. Coral gardens and their magic. 2 vols. London: Allen and Unwin Ltd.

MANCALL, M. 1968. The Ch'ing tribute system: an interpretive essay. In The Chinese world order. J. K. Fairbank, ed. Cambridge: Harvard University Press.

MARX, K. 1970. Contribution to the critique of political economy. New York: International Publishers.

MARX, K., and F. Engels. 1963. Gesamtausgabe. Bd. 22. Berlin: Dietz.

MATHUR, H. M. 1977. Anthropology in the development process. Atlantic Highlands, NJ: Humanities Press.

MEILLASSOUX, C. 1960. Essai d'interpretation du phenomene économique dans les societés traditionelles d'autosubsistance. Cahiers d'Etudes Africaines 4:38-67.

_____. 1972. From reproduction to production: a Marxist approach to economic anthropology. Economy and Society 1:93-105.

_____. 1975. Femmes grenier et capitaux. Paris: Maspero.

MIERS, Suzanne, and Igor Kopytoff. 1977. Slavery in Africa. Madison: University of Wisconsin Press.

MOORE, J. 1979. Marx on horseback: an application of rigid materialist concepts to Cheyenne ethnography. ms.

MOSELEY, K. P. 1979. The political economy of Dahomey. In Research in economic anthropology, vol. 2. G. Dalton, ed. Greenwich, CT: JAI Press.

MURRA, John Victor. 1980. The economic organization of the Inca state. Greenwich, CT: JAI Press.

ODNER, K. 1972. Ethno-historic and ecological settings for economic and social models of an iron-age society: Valdalen, Norway. In Models in archaeology. David L. Clarke, ed. London: Methuen.

PEUKERT, Werner. 1978. Der Atlantische Sklavenhandel von Dahomey (1740-1797). Wiesbaden: Steiner.

PITT, David C. 1976. Development from below: anthropologists and development situations. Chicago: Aldine.

POLANYI, Karl. 1944. The great transformation. New York: Rinehart.

_____. 1947. Our obsolete market mentality. Commentary 3:109-117. Reprinted in Polanyi, 1968.

_____. 1957. The semantics of money uses. Explorations (a magazine published by the University of Toronto). Reprinted in Polanyi, 1968.

_____. 1960. On the comparative treatment of economic institutions in antiquity with illustrations from Athens, Mycenae, and Alalakh. In City invincible: a symposium on urbanization and cultural development in the ancient Near East. C. H. Kraeling and R. M. Adams, eds. Chicago: University of Chicago Press. Reprinted in Polanyi, 1968.

_____. 1963. Ports of trade in early societies. The Journal of Economic History 23:30-45. Reprinted in Polanyi, 1968.

_____. 1964. Sortings and 'ounce trade' in the West African slave trade. The Journal of African History 4:382-393. Reprinted in Polanyi, 1968.

_____. 1966. Dahomey and the slave trade. Seattle: University of Washington Press.

_____. 1968. Primitive, archaic, and modern economies: essays of Karl Polanyi. New York: Anchor Books. Reprinted by Beacon Press, 1971.

_____. 1977. The livelihood of man. New York: Academic Press.

POLANYI, K., C. M. Arensberg, and H. W. Pearson. 1957. Trade and market in the early empires. Glencoe, Ill: Free Press.

PRICE, John A. 1980. On silent trade. In Research in economic anthropology, vol. 3. G. Dalton, ed. Greenwich, CT: JAI Press.

REY, P. P., and G. Dupré. 1978. Reflections on the pertinence of a theory of the history of exchange. In Relations of production. D. Seddon, ed. London: Frank Cass.

RICHARDS, A. I., F. Sturrock, and J. M. Fortt. 1973. Subsistence to commercial farming in present-day Buganda. Cambridge: Cambridge University Press.

RIESEBRODT, M. 1973. Zur Theorie diskussion in der Wirtschafts-ethnologie. Unpublished Ph.D. dissertation, Heidelberg University.

SABLOFF, J. A., and C. C. Lamberg-Karlovsky. 1975. Ancient civilization and trade. Albuquerque: University of New Mexico Press.

SEDDON, D., ed. 1978. Relations of production. Marxist approaches to economic anthropology. London: Frank Cass.

SIEVERS, Allen Morris. 1949. Has market capitalism collapsed? A critique of Karl Polanyi's new economics. New York: Columbia University Press.

SINGER, Hans. 1950. The distribution of gains between investing and borrowing countries. American Economic Review, papers and proceedings, May.

SLICHER VAN BATH, B. H. 1963. The agrarian history of western Europe, A.D. 500-1850. London: Edward Arnold.

SMITH, T. 1982. Wampum as primitive valuables. In Research in economic anthropology, vol. 5. G. Dalton, ed. Greenwich, CT: JAI Press.

STANFIELD, J. Ron. 1980. The institutional economics of Karl Polanyi. Journal of Economic Issues 14:593-614.

TERRAY, E. 1972. Marxism and primitive societies. New York: Monthly Review Press.

_____. 1975. Classes and class consciousness in the Abron kingdom of Gyaman. In Marxist analyses and social anthropology. M. Bloch, ed. New York: Wiley.

TORRENCE, Robin. 1978. Comment on "Ports of trade in early Medieval Europe." Norwegian Archaeological Review 11:108-111.

VAN LEUR, J. C. 1967. Indonesian trade and society. The Hague: W. van Hoeve.

VANSINA, Jan. 1973. The Tio kingdom of the Middle Congo, 1880-1892. London: Oxford University Press.

_____. 1978. The children of Woot, a history of the Kuba peoples. Madison: University of Wisconsin Press.

WACHTEL, Nathan. 1977. The vision of the vanquished. Hassocks, England: The Harvester Press.

WALLMAN, Sandra. 1969. Take out hunger, two case studies of rural development in Basutoland. London: The Athlone Press.

WHEATLEY, Paul. 1975. Satyanrta in Suvarnadvipa: from reciprocity to redistribution in ancient Southeast Asia. In Ancient civilization and trade. J. A. Sabloff and C. C. Lamberg-Karlovsky, eds. Albuquerque: The University of New Mexico Press.

WILKS, Ivor. 1975. _Asante in the nineteenth century_. Cambridge: Cambridge University Press.

WISSLER, Clark. 1914. The influence of the horse in the development of plains culture. _American Anthropologist_ 16:1-25.

III.   FACTORS UNDERLYING THE ORIGIN AND EVOLUTION OF MARKET SYSTEMS

Richard E. Blanton

Studies devoted to understanding the role of production and distribution in cultural evolutionary processes are notably on the increase in contemporary anthropological archaeology; the recent publication of two volumes on this topic attests to this growing orientation (Earle and Ericson, 1977; Sabloff and Lamberg-Karlovsky, 1975; cf. Adams, 1974). But severe gaps persist, in the double sense of a shortage of information and a lack of adequate theoretical development. The following quote from Paul Wheatley characterizes reasonably well the state of the art in studies of economic systems in archaeology (he refers here to work on the early Southeast Asian states, but the characterization can be applied with perhaps only slight amendment to the majority of work done in the field as a whole):

> So far as ancient commerce is concerned, such studies as exist have been undertaken with the limited aims of identifying within a more or less static framework the commodities traded, and charting the routes over which they moved. Only nominal attention has been devoted to exchange values, and none at all to the fundamental and exigent question of the precise modes of exchange involved and the manner in which they articulated with political, administrative, social, religious, and other institutions (Wheatley, 1975, p. 230).

Wheatley's critique applies particularly well to studies of ancient market systems as a context for exchange. This is unfortunate since, although market systems are not present in simple human societies, they are, generally speaking, present in early or archaic states (cf. Claessen and Skalník, 1978, Table II), and in some cases are to be counted among society's most important institutions. In spite of this, archaeologists interested in early civilizations have tended to devote most of their efforts to comprehending the evolution of centralized political forms. We have an abundance of theories and data pertaining to the origin of the state, yet our understanding of early market systems is probably best described as anemic. Most archaeologists simply ignore the problem, while others deny the existence of market systems in early times. This latter stance is attributable in large part to the very influential evolutionary theorists, especially Sahlins (1958) and Service (1975), who converted Polanyi's ideas about the redistributive economy into a scenario for early political evolution: they argue that centralized political institutions evolved under pressure to move goods between groups occupying contrasting environmental settings. We now know that attempts by evolutionary theorists and Polanyi to embed the economy in the early political institutions were, to say the least, overambitious (Earle, 1977; Adams, 1974).

Another excuse used for the nonattention to market exchange is the widely-accepted idea that the data, both archaeological and early literary, are biased against this aspect of human behavior, especially by comparison with the often times elaborate material remains of human action in the political sphere. To a certain degree this is true, but probably not to the extent that most people assume. As I see it, the real bias against market exchange does not derive from the data but from the anti-market mentality of anthropologists. When my colleagues and I decided to devote some effort to comprehending the role (if any) of market exchange in the evolution of Zapotec civilization in Oaxaca, answers were forthcoming to a gratifying degree. Pertinent information can be found, if archaeologists are willing to reorient field and analytical strategies away from more traditional approaches.

My purpose here is to correct this unwarranted bias in studies of early complex societies by emphasizing the role that market systems play in cultural change in a way that is not usually done in anthropological archaeology. I do not expect the following suggestions to be accepted by all of my archaeological colleagues, but I do hope, however, that they will be stimulated to think about a perspective that includes more than is traditionally considered in scenarios of cultural evolution. I approach this complex topic by making three proposals about the ways in which market systems evolve, and about the consequences of market system growth in the long-term evolution of civilizations. I developed these proposals in part based on my work on cultural evolution in the prehispanic Valley of Oaxaca (with my colleagues Steve Kowalewski, Gary Feinman, Jill Appel, and Laura Finsten), and in part on comparative studies of early markets and early states. These proposals are not to be construed as a general or complete theory of market origins and evolution, nor to be fully tested with data from Oaxaca. That would be a far more difficult task than I have assumed here. Instead, my goal is to identify several key factors we think were in operation in the long-term evolution of market systems in ancient Oaxaca, factors which, I think, may prove to have been at work in the evolution of market systems elsewhere.

At the outset, I want to make the distinction between market systems and what I will refer to as "border markets." In the past there has been a tendency to confuse these two classes of market exchange, which in some cases has led to confusion in discussions of market system origins, how they are structured, and how they function. Border markets may occur in many kinds of societies--even very simple ones where market systems are very unlikely (this distinction is discussed more fully in Blanton, et al., 1982a). They involve face-to-face exchanges by bartering, but they are exchange institutions that operate only along lines of cleavage in strongly segmented regions where there are social barriers to free movement. They typically involve exchanges of goods that are not uniformly distributed, i.e. production specialities based on contrasting environmental settings. Market system exchange, in contrast, while involving this category of production specialities to some degree, is exchange primarily of products that could be, but are not, produced by self-sufficient households. Market system development thus attests to a greater division of labor within society, rather than a division of labor between societies. My concern in the following is exclusively with market system exchange.

Before I present my hypotheses, I will give you a brief introduction to our Oaxaca findings. We think that the first market system exchange started in the Valley of Oaxaca during what is locally referred to as Monte Albán Period Early I, dating to about 500 B.C. We based this conclusion on the integration of four separate lines of evidence in our data and the data of other researchers which suggests the presence of market exchanges. Most of the evidence is ceramic because it is more abundant and can be more easily chronologically classified than any other category of manufactured items. Briefly, these lines of evidence are:

1) Formal changes in the pottery of the period suggest production by specialists and less household self-sufficiency (Winter, 1974).

2) This is the first period for which there is unequivocal evidence for ceramic workshops (Feinman, 1980; Blanton, et al., 1982a; Winter, 1974).

3) The distribution of these specialized ceramic production sites conforms to some of the elementary expectations of central-place theory. We assumed that in a market situation pottery producers would locate themselves so as to minimize the costs of moving the bulky, fragile, and heavy pots to distribution points. The clay needed for the production of the various ware types is present throughout the valley, so we can be sure that the distribution of pottery producing sites does not reflect the distribution of raw material. The distributional pattern of production sites, hence, should give a faint image of the spatial organization of the marketing points. We then classified the pottery according to whether the types would have been the equivalent of high, middle, or low order goods. We found that high order types were produced only in few places, located so as to be able to efficiently supply the whole population of the Valley. Lower order categories were produced in a larger number of places, scattered over a wider area, each workshop supplying a smaller, localized area. Families more distant from the suppliers of the high order goods had significantly less access to those same goods.

4) An architectural feature that suggests a marketplace and is dated Monte Albán I, was found. Adjacent to it we also found abundant evidence of pottery and lithic production. As far as we know this is the first of this type of structure so far discovered. There were undoubtedly more marketplaces, but they are difficult to identify archaeologically; furthermore, many of the early marketplaces were probably obliterated by later construction.

Using similar procedures (i.e. analyzing change through time in the formal and distributional aspects

54

of ceramic categories, and change in the distribution of ceramic production sites) we traced the history of market systems up to the end of the prehispanic sequence. While the complete story would be too long in the telling here, we reached several major conclusions about the long-term trajectory of market exchange in the Valley. First, a market system initially emerged in the context of a period of rapid evolutionary change in which the region became more integrated by the addition of a third level of administrative hierarchy, a change that was manifested by the construction of a new political capital. Second, while the market system at this initial date seems to have been largely free of administrative control, it was the case that during later periods closer linkages were forged between commercial and governmental institutions. Isomorphism of market system and state reached its peak during the Classic Period (A.D. 250-700) when society's most important institution at the regional level was a highly centralized state focused on a large, architecturally elaborate regal-ritual capital. Our final major conclusion about the long-term evolution of the market system was that the collapse of this centralized state resulted in a cultural landscape during the Postclassic that was quite unlike its Classic Period predecessor. I think that we can reasonably argue that by the end of the prehispanic sequence there was a degree of commercialization in the region not surpassed in any of the prior periods, and that the market system, rather than a political institution, provided society's most important linkages at the regional scale. The proposals that follow serve as a background to understand this set of changes. As the first proposal has to do with the origins of the market system, I will first say a few words about these theories.

Current theories of market system development can be divided into two schools (C. Smith, 1976, pp. 44-45): those that explain development from the "bottom up" or the "top down" (cf. Berry, 1967; Polanyi et al., 1957; C. Smith, 1974). The first approach views market development as the result of several factors operating among rural agriculturalists, especially the assumed propensity for humans to truck, barter and exchange goods. Although usually associated with the ideas of Adam Smith, this school also includes other proposed explanations that focus on local or "internal" changes, such as the development of surplus-producing technologies (Berry, 1967, p. 108), population growth (Skinner, 1964; Hodder and Ukwu, 1969) and topographic and climatic diversity (Sanders, 1956). Each of these explanations has in common the proposition that market exchange will develop without external stimulation when local conditions are appropriate.

Alternately, the "top down" school argues that market exchange is not likely to develop internally. It is, instead, the consequence of external influences. These external or foreign influences—such as long distance exchange (cf. Meillassoux, 1971; Vance, 1970), urban food needs (Appleby, 1976), and the demand of an elite class in stratified societies (C. Smith, 1974)—are viewed as the forces necessary for promoting market transactions among rural agricultural villagers.

Our Oaxaca data do not unequivocally support either the top-down or the bottom-up scenarios for market origins. We doubt, for example, that the market was instituted by the governing elite. While it will be difficult to demonstrate this conclusively, the fact that the early market and production sites that we have been able to identify are situated away from settlements that clearly had administrative functions suggests that markets were not instituted by governing elites. We think that the city was provisioned by non-market means, and we are by no means sure how the region's new capital was tied into the market system. It evidently had few if any commercial functions. As it was first developed, the market system may have been in large part a rural institution, providing certain household items to an emerging peasantry. This brings me to my first proposal.

Proposal 1. <u>The origin of market systems can be understood primarily as a consequence of the changing rhythm of work-time during the emergence of a peasantry</u>.

It is probably not coincidental that these first bits of evidence favoring a market system as a framework for exchange pertain to a time when, as our data indicate, there was a widespread shift from the one crop agricultural cycle of the Early and Middle Formative to the two crop cycle that characterized later times. This two crop cycle included a dry-season crop aided by small canal irrigation systems, already noted by Kent Flannery and his colleagues. This adaptation--prompted, no doubt, by the rapid increase in the urban population--would have involved a new rhythm of work-time for the emergent peasantry, with fewer periods completely free from agricultural labor. I suggest that in the context of altered work budgets, families must have devised strategies aimed at preserving at least some degree of non-work time in spite of the new demands. One of these strategies could have been to obtain certain household replacement items from specialized producers. The latter can provide them at low cost due to the scale advantages and skill advantages associated with specialized production. The market system, then, would have been a kind of labor-saving device for the primary producers.

Ethnographic and historical parallels can be mentioned. Eric Waddell (1972) noted the implications for the scheduling of household activities of intensive versus extensive agriculture in Highland New Guinea. Thomas Smith noted that in 18th century Japan an intensification of agricultural production had the following consequences for a rural family:

> In 1728, 45 man-days were spent gathering firewood, but only eight were used in this work in 1804; by that time the family presumably bought most of its fuel. There was also a shift from natural to commercial fertilizers, dried fish replacing grass gathered on the mountainside. The labor saved by this shift was employed in new tasks; in the care of the cocoons and in silk reeling, of course, but also in more intensive cultivation (T. Smith, 1959, pp. 85-86).

Viewed in this way, it could be argued that market systems provide advantages to a governing elite, since, as a kind of labor-saving device, peasant producers participating in a market system are able to devote more time to intensified agriculture and the production of surpluses to support that elite. This in some ways parallels Carol Smith's (1974, p. 193) suggestion that the urban elite will institute market systems to stimulate higher levels of agricultural production. As she put it, the market system allows the peasantry to become petty capitalists, therefore probably producing more surpluses than their tribute-paying forebearérs. But more complete appraisal of the advantages of market systems for an elite requires that we look at the nature of the political process in early states. This brings me to my second proposal, which has to do with the role market systems play in the growth of powerful states.

Proposal 2. A common product of the political process in early states is the evolution of a more elaborate market system.

A key aspect of the political process in early states is to be found in the mutual antagonism that exists between those at the center (the state), and those who govern at the level of the district or localized domain--by far the best discussion of this process and its outcomes is found in S. N. Eisenstadt's monumental Political Systems of Empires, 1969. The conflicts between these groups arise from the contrasting strategies used by the ruler, on the one hand, who wishes to solidify control at the regional scale, and the strategies used by the nobility, on the other hand, whose goal is to minimize the importance of the expansionist state apparatus so as to maximize the autonomy of the patrimonial domain. The key strategy of the state, Eisenstadt points out, is to bolster certain institutions whose activities are inimical to the continued autonomy of local level controls (e.g., a rationalized bureaucracy, a state army, etc.). Eisenstadt's comparative study demonstrates very nicely the importance that market systems assume in this regard: as a kind of "tool" in the arsenal of the state working to break down the traditional political system and replace it with a new, more centralized, regime.

A well-developed market system is important to the success of the state in two respects. The first has to do with the nature of labor control. The ideal form of labor control viewed from the perspective of the overlords of the local domains is one in which each domain is a tightly bounded administrative unit where peasants have only a limited degree of freedom of movement, and where their surpluses are regularly directed in vertical fashion to the overlords, according to traditional obligations. In contrast, a well-developed market system implies a regional-scale economy extending beyond the bounds of the local administrative districts. The fluidity of movement of peasants implied in a regional-scale market system, and the freedom of producers to direct their surpluses to the market, are inimical to the more structured requirements of the localized nobility. The market system is thus compatible with state goals. The compatibility of state and market is visible in a second sense. In order for rulers to extend their control over the larger territorial entity, they must mobilize resources of the sort referred to by Eisenstadt as "free-floating." That is, they must mobilize resources outside the framework of the traditional patrimonial domains. In early states, the market system is probably the single most important source of such funds. Market places as concentrated nodes of commercial activity are easily taxed with a minimum of administrative cost. As Gabriel Ardant puts it: "Tax collection and assessment are indissolubly linked to an exchange economy" (Ardant, 1975, p. 166). He goes on to say that:

> . . . seeing that taxation requires a certain economic structure, developed economic exchange, active commerce, and the division of labor, it behooves the state, and is in fact vital to its existence as a state, to bring its powers to bear upon that structure and to shape it into a structure better able to support taxation (Ardant, 1975, p. 196).

Ardant's conclusions are based on his study of the European experience since 1500, but they are not at all inconsistent with the results of Eisenstadt's comparative study, or with studies of other areas not touched on by Eisenstadt. For example, Elizabeth Brumfiel (1980) suggests that states might promote market system development in order to stimulate the agricultural production needed to support the state's urban centers (this parallels C. Smith's (1974) idea mentioned above).

A number of strategies may be employed by the state to promote market system development. Among the major strategies are the following: 1) The promotion of a free peasantry not tied to the obligations of the patrimonial domains; 2) The establishment of new markets and fairs under royal authority; 3) The establishment of a unified currency, which facilitates economic transactions over the whole of the larger spatial scale, and thus helps to break down the significance of local-level administrative boundaries.

(All of these points are discussed in passim in Eisenstadt (1969); Meillassoux (1971, p. 70) reached similar conclusions regarding currency in West Africa).

A Caveat: The preceding processes are evidently not inevitably a concomitant of the growth of strong states. In Russia, for example, the czars were not able to use the market in their state-building activities because there was virtually no pre-existing commercial framework on which to build (Ardant, 1975, p. 197). Their tactic was thus to freeze the peasantry and to create a patrimonial domain writ large.

To complete this section, I should point out that where the state/market symbiosis did develop, it should not be thought of as a kind of hand-in-glove harmony between the two institutions. Instead, the relationship becomes one of a dynamic interaction between potentially antagonistic forces. The augmentation of the market system may have the desired result of diminishing the influence of local-level controls, but the newly developed market system itself may come to resist the incursions and taxes imposed by the state. In essence, the political process simply shifts from one arena to another. An extremely strong state may resolve this problem by incorporating the market system into the official structure, as we think happened in Oaxaca, but if market institutions are powerful, they resist this level of state control. This brings me to my third proposition concerning the evolution of market systems.

Proposal 3. In the long-term evolution of civilizations, the degree of state control diminishes, in large part due to the growth of increasingly strong market systems.

Although market systems may become augmented in importance under the influence of an expanding state apparatus, they normally depend to a varying degree on that same apparatus for regulatory functions, such as adjudication. But the collapse of a state, while perhaps serious, does not always also lead to total collapse of the commercial system. In fact, I suggest that in some cases nearly the opposite occurs. I propose that it is in the context of the trauma that is brought on by collapse of central governments that market participants, wishing to preserve aspects of their traditional way of life in the light of drastically changed circumstances, engage in a flurry of innovation and institution-building so as to assure the continuation of some acceptable level of market functioning. The stress brought on by periods of weak government, in other words, provides the stimulus for the establishment of what Skinner refers to as "parapolitical" structures, capable of "informal governance" some in commercial contexts (Skinner, ed., 1977, pp. 336-344, 721, footnote 48)., Cross-culturally, probably the most common parapolitical institutions are the autonomous and autocephalous merchant cities, as well as other associations such as guilds. The establishment of the Khumseh confederacy by the merchant Ghavam, to keep commerce going in light of weakened state control of caravan routes, is a useful example (cf. Barth, 1961, pp. 86-8).

This proposed process of institution building has an important general consequence in the long-term evolution of civilizations. In all the early civilizations, the degree of state power varied through time. Periods of strong control were punctuated by periods of dynastic collapse and reorganization. However, market systems organized around parapolitical structures may have the capacity for a significant degree of self-regulation even when governments are weak. Furthermore, once such market institutions become established they can resist the reinstatement of strong centralized controls to a degree that would have been impossible during the initial stages of state building. Although the market provides a natural framework for the mobilization of resources needed for political centralization, historically later states often find the going much more difficult than what had been encountered by their predecessors: Early states built highly centralized structures in the context of much simpler cultural landscapes. This sequence produces the perhaps counter-intuitive result that the most definitive evidence for highly centralized control in the early civilizations usually pertains to the earliest periods of centralized control (e.g., the elaborate Old Kingdom monuments in Egypt vis à vis the more diminutive and poorly constructed later ones (cf. Rathje, 1975), or the decline in the degree of governmental effectiveness and involvement in commercial affairs in China from the mid T'ang up to the end of imperial times (Skinner, ed., 1977).

The Classic-Postclassic transition in Oaxaca and elsewhere in Mesoamerica illustrates this aspect of the secular change. The Postclassic states were never able to mobilize the labor for construction of public monuments on the scale of those of the Classic Period, nor were they able to direct the destinies of whole regional economies as had occurred in the Classic Period (cf. Blanton, et al., 1982b; Rathje, 1975). This is not to deny that strong centralized control can never be reinstituted. I suggest, however, that it is less likely, and there is a higher probability that the attempts to reestablish controls will be both unstable and short-lived.

CONCLUSION

My final point is a qualification of the third proposal. Although I think there are general trends in the early civilizations, leading to increased commercialization, the eventual outcome of this kind of long-term process is not identical everywhere. The kind of elaborated market system associated with capitalism was not independently developed in every area of early civilization, even though market institutions and merchants generally emerged with more significance in the later periods. Why this civilizational process has different outcomes in different places is not easy to understand, but several elementary points can be made. First, as Wallerstein (1974, Chapt. 1) pointed out, the ideal environment for the growth of capitalism is evidently a world economy like Western Europe, in which the economic system is of considerably larger spatial scale than the scale of any of the constituent political units. This condition was not met in China, which remained a world empire, with central governmental controls extending over the whole of the spatial scale of the economic system. But the idea of a world economy invites comparisons between Western Europe and prehispanic Mesoamerica. In 1500, both were world economies of similar scale. Steve Kowalewski pointed out to me that at that time both could be traversed with existing transportation in forty to sixty days. [2] Western Europe covers an area of some 2 million km^2, while Mesoamerica covers 1 million. Western Europe's population was about 70 million, Mesoamerica's roughly half that. So in some regards the two areas were not highly dissimilar. But while Mesoamerica was relatively highly commercialized in the late Postclassic, it did not seem to be moving in the direction, at least not very rapidly, of an independent development of capitalism. This is probably due largely to the fact that while Mesoamerica was an economic system of sorts over the whole of its geographical extent, the material flows across political boundaries were different from the flows across political boundaries in Western Europe. In Mesoamerica, most exchanges across political boundaries were exchanges of material pertaining to the Mesoamerican prestige system--i.e., elaborate goods consumed primarily by an elite. Europe had exchanges of this sort, too, but the movement of commodities destined for general consumption, things like cloth, wine, lumber, and grain, was much more important (there were some exchanges of bulk commodities in Mesoamerica, but not to this degree). In Mesoamerica, trade in preciosities was only slowly and to a minor degree converting itself into a bulk trade, as happened in Europe.

Does this mean that capitalism would never have developed in aboriginal Mesoamerica? Of course we will never know, but the character of the Mesoamerican world economy may have precluded a development of this sort. Consider for a moment just one factor: transportation. Since most long-distance exchange was in small, highly valuable items, it was not necessary to develop an elaborate technology for the long-distance movement of heavy, less valuable goods. Thus animals that could carry heavy loads were not domesticated, and the human carrier persisted as the basic machine of transportation.

This discussion needs to be greatly expanded, but I think what I have said illustrates the general point: that although there may be general long-term trends in the evolution of civilizations everywhere, their outcomes are by no means identical in each case.

Acknowledgments

I wish to acknowledge the stimulation provided by Steve Kowalewski, Gary Feinman, and Laura Finsten as I was preparing this paper; all errors are my responsibility. Funding for my work in Oaxaca has come primarily from National Science Foundation grants GS-28547, GS-38030, and BNS-19640.

References

ADAMS, Robert McC. 1974. Anthropological perspectives on ancient trade. Current Anthropology 15:239-258.

APPLEBY, Gordon. 1976. The role of urban food needs in regional development, Puno, Peru. In Regional analysis, volume 1: economic systems. Carol Smith, ed. New York: Academic Press.

ARDANT, Gabriel. 1975. Financial policy and economic infrastructure of modern states and nations. In The formation of national states in western Europe. Charles Tilly, ed. Princeton: Princeton University Press.

BARTH, Fredrik. 1961. Nomads of South Persia. Boston: Little, Brown and Co.

BERRY, Brian J. L. 1967. Geography of market centers and retail distribution. Englewood-Cliffs, N.J.: Prentice-Hall.

BLANTON, Richard E., Stephen Kowalewski, Gary Feinman and Jill Appel. 1982a. Monte Albán's hinterland, part 1: the prehispanic settlement patterns of the central and southern parts of the Valley of Oaxaca, Mexico. Museum of Anthropology, University of Michigan, Memoir 15.

_____. 1982b. Ancient Mesoamerica: a comparison of change in three regions. N.Y./Cambridge: Cambridge University Press.

BRUMFIEL, Elizabeth. 1980. Specialization, market exchange, and the Aztec state: a view from Huexotla. Current Anthropology 21:459-467.

CLAESSEN, Henry J. M., and Peter Skalník, eds. 1978. The early state. The Hague: Mouton.

EARLE, Timothy. 1977. A reappraisal of redistribution: complex Hawaiian chiefdoms. In Exchange systems in prehistory. T. Earle and J. Ericson, eds. New York: Academic Press.

EARLE, Timothy, and Jonathan Ericson, eds. 1977. Exchange systems in prehistory. New York: Academic Press.

EISENSTADT, S. N. 1969. The political systems of empires. New York: Free Press.

FEINMAN, Gary. 1980. The relationship between administrative organization and ceramic production in the Valley of Oaxaca, Mexico. Unpublished Ph.D. dissertation, Department of Anthropology, City University of New York.

HODDER, B. W., and U. Ukwu. 1969. Markets in West Africa. Ibadan University.

MEILLASSOUX, Claude. 1971. Introduction. In The development of indigenous trade and markets in West Africa. C. Meillassoux, ed. London: Oxford University Press.

POLANYI, Karl, Conrad Arensberg, and Harry Pearson, eds. 1957. Trade and market in the early empires. Glencoe, Illinois: The Free Press.

RATHJE, William. 1975. Last tango in Mayapán: a tentative trajectory of production-distribution systems. In Ancient civilization and trade. J. Sabloff and C. C. Lamberg-Karlovsky, eds. Albuquerque: University of New Mexico Press.

SABLOFF, Jeremy and C. C. Lamberg-Karlovsky, eds. 1975. Ancient civilization and trade. Albuquerque: University of New Mexico Press.

SAHLINS, Marshall D. 1958. Social stratification in Polynesia. Seattle: University of Washington Press.

SANDERS, William. 1956. The central Mexican symbiotic region. In Prehistoric settlement patterns in the New World. G. Willey, ed. New York: Viking Fund Publications in Anthropology 23.

SERVICE, Elman. 1975. The Origins of the state and civilization: the process of culture evolution. New York: Norton.

SKINNER, G. William. 1964. Marketing and social structure in rural China (part I). Journal of Asian Studies 24:3-43.

65

SKINNER, G. William, ed. 1977. The city in Late Imperial China. Stanford: Stanford University Press.

SMITH, Carol. 1974. Economics of marketing systems: models from economic geography. Annual Review of Anthropology 3:167-201.

_____. 1976. Regional economic systems: linking geographical models and socioeconomic problems. In Regional analysis, volume I: economic systems. Carol Smith, ed. New York: Academic Press.

SMITH, Thomas C. 1959. The agrarian origins of modern Japan. Stanford: Stanford University Press.

VANCE, James. 1970. The merchant's world. Englewood-Cliffs, N.J.: Prentice-Hall.

WADDELL, Eric. 1972. The mound builders. Seattle: University of Washington Press.

WALLERSTEIN, Immanuel. 1974. The modern world system: capitalist agriculture and the origins of the European world-economy in the sixteenth century. New York: Academic Press.

WHEATLEY, Paul. 1975. Satyarta in Suvarnadvipa: from reciprocity to redistribution in ancient southeast Asia. In Ancient civilization and trade. J. Sabloff and C. C. Lamberg-Karlovsky, eds. Albuquerque: University of New Mexico Press.

WINTER, Marcus. 1974. Late Formative society in the Valley of Oaxaca and the Mixteca Alta, Mexico. Paper presented at the XLI International Congress of Americanists, Mexico.

IV. SOME THEORETICAL CONSIDERATIONS ABOUT THE ROLE OF THE MARKET IN ANCIENT MEXICO

Pedro Carrasco

In Mesoamerican research, one normally understands by ethnohistory the study of pre-Spanish or Colonial societies on the basis of historical records, most of them the product of the early Colonial period. Thus a distinctive feature of ethnohistorical studies is that information exists about all aspects of culture and society, not only about those leaving material remains. It is therefore possible to study economic institutions such as property, markets, the organization of production and forms of labor, with actual descriptions of institutional arrangements, not only by inference from material remains as in archaeology.

Another feature is the heavy reliance on Colonial source materials. Most of these, even if they describe pre-Spanish conditions, are still written by Spaniards or by Spanish-influenced natives, and consequently call for careful examination for possible distortions caused by the mentality of the reporters. In the case of data referring to the early Colonial period, one also has to consider the modifications introduced by the Colonial regime.

Because of the level of complexity of the economy of ancient Mexico and because of the nature of ethnohistorical information, research in this field finds its closest affinity in the study of economic history, especially that of early and preindustrial civilizations.

In the theoretical literature of economic anthropology the approaches that are most relevant to the material that the student of early civilizations is concerned with are those associated with the work of Polanyi and Marx. Polanyi's interests in the economy of early empires--especially trade and markets--and in the origins of the modern economy are central to his outlook (Polanyi, et al., 1957; Polanyi, 1944, 1977). Marx's ideas about the existence of several modes of production have resulted in new interpretations of the economies of classical antiquity, feudalism, and especially of the Asiatic mode, where Wittfogel's work (1957) has made a particular impact. In this paper I refer mainly to Polanyi since I deal with the nature of the market. Were I to concentrate on the analysis of production, the approach would be more akin to Marx's (see Carrasco, 1978).

In contrast, it is striking that scholars using other theoretical approaches have not paid much attention to the comparative study of the economies of early civilizations. Herskovits's early survey of economic types was limited to the economies of "non-literate" societies and to the economic theory developed for the capitalist system (Herskovits, 1952). Economic history was neglected, especially as related to complex precapitalist societies, as well as the Soviet economy. A similar limitation as to economic types considered is still found in more recent works by writers with different approaches (e.g., Schneider, 1974). It seems that some economic anthropologists do not consider important the study of past or "moribund" economies and see the task of our discipline as the study of the spread of the "Western market economy," without taking into consideration the spread of command economies (Cook, 1966, pp. 325, 337).

This paper deals with economic systems of the past. It aims at identifying qualitatively different institutional arrangements of the economic process, and it takes into consideration the possibility that in the complex societies of the past, as in those of the present, features of a command economy may appear in all aspects of the economy including the market.

In studying the economy of ancient Mexico one is struck by the presence of contrasting forms of organization. A far-reaching tribute system coexisted with numerous and well-attended marketplaces. Household production was found side by side with large state-organized construction projects. Land was allocated according to the individual's place in the estate system, but there are also some references to the selling of the land. Corvée labor was a universal obligation of commoners and was systematically used on royal lands and for other public works; but it is also said that people were available for hire in the marketplace.

This situation calls for an evaluation of the contrasting types of organization in order to determine how they were articulated, and which one was the dominant one. In other words, which one integrated the economy.

Differences of opinion in the interpretation of Mesoamerican materials have been common, especially as concerns the existence of private property and the nature and importance of the market. These are issues similar to those that have developed in the study of other complex societies such as Classical Antiquity or Mesopotamia.

Some of these differences of opinion are due, of course, to the insufficient nature of the data; but perhaps more important are the different theoretical assumptions used in interpreting the data. It is my purpose in this paper to outline the theoretical issues in the analysis of market systems that pertain to the interpretation of the Mexican material.[1]

This calls, first of all, for a definition of market and an identification of the various activities and forms of organization that can be found in a market system. As LeClair remarked (1962, pp. 1185-1186), the concept of market is often not defined, but efforts to define and refine it in ways that will improve the understanding of archaic preindustrial economies have been made, especially in the work of Polanyi and his followers. I understand "market" to mean a system of exchange in which the participants are a supply crowd offering certain goods and a demand crowd wanting those goods, all of whom are free to choose the counterpart with whom the exchange will be made (cf. Polanyi, 1957, pp. 167-169). This freedom, or lack of prior definition, of the parties who make the exchanges is the diagnostic trait of markets, in contrast with exchanges based on political or kinship arrangements in which the parties to the exchanges are rigorously defined and obliged to effect them by reason of their status--for example, the exchange of tribute for protection between a ruler and his subject, or the reciprocal giving that takes place within the family. Thus the market is a system of relations binding people who participate in status-free acts of exchange.

The contrast between a status and a market economy is part of the familiar status vs. contract, or ascription vs. achievement dichotomies. The market principle in an economy with freedom of choice and the supply-demand mechanism is comparable to the election of competing candidates for office, to the selection of mates in a complex marriage system, or to the exchange of ideas under freedom of thought and speech. As is true of all these processes, the market cannot be assumed to be a universal feature of society. It is of necessity institutionalized, mainly on the basis of rules regarding property and contracts, and very different types of market institutions are known from the human record, past and present.

The analysis of different types of market systems requires the consideration of a wide variety of questions such as: the social and geographical boundaries of the people participating in the exchanges (including, to put it in other terms, the possible existence of barriers to the movement of goods and people); the kinds of goods that circulate in the system; the way in which equivalency rates (prices) are arrived at; and also, the locale where the exchanges take effect, whether in marketplaces or stores, or with itinerant traders, etc. This latter issue has been the subject of an abundant literature on marketplaces in various parts of the world.

Of the many issues relating to the market system I will discuss some which are essential in ascertaining the importance of the market within the total economic system of ancient Mexico: a) The extent to which the market enters into the handling of factors of production as well as of finished products; b) the degree of specialization in different market activities; c) the extent of political control of the market.

I. THE MARKET SYSTEM AND PRODUCTION

The basic issue is whether there was a market for factors of production as well as for finished products. In this respect a few points stand out clearly in our data about ancient Mexico. It is clear that finished products were handled both by the tribute system and the market. Descriptions of marketplaces emphasize the fact that every kind of product was offered for sale, and the Matrícula de Tributos (1980)--Montezuma's tribute roll--lists tribute in kind including all sorts of items, especially staples, textiles, and luxury objects. However, a comparison of the goods included in the

Matrícula and the lists of items offered in the marketplace shows some interesting differences. The major one is that items not in the tribute roll occupy a prominent place in the market: fresh food (vegetables, fruit, game, fish, dogs) and cooked food, as well as pottery and a few other commonly used items such as flint knives, medicinal herbs, or sandals.

This does not mean that all those items could not be obtained as tribute. Sources other than the tribute roll show the existence of tribute paying units, apparently not considered in that document, which provisioned the palaces with items such as food and pottery (Ixtlilxochitl, 1952:II, p. 168; Zimmermann, 1970, p. 5). Yet, the royal palaces and the households of members of the ruling estate may have obtained goods from the marketplace. There is no doubt, however, that the main source of their supplies was tribute payment in kind. The major conclusion to be drawn from this comparison is that consumption items for the mass of the population predominated in the marketplace.

There is no basis for thinking of the existence of factor markets in either land or labor. There were different types of land for the use of members of the different social categories, basically kings, temple personnel, noblemen-officials, and commoners. Transfers of land took place as the result of conquests, administrative decisions, and inheritance. There are also some references to gambling and to renting and selling. The latter were bound by restrictions as to estate membership and locality and required the approval of local authorities. There is no information as to frequency of sales. It does not seem possible to think of a land market as a major procedure for the transfer of land. The distribution of land was essentially the result of political allocations according to status.

Labor also was organized without reference to the market principle. Household production in agriculture and crafts took place on the basis of the labor of family members. Some households included servants or slaves, and reciprocal labor exchange was also practiced. Commoners had the general obligation of providing labor services, in addition to tribute in kind, to the ruler or the noblemen whose dependents they were. Large scale production in the royal lands, or in public work projects, was based on such labor services.

Descriptions of the marketplace mention that porters were available for hire, as well as craftsmen of all trades. Since no production units are described as being based on wage labor, I think such statements refer to the occasional employment of porters and craftsmen. In the case of craftsmen we would have to know to what extent, in addition to the buying of finished products, the customers might have placed their orders with the craftsmen in the marketplace.

Labor organization was based on household membership, personal dependence, and the labor services required from the commoners. There was no significant wage labor, hence no labor market.

II. SPECIALIZATION IN MARKETING

As to specialization in market activities, it is clear that a large number of the attendants at the marketplace were producers who brought their own products for sale. In addition, there were retailers (tlanecuilo) who acquired goods for resale.

A salient fact in all descriptions of pre-Spanish commerce is the existence of professional merchants called pochteca, or oztomeca when they went to distant areas. We have descriptions of foreign expeditions in which professional merchants were sent as agents of their sovereign to exchange goods with the rulers of the visited area. On these expeditions they also took goods for the common people, which they sold in the marketplace. In some cases, the latter is the only type of trading reported.

No complete information is available as to the relationship between these professional merchants and the retailers. We do not know whether all retailers were pochteca or whether they may have been outside the merchant group. I am inclined to think that dealers in the products of the skilled craftsmen, such as feather workers, lapidaries, or goldsmiths, were pochteca or closely related to the pochteca's organization, but that dealers in articles of common use for the local population would not necessarily be pochteca.

In any case there were, on the one hand, barter and exchanges mediated by money objects such as cacao and blankets, that took place between producers (C-C; C-M-C). On the other hand, there was merchant capital in the case of the retailer who bought to sell (M-C-M). There are no reports, however, about the existence of industrial capital. That is, there were no entrepreneurs buying tools and raw materials and paying wage laborers in order to organize production for the market.

III. POLITICAL CONTROLS OF THE MARKET

Political control may take the form of barriers to the free movement of goods and people, or--just the opposite--the requirement to participate in the market by the offering or buying of specified kinds of goods. The contrast between freedom and compulsion in different types of markets also appears in the establishment of equivalencies, that is, in the contrast between prices resulting from free supply and demand, and the set prices imposed by a political authority. This is a crucial point in Polanyi's work (1957, pp. 267-69; 1977, pp. 71-72, 77-78, 123 ff.) which has not been sufficiently pursued even by followers of his approach (Bohannan and Dalton, 1962. See, however, Belshaw, 1965, pp. 102-03).

Usually the theoretical model of a market system assumes freedom of access to dealers and goods and freedom of contract so that prices develop from the free play of supply and demand, and the distribution of the social product follows from the play of the market. Natural and social restrictions are seen as imperfections that circumscribe or modify the way and the extent to which the model operates.

This concept of a market is, of course, a theoretical construct. In every known society there are natural limitations to the availability of land and labor; there is a distribution of property previous to the operation of the market; and there are transfers of property on the basis of principles other than the market, such as, for instance, inheritance and taxation. Taking all these restrictions into account, a sphere can be defined within which this market model operates.

It is clear, however, that in complex economies of both the preindustrial and the modern world, market systems exist in which regulations interfere with the freedom of the market, and as a consequence the market takes different forms and operates in different aspects of the economy (e.g., Lindblom, 1977). It is convenient then to think of another type of market--the controlled market--that instead of freedom has as essential features compulsion and regulation. Instances of freedom of the market will then be seen as the imperfections to be found in areas where compulsion is not applied or cannot be enforced. The free and the controlled market models can be used as polar concepts for the analysis of the real markets under investigation.

Features of the controlled market include, primarily, the existence of regulated prices. Prices are established by an authority in order to achieve given policy goals. In some cases this means prices that will enable participants in the market to maintain the living standards appropriate to their status. For example, the price of staples may be controlled for the benefit of the consumers, or, as in the medieval guild regulations, minimum prices may be set to assure sufficient income to the producers. In other cases, prices may be set in such a way that they will allow the accumulation of wealth for public use--for example, the government monopolies established to raise revenue. With these procedures taxation and welfare are built into the market. The market is thus not in opposition to a politically run sector of the economy but is an instrument of state policy.

Set or regulated prices are not necessarily immovable. They may be changed according to changing social needs and policies, and according to the availability of goods, but this is not the same as the supply and demand mechanism of the free market. Under a system of set prices, market participants are not free to negotiate the terms of the transaction, or may do so only within the limits imposed by minimum or maximum set prices. In a free market the play of supply and demand determines the distribution of goods; in a controlled market it is the distribution being aimed at that decides how prices are set.

Another feature of the controlled market may be obligatory participation, i.e. forced selling or forced buying, as long as this does not entirely suppress the freedom to select the trading partner

74

otherwise we would no longer be dealing with a market transaction. Let us keep in mind that the freedom to select the trading partner and the freedom to negotiate, or bargain, are separate variables. Thus, in some cases one can have supply and demand crowds without freedom to negotiate. On the other hand, there can be bargaining in nonmarket transactions in which the parties are strictly defined by status such as tribute, war reparations, dowry or alimony payments.

The use of two polar concepts of the market--free and controlled--has a number of advantages for the analysis of concrete economies:

1) It forces equal consideration of two sets of characteristics that are present, although in varying relative extent, in all real societies.

2) It keeps us from assuming that any one free market feature requires the presence of other features of the free market model.

3) It helps us to avoid thinking that the normal course of development must be towards a free market. Changes can occur in the direction of either a free market or a controlled market.

All this is especially important in ethnohistorical research, since incomplete records so often oblige us to interpret data and fill in the gaps in our information through inference and analogy.

I will mention briefly the various features of the market in ancient Mexico that show the usefulness of working with the concept of a controlled market.[2]

The establishment of markets is several times described in our sources as the result of political decisions connected with changes in the balance of power relations between different city-states and related to the migration of people specializing in trade. The creation of a market was one of various ways used to strengthen the political power of the city that established it. For example after the Aztec conquest of Tepeaca, it was required that a large marketplace be established there which all merchants could attend, and that help be provided to the merchants going beyond Tepeaca to the outer boundaries of the empire at Xoconochco.

Markets were held at stipulated places and times, and all commerce had to take place in the marketplace. Transactions outside the marketplace were forbidden and punished. Furthermore, regulations restricted the dealing in some commodities to specific localities.

In the capital, commerce was watched over by market authorities. There were "market leaders" (tianquizco teyacanque) for each kind of goods, and the "market lords" (pochteca tlatoque) formed a court with jurisdiction over the market that decided in situ all cases. In the Tlatelolco market in Mexico, the teyacanque are also described as labor commanders (tequitlato) who organized the market people to prepare the war supplies that it was their responsibility to provide. It is not clear to what extent these teyacanque might have been selected from among the professional merchants, or whether they were members of the same groups they were in charge of.

Sahagún twice mentions that prices were set but gives no information as to precisely how or on what basis this was done.[3] The data are equally vague regarding the existence of free bargaining. A statement from Torquemada (1969:II, p. 580) describes silent bargaining in the marketplace, but this report resembles descriptions of Inca markets (cf. Cobo, 1946:II, p. 25), and it might be one of the cases in which Torquemada deals with data from different places without making clear his reference.

Calnek (1974, p. 191) has drawn attention to the fact that shelled corn is described as being expensive (tlaçoti, literally "dear") during the celebration of Uey Tecuilhuitl (July) before the major harvest period (September to December). This may indicate seasonal price fluctuations but does not tell us anything about price setting versus free bargaining as price making mechanisms.

The evidence about pricing is thus very flimsy. I see no reason not to admit both price setting and bargaining in pre-Spanish times. Price setting does not have to be rigidly imposed as unchanging prices for all commodities at all times, nor does the presence of one necessarily preclude the existence of the other. In this respect a useful comparison can be made between the pre-Spanish situation and that of early colonial times, when both price fluctuations and

price setting are better documented as existing at the
same time.

There is a story told of King Nezahualcoyotl of
Tetzcoco that indicates how the ruler might intervene
in the market process. It is said that he used to
watch the marketplace and when he saw poor people who
were not selling the goods they were offering (such as
salt, firewood and vegetables) he would send his
stewards to buy everything they had at twice the price
in order to give it to others (Ixtlilxochitl, 1952:II,
pp. 233-234, 243). The story is given as illustrating
the king's policy of providing for the poor, who were
also fed from his granaries in times of famine
(Ixtlilxochitl, 1952:I, p. 322). It is a clear
example of redistribution. To the extent that it
might reflect a price policy, it certainly does not
speak in favor of a free market but would constitute
an example of price support. If we were to generalize
from this case, we would say that producers took their
goods to market to be sold to other participants and
the unsold goods were bought up by the royal treasury.

Another question is the extent to which there was
freedom of access to the market. Ancient Mexico was
divided into a large number of political units, and
although, in some instances, traffic was possible
across boundaries, the information available does not
allow us to generalize with certainty.

The professional merchants (pochteca) travelling
within the empire and beyond were located in several
cities that were part of the three realms of the
empire. Traffic to independent cities beyond the
empire was in some cases (as in Xicalanco) carried on
openly as embassies to the foreign lords. In other
cases entrance was forbidden to Aztec merchants, and
they were able to enter the market only in disguise as
merchants from other areas. There are no reports of
important traffic between the empire and the enemy
cities of Tlaxcala, Cholula, and Huexotzinco. In the
case of Tlaxcala, it is said that the Aztecs imposed
an economic blockade and the Tlaxcallans had a
scarcity of salt.

Imperial expansion seems to have fostered the
development of long distance trade within the empire
and with friendly neighbors; the creation of the
market at Tepeaca and the expeditions to Xicalanco are

good examples. Data are weaker on the movement of
common people and consumer goods at the local level.

As has been mentioned, all commerce had to take
place in the marketplace where it was watched over by
the market authorities. This raises the question of
whether we should look at participation in the market
as a requirement as much as a right. It might be
useful to consider a few features of the colonial
period that imply compulsion to participate in the
market.

In order to assure supplies for the cities,
Indian communities were obliged to cultivate
stipulated areas of communal land and to take their
wheat or maize to the market, keeping their earnings
for their local communities' treasury (Gibson, 1964,
p. 203). Somewhat similar requirements existed for
the supply of other goods (Gibson, 1964, p. 355). In
one particular town, Xochimilco, stone workers and
carpenters were obliged to sell stone and timber in
Mexico City and to use their earnings from these sales
for the public expenditures of their communities
(Scholes, 1958, pp. 113-115).

Indian communities also had the obligation to
provide stipulated numbers of workers for Spanish
employers. The details of this repartimiento system
varied in different places and times, but in the late
sixteenth and early seventeenth centuries in Central
Mexico, it was not simple corvée. Some elements of a
market had developed. Indians went to the marketplace
to be hired and were paid set wages (Zavala y Castelo,
1939-46, Introduction to vols. 4, 5, 6; Gibson, 1964,
pp. 224-236, 387-389). Indian communities were also
required to buy stipulated quotas of imported goods
(Gibson, 1964, pp. 94-95).

All these regulations were clearly connected with
the needs of the colonial regime, but one should admit
the possibility that they also reflect policies
already present in pre-Spanish times, in the same way
as colonial tribute and labor institutions are known
to have developed from pre-Spanish practices. These
market regulations show how forcing the circulation of
goods in a controlled market can be an alternative to
a tribute and redistributive system without destroying
the political control of the economy.

Another kind of political intervention in the market is the control of the supply of money. In pre-Spanish times the main money objects were blankets and cacao beans. Large quantities of both came to the royal storehouses as tribute, and blankets were an important means of payment by the ruler. Thus, the use of these money objects served to link the tribute and the market systems, but there are no data available to examine supply fluctuations of such money objects in the market.

CONCLUSION

In conclusion, the economy of ancient Mexico was a command economy based on a system of production that relied on the political control of land and labor, and on a tribute system for the accumulation of social surpluses. Since the market did not determine the allocation of the basic factors of production, land and labor, it was essentially an adjunct mechanism. Its operation was limited primarily to consumer goods and, to some extent, tools and raw materials.

Some of the recent work on the market in ancient Mexico (as in similar societies) has improved our understanding of it by concentrating on the distinction between marketplace and market system, and by exploring the various forms of long distance trade. I suggest that making a distinction between free and controlled market systems will also contribute to our understanding of the economy and society of ancient Mexico, and of other societies of a similar level of complexity. It highlights the existence of market controls, including price setting; it shows the insertion of the market within the politically run economy; and it explains why there was a minimum of conflict between the tribute and the market sectors of the economy.

Notes

[1] I discuss in more detail the entire economy of ancient Mexico in Carrasco, 1978. In reference to the market, see also Carrasco, 1980. For other discussions of the pre-Spanish markets, see Kurtz, 1974; Berdan, 1975; and Calnek, 1978.

[2] See note 1 for the main recent literature on the market. I give detailed references here

only for those points not treated in Carrasco, 1978.

[3] This is an important point. Both the nahuatl text and Sahagún's own Spanish version have to be considered. The relevant passages are in Book 8, chapter 19 (Sahagún, 1954, p. 67; 1956:II, p. 325) and in Book 9, chapter 5 (Sahagún, 1959, p. 24; 1956:III, p. 32).

References

BELSHAW, Cyril S. 1965. Traditional exchange and modern markets. Englewood Cliffs, N.J.: Prentice-Hall.

BERDAN, Frances F. 1975. Trade, tribute and market in the Aztec Empire. Unpublished Ph.D. dissertation, The University of Texas at Austin.

BOHANNAN, Paul, and George Dalton. 1962. Introduction. In Markets in Africa. Paul Bohannan and George Dalton, eds. Evanston, Ill.: Northwestern University Press.

CALNEK, Edward E. 1974. The Sahagún texts as a source of sociological information. In Sixteenth-century Mexico: the work of Sahagún. Munro S. Edmonson, ed. Albuquerque: University of New Mexico Press.

_____. 1978. El sistema de mercdo de Tenochtitlan. In Economía política e ideología en el México prehispánico. Pedro Carrasco and Johanna Broda, eds. Mexico: Editorial Nueva Imagen.

CARRASCO, Pedro. 1980. La economía del México prehispánico. In Economía política e ideología en el México prehispánico. Pedro Carrasco and Johanna Broda, eds. Mexico: Editorial Nueva Imagen.

_____. 1980. Markets and merchants in the Aztec economy. Journal of the Steward Anthropological Society 11:249-269.

COBO, Bernabé. 1956. Historia del Nuevo Mundo. In Obras Biblioteca de Autores Españoles. vols. 91, 92. Madrid: Atlas.

COOK, Scott. 1966. The obsolete 'anti-market' mentality: a critique of the substantive approach to economic anthropology. American Anthropologist 68:323-345.

GIBSON, Charles. 1964. The Aztecs under Spanish rule. Stanford: Stanford University Press.

HERSKOVITS, Melville J. 1952. Economic anthropology. New York: Knopf.

IXTLILXOCHITL, Fernando de Alva. 1952. Obras históricas. 2 vols. Mexico: Editora Nacional.

KURTZ, Donald W. 1974. Peripheral and transitional markets: the Aztec case. American Ethnologist 1:685-705.

LECLAIR, Edward E., Jr. 1962. Economic theory and economic anthropology. American Anthropologist 64:1179-1203.

LINDBLOM, Charles E. 1977. Politics and markets. New York: Basic Books.

MATRÍCULA DE TRIBUTOS. 1980. Matrícula de tributos (Códice de Moctezuma). Kommentar Frances F. Berdan, Jacqueline De Durand-Forest. Graz, Austria: Akademische Druck--u. Verlagsanstalt.

POLANYI, Karl. 1944. The great transformation. New York: Holt and Rinehart.

_____. 1957. The economy as instituted process. In Trade and markets in the early empires, K. Polanyi, C. Arensberg, and H. Pearson, eds. Glencoe, Ill.: The Free Press.

_____. 1977. The livelihood of man. Harry W. Pearson, ed. New York: Academic Press.

POLANYI, Karl, Conrad M. Arensberg, and Harry W. Pearson, eds. 1957. Trade and markets in the early empires. Glencoe, Ill.: The Free Press.

SAHAGÚN, Bernardino de. 1954. Florentine codex: general history of the things of New Spain. Translated by A. J. O. Anderson and C. E. Dibble.

Book 8: Kings and lords. Santa Fe: University
of Utah and School of American Research.

_____. 1956. Historia general de las cosas de
Nueva España. 4 vols. A. M. Garibay, ed.
Mexico: Porrúa.

_____. 1959. Florentine codex: general history
of the things of New Spain. Translated from the
Aztec into English by A. J. O. Anderson and C. E.
Dibble. Book 9: The merchants. Santa Fe:
University of Utah and School of American Research.

SCHOLES, F. V., and E. G. Adams. 1958. Sobre el
modo de tributar los indios de Nueva España a su
Majestad, 1561-1564. Mexico: Porrúa.

SCHNEIDER, Harold K. 1974. Economic man. New
York: Free Press.

TORQUEMADA, Juan de. 1969. Monarquía indiana. 3
vols. Mexico: Porrúa.

WITTFOGEL, Karl A. 1957. Oriental despotism. New
Haven: Yale University Press.

ZAVALA, Silvio, and María Castelo, eds. 1939-46.
Fuentes para la historia del trabajo en Nueva
España. 8 vols. Mexico: Fondo de Cultura
Económica.

ZIMMERMANN, Günter, ed. 1970. Briefe der
indianischen nobilität aus Neuspanien an Karl V
und Philipp II um de Mitte des 16 Jahrhunderts.
Hamburg: Museum für Völkerkunde und
Vorgeschichte.

V. THE RECONSTRUCTION OF ANCIENT ECONOMIES: PERSPECTIVES FROM ARCHAEOLOGY AND ETHNOHISTORY

Frances F. Berdan

In their analyses of ancient economic systems, archaeologists and ethnohistorians have been faced with similar problems of analysis: the data are frequently fragmentary, contradictory and perplexing. To aid in their interpretation of these data, researchers have devised a variety of theoretical models. These models, based on specific assumptions, have served the useful purpose of expanding our reconstructions of ancient economic life from descriptions of known fragments to portrayals of integrated, functioning systems. Nonetheless, the details of this procedure have generated vigorous controversies; the most spirited of these focuses on the Aztecs of central Mexico.

During the past decade the Aztec economy has received considerable attention from ethnohistorians, and more recently from archaeologists. This topic has indeed provided a lively forum for discussing controversies in data-interpretation, model-building, and the relative merits of opposing theoretical persuasions. Considering the vigorous quality of this field, my primary goal here is to reassess the models and theoretical approaches that archaeologists and ethnohistorians have been using in reconstructing the Aztec economy, society and polity. In addition, I will suggest how an alternate model may prove useful in more fully accounting for the data currently available; in particular, my intent is to isolate the underlying principles guiding economic processes and activities, and to determine along what nexuses these processes are linked with the social and political world encompassed by the Aztec, or Triple Alliance, empire.

But first, a word about the term "Aztec." I am using this problematic term here to refer to the Triple Alliance of Tenochtitlan, Texcoco and Tlacopan. I fully recognize the considerable ethnic variation and political "disunity" that pertained in the area of the Aztec empire. When discussing particular cultural groups or political entities, I will refer to them by their specific names.

I. THEORY AND MODELS

The key in economic analyses of past societies is "reconstruction." And, in the absence of complete, inviolable data,[1] ethnohistorians and archaeologists have resorted to, and come to depend heavily on theoretical positions and the models based on them. The constructs most avidly applied to the central Mexican economy of the sixteenth century tend to be "ideal models," or models of ideal types. A model of a politically-controlled economy in its production, exchange and consumption aspects (Carrasco, 1978; Evans, 1980) has been juxtaposed with a model of a theoretical "free market" where supply and demand are operative and influential forces (Calnek, 1978; M. Smith, 1979, 1980; Offner, 1981a, 1981b). In this latter context, the central place model has been applied to the central Mexican region, an application which has resulted in a spirited debate in the recent literature (Smith vs. Evans). The use of these models (and others, but these in particular) illustrates attempts to work from the known (or better known) to the unknown. For example, if the central place model closely approximates in settlement distribution the settlement pattern of a region (say, central Mexico), it is then projected that the assumptions of the model also apply, although we do not have direct archaeological or ethnohistoric knowledge (e.g., "market centers exist for the express purpose of facilitating market exchange and are located so as to minimize the frictional effects of distance," or "market suppliers are knowledgeable and rational in seeking to maximize profits, and market consumers are equally knowledgeable and rational in seeking to minimize costs"). Likewise, the "political control" approach expressed by Pedro Carrasco (1978) among others, views the polity as the most powerful element in the economic equation; hence, it is concluded that the role of markets is minimal in integrating the economy, and that redistribution and the rules surrounding it governed the allocation of resources, including land and labor (see also Dalton, Chapter I in this volume).

Each of these models has been of use, allowing systematic representations of large, but somewhat differing sets of data. But given the continuing controversies, it may be useful to reassess the theoretical questions being asked of the economies of past societies, to see if the models based on them will continue to provide useful generalizations as data continue to accumulate. The general theoretical question which has dominated the recent discussions of the central Mexican economy has been: "What principle is dominant in the operation of the economy?" This question has put Mesoamericanists at a theoretical impasse. It has resulted in recent controversies between, for example, Pedro Carrasco who supports the position that the market did not integrate the economy, the polity did, and Jerome Offner who has recently stated that "the state alone did not integrate the economy" (1981b, p. 72), but that market forces were also operative. Indeed, in a single book (Carrasco and Broda, 1978), Pedro Carrasco and Edward Calnek paint dramatically different pictures of the central Mexican economy in regard to the operation of political or economic principles.

II. A "COMPROMISE MODEL" OF THE AZTEC IMPERIAL ECONOMY: A PRELIMINARY FORMULATION

Rather than ask the question, "Which of the exchange principles dominates?", I believe we are at a stage now where we can better ask "How do the many variables involved in the economic system interact, influence one another, interplay in a fashion so that the system 'works'?" Those who advocate the central place model do in fact recognize that political factors are involved in and influence settlement patterns and market orientations (M. Smith, 1980, p. 120); those who advocate the political control model likewise recognize that all marketplaces may not have been as closely monitored as those in the largest urban centers, the centers of political control. There is no reason why a fairly free market, in some areas and in some of its aspects, cannot operate within a state-directed economy. Indeed, the Aztec professional merchants, or pochteca, operated as both state agents and private entrepreneurs. These roles are not necessarily incompatible.

In a slightly different vein, Blanton (Chapter III in this volume) presents a longitudinal model for economic change in the Valley of Oaxaca, spanning some 2000 years. His model, portraying the fluctuating relationships between the "market system" and "political institutions," implies that both forces were present in this lengthy time frame; they waxed and waned in importance as conditions in and around the valley changed.

It is clear that no actual economic system matches in detail the ideal types of "political control" or "free market": these are idealizations, as Pedro Carrasco has noted with his construct of free vs. controlled markets (Chapter IV in this volume). Taking Carrasco's recognition of this a bit further, it may be useful now to construct models, perhaps of a more systemic nature, that would more closely resemble "actual" empirical systems. Warwick Bray (1980), referring to the work of Conrad (1978) in Peru, has recently called for the need to develop a "compromise model" to resolve these impasses in theory. Such a model could unify, for example, politics, economics and settlement patterns, recognizing that each has its own impact on the real-world appearance and functioning of any given system as a whole; all of these "conflicting (although sometime is compatible) tendencies" will tend to be resolved as a "compromise," rather than in a singular deterministic sense (Conrad, 1978, p. 281). I agree with Bray that such a model could well apply to complex economies such as that of sixteenth-century central Mexico. Then, instead of rejecting aspects of market or polity, they could be built into this more holistic model as variables. In so doing, such a model should achieve a better "fit" with real-world economic systems.

What factors, then, conditioned the production and circulation of goods in the Aztec imperial setting? And what principles guided the dynamic interplay of these factors in different realms of the empire?

In a general and very preliminary sense, the relevant dimensions underlying the dynamics of the imperial economy might include: special adaptations to particular environmental circumstances, population structure, the organization of labor, unique historical backgrounds and cultural traditions, social stratification and its role in the control of resources, maximization of economic effort, available distribution networks, political goals, and military forces. Additionally, the imperial state affected different regions under its domain differently--and to analyze this we may further add "imperial conditioning factors," such as 1) length of time under Aztec or other domination; 2) perceived importance of the region to the empire (access to trade routes, availability of critical resources); and 3) distance from the centers of political power.

To shed light on the interplay among these many factors, some propositions about the Aztec imperial economy may be posited. Each, if adequately demonstrated, could be considered a principle underlying the changing form of the imperial economy.

A. The Structure of Production

Whether to satisfy tribute/tax demands or personal needs, production tends to be decentralized at the local community level, and more specialized in the larger, more complex settlement units. This reflects the ability of urban settlements to attract and coordinate organized, specialized labor: population density; accessibility to necessary materials, services, and information; political advantages; and a high proportion of elite consumers to support luxury manufactures are all forces encouraging such a concentration.

It appears that for many products, decentralized production in the imperial provinces was the rule (as in archaeological interpretations of Coatlan Viejo: Mason and Lewarch, 1981). Ethnohistorically there only exist aggregate data for tribute assessments, through tribute lists. Some of these are as gross as the provincial level, some by towns, but beyond the caluplli level, it simply is not clear how tribute was assessed and paid. It could be that decentralized production for tribute was the mode, with a small amount being demanded from each household, rather than through specialized workshop arrangements. This was apparently true of the production of cotton cloth, women's work in fifteenth and sixteenth century central Mexico. Where special goods (such as ornate warriors' costumes) could not readily be produced by single unspecialized households, assessments in other goods, such as cotton cloth, may have been made to underwrite the production or purchase of such goods.

B. The Embeddedness of the Economy in Society and Polity

The degree of political control exercised over economic production and distribution networks varied with distance from the centers of political power (most notably, the imperial capitals). If this can be

clearly demonstrated, it would suggest that the strict
regulations governing the Tlatelolco marketplace
(e.g., permanent judges, price controls) would not
pertain in such strength, if at all, to outlying
districts. Likewise, greater political supervision
would have been exercised over the specialized craft
and merchant guilds concentrated in the urban centers
than over outlying household production units. The
extent of this political control would have been
somewhat mitigated by the crucial military and
espionage roles played by the professional merchants,
and by the social and economic dependence of the elite
on the luxury artisans. These artisans crafted the
rich, ornate objects so important in overtly
symbolizing high status and privilege in Aztec
society.

Partly as an artifact of the state-level
orientation of ethnohistoric sources, Mesoamericanists
have often called all merchants pochteca or oztomeca.
Yet the pochtecatl is a very special type of
professional merchant, operating through guilds
concentrated in the major cities of the Basin of
Mexico, with important political affiliations and
functions. He was a long-distance merchant, although
he also operated in the imperial capitals; he served
the state in the political and military arena,
although he also served himself as an economic
entrepreneur. Yet it is clear that another type of
merchant, the tlanecuilo, also operated in the central
Mexican marketplaces. He has no known special
political obligations, and while he is found
occasionally in the Tlatelolco marketplace as a
purveyor of distant goods (e.g., Sahagún, 1950-82,
book 10, pp. 67, 75, 77), he probably was a prominent
feature of the economic landscape in outlying regions.
We know little of what goods he may have carried, but
goods that would have had a noticeable exchange
advantage over distance, such as salt, cacao and
cotton, are likely candidates (Berdan, 1980, p. 39).
And, given the proposition suggested above, he
probably was more of an entrepreneur than a political
agent. Hence, this professional merchant is in marked
contrast to the pochteca in the manner in which his
activities articulated with the state, the system of
social stratification, the military hierarchy, and
other units of social structure. His greatest impact
on the economy was probably in areas at some distance
from the center of imperial power.

C. Patterns of Economic Distribution

Some goods underwent a complex process from raw material to finished good, a process I will call "the sequential movement and modification of goods." Mason and Lewarch (1981) and Byland (1981) have observed, with obsidian, that raw materials were obtained in one locale, transported to another for manufacture, and then distributed as finished products. The same pattern is documented ethnohistorically for the production and distribution of cotton cloth. Consider these patterns, recorded in the colonial period, but referring to native persons, goods, and surely indigenous patterns.

> For example, the people of Tepeaca journeyed to the tierra caliente, upwards of 120 kilometers away, to obtain cotton; the women of Tepeaca then wove that cotton into cloth, proceeding to sell it, supposedly in nearby regional marketplaces (PNE V:40-41). In another case, the people of Papaloticpan in the Oaxaca area traveled approximately 96 kilometers to the Rio de Alvarado to purchase cotton. The women then wove the cotton into skirts and mantas which they either used themselves, sold locally, or carried them back to the Rio de Alvarado (where they had obtained the cotton in the first place) and sold the finished goods there. In this manner they gained sufficiently to be able to pay their tribute (PNE IV:93). The people of Tequisistlan near Texcoco also engaged in the highland-lowland symbiosis, obtaining their cotton in the Cuernavaca region, weaving mantas and huipiles, and subsequently selling them (PNE VI:230). (Berdan, 1980, p. 39)

This sounds, in outline, very much like the cases of obsidian. The pattern may hold for other goods as well. It is in this realm that the tlanecuilo may have been particularly instrumental in moving goods.

D. The Role of the Economy in Imperial Expansion

Imperial expansion strategies varied to meet differing ecological and economic conditions. It must of course be kept in mind that variables other than economic ones also play important roles in expansion strategies, and that such variables may be combined with economic conditions.

For example, the Aztec empire never succeeded in conquering its near-neighbors, the powerful Tlaxcalans. Given the frequent disastrous results of the periodic "flowery wars" with Tlaxcala, it could well be that the Aztecs were simply not powerful enough militarily to conquer this area, particularly during the fifteenth century. As the empire expanded and consolidated the immediate Valley of Mexico region, it developed an increasing ability to mobilize more manpower for warfare. By sheer bulk of troops, it may have been powerful enough by the early sixteenth century to indeed conquer Tlaxcala (also somewhat weakened by economic "embargos"), but the economic reward to the Aztecs would probably have not been worth the effort. With an expanding nobility, the Aztecs were increasingly interested in luxury goods such as precious feathers, gold, and turquoise. Tlaxcala could offer none of these; it would have been an extremely expensive venture to undertake the conquest of Tlaxcala, with a lack of comparable rewards at the end. The "flowery wars," therefore, maintained the warlike intent but did not require any attempt at conquest, which would have cost the "flower of Tenochtitlan" dearly.

A second example more specifically addresses the economic correlates of imperial expansion. As the empire expanded, it gained control over the goods produced in newly conquered areas through the institution of tribute requirements. It also gained access to goods produced in areas beyond those boundaries. Among the goods required in tribute were those that were not produced in the conquered province itself, but had been traditionally brought into the area through the more ancient market system, and then sent to the imperial capitals as tribute (Berdan, 1975). This pattern of tribute exactment would be highly adaptive in areas boasting an extensive market system, and patterns of both markets and tribute characterized the area included in imperial territories in 1519. In the process of expansion, ultimately the empire would have to determine whether to continue to obtain foreign goods indirectly through markets and subsequently by tribute, or to initiate conquest of the source areas and collect the goods directly through tribute.

A decision to conquer would be effective only if desired goods were actually produced in the area to be conquered; or, if more distant goods were desired, that they be available to the conquered populations through the market or similar network. The expansion strategy of conquest and tribute exaction, then, would be most effective in areas where markets were common, frequent and active. When the empire reached the southern limits of this active market area, it encountered a quite different zone of economic activity, a zone which called for a re-emphasis of expansion strategies on the part of the Aztecs.

The lowland Maya areas were characterized, overall, by a less intensely developed market system. Markets certainly did exist, yet they appear for the most part to have been highly localized and did not serve to integrate regions. Flows of goods from region to region, especially the luxury goods in which the Aztecs were so interested, were primarily the concern of professional merchants. In these lowland Mayan areas and Gulf coast port-of-trade districts there was no well-developed exchange mechanism which would have allowed goods to flow across Aztec political boundaries. Foreign (Mayan) merchants, not allowed to penetrate Aztec territory, would not have been able to import goods. Similarly, the Aztec merchants were restricted from entering many Mayan areas, and their trekking into non-Aztec controlled districts was a risky enterprise in any event. Therefore, in situations where a highly developed market system exists, foreign as well as locally-produced goods could be obtained through conquest and the institution of tribute. However, in areas with a weakly-developed market system (along with the non-admittance of foreign merchants), foreign goods could not be obtained through conquest and tribute. In this case, the emphasis on foreign trade, state-controlled, becomes a viable alternative strategy for gaining access to those external resources, and moderately protected ports-of-trade become viable centers of exchange.

E. The Many Determinants of Tribute Assessments

Tribute assessments were the result of both political and nonpolitical factors. Tribute, as institutionalized in imperial systems, is a political device to control economic production. Therefore the goods demanded in tribute will be geared to the needs and goals of the state. As the elite sector of the Aztec population increased, so did its need for prestige goods: as the empire expanded, it increasingly encompassed provinces from which it could demand these goods in manufactured form or as raw materials (e.g., gold, feathers, jade). Similarly, the assessment of warriors' costumes is closely linked to the Aztec system of military rewards. A perhaps inadvertent consequence of the Aztec style of warfare was to disproportionately reduce the male provincial population in each newly-conquered province. Interestingly, accounts of "immediate" tribute demands emphasize cloth and clothing, strictly women's work throughout Mesoamerica (Alva Ixtlilxochitl, 1965, v. II, pp. 196-7). Over time the demands diversified, indicating a) a restoration of the population balance, and/or b) stimulation of specialized production in the province through increased contact with imperial agents and institutions.

Yet tribute demands reflected not only the needs and goals of the dominant society. Quite to the contrary, the Aztec tribute system relied heavily on pre-existing production styles and exchange modes. As discussed above, many tribute assessments relied heavily on the circulation of goods through marketplace exchange. Furthermore, it appears that the imperial tribute demands of many items more closely reflected the style of the conquered than that of the conqueror (Anawalt, 1981). Many cloak designs, for example, were intimately tied to the ethnic groups that produced and delivered them as tribute. Where these same designs are found more widely distributed, it may be due more to the activities of merchants such as the tlanecuilo than to any imperial imposition of styles. If this was the case, the role of regional merchants in transmitting cultural styles over broad areas (and, hence, influencing production) must be taken into consideration.

These processes, it must be kept in mind, are not simplistic nor necessarily uniform throughout the empire. Certainly a variety of factors, in interaction with one another, produced singular patterns for each region. In unraveling these relationships, it should be most productive to emphasize dynamic models, not static ones. By viewing these relationships over time, the principles behind them should begin to emerge. Processual integrative models can draw on both archaeological and ethnohistorical materials, yielding very productive answers. And, in the course of relating the accumulating sets of data on Aztec economics to the propositions suggested above, it will become apparent to what extent these principles can account for the data in a meaningful way. They may well require modification, and will surely be joined by other general principles.

Notes

[1] Several "data problems" face the Mesoamerican ethnohistorian. First, the bulk of the data are post-conquest in origin, and must be carefully sifted for Spanish influence. Second, the classic documentation stems from elite-level sources, presenting an incomplete picture of Aztec culture and society. Increasingly, however, local-level documentation is being found and used. Third, the documentation often consists of accounts of events or special circumstances: to what extent are these indeed unique events or can they be expanded into general, repetitive patterns? Fourth, there is a frequent temptation to generalize cultural and social patterns from one Mesoamerican region to others--yet given the vast ethnic variety of Mesoamerica, it is still uncertain to what extent such generalizing is justified. For a fuller discussion of these and similar problems, see Berdan, 1982.

References

ALVA IXTLILXOCHITL, Fernando de. 1965. _Historia Chichimeca_. Mexico: Editora Nacional.

ANAWALT, Patricia. 1981. Textile production and distribution in the Aztec Empire. Paper presented at the 1981 meeting of the American Anthropological Association, Los Angeles.

BERDAN, Frances. 1975. Trade, tribute and market in the Aztec Empire. Unpublished Ph.D. dissertation. The University of Texas at Austin.

_____. 1980. Aztec merchants and markets: local-level economic activity in a non-industrial empire. _Mexicon_ II(3):37-41.

_____. 1982. The Aztecs of Central Mexico: an imperial society. New York: Holt, Rinehart and Winston.

BRAY, Warwick. 1980. Landscape with figures: settlement patterns, locational models and politics in Mesoamerica. Paper presented to the Burg Wartenstein Symposium No. 86: Prehistoric Settlement Pattern Studies: Retrospect and Prospect.

BYLAND, Bruce. 1981. Economy, politics, and the expansion of the Aztec Empire in the Mixteca Alta. Paper presented at the 1981 meeting of the Society for American Archaeology, San Diego.

CALNEK, Edward. 1978. El sistema de mercado de Tenochtitlan. In Economía política e ideología en el México prehispánico. Pedro Carrasco and Johanna Broda, eds. Mexico: Editorial Nueva Imagen.

CARRASCO, Pedro. 1978. La economía del México prehispánico. In Economía política e ideología en el México prehispánico. Pedro Carrasco and Johanna Broda, eds. Mexico: Editorial Nueva Imagen.

CARRASCO, Pedro and Johanna Broda, eds. 1978. Economía política e ideología en el México prehispánico. Mexico: Editorial Nueva Imagen.

CONRAD, G. W. 1978. Models of compromise in settlement pattern studies: an example from coastal Peru. World Archaeology 9:281-298.

EVANS, Susan T. 1980. Spatial analysis of basin of Mexico settlement: problems with the use of the central place model. American Antiquity 45:866-875.

MASON, Roger D., and Dennis E. Lewarch. 1981. Structural analysis of the late horizon settlement system in the Coatlan del Rio Valley, Morelos, Mexico. Paper presented at the 1981 meeting of the Society for American Archaeology, San Diego.

OFFNER, Jerome. 1981a. On the inapplicability of 'oriental despotism' and the 'Asiatic mode of production' to the Aztecs of Texcoco. American Antiquity 46:43-61.

_____. 1981b. On Carrasco's use of 'first principles.' American Antiquity 46:69-74.

SAHAGÚN, Bernardino de. 1950-82. Florentine codex: general history of the things of New Spain. Translated by Arthur J. O. Anderson and Charles E. Dibble. Santa Fe: University of Utah and School of American Research.

SMITH, Michel E. 1979. The Aztec marketing system and settlement pattern in the Valley of Mexico: a central place analysis. American Antiquity 44:110-124.

_____. 1980. The role of the marketing system in Aztec society and economy: reply to Evans. American Antiquity 45:876-883.

PART TWO

MARXIST ECONOMIC ANTHROPOLOGY

Economy and society remained the central concern of economic anthropologists during the fifties and sixties. Nash, Geertz, Firth, Belshaw, Dewey, Epstein, Douglas, Bailey, Cancian, Richards--all wrote classic monographs about social relations, political arrangements, relations of productive units, and modes of distribution. But in their writings they turned not to Marx but to Weber, Veblen, and Durkheim for a focus, an analytical framework, or an hypothesis to explore. Anthropologists were more concerned with the formulations of holistic explanations, with the understanding of adaptive and equilibrating mechanisms, than with the analysis of historical process. They were much more concerned with a timeless comparative study of other cultures than with those cultures' changes. They thought that comparison would better reveal the functioning of basic economic structures. (See Firth, 1975, for descriptions of each tradition.)

Sahlins and Wolf, however, retained an interest in an evolutionary-historical perspective. Their contribution to the study of the evolution of political and economic systems is still influential. Wolf's (1966) discussion of extraction of surplus throughout the colonial experience has inspired many monographs; and Sahlins's (1972) essay on the emergence of trade and what he called "negative reciprocal exchanges" deserves a wider audience. But their thoughts, though influenced by Marx's and Marxists' writings, did not follow all of Marx's central arguments.

The substantivists likewise shared with Marx an interest in the historical study of economic processes. Polanyi's The Great Transformation (1957, 249-258) revealed an interest in social dislocation, below-subsistence wages, unemployment, the dependence of nations and people on market forces beyond their control, and the disintegration of a uniform market economy. Yet because their approaches were so different, Marxists and substantivists found it difficult to communicate. Marx argued logically about what he thought were historical inner processes. Polanyi argued historically about what he believed to be observed sequences and relations. Dalton's postscript to Chapter I in Section One and Hart's chapter on Marx attest to the wide difference between these two traditions.

It was not until the seventies, when substantivism was well established, that economic anthropologists began to read Marx. As Hart points out, Marx reentered anthropology through a structuralist's (Godelier's) translation of his writings. Many empirically minded economic anthropologists in Britain did not at first accept Godelier's rationalistic-structuralist writings (1969). Slowly, however, they too became concerned about self-action and the inner logic of ideal modes of production. The breakthrough came when a number of major empirical monographs presented theory in a guise more amenable to the academic heritage of Anglo-American anthropologists. Keith Hart in Chapter V traces the evolution of Marxist ideas and the growth of Marxist economic anthropology, and discusses how this school of thought has influenced the writings of economic anthropologists who, strictly speaking, may not be considered Marxists.

Hart ends his chapter on a polemical note that echoes a question raised in recent books and reviews: Can there be a new Marxist economic anthropology? Perhaps someday, Hart suggests, but not quite yet. We are still laying the foundation of a new and different understanding of how economies and societies develop. Together with Marx's ideas, the studies now being published will form part of that foundation. Hart reviews these studies in Chapter V. But these recent theories require further development; they do not yet fully define the intellectual matrix of economic anthropology. Hart believes this matrix should be firmly embedded in an historical perspective of the economic process. Donald Donham (in comments at the conference) added other research suggestions to those listed by Hart. Donham's suggestions point to what he considers key issues in the development of the new synthesis: clarification of the meaning of determination; clarification of the concept of domination so that it can encompass more than class; an exploration of the relation between ideal models of modes of production and historical reality.

There are, of course, a number of scholars who feel we have already neared a synthesis. John Clammer

felt confident enough to title the book he edited the
New Economic Anthropology. Crumney and Stewart
imply the existence of a cogent Marxist approach in
the introduction to Modes of Production in Africa.
Yet this economic anthropology has so far managed to
tackle only some aspects of what should be the
concerns of economic anthropologists: development and
variations in economic organization. Starting from
the assumption that the forces and relations of
production may engender different modes of production,
they argue logically about transformation or
reproduction of these modes. They also argue
logically about the potential coexistence of various
modes of production and manners in which they
articulate with each other. In turn these arguments
lead to discussion about the consequences of the
articulating processes. The contributors to Crumney
and Stewart's (1981), as well as Wolpe's (1978) and
Seddon's (1978) volumes select for topics of
discussion the transformations of classless societies,
changes in modes of surplus production, the
reproduction or instability of systems in the face of
inequalities, the coexistence of systems, the modes of
surplus extraction, and the control of such surpluses.
More recent writers have taken these arguments in a
new direction: the analysis of legal in addition to
political relations. Snyder (1981) examines the legal
forms that define units of production, ensure the
extraction of surplus value, and determine the flow of
labor and commodities. He also considers how changes
in commodity relations and social forms of labor power
have altered legal forms of transaction and the
relations of production.

But another problem in economic anthropology
could also be argued from a Marxist point of view:
cyclical dynamics. This area has not yet attracted
the attention of many scholars. Marx's theory of
value allowed him to examine not only the dimensions
of exploitation but also the dynamics of capitalist
systems. It is true that Becker (1977) has dedicated
several chapters in a recent book to a reexamination
of the labor theory of value, and that Morishima has
written an entire book on the subject. Nevertheless,
most anthropologists have carefully avoided the
subject. Perhaps we are not yet ready to enter this
controversial area of Marx's writings. Nevertheless,
whether through the labor theory of value or new
frameworks, Marxist economic anthropologists should
begin to examine shorter-term cyclical processes.

101

One of the few economic anthropologists to be concerned with fluctuations has been Scott Cook. Both in his comments on Hart's paper (a conference communication) and in a recent book (1982), Cook argues for the centrality of the labor theory of value. The theory helps explain the equilibrating movements of price in simple commodity production, as price should still reflect the labor value of commodities. But when producers are incorporated into market exchanges, as happened to the metate producers, Cook studied in Oaxaca, the potential for accumulation and expansion emerges and petty commodities production may suffer a transformation.

Kahn (1980) discusses this same problem in a recent book, albeit in a general rather than an ethnographic context. He discusses logically the cost entailed in simple reproduction with different organic compositions of capital. It is unlikely, he argues, that the simple commodity producer places a higher reliance on capital than on labor; such producers avoid capital-intensive enterprises with higher productivity. Kahn describes as well the possible cyclical movements that would ensure a return to petty commodity production rather than accumulation and differentiation (see Chapter XI for a critical review of his analysis).

Except for Cook, Kahn, and Godelier (1971), no Marxist economic anthropologists have fully incorporated labor theory into their analyses. Nevertheless, some have used the principles implied by the theory in arguments about transfer of value, inequality in exchange, and exploitation and dependence. In Chapter XI, Carol Smith examines in detail some of these arguments and shows how they link to dependency theories of development.

There is yet another reason why some Marxist political economists and economic anthropologists have reexamined the labor theory of value. The theory provides a numerarire that allows the analyst to reduce a heterogeneous assemblage of commodities and services to a single quantity. Becker believes that the measurement of value is important for a political evaluation of exchange and development. Others disagree. Morishima (1973) alerts us to some serious problems entailed in the aggregation of values in capitalist systems; Firth (1979) discusses the difficulties of dealing with the concept of value; and Ortiz (1979) discusses problems in determining labor value in precapitalist systems.

References

BECKER, James F. 1977. Marxian political economy. London and New York: Cambridge University Press.

CLAMMER, John, ed. 1978. The new economic anthropology. London: The Macmillan Press.

COOK, Scott. 1982. Zapotec stoneworkers. Lanham, Md.: American University Press.

CRUMNEY, Donald and C. C. Stewart. 1981. Modes of production in Africa. Beverly Hills: Sage.

FIRTH, Raymond. 1975. The sceptical anthropologist? Social anthropology and Marxist views on society. In Marxist analysis and social anthropology, Maurice Bloch, ed. London: Malaby Press.

_____. 1979. Work and value. In Social anthropology of work. S. Wallman, ed. A.S.A. Monograph 19. London: Academic Press.

GODELIER, Maurice. 1969. Rationalité et irrationalité en économie. Paris: Maspero.

_____. 1971. Salt currency and the circulation of commodities among the Baruya of New Guinea. In Studies in economic anthropology. G. Dalton, ed. Anthropological Studies No. 7. Washington, D.C.: American Anthropological Association.

KAHN, Joel S. 1980. Minangkabau social formations. London: Cambridge University Press.

MORISHIMA, Michio. 1973. Marx's economics, a dual theory of value and growth. London and New York: Cambridge University Press.

ORTIZ, Sutti. 1979. The estimation of work. In Social anthropology of work. S. Wallman, ed. A.S.A. Monograph 19. London: Academic Press.

POLANYI, Karl. 1957. The great transformation. Boston: Beacon Press.

SAHLINS, Marshall. 1972. _Stone age economics_. Chicago: Aldine.

SEDDON, David., ed. 1978. _Relations of production_. London: Frank Cass.

SNYDER, Francis G. 1981. _Capitalism and legal change_. New York: Academic Press.

WOLF, Eric. 1966. _Peasants_. Englewood Cliffs: Prentice Hall.

WOLPE, Harold, ed. 1978. _The articulation of modes of production_. London: Routledge and Kegan Paul.

VI. THE CONTRIBUTION OF MARXISM TO ECONOMIC ANTHROPOLOGY

Keith Hart

The idea of assessing the contribution of Marxism to economic anthropology is a bit odd when we consider their relative significance in world history as organized bodies of thought. It might be more appropriate to ask if economic anthropology has made any contribution to Marxism. But, even taking the direction of this paper's title seriously, there are still some major choices facing the reviewer. Economic anthropology is an Anglo subject, i.e., its main practitioners have been English-speakers from the U.S.A. and Britain. Marxism has had a serious impact on Anglo social science only during the last decade and then only fitfully. The option of searching the literature of economic anthropology for Marxist references seems rather unpromising on several grounds. First, Marxist ideas have been incorporated in an extremely unsystematic and casual fashion. Second, few writers who have been influenced by Marxism have had a coherent notion of what economic anthropology is or might be. And third, if one were to focus on the significant outburst of Marxist economic anthropology in the 1970s, the danger is that the discussion would be trapped in a narrow and ephemeral parochialism. For these and other reasons I have chosen a framework which considers Marxism in world historical perspective as it contributes actually and potentially to an economic anthropology whose definition is ideal and which has only partially been realized in work that has been done so far. In this construction Marxism may even be identified as a kind of economic anthropology.

If economic anthropology is the study of the evolution of human society in its material aspect, the organized interaction of man and nature (subject/object), this comes close to the definition of historical materialism in Marxist theory. A more explicitly Hegelian version would emphasize the progressive emancipation of rational economic life from its original matrix of organic symbiosis between living things and the material world. The idea of economy in this formulation entails a cumulative separation of human social activity from material life (cf. Levine, 1978).

The original conditions of production cannot initially be themselves produced. What requires explanation is not the unity of living and active human beings with the natural, inorganic conditions of their metabolism with nature and therefore their appropriation of nature; nor is this the result of a historic process. What we must explain is the separation of these inorganic conditions of human existence from this active existence, a separation which is only fully completed in the relationship between wage labor and capital. (Marx, <u>Grundrisse</u>, 1973, p. 489)

The poles of formal and substantive definitions of the economy are thus seen to stand in a dialectical relationship to each other as expressions of evolving subject-object relations. Much more could and should be said on this topic. But the main point is that this anthropology is concerned with human economy as a whole and especially with its culmination in the present moment of world history, i.e., with the rise of industrial capitalism as the dominant force of our age. There is no room in such an economic anthropology for a division of labor which accords to other social sciences the study of industrialized societies and to anthropology other societies considered in isolation. The anthropology of preindustrial economies must be secondary to the anthropology of global industrialization, since it is the latter that makes anthropology possible.

The discussion is organized as follows. First, Marx's anthropological ideas will be summarized, with only minor reference being made to Engels. Then an outline of the intellectual history of Marxism will be used to justify emphasis on two periods of innovation--the late nineteenth/early twentieth centuries in Germany and Russia and the period since World War Two which has seen new departures in Third World underdevelopment theory, French structuralist Marxism and Anglo social history. Each of the movements has significance for economic anthropology. The paper concludes with a review of recent trends in Marxist economic anthropology and proposes some directions for future initiatives.

I. THE ECONOMIC ANTHROPOLOGY OF KARL MARX

Having redefined the subject as historical materialism, it should come as no surprise that I consider the greatest economic anthropologist of all time to have been Marx himself. Most of his relevant writings are to be found in a small number of works--specifically, Capital (especially the early chapters of Vol. 1 and parts of Vol. 3), Grundrisse (especially the Introduction to the Critique of Political Economy and Precapitalist Economic Formations), Economic and Philosophical Manuscripts of 1844 and German Ideology (written with Engels). Marx's relationship to Engels is a complex one: so much of their writing as individuals came out of intense collaboration that it is both difficult and unnecessary to seek to separate them out. Engels's specific contribution to historical materialism conceived of as economic anthropology is relatively minor. His most famous works--The Origin of the Family, Private Property and the State (1972), Condition of the Working Class in England (1971), The Anti-Duhring (1939), The Peasant War in Germany (1926)--have none of the focus on economy which gives Marx's principal writings their distinctive rigor. One essay, however, The Part Played by Labor in the Transition from Ape to Man (Marx and Engels, 1962), is a wonderfully succinct rendition of the Marxist vision of anthropology. And Engels's wide ranging knowledge of history and ethnography was often vital to the concretization of Marx's philosophical speculations as empirically plausible hypotheses, as their correspondence testifies over and over again. Their partnership had many of the elements of a mature division of labor in which Marx devoted more energy to abstract economic philosophy and Engels was nearer in approach to the polymath historians of his day. From the standpoint of intellectual history, therefore, we lose little by concentrating on Marx's principal theoretical writings and by downplaying the massive contribution of his great colleague.

I shall try to organize Marx's economic anthropology as a sequence of points, any one of which could be expanded from a compressed paragraph to a paper in its own right. The emphasis is necessarily selective and it reflects my own preferences. There are as many Marxes as there are interpretations of the Bible.

1. Economic anthropology (and economics or
political economy) is made possible by our historical
experience of industrial capitalism, which brings the
bulk of human labor for the first time into the
circuit of commodities.[1] The history of precapitalist
economies can reveal elements of the basic categories
of economic life--value, labor, wages, capital,
etc.--but only modern capitalism makes them a
coherent, objective system of commoditized social
relations. In this way economy takes on a general
subjective dimension which was previously confined to
the unsystematic calculations of merchants and other
specialists in the narrow sphere of precapitalist
commodity relations. This evolution should be
intrinsic to any self-conscious theory.

2. Economy is first labor (divided labor,
surplus labor, etc.) whose activity is production, the
embracing category of Marx's system--see Introduction
to the critique of political economy in Grundrisse.
Production is both all material activity and one side
of an economic process which also includes
distribution, exchange, and consumption. The
definition of production in general is always colored
by the mode of production characteristic of our
epoch--in this case, capitalism. Thus productive
labor is, for us, whatever produces value for capital.

3. The commodity is abstract social labor: its
highest form is capital.[2] The simple circuit of
commodities (C-M-C) is one in which units of divided
labor produce a specialized range of commodities that
are exchanged through the medium of money sales for
the whole range of subsistence needs making up the
consumption of each unit. There is no room for
expansion in this circuit which leaves a small niche
for merchant and usurer's capital to occupy. The
capitalist circuit of commodities (M-C-M') is one in
which owners of money use it to make more money by
purchasing commodities. This circuit is inherently
dynamic and accumulative. Only one commodity can
produce extra value and that is human labor. Hence
the revolutionary significance of the entry of capital
into the organization of production (especially
agriculture). Marx's greatest discovery, in his own
eyes, was that wage labor produced surplus value for
capital and thereby transformed the rate and
conditions of accumulation. His economic theory
hinges on the law of value which describes the

necessary behavior of capital and labor under a system of generalized commodity production and market competition.

4. Commodity relations and productivity are intrinsically connected, especially under industrial capitalism. Only when the market becomes the main means of social reproduction does the law of value operate effectively and then the stimulus of competition acts directly to make technological innovation a condition of survival. The combination of money capital and wage labor under conditions of juridical freedom is thus fundamental to an accumulation process which revolutionizes the productivity of human labor, making it possible for the first time to produce with machines much more with less work. This formula is sometimes expressed as a statement about relations and forces of production, the former acting as "fetters" on the latter in precapitalist systems. It is central to Marx's version of the subject/object dialectic.

5. In the extraordinary passage of Grundrisse known as Precapitalist Economic Formations (cf. Hobsbawm, 1964; Marx, 1973), Marx lays out a vision of human history in which capitalism is seen as the final dissolvent of those forms of society linking us to an evolutionary past that we share with the animals. In making that break, capitalism is the enabling force for the emergence of a human society fully emancipated from our primitive dependence on nature. It is, of course, not that society, but its midwife. Two processes mark human evolution up to the epoch of capitalism--the individuation of the original animal herd and the separation of social life from its original matrix, the earth as natural laboratory. The logic of these passages is markedly Hegelian and somewhat unfashionable to twentieth century taste: it is, however, the essence of Marx's anthropology.

6. In contrast, the concept of class plays a minor role in Marx's economic anthropology. The Communist Manifesto (Marx and Engels, 1945) is quite explicit in pointing to the plurality and confusion of classes, estates and orders in precapitalist societies. Only when the logic of accumulation and commodity economy penetrates the bulk of production does class struggle define social evolution in a clear cut way, as the two great classes of bourgeoisie and proletariat are fashioned out of the polarized

movement of the capitalist mode of production. Even then, this is more of a potential dualism, a tendency, than an historical actuality, since residual classes often play a significant part in the struggles of industrial capitalist societies (see Marx, 1907).

7. Marx's ideas about a sequence of modes of production in history are at best sketchy, contrary to the efforts of his successors to generate a formal scheme out of his occasional references to Asiatic (oriental/Slavonic), ancient, Germanic, feudal and similar precapitalist modes (cf. for example, Krader, 1975). Since the economy is only dominant under capitalism, the economic determination of precapitalist social forms is at best indirect. Rather than seek to uncover the functional underpinnings of specific cases, Marx's method was more normally to trace out the logic of the tendency of world history, using extremely idealized examples as reference points along the way. Indeed he makes it clear in Grundrisse that the historical explanation of particular cases must draw on an ad hoc series of ecological, political and other variables--a task which differs greatly from the exegesis of logical pathways out of the primitive commune to the threshold of modern capitalism. This dualism between empirical analysis and philosophical speculation is a weakness that Marx himself did not resolve.

8. Marx's method is to start with the concrete as a basis for making abstractions which only attain their fullest significance when they are reinserted into the concrete as analysis and explanation or as the basis for informed social action.[3] In this he opposed Hegel and all others who give priority to the abstract in itself. He also stressed the inadequacy of any social theory which failed to explain the social theorist ("why me?") as part of its field of enquiry. This is doubly a criticism of those anthropologies which do not even include an analysis of modern western society in their accounts of the primitive and the exotic (e.g. Sahlins, 1972).

9. Marx's economic anthropology is a special theory of industrial capitalism, one which conceives of our epoch as having general world historic significance, as being a turning point in human social evolution. It is not a case study of western society, as Godelier (1972b) implies in his absurd juxtaposition of Marx on capitalism with Lévi-Strauss

on the Murngin. Rather industrial capitalism has set
in train a series of events which must bring the rest
of the world under its contradictory logic, if only in
the form of its negation, socialism. It is not
ethnocentric to deny non-western societies their
autonomous evolution; history has already done that.

10. For Marx then, economic anthropology becomes
a set of analytical constructs of the capitalist mode
of production, modified by an awareness of the world
that preceded and lies outside capitalism. It should
be noted that some consider the greatness of Marx's
work to lie not in his theoretical discoveries, but in
the fine historical and ethnographic sense that he and
Engels brought to their study of Victorian capitalism
(Lange, 1968). Others have identified a break
(coupure) between Marx the Hegelian and Marx the
mature economist, treating Capital as a positive
text which escapes from the dialectical subjectivity
of the earlier economic manuscripts (Althusser and
Balibar, 1965). The point can be sustained, but it
should be minimized if the whole corpus of Marx's work
is to be taken as a basis for reading him as an
economic anthropologist.

II. AN OUTLINE INTELLECTUAL HISTORY OF MARXISM

In the century since Marx's death ended his
collaboration with Engels,[4] the accumulated work of
his self-acknowledged followers has assumed
proportions paralleled only by the traditions
initiated by Buddha, Christ and Mohammed. This is not
to say that Marxism is a religion, only that its
organization and impact share many of the features of
the great world religions. The specific historical
vehicle for this extraordinary rise to global
prominence has been the emergence of the Soviet Union
and secondarily of China to challenge the hegemony of
the U.S.A., Britain and other western industrial
powers in the name of worldwide communist revolution.
DeTocqueville (1839) predicted long ago that America
and Russia were destined to carry on the two thousand
year old struggle between west and east to dominate
European civilization. This somewhat parochial
dialectic has been transformed in our time by the
struggle to dominate the whole world under the cover
of competing abstract ideologies of economic
organization and state power. And for the last thirty
years this struggle has threatened to end all life on
the planet before it is resolved. Marxism is thus not

just an intellectual tradition and, in assessing its contribution to economic anthropology, we would be unwise to gloss over the political context within which Marxist writing is carried out.

The evolution of Marxism after Marx may conveniently be divided into three periods, using the political history of the Soviet Union as a benchmark for more general trends in world history. The first (1883-1917) ends with the Bolshevik revolution and the formation of a state dedicated to Marxist principles. This was more generally the most significant period of transformation since the last quarter of the eighteenth century; it saw the second industrial revolution, imperialism, the emergence of modern art, music, social science and much else. The second (1917-1948) sees the completion of the Russian empire after three decades of unremitting disaster--two world wars, global depression, fascism, Stalinism and the Holocaust.[5] The third (1948-   ) might well be seen later to have ended in the energy and commodities crisis of 1973, making our own day the dim beginning of a fourth phase in the above sequence. This postwar period has witnessed the greatest economic boom in history, decolonization and the construction of a system of some 150 nation states, domination of global politics by the two antagonistic superpowers and the elements of a third industrial revolution (computers, biological engineering, space transport). Marxism has evolved through stages which reflect this history; indeed a principle of synchronicity might well be invoked to suggest that Marxist thought often more closely resembles non-Marxist thought of the same era than it does previous phases of its own development.[6] This is not to deny the coherence of the Marxist tradition, but to warn the simple-minded against assuming that anyone wearing a Marxist label is necessarily a profound exegete of Marx's thought.

In seeking to trace the actual and potential contribution of Marxism to economic anthropology, I intend to concentrate on the first and third periods listed above. The few decades before World War I were filled with excitement--political, technological, cultural--and intellectual life reflected this. A new cadre of Marxists arose in Germany and Russia whose writings reflect the realistic ambitions of the Social Democratic Party, Bolsheviks and others to win political power in their respective countries. Just as orthodox social scientists today look to Weber,

Durkheim, Freud and other giants of the period for their main inspiration, so too the Marxist intellectuals at this time stand out for the clarity and innovation of their thinking. Lenin is the greatest of these, but I would like to draw attention to some of the others too--Luxemburg, Kautsky and Bukharin, for example.[7]

The blight of what Winston Churchill called the second thirty years war (1914-1945) is similarly reflected in what happened to Marxism after Russia assumed a worldwide responsibility for its dissemination. The historical theories of determinate economic stages, initiated by writers like Plekhanov (1934, 1980) and systematized between the wars by Stalin (1952), gave Marxism the mechanical reputation it enjoyed in much of the west until the partial dismantling of the Cold War a decade ago. Official Russian Marxism will not be considered in this paper, although important work in economic anthropology has been undertaken by Russian ethnologists (e.g., by Semenov, 1980). Equally the whole output of Eastern Europe and Communist Asia will be ignored, in part because of my lack of knowledge, but also because communist intellectuals and Anglo economic anthropologists have lived in separate sealed compartments. It should be said, before leaving this unfortunate second period of Marxist development, that what Stalin did to the dynamic philosophy of Marx, Engels and Lenin was paralleled by the emasculation of classic social thought in the west, where structural-functionalism and static equilibrium theories replaced the vision of the nineteenth century founding fathers. Finally, I have omitted the few great Marxist figures who emerged in this period, such as Lukács and Gramsci, mainly because their emphasis is more political and cultural than economic.

The post-war period is the most interesting to us, because of its recency and because of its relative eclecticism, even pluralism. The intensification of military and ideological conflict between east and west, when combined with a plethora of decolonization struggles and the entry of third world nations into global politics, has made it virtually impossible any longer to identify a coherent body of Marxist thought. Within the U.S.A., many intellectuals who were sympathetic to Marxism felt themselves unable to express this sympathy openly in their writings during the 1950s and 1960s. In many other countries the opposite conditions held, so that intellectuals of all persuasions often found it necessary to claim the label "Marxist" as a source of political legitimacy. It is no exaggeration to state that almost any idea can now be found on both sides of the great divide between western orthodoxy and Marxism: only the self-appointed symbols of identification vary. To take a prominent example, the Frankfurt School of Horkheimer, Adorno, Habermas, etc., labels itself "historical materialist" and "critical of bourgeois theory."[8] This is fighting Marxist talk and the naive may be led into supposing critical theory to be Marxist. But far more important to the Frankfurt School than Marx is the left-tendency of German social thought derived from Weber.[9] New syntheses of this kind are vital to intellectual growth, but they obscure the history of Marxism, except to make it clear that it should now be thought of as a vast church capable of embracing many creeds and constantly challenged by usurping apostasies.

Despite a recent increase in the international flow of ideas, any Marxism is usually best described within the context of a national intellectual culture. French Marxism is French before it is Marxism and the same goes for Anglo, Latin American and Chinese versions. The most catholic, diffuse and, in some sense, unmarxist Marxism is the body of writing on third world economic and political emancipation from western domination which may be loosely labeled "underdevelopment theory." This comes out of Latin American and Africa in the main, with "dependency" theorists like Frank (1969, 1978), Cardoso (1979) and the Egyptian political economist Samir Amin (1974, 1976) leading the way. We might add to this corpus the revolutionary writings of Fanon (1963), Cabral (1972) and, of course, Mao (1971). A later variant of this school is Wallerstein's (1974, 1979) world systems approach which has inspired many imitations in recent anthropological work (cf. Smith, 1976; Schneider, 1976). By far the most prominent Marxist influence on anthropology has been French structuralist Marxism initiated by Althusser and his colleague Balibar (1965) and carried on by a number of people who are professionally employed as anthropologists--Godelier, Terray, Meillassoux, Rey, etc. Less obviously, the stream of Marxist historical writings that has come out of Britain (and to a lesser extent America) since the war constitutes a major source of intellectual influence for anthropology--Hobsbawm,

Dobb, Hilton, Thompson, Williams, Anderson, etc. In all three cases the prevailing trends of national intellectual life ("Yanqui go home," structuralism, empiricism) transform the century-old heritage of Marx's thought into distinctly novel systems containing many ideas that Marx spent his lifetime seeking to demolish.

Before concluding this section with some general thoughts on the evolution of Marxism, I should make some reference to the cultural materialist wing of American anthropology. None of the works embraced by this label has achieved the international currency of the schools of Marxist thought I have referred to above; but in this context some may think a nod in their direction appropriate. American anthropology produced in the 1950s and 1960s an evolutionary conception of culture which was both materialist and, to a degree, historical. The followers of White and Steward at Michigan and Columbia were responsible for a coherent body of comparative work that has obvious affinities to Marxism.[10] Wolf, Sahlins, Service, Mintz, Fried and Harris--to name but a few--were all affected by Marxist thought to some extent, even as their work departed from anything resembling mainstream Marxism. Who knows what their output would have looked like if there had been no Red Scare or Cold War? As it is, only Wolf[11] has taken advantage of the warmer climate of the 1970s to locate his anthropology as a thoroughgoing Marxism along lines promulgated by the great Belgian theorist, Ernest Mandel (1968). As an outsider to American anthropology I am reluctant to enter the maze of covert intention and overt periphrasis that national politics has imposed on its postwar intellectuals. For that reason I have left the relationship between Marxism and cultural materialism out of the discussion.

To summarize this cavalier sweep through a century of Marxism, I would draw attention to the enormous gap between Marx's world and that of his latterday followers. Marx's thought is truly synthetic, combining German dialectical philosophy, English political economy and French socialism. His vision is of a world history culminating in the revolutionary transitions of his own time. His language reflects the fluidity and flexibility of his practice--he had no intention to lay down the formal language of a self-replicating doctrine. His followers, on the other hand, have usually been lesser men and women, incapable of transcending the limits of national culture, preoccupied with the bureaucratic affairs of parties and states, devoted to institution-building and above all else looking to Marx for legitimation of a fixed, formal vocabulary capable of drawing lines between enemies and of defining what is right between friends. And then we have the academics, an enormous effusion of proletarianized intellectuals who have lately come to Marxism as yet more grist for their introspective mill. The fact that about a hundred people can sign up in North America alone for a Society of Economic Anthropology is just one indication of this astonishing post-war phenomenon. Such people cannot handle Marx's protean use of language and ideas, any more than their bureaucratic counterparts can.

The result is a formalization of Marx's thought that brings it in line with western social science as it drives a wedge between us and Marx. Thus an epithet like kleinstädtich ("small town like") acquires the fixed frenchified English translation "petty bourgeois" and its precise referents in a typology of class categories are debated with scholastic fervor. More serious is the fate of "mode of production." Even the most casual reading of Grundrisse reveals how subtle and nuanced was Marx's understanding of the concept "production": that subtlety is sacrificed by the unending attempts of his followers to construct types of production (which they are pleased to call "modes" following Marx's unsystematic use of the expression) whose positivist logic is foreign to Marx's way of thinking.[12] The question of translation just between German, French and English is almost never brought up, since this would unleash a storm of semantic confusion that the universalizing pretensions of latterday Marxism could not tolerate.

When Marx said that he was not a Marxist he could not possibly have anticipated the gap that the twentieth century would introduce between the spirit and letter of his works and the intellectual activities of those claiming descent from him. Some say (e.g., Lichtheim, 1961) that Lenin converted Marxism from an enlightenment theory of general world history into a political tool for the forced industrialization of backward economies, beginning on the European periphery and extending in this century to the third world. That is as may be. Certainly the institutionalization of Marxism as an ideological weapon in the most important confrontation of our times, when combined with the fragmentation of national and regional cultures, has led to a state of affairs in which the original coherence of Marx's thought has been all but dissipated.[13]

III. GERMAN AND RUSSIAN MARXISM AT THE TURN OF THE CENTURY

The fragmentation or, more charitably, differentiation of Marxist thought began with its incorporation into the left-wing political struggles of the late nineteenth century. The three great continental empires of Germany, Austria-Hungary and Russia (which at one time formed a league, the Dreikaiserbund) proved to be more fertile ground for Marxism than England, France, America or the Mediterranean and Scandinavian peripheries of Europe. Here the problem of socialist transformation became inextricably linked to the issue of economic backwardness, particularly to the analysis of the incipient effects of capitalism on varied, predominantly rural economies. In this period, then, several writers (all very prominent political figures) addressed the question of the "transition" to capitalism which Marx had been content to leave as a secondary aspect of his enquiry into the workings of an advanced capitalist structure in Britain. Very little has been written since about the Marxist theory of economic development that improves upon the work of Lenin, Luxemburg and Kautsky on the transition to capitalism.

The German Social Democratic Party was the first Marxist organization to mobilize a significant portion of the industrial working class. It was a cauldron of intellectual innovation at the turn of the century, producing great revolutionaries (Luxemburg) and revisionists (Bernstein, Kautsky). Rosa Luxemburg's The Accumulation of Capital (1951) has been derided, e.g., by Bukharin, as a conceptual mess in the formal sense; but she opened up the closed model of capitalism current then and now, so that Marxism could deal with the historicity of global accumulation. She explicitly addressed the question of how commodity economy is inserted into social formations governed by other principles. This was not just a matter of capitalist origins in feudalism, but recognition of the continuing significance of imperialism, colonialism and the incorporation of peasantries for the reproduction of capitalist social relations. In this way she challenged that tendency of Marxist economic thought to replicate liberal economics in postulating a closed sphere of capitalist commodity relations whose logic could be understood as a system sui generis and she focused attention on the mechanisms which joined that system in an accumulative dynamic to a world that was still in many ways its negation. Luxemburg's book is indispensable to any economic anthropology of the ongoing transition that forms the matrix of modern ethnographic study in the third world. Her satirical descriptions of North American and South African modes of expansion add a lively historical dimension to her central arguments concerning the peaceful and violent forms of capitalist development around the world.[14]

Karl Kautsky's several works include Die Agrarfrage (1899) (The Agrarian Question), a book which has been translated into every major European language except English.[15] It is the best account to date of the evolution of an industrial capitalist economy out of an agrarian one. His main thesis is that variations in agrarian structure are central to the course of capitalist development, generating the dominant problem of politics in each specific country. Thus English feudalism and the parliamentary gentry who led the seventeenth century revolutions shaped the future course of British industrialism. In the German imperial state an alliance of East Prussian junkers and Rhineland industrialists created an entirely different setting for working class politics. These and similar considerations led Kautsky to solutions that brought him into sharp conflict with Lenin on political strategy, and "Kautskyism" became for the latter synonymous with apostasy from the communism envisaged by Marx. Nevertheless, Die Agrarfrage is one of the great intellectual contributions to the theory of economic evolution and it should be read alongside Eduard Bernstein's more general work, Evolutionary Socialism (1898).

Lenin's short popular works, such as Imperialism (1916) and The State and Revolution (1917), offer ready access to his social thought. Indeed, the former may well come back into vogue, since the crisis of finance capitalism and its imperialist solution in the late nineteenth century look not unlike the phase of the global cycle that we ourselves are entering. If so, the fuller work on the same subject by the English radical, Hobson (1902), should be read as a companion text. But Lenin's great work--in my view the finest study of its kind--is The Development of Capitalism in Russia (1899). In order to write this piece of over 600 pages, he spent three years reading the literature and absorbing the Zemstvo statistics on rural communities compiled after the Alexandrine reforms of 1861. His economic sociology has a clarity that recalls Mao's discussions of the Asian peasantry and it is much more detailed. More important is his polemic against the Narodniks advocates of peasant communalism in the countryside. He shows how Russia's involvement in the growing world capitalist economy has already set in train class forces that are transforming agriculture and that make such ideologies mere mystification. His arguments and his demonstrations are profoundly germane to present day disputes over the development of rural peoples in the third world, where Narodism still lives in the pronouncements of both international bureaucracies and dependent governments.

Lenin's thesis was the occasion for A. V. Chayanov's better known refutation, The Theory of Peasant Economy (1966), a marginalist analysis resting on the assumption of homogeneity in Russia's peasant labor force. Instead of endlessly aping Sahlins's ingenious application of Chayanov's formal analysis to primitive economies (see Sahlins, 1972, Chapters 2, 3), economic anthropologists might more profitably set about trying to discover which of Lenin and Chayanov's issues were central to their debate and why.

These three works define a more historically specific economic anthropology which addresses the contradictory advance of capitalism and of its negation, socialism, in backward areas. One more study from a slightly later period is worth mentioning here, even though its subject concentrates on developments internal to the advanced capitalist societies. That study is Bukharin's Economic Theory of the Leisure Class (1927), which turns the lens of Marxism on the rise of modern marginalist economics as a specific social ideology. Others, notably Thorstein Veblen (1948), had noted the ascendancy of the new marginalism since it was independently invented in the 1870's by Jevons, Walras and Menger (see Schumpeter,

1954, part IV). In place of the dynamic, class-based, structural theory proposed by classical political economy from Smith to Marx, modern economics had constructed a static, individualist, micro-theory of economic action based on the calculation of subjective utilities. Bukharin argued that this shift in economic thinking reflected a real change in the interests and composition of the capitalist class, which, having once been entrepreneurial and productive, was now a rentier class of stock managers for whom calculation of yields at the margin was truly meaningful. Mandel's chapter in <u>Marxist Economic Theory</u> (1968), entitled "The origins, rise and withering away of political economy" is a much broader essay on the general topic of the historical foundations of economic ideas. It is a topic that should be central to economic anthropology, making the social history of intellectual trends one of its most important contributions to the critique of western society's pretensions towards universalism. (See Dumont, 1977, for a step in this direction.)

There is another reason to embrace a thoroughgoing intellectual history as part of our task: to help us set our own enquiries in a more relative context. Most of the authors discussed in this section routinely have investigated the history of their problem and concepts, so that they would be more aware themselves of the specificities and generalities in their definition of the problem. Thus Luxemburg starts her work with a review of historical debates on capital and Lenin's theories of the state which led him to consider why More and Hobbes had come up with their solutions to the problem at their time in history. This is one of the greatest legacies of Marxism, that its major thinkers have always thought of themselves as living in history rather than as inventing an abstract, static doctrine of no historical specificity. Given the fragmentation of the intellectual division of labor in our day, perhaps only anthropology can reconstitute the task of placing western social thought in the appropriately relative context of its own particular history.

IV. UNDERDEVELOPMENT THEORY

The theory that much of the world has become "underdeveloped" as a result of capitalism, acquired wide currency in the late 1960s. The thesis of Latin American "dependistas," such as Cardoso and Frank, was

that the poor countries were being made poorer by a
process of capitalist development which benefits the
rich countries; that this exploitation was intrinsic
to the origin and growth of the modern world economy;
and that the blockage to their emancipation could only
be removed by some sort of withdrawal from that
economy. The polemical force of this position derived
from its critique of prevailing American and Western
European assumptions about development, sometimes
called modernization theory, which held that the
diffusion of the bourgeois institutional
package--capital, cities, science, democracy, law and
education--would eventually and without contradiction
bring the poor countries into the fold of civilized
affluence, by osmosis as it were.[16] Amin's several
books reflect a similar point of view to that of the
dependency theorists; the idea that capitalist
penetration of third world regions actually retards
their development is expressed in the title of one of
the books: L'Afrique de l'ouest est Bloquée
(1971). Somewhat later Immanuel Wallerstein, a
political sociologist specializing in Africa, wrote an
influential work entitled The Modern World System
(1974) in which he explained western economic history
in terms of the exploitation of a dependent periphery
by a metropolitan core originating in Northwest
Europe. In outline his argument shares much in common
with underdevelopment theory.

All of these writers were influenced heavily by
the work of Marx and his followers and most would
identify themselves as Marxists. Many social
scientists, historians and anthropologists who have
been influenced by them in turn no doubt consider
themselves receptive to what by all accounts is a
version of mainstream Marxism. Yet, in its central
premises, underdevelopment theory is profoundly
divergent from the historical materialism propagated
by Marx, Engels and Lenin. In particular, the latter
placed emphasis in the process of capital accumulation
on the social determinants of productivity (the
dialectic of man and nature), whereas the former focus
on the extraction of surplus from the periphery (a
kind of economic geography). Where the founders of
Marxism, perhaps erroneously, embraced capitalism as
the temporary salvation of backward areas--see, e.g.,
Marx on India (Marx and Engels, 1962), Lenin on Russia
(1956)--underdevelopment theory has it that these
areas are made worse off and trapped into specialized
forms of dependent immobility.

Several critics, notably Brenner (1977), have pointed out that underdevelopment theory has shifted attention away from production to the sphere of circulation (distribution and exchange), thereby committing the classical error of orthodox economics--hence Brenner's phrase "neo-Smithian Marxism." It was essential to Marx's theory of development that emphasis be placed squarely on the market effects of uneven gains in labor productivity. He was aware that mercantilist colonialism generated "primitive accumulation" of capital by direct transfer, but "capitalist accumulation" proper takes place when capital organizes production itself and is driven by competition to reduce costs through improving the efficiency of labor (see Marx, 1954, v. 1). Thus the growing gap between industrial capitalist countries and the rest is more the result of a rising productivity curve than of continuing primitive accumulation in the third world. Moreover, it can be shown historically, by pointing to such countries as Korea, Taiwan, India, Mexico and Brazil today (not to mention Russia, Hungary, Italy, Chile and other "peripheral" countries from an earlier era), that underdevelopment theory's representation of the capitalist world economy as a static zero sum game is badly misplaced rhetoric.

The prototype for underdevelopment theory is not Marxism, but various nineteenth century writings in nationalist economics--that emerged in response to Britain's industrial pre-eminence over the U.S., Germany, and other countries--as attempts to consider ways of recovering from a position of relative backwardness. Hamiltonian economics and the writings of the father of German economic nationalism, List, stressed a combination of protectionist and liberal measures in order to promote their country's manufactures.[17] Their impulse was the same as that which drives much of the writings on third world underdevelopment today. The strongly geographical bent of this kind of thinking, with its focus on existing state boundaries and trade within and across them, is one significant divergence from Marxism. Anthropologists who borrow from this stream of modern thought may find it congenial because it gives a larger framework for their own intuitive identification with the people they study and because it both confirms their habitual tendency to think in terms of exchange before production and avoids confrontation with a truly dialectical materialism. The proliferation of Marxist terms in underdevelopment theory suggests a possible synthesis between the two and, if we are to be charitable, it must be granted that it has a place in the history of Marxism.

V. FRENCH STRUCTURALIST MARXISM

By far the greatest source of Marxist influence within post-war anthropology has been the structuralist version that emanated from Paris in the late 1960s and early 1970s. As such it shared many of the features of French intellectual life in this period. Cartesian rationalism shapes the contours of all modes of thought in what is an extremely centralized system of national politics and education. Structuralism gave them a Kantian twist, finding forms beneath appearances and structures whose coherence was only accessible to the analytical mind. The hidden logic of language patterns seemed to offer a powerful example of the need for structuralist method; linguists, social scientists, including anthropologists, literary critics, psychologists and historians all took up the crusade to modernize thinking in their disciplines (e.g., Lane, 1970). Lévi-Strauss (1963) was, of course, a leading light in the movement; but, for our purposes, the crucial figure is Louis Althusser, a Marxist philosopher who set out in the 1960's to bring Marx up-to-date by making him a structuralist.

Althusser and Balibar (1965) produced a reading of Capital which divested it of any residual elements of Hegelian philosophy and brought it into line with both structuralist methodology and the most modern "scientific" approaches emanating from the Anglo world, notably systems theory. The phenomenology of the human subject, the dialectic and, indeed, history itself were in effect dropped from their scheme. In their place a deep structure of the ideal mode of production was outlined, having three elements--producers, non-producers and means of production--whose variable combination was realized as concrete modes of production (Balibar, 1970). Much attention was paid to the relationship between economic, political and ideological levels of the mode of production and to the question of which was dominant and/or determinant in any given case. Althusser abandoned the ideological notion of "society" in favor of "social formations" in which, it was recognized, more than one mode of production was normally combined. Many concepts were clarified and new, often penetrating, vocabulary honed for potential use in the analysis of real political conflicts.

Several anthropologists made substantial contributions to structuralist Marxism at about this time. Maurice Godelier claimed a direct line from Marx and Lévi-Strauss, unmediated by Althusser's philosophy. Indeed his great work, Rationalité et Irrationalité en Economie (English translation 1972a), was published in 1966 and much of it written some years earlier. Godelier entered anthropology via economics and philosophy and this is reflected in his book, two parts of which are a sensitive analysis of the history of economic (especially Marx's) ideas. The third part, "Objets et méthodes de l'anthropologie économique," is a fairly conventional attempt to struggle with the poles of formalism and substantivism as defined by the Polanyite wing of Anglo anthropology.[18] The notion of rationality is applied not only to persons but to systems, thereby setting up a contradiction which the author is unable to resolve. The introduction to the English edition sets out a revealing comparison between Marxism, structuralism and functionalism. Marxism, says Godelier, can add a specific kind of function to Lévi-Strauss's structures, thereby allowing a complete anthropological analysis of social systems. The result, however, looks more like an ecological version of structural-functionalism than Marxism and Godelier's scheme has never been successfully applied to a moving, historical society. In his later writings Godelier (1977) has returned to the classical comparative topics of social anthropology, such as the role of religion and kinship in shaping primitive societies. His early book (1972a), however, can stand with Lire le Capital (Althusser and Balibar, 1965) as the most formative influence in opening up Anglo economic anthropology to Marxist ideas.

Claude Meillassoux, Emmanuel Terray and Pierre-Philippe Rey have all acknowledged their debt to Althusser, but they sustained a lively debate among themselves for over a decade, often based on conflicting interpretations of their common ethnographic area, West and Central Africa. All three wrote major field monographs, but Meillassoux's L'anthropologie économique des Gouro de Côte d'Ivoire (1964) became the locus classicus for application of rival schemes, much as Evans-Pritchard's <u>The Nuer</u> (1940) continues to exercise the theoretical imagination of Anglo social anthropologists. Meillassoux's ethnography is sound, but not remarkable in itself, except for its explicitly Marxist framework. His various journal articles of the 1960's and 1970's (Meillassoux, 1960, 1971, 1972, 1975b) attracted widespread attention for their relevance to third world peasantries in general; and two editorial essays on West African indigenous commerce and precolonial slavery reveal a masterly control of the sweep of the region's history which are enormously suggestive. One tendency of Meillassoux's thought is summarized in a later book, <u>Femmes, Greniers et Capitaux</u> (1975a), which sets out an evolutionary scheme similar in many ways to the band-tribe-state sequence worked out by Sahlins (1968), Service (1966) and other cultural materialists. His three stages highlight the key sources of power in each--marriageable women, food granaries and money capital. Meillassoux has also been a radical critic of the western powers in Africa. His persisting intellectual interest is the relationship between production and reproduction, and it is for this that his work will be largely remembered.

Terray's essay reinterpreting the Gouro ethnography (Terray, 1972) is in many ways the most interesting piece to emerge from the Althusserian school of West African ethnology. In it he argues that Marxist analysis is often too crude, labelling all primitive societies in much the same way, so that idealist ethnographers are left free to explain their specificity by reference to kinship structures and the like. Instead he lays out a method for classifying the material base of a society in great detail, so that its modes of production may be inferred empirically and concrete particulars may be incorporated into a materialist analysis. The results in this case are quite impressive, as is the abstract theorizing that he brings to such matters as kinship and class, the authority of elders and the relative significant of production organization and marriage exchanges. The methodology appears to be trapped in the same static synchronicity that plagued British structural-functionalist ethnography in the same region. Indeed there is little history in this version of historical materialism. But it has many virtues and I suspect that anthropological archaeologists and ethnologists would find in this piece a goldmine of ideas about how to investigate empirical economies systematically. Terray's (1974, 1975) theoretical essays on the Abron kingdom of Gyaman in the nineteenth century, in marked contrast, are extremely sensitive to history and offer many substantive insights into the application of Marxist class analysis and similar ideas to the study of preindustrial complex societies. The trend of his work seems to be towards more concrete, particular studies, but Terray's theoretical contribution has already been large, if not as widely touted as that of his colleagues.

Least known to Anglos (because of the failure of his books to be translated) and in my view the most significant of the French Marxists is Pierre-Philippe Rey. His long monograph on a matrilineal tribe of the French Congo, entitled somewhat grandiosely Colonialisme, Néo-colonialisme et Transition au Capitalisme (1971), is seminal in a number of respects. First, it marked an original contribution to the regional literature on matriliny, slavery and European penetration of the Congo, unlike many Marxist interpretations which merely restate what is known in a new jargon. Second, Rey outlines here his idea of a "lineage mode of production" (see also Rey, 1975) which has been taken up widely since. Third, he spells out the issue of "articulation of modes of production in a structure of dominance," showing concretely how colonial capitalism restructures the lineage and petty commodity modes of production to reproduce its own interests. This argument is partly replicated in a seminal article he wrote with Dupré "Reflections on the pertinence of a general theory of the history of exchange" (Dupré and Rey, 1978), where they savage Polanyi's school of economic anthropology, using Bohannan and Dalton's introduction to Markets in Africa (1962) as primary target. They claim that elders control the labor of youths in the lineage mode of production by rationing access to marriageable women; this exploiting class is then suborned by the colonial ruling class to supply labor to plantations, mines, etc., thereby showing how two formally separate structures may be combined to produce an effect beneficial to both of the dominant classes. This line of thought is made much more general in Rey's Les Alliances des Classes (1973), where a putative collaboration between the landed aristocracy and the bourgeoisie in England's drive to industrial capitalism is adduced as comparative evidence supporting the thesis advanced for colonial Africa. Finally, in an essay introducing a volume called Capitalisme Négrier: La Marche des Paysans vers le Prolétariat (Lebris, Rey, Samuel, 1976), Rey calls for greater ethnographic particularism in analyses of the social forces extruding migrants from the countryside: it is not enough to speak of capitalism sucking its proletariat out of agriculture; who goes and who stays? and what variable effects do rural social structures have on the process? The scope of Rey's work is always magisterial and there is obviously much more to come from this, perhaps the most original mind to have contributed to French Marxist anthropology.

We are left with a mystery: why should this small band of men have had such a disproportionate effect on Anglo anthropology, as they surely did in the 1970's. It cannot be that they clarified a number of concepts nor that they wrote a few untranslated monographs. Neither is it likely that their concern with and participation in Parisian left-wing politics stirred up sympathy in the Anglo breast. Yet a whole journal, Economy and Society, was devoted principally to disseminating their shorter works throughout the English speaking world; another, Critique of Anthropology, frequently translated important passages by Rey and others; and Frank Cass published a collection of translated writings in 1978 (Seddon, 1978). A derivative work by Hindess and Hirst, Precapitalist Modes of Production (1975), achieved wide notoriety, if not acclaim. This openness of Anglos to structuralist Marxism requires explanation. I believe that its success was owed to the explicitly synthetic position it occupied between German, especially Marxist, philosophy and Anglo scientific empiricism. The modernization of Marx, by incorporating systems theory and dumping the dialectic, produced a version of structural-functionalism sufficiently different from the original to persuade Anglos they were learning Marxism and similar enough to allow them to retain their customary mode of thinking which had been temporarily discredited. The long-run effects are almost all beneficial: by now most Anglos are aware of structuralist Marxism's limitations, but some of them have stayed in continental discourse long enough to explore Italian Marxism, neo-Kantian philosophy and much else. The intellectual world is a more open, more international place as a direct result of the efforts described in this section.

VI. ANGLO HISTORICAL MARXISM

The most prominent spokesmen for Marxist ideas in the English-speaking world have usually been historians. E. P. Thompson (1963, 1978), has recently moved from writing the cultural history of the English working class to launching a virulent attack on Althusserian Marxism (as well to compaigning vigorously against nuclear weapons). For all his prominence, Thompson has not had much influence on economic anthropology--mainly because his interests are not particularly economic. Eric Hobsbawm's output is perhaps the most impressive. His introduction to Marx's Precapitalist Economist Formations (1964) has long been an essential part of economic anthropology courses and his book Primitive Rebels (1959) offers many anthropological insights into the comparative study of politics and religion. But his larger works on nineteenth century social and economic history are more works of reference than models of enquiry and Hobsbawm's influence on the formation of economic anthropology has been slight. The same could be said of Raymond Williams's sustained application of Marxist ideas to English literature and culture history (Williams, 1966, 1977). Several of the most prominent figures, then, in the post-war revival of English Marxism are not central to the intellectual history that concerns us here.

The seminal work in Anglo Marxist economic history is Maurice Dobb's Studies in the Development of Capitalism (1947). For all the criticisms levelled against it, Dobb's book is still the essential starting point, if only in order to allow the student to trace the threads of subsequent debate. That debate is conveniently summarized in Hilton's collection The Transition from Feudalism to Capitalism (1976). Dobb's initial critic was the great American Marxist economist Paul Sweezy (whose book The Theory of Capitalist Development (1942) is the best introduction to Marxist economics), followed by at least half a dozen others. The details of the argument cannot be repeated here, beyond commending Merrington's admirable attempt as a latecomer to set the field straight in the last essay. Marxists have a lot at stake in the case of English capitalism, since it was the main preoccupation of their mentor; hence the liveliness of the discussion. Moreover, non-Marxist historians--e.g. Macfarlane (1978) and Stone (1972)--have seen fit to enter the fray and dispute the facts. In consequence this is a most historical and empirical branch of Marxist discourse and one from which economic anthropologists can learn a great deal about preindustrial societies. Best of all it provides the original concrete context in European history for many of the abstractions about economic development that today come to us directly from ahistorical textbooks.

Many specialist books and journals have arisen to publicize left-wing Anglo history: but the New Left Review has published consistently intelligent work of a historical and theoretical nature. I have already mentioned one such article by Brenner (1977). Later periods of social history than that covered by the "transition" debate are well represented here. Out of many regular contributors, I would single out Gareth Stedman Jones's work as outstanding (see, e.g., Outcast London, 1971). The New Left Review's editor for a number of years was Perry Anderson, an American whose publication in 1974 of two synoptic books on European history--Passages from Antiquity to Feudalism and Lineages of the Absolutist State--were probably the event of the decade as far as Anglo Marxist history is concerned. The second of these volumes includes two long appendices on "The Asiatic mode of production" and "Japanese feudalism" that are of particular importance to economic anthropologists. But their principal contribution is that, together, they show how we can begin to write an anthropological history of European political economy that situates it in a larger process of world history. This then is the promise that Anglo Marxism opens up for economic anthropology, a regional history of the west which is both extremely significant for universal world history and greatly in need of relativizing treatment within a more complete history of the human economy than western historians have previously been able to compile.

VII. A MARXIST ECONOMIC ANTHROPOLOGY?

The great majority of professional anthropologists in the world today live in the United States. This holds true for economic anthropology, but not for Marxism. Only recently have American openly professed an interest in Marx with relative impunity; their Anglo colleagues in Canada, Britain and Australia may have encountered this intellectual freedom slightly earlier, but an explicitly Marxist economic anthropology, carried out by English speakers, has only arisen in the 1970s. Despite the waning of what became almost a messianic cult of French structuralist Marxism in the mid 1970s, the number of new Anglo works bearing a recognizable Marxist influence continues to multiply apace. This, presumably, was why Marxism was chosen as one of the basic categories dividing up the field of economic anthropology for the purpose of this inauguration of our Society. Even if we are all confused about what Marxism actually is any more, its institutionalization in American academic life seems to be well under way and in Britain Marxist social science may even be said to exercise a kind of intellectual hegemony at the beginning of the 1980's. Any serious deterioration in world politics would be likely to disrupt this cosy assimilation, but, for now, we may speak of a resurgent Anglo Marxism that has taken root in economic anthropology at least as strongly as in any other field.[19]

London was the main conduit for bringing French Marxism into anthropology, specifically a group of young lecturers and graduate students at University College in the early 1970s. They founded a journal, Critique of Anthropology, which has maintained a high standard of abstract discourse throughout the period of its existence. The most prominent members of this circle were not English, but from America. Joel Kahn and Jonathan Friedman--the one more influence by Althusser, the other by Godelier--made important contributions to a collection arising out of the Decennial Conference of the Association of Social Anthropologists in 1973 (Bloch, 1975). Kahn's work (1975, 1980) is the more explicitly economic of the two, but Friedman's (1975) highly schematic reconstruction of the Highland Burma case can easily be assimilated into a holistic economic anthropology of the kind established by ethnographers such as Raymond Firth. Kahn, in a series of articles and a recent book, has been concerned to show how the cycle of artisan production in West Sumatra (specifically Minangkabau blacksmiths) can only be understood through a longrun historical approach to the interaction of traditional agriculture and varieties of colonial and post-colonial capitalist penetration. His work bears some resemblance to Rey's early Congo ethnography. Friedman is brilliant, eclectic and less securely anchored in the empirical materials of his chosen area. His theoretical polemics reflect the style of his two teachers, Harris and Godelier, which is to say that they are not marked by diffidence. A third member of this University College group is Jose Llobera who has worked extensively on the scattered Marxist texts dealing with precapitalist economies, focusing in particular on the possibility of systematizing the modes of production characteristic of the hunter-gathering phase of human evolution (see Kahn and Llobera, 1981).

In America, Stanley Diamond's journal, Dialectical Anthropology, pursues a humanistic line, but regularly prints articles synthesizing the concerns of Marxism and economic anthropology. Marshal Sahlins's coinage of the phrase "domestic mode of production" in his Stone Age Economics (1972)--still the last major original work in economic anthropology--brought the appearance, but not the substance of Marxist thinking into the consciousness of many Americans. Bridget O'Laughlin's brave summary of the Althusserian position in Annual Review of Anthropology (1975) went much further in laying out the kind of intellectual transformation that would be necessary to a creative incorporation of Marxist ideas into normal discourse. Scott Cook (1966), who entered the decade as a harsh formalist critic of Polanyi, left it as a rigorous exponent of how to apply some of Marx's formal economic concepts to precapitalist societies: specifically he and his associates in Oaxaca (Cook and Diskin, 1976) have been concerned to interpret small-scale production patterns and price movements in Mexican markets through Marx's law of value, as laid out in his mature writings. In less sophisticated hands such an approach can easily lend itself to a conflation of the epistemologies of Marx and orthodox economics.

Many anthropologists maintain a radical stance toward their own society and find an outlet for their alienation in the opportunities that our discipline offers to investigate the third world and its discontents. Marxist rhetoric often enters into critical discourse of this sort, but it does not usually add up to a sustained economic analysis along Marxist lines. I have therefore chosen to omit from consideration here the growing body of anthropological writing that deals with unemployment, poverty, famine, business corporations, development agencies and public corruption in the third world. Peter Gutkind deserves mention for the part that he has played in assembling collections of radical critique, as well as for his encouragement of systematic Marxist analysis of political economy (see, e.g., Gutkind and Wallerstein, The Political Economy of Contemporary Africa, 1976). But intellectual leadership on this wing of American anthropology lies unequivocally with Eric Wolf. His early work on peasants (1966), peasant wars (1969) and Latin American social structure (Wolf, 1959) carved out the way for anthropologists to study the important political and economic movements of the third world in our day. For some time now he has been engaged in a synthetic work on the Atlantic economy and imperialism since late medieval times, the publication of which will mark another major step forward for American anthropologists. Michael Taussig's (1978) smaller-scale study of the transition problem in southwest Colombia, dealing at first with capitalist penetration of peasant agriculture and in a recent book (1980) with the cultural dimensions of incorporation into a capitalist economy, offers a fresh look at problems touched on by Wolf. Finally, several anthropologists have combined a world systems approach derived from Wallerstein with other elements of Marxism, economic geography, and cultural analysis to produce fascinating regional case studies, such as the Schneiders' on Sicily (1976) and Carol Smith's on Guatemala (1976). These works need not be judged by the canons of Marxist orthodoxy, but their success depends in part on their authors' openness to Marxist ideas.

There is a growing body of scholarship dealing with the anthropological and historical writings of Marx and Engels. A recent Moscow publication brings into one convenient 600 page volume most of the passages anthropologists would be interested in--Precapitalist Socio-Economic Formations (1979). Before this we were indebted to the editorial labors and scholarly commentary of Lawrence Krader (1974, 1975) for the founders' thoughts on such matters as the Asiatic mode of production and primitive communism. Marx and Engels were themselves highly receptive to new anthropological ideas, especially of course to those of L. H. Morgan (1877). In recent years it would not seem that Marxists have drawn any similar inspiration from anthropology, even though one would expect that a major task of economic anthropology would be to make such an impact one way or the other. A major exception is Ernest Mandel, one of the most prolific of European Marxist writers and the author of Marxist Economic Theory (1968), which, with Sweezy's text mentioned above, makes an admirable introduction to the subject. In the first few chapters of this book, as a way of developing his conceptual framework, Mandel draws heavily on the classics of economic anthropology--Malinowski (1922), Firth (1965), Nadel (1942) and Douglas (1963)--to support his various positions. It would be nice to think that the Marxist economic anthropology of the 1980s would be even more useful to someone seeking to replicate his task.

CONCLUSION

An essay of this length should end on a programmatic note. What do I think a Marxist economic anthropology should do?

1. Its main task is to write the history of the human economy taken as a whole.

2. Within that task, the secondary need is for large-scale regional histories.

3. It should join the mainstream debates on industrial capitalism's past, present, and future.

4. It should continue where it is already strong, namely dealing with the transition problem in the third world.

5. But it should also study the unfinished dialectic of commoditization in those countries where the division of labor is advanced.[20]

6. An urgent task is to devise comparative studies capable of assessing both claims about and real differences in economic organization between capitalist and communist countries.

7. The social history of economic ideas permits an ongoing critique of economics (and cognate disciplines like sociobiology) as ideology.

8. It is still important to reconstruct primitive economies that are available only through archaeological, historical and ethnographic research.

9. It would be useful to find ways of describing global industrialization--in terms of energy, population, cities, commodity flows, etc.--that facilitate an informed grasp of the dilemmas facing us today.

10. Our aim should be to construct an anthropological vision of alternative human futures that are economically sound and just.

Marx obviously plays a big part in any attempt to carry out such a program, but his ideas cannot possibly be sufficient to define the intellectual matrix of economic anthropology. Eclecticism is essential to any new synthesis. If there is any message conveyed by the foregoing review it is that the field can only be made coherent through the exercise of one man's selective judgment. It is not a failure of Marxism that its doctrines can no longer be identified unequivocally: it means that many intellectuals have let go of the obsessive idea of a pure party line and that many others learn from Marx without signing up for the world revolution. Such a stage of disintegration and rebuilding is never glorious, but we who occupy it have the opportunity to lay the foundations of new synthetic breakthroughs advancing our practical comprehension of human society. I hope and expect that the ideas of Marx, economics and anthropology will be important elements in that synthesis.

Notes

[1] See the Introduction to the critique of political economy (Grundrisse) for this and the next paragraph (Marx, 1973).

[2] Capital, Volume 1, especially chapter 1 (Marx, 1954), is the main source for this and the next paragraph.

[3] Again the Introduction to Grundrisse (Marx, 1973) lays out the approach clearly.

[4] Marx died in 1883.

[5] 1948 was chosen over 1945 as the dividing line between periods, since 1945-48 saw political developments that ought to be considered an

extension of the second world war, notably the consolidation of Eastern Europe as a Russian province. 1948 was the beginning of the post-war economic revival proper.

[6] With apologies to De Jouvenel's (1949) observation that the members of a post-revolutionary Chamber of Deputies had more in common with each other than with members of their own parties outside.

[7] I have left Trotsky off this list because he has so far played a small part in my reading of Marxist literature. There is no explicit ideological bias behind the choice.

[8] Habermas (e.g., 1971, 1979) is perhaps the school's most prominent member.

[9] Weber (1978). There is a right and a left tendency of interpretations following Weber; the one stresses authority, control and cohesion, the other domination (Herrschaft) and social conflict. The former has been influential in American sociology thanks to Parsons, but in Germany Weber's work has inspired many intellectuals of the center-left.

[10] White (1959); Steward (1977); Sahlins and Service (1960).

[11] Wolf's work is still in progress, but near publication.

[12] This is especially true of French Structuralist Marxism and of Anglo imitations.

[13] See Kolakowski's account of "the rise, growth and dissolution" of Marxism (1978).

[14] Part III of Luxemburg (1951) contains the concrete historical description and analysis supporting her general argument.

[15] See Hussain and Tribe (1980) for an excellent summary of the agrarian question in Germany and Russia.

[16] Frank's critique of modernization theory (1969, chapter 1)--in places more a lampoon than a

critique--was devastatingly successful. Within a
year or two the hegemony established by such works
as Rostow (1960) and Apter (1965) was in ruins and
the way opened up for a more explicitly Marxist
approach to development in the Anglo intellectual
circles of the 1970s.

[17] Hamilton (1913), List (1856); Schumpeter
(1954).

[18] See LeClair and Schneider (1968) for the
context of debate in economic anthropology during
the 1960s.

[19] The selection of names in what follows is
often casual and may be ill-informed. There is no
political or personal animus behind any omission.

[20] I have written on this subject in several
papers, e.g. Hart, 1983.

References

ALTHUSSER, L., and E. Balibar. 1965. Lire le
capital. Paris: Maspero. Eng. trans. 1970,
Reading "Capital". London: New Left Books.

AMIN, S. 1971. L'Afrique de l'ouest est bloquée.
Paris: Les Editions de Minuit.

_____. 1974. Accumulation on a world scale.
New York: Monthly Review Press.

_____. 1976. Unequal development. New York:
Monthly Review Press.

ANDERSON, P. 1974a. Passages from antiquity to
feudalism. London: New Left Books.

_____. 1974b. Lineages of the absolutist state.
London: New Left Books.

APTER, D. 1965. The politics of modernization.
Chicago: University of Chicago Press.

BALIBAR, E. 1970. The basic concepts of historical
materialism. In Reading "Capital". L. Althusser
and E. Balibar, eds. London: New Left Books.

BERNSTEIN, E. 1961 (c. 1898). Evolutionary socialism. New York: Schocken Books.

BLOCH, M., ed. 1975. Marxist analyses and social anthropology. New York: Wiley.

BOHANNAN, P., and G. Dalton, eds. 1962. Markets in Africa. Evanston, Ill.: Northwestern University Press.

BRENNER, R. 1977. The origins of capitalist development. New Left Review 4:25-91.

BUKHARIN, N. 1972 (1927). The economic theory of the leisure class. New York: Monthly Review Press.

CABRAL, A. 1972. Revolution in Guinea: selected texts. New York: Monthly Review Press.

CARDOSO, F. H. 1979. Dependency and development in Latin America. Berkeley: University of California Press.

CHAYANOV, A. V. 1966. The theory of peasant economy. Homewood, Ill.: R. D. Irwin.

COOK, S. 1966. The obsolete 'anti-market' mentality: a critique of the substantive approach to economic anthropology. American Anthropologist 68:323-345.

COOK, S., and M. Diskin, eds. 1976. Markets in Oaxaca. Austin: University of Texas Press.

DOBB, M. 1947. Studies in the development of capitalism. New York: International Publishers.

DOUGLAS, M. 1963. The Lele of Kasai. London: Oxford University Press.

DUMONT, L. 1977. From Mandeville to Marx. Chicago: University of Chicago Press.

DUPRÉ, G., and P.-P. Rey. 1978. Reflections on the relevance of a theory of the history of exchange. In Relations of production. D. Seddon, ed. London: Frank Cass.

ENGELS, F. 1926. The peasant war in Germany. New York: International Publishers.

_____. 1939. Herr Eugen Dühring's revolution in science. New York: International Publishers.

_____. 1962. The part played by labor in the transition from ape to man. In Marx and Engels, Selected works.

_____. 1971. The condition of the working class in England. London: Oxford University Press.

_____. 1972. The origin of the family, private property and the state. New York: Pathfinder Press.

EVANS-PRITCHARD, E. E. 1940. The Nuer. London: Oxford University Press.

FANON, F. 1963. The wretched of the earth. New York: Grove Press.

FIRTH, R. 1965. Primitive Polynesian economy. London: Routledge and Kegan Paul.

FRANK, A. G. 1969. Capitalism and underdevelopment in Latin America. New York: Monthly Review Press.

_____. 1978. Dependent accumulation and underdevelopment. London: MacMillan.

FRIEDMAN, J. 1975. Tribes, states and transformations. In Marxist analyses and social anthropology. M. Bloch, ed. New York: Wiley.

GODELIER, M. 1972a (c. 1966). Rationality and irrationality in economics. London: New Left Books.

_____. 1972b. System, structure and contradiction in Das Kapital. In Ideology in social science. R. Blackburn, ed. London: Fontana.

_____. 1977. Perspectives in Marxist anthropology. Cambridge: Cambridge University Press.

GUTKIND, P., and I. Wallerstein, eds. 1976. The political economy of contemporary Africa. Beverly Hills, Ca.: Sage.

HABERMAS, J. 1971. Knowledge and human interests. Boston: Beacon Press.

_____. 1979. Communication and the evolution of society. Boston: Beacon Press.

HAMILTON, A. 1913 (c. 1791). Report on manufactures. Washington: Government Printing Office.

HART, K. 1983. On commoditization. In From craft to industry. E. Goody, ed. Cambridge: Cambridge University Press.

HILTON, R., ed. 1976. The transition from feudalism to capitalism. London: New Left Books.

HINDESS, B., and P. Hirst. 1975. Precapitalist modes of production. London: Routledge and Kegan Paul.

HOBSBAWM, E. 1959. Primitive rebels. Manchester: Manchester University Press.

HOBSBAWM, E., ed. 1964. Karl Marx: precapitalist economic formations. London: Lawrence and Wishart.

HOBSON, J. 1902. Imperialism: a study. New York: J. Pott.

HUSSAIN, A., and K. Tribe. Marxism and the agrarian question, volume 1, 2. London: MacMillan.

DE JOUVENEL, B. 1949. On power, its nature and the history of its growth. New York: Viking Press.

KAHN, J. 1975. Economic scale and the cycle of petty commodity production in West Sumatra. In Marxist analysis and social anthropology. M. Bloch, ed. New York: Wiley.

_____. 1980. Minangkabau social formations. Cambridge: Cambridge University Press.

KAHN, J. and J. Llobera, eds. 1981. The anthropology of precapitalist societies. London: MacMillan.

KAUTSKY, K. 1899. Die Agrarfrage. Hanover: J. H. W. Dietz.

KOLAKOWSKI, L. 1978. Main currents of Marxism: its rise, growth and dissolution (3 vols.). Oxford: Clarendon Press.

KRADER, L. 1974. The ethnological notebooks of Karl Marx. Assen: Van Gorcum.

_____. 1975. The Asiatic mode of production. Assen: Van Gorcum.

LANE, M. 1970. Structuralism: a reader. London: Cape.

LANGE, O. 1968. Marxian economics and modern economic theory. In Marx and modern economics. D. Horowitz, ed. London: MacGibbon and Kee.

LEBRIS, E., P.-P. Rey and M. Samuel. 1976. Capitalisme négrier: la marche des paysans vers le prolétariat. Paris: Maspero.

LECLAIR, E., and H. Schneider, eds. 1968. Economic anthropology. New York: Holt, Rinehart, Winston.

LENIN, V. 1917. The state and revolution. London: British Socialist Party.

_____. 1956 (1899). The development of capitalism in Russia. Moscow: Foreign Languages Publishing House.

_____. 1963 (1916). Imperialism: the highest stage of capitalism. New York: International Publishers.

LÉVI-STRAUSS, C. 1963. Structural anthropology. Garden City, N.Y.: Doubleday.

LEVINE, D. 1978. Economic theory: volume 1. The elementary relations of economic life. London: Routledge and Kegan Paul.

LICHTHEIM, G. 1961. Marxism: an historical and critical study. London: Routledge and Kegan Paul.

LIST, F. 1856. National system of political economy. Philadelphia: J. B. Lippincott.

LUXEMBURG, R. 1951. The accumulation of capital. New Haven: Yale University Press.

MACFARLANE, A. 1978. The origins of English individualism. Cambridge: Cambridge University Press.

MALINOWSKI, B. 1922. Argonauts of the western Pacific. New York: E. P. Dutton.

MANDEL, E. 1968. Marxist economic theory. New York: Monthly Review Press.

MAO ZEDONG. 1971. Selected readings from the works of Mao Tsetung. Peking: Foreign Language Press.

MARX, K. 1907. The eighteenth brumaire of Louis Bonaparte. Chicago: C. H. Kerr.

_____. 1954. Capital: a critical analysis of capitalist production. Moscow: Foreign Languages Publishing House.

_____. 1964. The economic and philosophical manuscripts of 1844. New York: International Publishers.

_____. 1973. Grundrisse. New York: Vintage Books.

MARX, K., and F. Engels. 1942. The German ideology. London: Lawrence and Wishart.

_____. 1945. Manifesto of the Communist Party. Chicago: C. H. Kerr.

_____. 1962. Selected works. Moscow: Foreign Languages Publishing House.

_____. 1979. Precapitalist socio-economic formations. Moscow: Progress Publishers.

MEILLASSOUX, C. 1960. Essai d'interprétation du phénomène économique dans les sociétés traditionelles d'autosubsistence. Cahiers d'Etudes Africaines 4:38-67.

_____. 1964. Anthropologie économique des Gouro de Côte d'Ivoire. Paris: Mouton.

_____. 1972. From reproduction to production. Economy and Society 1:93-105.

_____. 1975a. Femmes, greniers et capitaux. Paris: Maspero.

MEILLASSOUX, C., ed. 1971. The development of indigenous commerce in West Africa. London: Oxford University Press.

_____, ed. 1975b. L'esclavage en Afrique précoloniale. Paris: Maspero.

MORGAN, L. H. 1877. Ancient society. London: MacMillan.

NADEL, S. F. 1942. A black Byzantium. London: Oxford University Press.

O'LAUGHLIN, B. 1975. Marxist approaches in anthropology. Annual Review of Anthropology 4:341-370.

PLEKHANOV, G. 1908. Fundamental problems of Marxism. London: Lawrence and Wishart.

_____. 1934. Essays in historical materialism. London: John Lane.

REY, P.-P. 1971. Colonialisme, néocolonialisme et transition au capitalisme. Paris: Maspero.

_____. 1973. Les alliances des classes. Paris: Maspero.

_____. 1975. The lineage mode of production. Critique of Anthropology 3:27-79.

ROSTOW, W. W. 1960. The stages of economic growth: a non-communist manifesto. Cambridge: Cambridge University Press.

SAHLINS, M. 1968. Tribesmen. Englewood Cliffs, N.J.: Prentice Hall.

_____. 1972. Stone-age economics. Chicago: Aldine.

SAHLINS, M., and E. Service, eds. 1960. Evolution and culture. Ann Arbor: University of Michigan Press.

SCHNEIDER, J., and P. Schneider. 1976. Culture and political economy. New York: Academic Press.

SCHUMPETER, J. 1954. History of economic analysis. New York: Oxford University Press.

SEDDON, D., ed. 1978. Relations of production: Marxist approaches to economic anthropology. London: Frank Cass.

SEMENOV, Y. 1980. The theory of socio-economic formations and world history. In Soviet and Western anthropology. E. Gellner, ed. New York: Columbia University Press.

SERVICE, E. 1966. The hunters. Englewood Cliffs, N.J.: Prentice Hall.

SMITH, C., ed. 1976. Regional analysis (2 vols.). New York: Academic Press.

STALIN, J. 1952. Works. Moscow: Foreign Languages Publishing House.

STEDMAN-JONES, G. 1971. Outcast London. Oxford: Clarendon Press.

STEWARD, J. 1977. Evolution and ecology: essays on social transformation. Urbana: University of Illinois Press.

STONE, L. 1972. The causes of the English revolution. London: Routledge and Kegan Paul.

SWEEZY, P. 1942. The theory of capitalist development. New York: Oxford University Press.

TAUSSIG, M. 1978. Peasant economics and the development of capitalist agriculture in the Cauca

143

Valley, Colombia. Latin American Perspectives 5:62-91.

_____. 1980. The devil and commodity fetishism. Chapel Hill: University of North Carolina Press.

TERRAY, E. 1972. Marxism and 'primitive' societies. New York: Monthly Review Press.

_____. 1974. Long-distance exchange and the formation of the state: the case of the Abron kingdom of Gyaman. Economy and Society 3:315:345.

_____. 1975. Classes and class consciousness in the Abron kingdom of Gyaman. In Marxist analyses and social anthropology. M. Bloch, ed. New York: Wiley.

THOMPSON, E. P. 1963. The making of the English working class. New York: Pantheon Books.

_____. 1978. The poverty of theory and other essays. New York: Monthly Review Press.

DE TOCQUEVILLE, A. 1839. Democracy in America. New York: G. Adlard.

VEBLEN, T. 1948. Why is economics not an evolutionary science? In The pocket Thorstein Veblen. M. Lerner, ed.

WALLERSTEIN, I. 1974. The modern world-system. New York: Academic Press.

_____. 1979. The capitalist world-economy. Cambridge: Cambridge University Press.

WEBER, M. 1978. Economy and society (2 vols.). Berkeley: University of California Press.

WHITE, L. 1959. The evolution of culture. New York: McGraw-Hill.

WILLIAMS, R. 1966. Culture and society, 1780-1950. New York: Harper and Row.

PART THREE

ECOLOGICAL ADAPTATION AND

ALLOCATION OF RESOURCES

Adam Smith in The Wealth of Nations spoke of
the interrelationship of wages, demand for workers,
propensity to procreate, infant morality, and
population trends. Ricardo noted that produce prices
rose as the fertility of the soil decreased and cost
of production increased. Malthus argued that as soil
fertility decreases or as agriculturalists are forced
to bring marginal lands into production, the profits
of agriculture will decrease and capital will be
shifted to industry. Demand for labor, he reasons,
will continue to rise until a market glut makes
capital investment in industry equally unprofitable.
At that point, laborers may be thrown out of work;
soon famine and disease will spread; and eventually
high mortality will deplete the population until it
has a more favorable relationship to agricultural
resources. Later, Malthus altered this pessimistic
view of the relation of population to productivity and
human disaster. In Principles of Political Economy
(1836) he argued that population pressures are likely
to cause only temporary unemployment periods; in the
long run they will encourage further production
cycles.

Thus by the nineteenth century, a framework for
examining the relation of nature to population, and
economy had been outlined. It could yield either
optimistic or pessimistic predictions about future
social conditions and the growth potential of the
economy. Cultural anthropologists and archaeologists,
using a similar framework, have often favored the more
optimistic predictions. They have suggested that
societies adapt to ecological constraints by devising
institutional means of population control and adopting
appropriate resource management practices. Assuming
homeostasis, they have examined the relationship among
techniques of production, fertility of soil, rate of
population growth, and pattern of settlement and
migration. Conklin's (1957) study of swidden
agriculture and Rappaport's (1967) study on the
relation of human to animal populations have now
become classics, but many other studies explore and
qualify the nature of that relationship (Richard Lee,
1972; Gross, 1975; Meggers, 1971; Ucko and Tringham,
1972; Kunstadter, 1972) (see Chapters VII and VIII).

Assumptions about the carrying capacities of ecological niches, given specific technological practices, have been helpful to archaeologists trying to reconstruct past demographic patterns and systems of resource exploitation. But assumptions do not suffice, and ecologists have had to devise means of determining carrying capacity (Brush, 1975), ecological possibilities (Harris, 1969), demographic pressures (Binford, 1968; Sanders and Price, 1968) and the risks of temporary resource depletion (Flannery, 1973).

Stimulated by new studies on ecology and population, cultural anthropologists began to explore the institutional and cultural mechanisms that ensure a homeostatic balance or an ecological adaptation (Vayda and Rappaport, 1968). Gross (Chapter VII) examines the premises of the cultural ecology approach and the technical and cultural mechanism for sustaining and enriching human life. But unlike economic anthropologists, cultural ecologists do not focus on the interrelation of, for example: price and nature; exchange rate and production; or availability of labor, distribution of nutrients, productivity, returns, and scarcity of opportunities. Not surprisingly, Gross regards the cultural ecological approach as parallel to that used in economic anthropology. Although they may sometimes be combined, neither should be subsumed under the other.

The cultural ecological approach that Gross outlines may be useful to economic anthropologists, but is not economic anthropology. As he himself implies, it has more to do with Darwin than with Malthus, though it may echo Malthus's early pessimism. Luckily, another aspect of ecology reflects the concerns of economic anthropologists: human ecology. In Chapter VIII Lees describes this approach as the study of environmental events and human responses to them. This perspective allows the analyst to examine environmental changes and their impact dynamically. Furthermore, it avoids the assumption that populations can adapt only by constraining growth. The writings of Knight (1974), Netting (1968), Neitscham (1973), Brush (1977), Collier (1975), and Bennett (1969) carefully analyze the adaptive strategies that farmers developed to deal with ecological and economic changes in their environment. These illustrations of the adaptiveness of human societies offer more than just theoretical interest. They provide development

148

planners with important information about alternative strategies that are economically and ecologically viable.

Lees also proposes that the microperspective of decision analysis may be a useful format in which to integrate environmental, social, and economic variables. It may help us determine why people persist in certain behaviors and abandon others. In an earlier publication Bennett had addressed the same problem: "Adaptive strategies," he wrote, "are generally at the conscious level in the behavior of the people involved" (Bennett, 1976, p. 14). Following this line of thought, Rutz (1977) examined household decisions in Fiji, and McCay (1978) looked at individuals' reactions to the decline of nearby fisheries. Orlove (1980) also believes that the microperspective is a helpful format for linking demographic developments to environmental issues and adaptive strategies.

Not all anthropologists who have used this approach, however, share the optimism of Lees and Orlove (see Gross in this volume). Rutz doubts that some hypotheses from ecology can be transposed to economic decision models because ecological anthropologists

> look at problems of adaptive behavior from the standpoint of energy efficiency, whereas economic anthropologists have emphasized labor efficiency, and how various choices in production maximize output per unit of labor employed. Often it is not apparent why one measure of efficiency is adopted over another. Selection of a technology from the standpoint of its energy efficiency with respect to alternative sources of fuel may result in inefficient use of labor time when measured against the opportunity cost of foregone earnings. More attention should be paid to competing efficiencies operating in complex phenomena, and models should be constructed to show implications of cultural behavior. Smith (1979), for example, has raised important issues about the relationship between optimal foraging theory and adaptation, and in another context Granovetter (1979) has questioned the possibility of using any measure of "overall" efficiency in a meaningful way. Economic

anthropologists have approached the problem of
efficiency, competing efficiencies and overall
efficiency from the perspective of risk and
uncertainty, satisficing versus maximizing
assumptions about strategies, and notions of
welfare or distributive justice that get beyond
the unidimensional notions of performance
evaluated by efficiency. (Rutz, 1981,
conference comment)

Another limitation to the use of decision
analysis, as Bennett (1976) reminds us, is that
consciousness of the importance of conservation does
not always ensure that it will be adopted. We are
faced with the same problem economists face.
Short-run maximization may sometimes give way to
preference for average returns over the long run.
Although shifting cultivators may not have to be
concerned over depletion of resources, small farmers
do; yet they may be forced to overexploit their farms
to satisfy basic income needs. Ecologists thus have
to solve two problems to use a decision format
correctly: they must first determine when long-range
strategies are likely to be preferred, and then decide
how decision makers evaluate the significance of
steady income trends against that of future risks
whose value is as yet undetermined (see Ortiz, Chapter
X). We have to ascertain that the task is possible
for we can assume it to be a step in the farmers'
decisions. One hopes we can avoid the trap of
ascribing differential selection of strategies to
different types of farmers. Bennett (1976 and 1982)
offers us some useful suggestions for doing so.

Thus, the microperspective, though useful, cannot
give us a complete picture of the changing trends in
man's adaptation to his changing environments. The
problem must also be examined at the macrolevel, as is
illustrated in Gross's example of changes in the use
of fertilizers. Lees adopts from cybernetics the
concept of feedback--see Bennett (1976)--using it to
link the findings from the micro to the
macroperspective. In this way she avoids some of the
problems of aggregation alluded to in Chapters IX and
X. She makes the intriguing suggestion that by
studying environmental hazards we can glean
stimulating data with which to elaborate models and
study feedback responses. Only then can we reexamine
the subjects that have been of concern to
evolutionists and developmental economists: the

growth and transformation of economic systems, and the relation of population pressure to development and frontier expansion (see Bender, 1975; Geertz, 1971; Boserupt, 1965; Hutchinson, 1972; Polgar, 1975; Durham, 1979; Kunstadter, et al., 1978).

References

BENDER, Barbara. 1975. Farming in prehistory. London: John Baker.

BENNETT, John W. 1969. Northern plainsmen. Chicago: Aldine.

_____. 1976. The ecological transition. New York: Pergamon Press.

_____. 1982. Of time and the enterprise. Minneapolis: University of Minnesota Press.

BINFORD, Lewis. 1968. Post-pleistocene adaptations. In New perspectives in archeology. S. R. Bindford and L. R. Bindford, eds. Chicago: Aldine.

BOSERUPT, Esther. 1965. The conditions of agricultural growth. Chicago: Aldine.

BRUSH, Stephen. 1975. The concept of carrying capacity for systems of shifting cultivation. American Anthropologist 77:799-811.

_____. 1977. Mountain, fields and family. Philadephia: University of Pennsylvania Press.

COLLIER, George A. 1975. Fields of the Tzotzil. Austin: University of Texas Press.

CONKLIN, Harold C. 1957. Hanunóo agriculture. FAO Forestry Development Paper No. 12. Rome: Food and Agriculture Organization of the United Nations.

DURHAM, William H. 1979. Scarcity and survival. Stanford: Stanford University Press.

FLANNERY, K. U. 1973. The origins of agriculture. Bienniel Review of Anthropology 2:271-310.

GEERTZ, Clifford. 1971. Agricultural involution. Berkeley: University of California Press.

GRANOVETTER, Mark. 1979. The idea of 'advancement' in theories of social evolution and development. American Journal of Sociology 85:489-516.

GROSS, Daniel. 1975. Protein capture and cultural development in the Amazon basin. American Anthropologist 77:526-549.

HARRIS, D. R. 1969. Agricultural systems, ecosystems and the origins of agriculture. In The domestication and exploitation of plants and animals. P. J. Ucko and G. W. Dimbleby, eds. Chicago: Aldine.

HUTCHINSON, J. 1972. Farming and food supply. Cambridge: Cambridge University Press.

KNIGHT, C. Gregory. 1974. Ecology and change. New York: Academic Press.

KUNSTADTER, Peter. 1972. Demography, ecology, social structure and settlement patterns. In The structure of human populations. G. A. Harrison and A. J. Boyce, eds. Oxford: Clarendon Press.

_____, E. Chapman, and Sanga Sabhasri. 1978. Farmers in the forest. Honolulu: The University Press of Hawaii.

LEE, Richard B. 1972. Work effort, group structure and land-use in contemporary hunter-gatherers. In Man, settlement and urbanism. Peter J. Ucko, Ruth Tringham and G. W. Dimbleby, eds. London: Gerald Duckworth & Co., Ltd.

MALTHUS, Thomas R. 1936. Principles of political economy. London: William Pickering.

MCCAY, B. J. 1978. Systems ecology, people ecology and the anthropology of fishing communities. Human ecology 6:397-422.

MEGGERS, Betty J. 1971. Amazonia. Chicago: Aldine.

NETTING, Robert McC. 1968. Hill farmers of Nigeria. Seattle: University of Washington Press.

152

NIETSCHMANN, Bernard. 1973. Between land and water. New York: Seminar Press.

ORLOVE, Benjamin S. 1980. Ecological anthropology. Annual Review of Anthropology 9:235-273.

POLGAR, Steven. 1975. Population, ecology and social evolution. The Hague: Mouton.

RAPPAPORT, Roy A. 1967. Pigs for the ancestors. New Haven: Yale University Press.

RUTZ, H. J. 1977. Individual decision and functional systems: economic rationality and environmental adaptation. American Ethnology 4:156-174.

SANDERS, William T. and Barbara J. Price. 1968. Meso-America: the evolution of a civilization. New York: Random House.

SMITH, E. A. 1979. Human adaptation and energetic efficiency. Human ecology 7:53-74.

UCKO, Peter J., Ruth Tringham, and G. W. Dimbleby. 1972. Man, settlement, urbanism. London: Duckworth and Co.

VAYDA, Andrew P. and R. A. Rappaport. 1968. Ecology: cultural and noncultural. In Introduction to cultural anthropology. J. Clifton, ed. Boston: Houghton Mifflin.

VII. THE ECOLOGICAL PERSPECTIVE IN ECONOMIC ANTHROPOLOGY

Daniel R. Gross

Ecological anthropology is primarily concerned with explaining sociocultural differences and similarities in terms of the ways in which human societies adapt to the material conditions of existence over time. "Material conditions" may be defined broadly as all variables which demonstrably affect the capability of human organisms and populations to survive, produce, reproduce, and grow. Ecological anthropology is concerned with causality and tends to be nomothetic and deterministic. While it does not replace all the other concerns in sociocultural anthropology, the ecological model provides a window which can be used to view virtually any human phenomenon including ideational ones. It provides an important perspective concerning the linkage between the biological nature of humans and their culture without reverting to the racism or psychological reductionism of nineteenth century anthropologists. Most ecological anthropologists accept and consider legitimate other paradigms whose aims are to demonstrate the variability of human cognition, and to provide detailed empathetic descriptions of human beings in other cultural traditions, or to explicate the symbolic systems by which people become aware of their condition and express themselves.

The relationship of ecological anthropology to economic anthropology is complex and will be explored to some extent in this paper. To the extent that economic anthropologists are concerned with models of rationality, one could say that ecological anthropologists are primarily concerned with explicating the conditions which underlie or cause systems of rationality. Ecological anthropology also has an affinity with the definition of the economic as an embedded process in society concerned mainly with provisioning (production and exchange). But it would probably be fair to say that ecological anthropologists part company with economic anthropologists who wish to consider factors other than material conditions of life as primary in an analysis. Ecological anthropology may be seen as part of a broader field of inquiry whose basic approach was defined by the Darwinian synthesis. In less than

155

thirty years as a recognized subdivision of ethnology, ecological anthropology has made strides in applying evolutionary concepts to sociocultural phenomena. Almost from its inception, however, critics demanded reexamination of the basic assumptions and methods used. Ecologists had to relearn the distinction between function and origin, between logical and empirical validity, and they had to rethink the relationship between individual action and individual consciousness on the one hand, and cultural patterning and behavior on the other. With some of these problems resolved and solutions to others in sight, ecological anthropology stands on the threshold of new advances, particularly as it tackles problems associated with complex societies. In this paper, I am going to review some of the major obstacles to progress in ecological anthropology and how I think they have been or may be overcome.

I.   SELECTION THEORY AND SOCIAL SCIENCE

Darwin presented a comprehensive approach to understanding the rise of new forms and their persistence. The core of his theory was the principle of natural selection, a model of stability and change in which environmental factors favor the reproduction of organisms whose phenotypes provide them with a better "fit" with the environment, while hindering the reproduction of others. The organizational pattern of the better adapted is transmitted, more or less faithfully, to the next generation, providing for stability so long as environmental conditions do not change.

In culture, as in nature, variation and selection[1] occur constantly. The mechanics of natural selection are not identical for culture: selection among variants occurs opportunistically, but the variants themselves do not occur randomly as do mutations. They may be designed deliberately or they may be introduced by diffusion from somewhere else. Traits, or cultural patterns, may suffer negative selection when the culture carriers themselves decline in reproductive fitness. An example can be drawn from the numerous native societies of the Americas whose cultural patterns disappeared when the last members of their group died. But a cultural pattern or trait may also become extinct without any decline in biological fitness on the part of the people who formerly carried the trait. An example of this is the use of draft animals for transport in the urban United States.

Notions of selection have long exercised strong influence in social science. Classical economics proposed the idea of an "invisible hand" of market forces, leading actors this way or that in their economic behavior. Marxian economics stressed the selective influence of a process of struggle in which the forces of production set into motion social events, destroying old forms and creating new ones. In fact, it has been suggested that social thinkers were the ones to introduce the principle of natural selection to the biological sciences (Harris, 1968). Structuralist thought, for example, bears an imprint of selection in its concern for the relative viability of different kinds of solidarity.

Thus, there are major parallels in these diverse intellectual traditions. All of them embody an environment, or selective force, outside the individual actor and usually beyond his or her ability to influence. This external force effects the selection of <u>traits</u>, or characteristics of populations which persist through time (across generations) and which bear on the adaptation of the individual or group to its environment. Some paleontologists have recently challenged the assumption that evolution proceeds as a smooth and gradual transition of forms (Eldredge and Gould, 1972). The notion of punctuated equilibria actually makes social science theories of selection even more compatible with Darwinian evolution, as social change often occurs in a relatively jumpy, discontinuous fashion.

The survival of a trait (whether transmitted genetically or culturally) depends on the capabilities it confers on its carriers, in a given environment. One such capacity must be the ability to use resources without using them up. Where there is competition, the spoils (greater reproductive success) go to the holders of the pattern which uses resources most efficiently. Thus, all these forms of selection theory require a kind of maximization which can be stated in various ways. Two organisms, two societies, two modes of production will compete in terms of which can make the best use of available resources. In these temrs, there ought to be broad areas of agreement among ecological anthropologists, economists and political economists. But, as scarcely needs saying, there is no such agreement.

II. THE ECOLOGICAL PARADIGM

In this paper, I shall review some of the principal aspects of ecological anthropological research from the standpoint of various critics of the approach. The major issue at stake is the bearing of these questions on the development of a viable ecological paradigm in social science. Space does not permit me to elaborate on what I mean by a "viable" paradigm, other than to indicate that I intend an empirical approach to phenomena which can be intersubjectively verified and in which hypotheses are proposed and tested against data. I also want to clarify what I mean by "ecological" anthropology. The term appears to restrict the field of inquiry to situations in which only the traditional tools of biological ecology are applicable, such as the concepts of energy flow, homeostasis, nutrient cycling, etc. For some, the term limits the field to situations in which groups of people live in narrowly bounded environments, engaging in direct material exchanges with the living and non-living surroundings. The term might also be taken as restricting inquiry to "natural ecosystems," thereby excluding "man-made" environments. As I will argue at greater length below, these restrictions are based on a set of distinctions difficult to maintain in practice.

I elect to maintain the label "ecological" anthropology discarding some of the restrictions which may connotatively apply to it. I think that ecological anthropology refers to a field of inquiry which possesses a certain theoretical and methodological coherence. It is devoted to the examination of cultural behavior and the cultural patterns which underlie it, as adaptations to material conditions that are external to the culture carriers themselves. It is of no major importance for the practice of the ecological paradigm whether these conditions are themselves the products of human action. The ecological paradigm is not disturbed by the fact that the environment was structured, to a greater or lesser extent, by human actors. Furthermore, the fact that the environment itself may change frequently or even continuously, is not necessarily a stumbling block. Finally, the frequent or continuous reinterpretation of environments by human actors is also not an obstacle to an ecological approach. It may be worth stressing that the ecological paradigm treats phenomena as if they were objectively real and does not interpret the universe as a seamless whole in which the observer and observed are inseparable and, ultimately, indistinguishable. Some anthropologists may object to this approach on philosophical grounds and therefore to the entire empirical enterprise in social science. I know of no way of dealing with such an objection, however, other than to simply recognize it as an alternative way of looking at the world.

A.   Economy of Nature or Fetishized Utility?

One recent critique of ecological anthropology locates the field in an historically bound moment of western cultural development. It views cultural ecology as a kind of "commodity fetishism," reflecting the concern with maximizing profits which dominates the thinking of capitalists. Sahlins (1976) says there is no economy of nature, just an economy of man: what ecological anthropologists do is to superimpose capitalism onto nature through a fetishized notion of utility. This critique derives from the insight of Marx, further developed by Habermas, that all economic systems, through their implicit theory of value, fetishize reality in a certain way, treating certain phantasmas as real. In the case of capitalism, money and profits are treated as if they have lives of their own.

Some of the above comments may be helpful in constructing a critical sociology of knowledge for anthropological thought. Every scientific paradigm reflects aspects of the social milieu in which it arises. But such insights do not address the question of the validity of the assumptions of the approach. To identify cultural ecological thought with capitalist accounting, does not weaken the analytic power of ecological theories, any more than a discovery that the apple which fell on Newton's head was really a tomato thrown by a small boy would destroy Newtonian physics. Neither does it release critics from the responsibility of addressing the scientific as well as the social aspects of a paradigm. What seems to disturb Marxist critics of ecological and economic anthropology the most is that these approaches are reductionist. But all science is reductionist, including symbolic and phenomenonological approaches.

Nature <u>does</u> have an economy. Life processes occur only within specifiable ranges of temperature, altitude, nutrient availability and other environmental parameters. The competition which occurs within an ecological niche obliges organisms to adapt by making optimal use of the available resources. Much recent research has shown the contingent nature of limitations imposed by nature and stressed the complex interactions between organisms and their surroundings.[2] Studies have shown that organisms must satisfy multiple and sometimes conflicting requirements simultaneously, e.g. speed and power for a predator (Sih, 1980). Such conditions further complicate the process of adaptation as well as the task of understanding it. But none of these discoveries shows that life has no limits or that limits are infinitely flexible. If someone in Chicago tries to plant a tomato in their back yard in January, they will have no fruit in July good for eating or for throwing.

Human life and the myriad cultural means for sustaining and enriching it are not exempt from these constraints. The economy of nature is observable in the cultural arrangements to obtain dietary protein (Gross, 1975). In the recent debate on protein capture in Amazonia, most parties have accepted the possibility that protein availability could influence settlement patterns. A few have attacked the very notion of minimum protein requirements. They suggest that protein requirements are variable among human populations and that some populations persistently reproduce under conditions of extreme protein deprivation. My analysis (Gross, 1975, 1981) insists that limits exist, even if they are difficult to determine in specific situations. The exploration of such limitations must proceed through comparative studies utilizing an assumption of ceteris paribus (Lewontin, 1978). Until someone shows that humans can safely ignore the limitations imposed by natural selection, there is no reason to discard the assumption of an economy of nature in which living forms make optimal use of resources and strive to minimize effort.

B. Core and Superstructure

A second, related criticism is that ecological anthropology is a "vulgar" form of materialism because it accepts a simplistic distinction between core and superstructure, relegating such cultural features as religion and kinship to mere epiphenomena (Godelier, 1977; Friedman, 1974). Two aspects of this criticism deserve attention. The first concerns the nature of epiphenomena as opposed to phenomena themselves. The muzzle flash and smoke following a gunshot are, from the point of view of a ballistics expert, epiphenomenal. This does not deny that a nomothetic explanation of these phenomena can be offered, although they have little to do with the velocity and path of a bullet. If something is treated as epiphenomenal, it is not unrelated to the other aspects of a phenomenon. It simply has not been given equal weight in the investigator's agenda.

The second aspect of the criticism grows out of the first. The structural Marxists accept materialist notions of core and superstructure, but object to the exclusion of certain elements (for example, kinship and religion) from the core. They prefer a flexible concept of infrastructure adaptable to a variety of ethnographic circumstances in which one feature or another appears to be fundamental. This preference is consistent with the idiographic thrust of twentieth century Euro-American ethnology. While affirming the fundamental importance of infrastructure as a determinant of social formations, the concept of infrastructure is so relativized that it ceases to guide investigators in the search for cross-cultural regularities. Thus the "laws" which structural Marxists formulate are not nomothetic formulations, but rather structural principles which succinctly describe the functioning of specific social formations at single moments in time.

The "core" of the cultural ecologists is not eclectically composed, but consists of a definite set of items which can be identified in any society. The set includes the physical and the biotic environment, the tools and techniques available for using that environment, and the material transactions between human populations and the environment and among people themselves. All of these items can be operationalized and quantified in any society. Theory, for ecological anthropologists, being nomothetic and cross-cultural, has a very different meaning than for the structural Marxists.

C. Cognitive Salience

Another source of concern with ecological anthropology is its failure to comprehend behavior in terms which are significant to the actors themselves. It is impossible to ignore the actor's point of view as an element of human behavior. It is essential to treat it, if we expect to gain a sense of empathy with actors from alien cultures, and empathy is an important part of understanding. Another approach, ethnoscience, sees cognition as the key to understanding behavior. Its practitioners argue that human action is governed by values, plans, mazeways and other features of the human cognitive apparatus. It follows that underlying any patterned cultural act, there stands a mental prescription for that act (see Harris, 1975). This should, in principle, be discoverable by an empirical procedure that utilizes the statements made by actor/informants in an appropriate eliciting context.

Some of the earlier approaches to cognition have encountered difficulty because they were never related to behavior in a systematic way. Questions have been raised about the methodological assumptions and sample adequacy of ethnoscience techniques (Kessing, 1972; Sanjek, 1971). In some cases, investigators may have worked "backward" and inferred cognitive orientations from behavior (e.g., Foster, 1965). Recent work in ecological anthropology has not discarded the actors' point of view, but there is a realization that cognitive and other psychological models can be no more than approximations of the mental states of actors. Studies like Chibnik's (1980) make reference to "decisions" without claiming to have grasped the psychological reality of the process. No matter how anthropologists paint pictures of cognition or motivation, they, in effect, build models. That is, they construct a coherent set of statements (formalized or not) designed to portray plausibly the actor's perceptions, feelings, cognitive categories, values or goals. The set is invariably selected from a larger corpus of statements and other data. Such models, if they are to be related to behavior must yield testable predictions about behavior.

Some strides have been made in developing a semantic approach to ecologically relevant behavior, but there remain certain methodological problems. In one influential study, Allen Johnson (1974) elicited the categories of land types significant to Northeastern Brazilian sharecroppers, as well as what kinds of crops grew best in each type. He then questioned the farmers as to the crops they had actually sown in each type of land they controlled. There was a high degree of conformity of crop mix to emically designated appropriate land. However, since the informants were the same people whose crop mix was examined, it is possible that the emic prescriptions were actually ex post factor rationalizations of how farmers had distributed their crops.

D. Ecology in Complex Societies

Some anthropologists assume that the ecological approach is useful for dealing with relatively simple societies living "close to nature," but that it cannot deal with the complexities of modern industrial societies in which the environment is man made. This viewpoint requires that a distinction be made between "natural" and "artificial." A modern city like New York, where people breathe polluted air, dine on feedlot beef and travel underground in electric trains, is defined as an artificial environment. By contrast, the Kalahari desert where the !Kung San hunt the wild kudu is defined as a "natural setting." In fact, both environments have been modified by human activities. The physical, chemical and biological processes on which humans depend--in both settings--are substantially the same (for example, the dependence of humans on animal converters to produce meat from plants). Most important, the environments of each can be treated in the same fashion in analyzing how people adapt to them behaviorally and culturally. The adaptation of the urban poor living in ghettos and slums as described by Lewis (1966), Valentine (1969), and others is ecological in much the same terms as Lee's (1969) discussion of the adaptation of the !Kung San to the Kalahari. Very different environments can present quite similar "problems" to people as in Murphy and Steward's (1956) comparison of South American rubber tappers to Athabaskan fur trappers. The solutions will depend not only on the restrictions imposed by the environment at a given moment in time, but also on the existing structure and organization of the societies which adapt.

163

When it comes to production, exchange and consumption, the !Kung are no less dependent than New Yorkers on an organization which evolved over a long period of time in response to many influences, only one of which was the need for subsistence. For the !Kung, we must take into account the influence of nearby cattle-breeding and farming peoples,and of the ceremonial and kinship structure of !Kung society in order to understand how any environmental pertubation might influence their future development. In New York, there may be more influences to consider, but the structure of an ecological approach would be substantially the same. The productive and reproductive systems of industrial societies and hunter-gatherers can be analyzed in terms of a number of common elements. In both, there is a requirement for energy and materials drawn from the earth, from living forms and by the transformation of these by physico-chemical processes. Access to materials is regulated by both social and nonsocial (e.g., geographical) factors, and their abundance is regulated by the same set of factors (e.g., demand in the marketplace and rainfall). An excellent case in point is Eric Ross's study of meat eating patterns in U.S. society (1980). Responding to a challenge by Marshall Sahlins (1976), Ross provides a detailed and compelling argument that the contemporary preference for beef in the U.S. is not the outcome of a dialectic between sex and food deeply rooted in an ancient Indo-European tradition. Ross does not explain the ascendence of the cattle industry simply as the most effective use of new territories acquired by a nation expanding westward. Instead, he shows that

> it was actually pork which dominated the American diet until comparatively recently and . . . the significance of beef is attributable to a shift in the material conditions of food production as American agriculture was integrated into a maturing capitalist system. (Ross, 1980, p. 182)

In his study, Ross reviews the impact of regional specialization and exchange, the rise of urbanism, the tendency toward monopoly control in agribusiness, the growth of highways and fast-food enterprises, the influence of rising fossil-fuel prices, the opening of rangeland in Latin America to supply foreign markets, and finally the impact of the financial institutions which accompany and condition the aforementioned developments. The antecedent state of the U.S. food production system is the baseline from which to gauge the influence of multiple selective pressures emanating from the natural environment, emerging technologies, the transportation system, and political-economic conditions. Incidentally, by handling such an impressive list of complex variables, Ross also effectively demolishes the myth of "monocausal" explanations in ecological anthropology.

E.   Ecology and Synchronic Functionalism

One of the most devastating criticisms of the ecological approach focuses on the use of functionalist type models or the concept of negative feedback (Friedman, 1974). Studies like those of Vayda (1962), Harris (1966), Rappaport (1968), Suttles (1960) and others are seen as incapable of accounting for the origins of institutions which they appear to purport to explain. In each case, it is suggested that a social institution maintains the value of a crucial variable within tolerable limits, sometimes as if the institution were the only one capable of fulfilling that function. Moore (1957), for example, suggests that the Montagnais-Naskapi of Labrador are able to avoid overhunting the caribou in their region by randomizing their hunting patterns. The cultural device involves "reading" the direction the hunt should take from cracks in burnt caribou bones. Such models also presume, without demonstrating, that populations are in fact regulated and are not degrading their environments (Bates and Lees, 1979).

Ecological anthropologists have admitted that it is not possible to retrodict the specific mechanisms which will fulfill specific functions simply from the knowledge that a "functional need" exists. They have also recognized how difficult it is to demonstrate that a population, or any variable associated with one, is regulated. Once functional requisites are established, it is still theoretically possible that they can be fulfilled by a range of functional alternatives. For example, a society faced with aggressive invaders who threaten to displace it can respond in various ways: it can resist militarily, it can surrender, it can call upon allies, it can negotiate. No imperative of survival, no matter how powerful can by itself predict which alternative will be selected. How can anthropologists generate predictive statements in the face of such open-ended

165

possibilities? Darwinian theory provides the answer. The range of alternatives open to a group facing a novel challenge is not, in fact, open-ended. It is restricted by the formations already in place and possibly also by the degree to which these formations are enmeshed in other aspects of the society. If the threatened group in the example had a military tradition, it could theoretically defend itself aggressively unless such militancy jeopardized trading relations maintained with a third group. By the same token, certain mammals became adapted to fully aquatic life (e.g., whales), while others became adept at flying (e.g., bats). But they did not become swimmers by the same means as fish or flyers as did the birds. Rather the mammalian pattern of limbs and digits became adapted for swimming and flying and the pattern can still be observed vestigially. The demonstration of such convergences is similar to certain kinds of comparative analyses in ecological anthropology.

The analysis required to determine what cultural material is available for selection to act upon is already familiar to most anthropologists, including historical particularists. The latter were concerned with the cultural conditions which influenced the acceptance or rejection of innovations. The ecological orientation, with its materialist bias, stresses behavioral aspects of culture over mental aspects, but its basic outlines are found in mainstream Euro-American ethnology. This approach is consistent with the evolutionary principle that selection acts upon the phenotypic variation present in a population and does not itself call forth new forms. Functionalist models cannot, then, explain the origins of cultural institutions unless they are conjoined with a kind of historical analysis which examines not only the selective forces but also the cognitive and behavioral repertoire on which selection can operate. A good example of such an approach can be found in Kottak's (1980) treatment of cultural evolution in Madagascar where the evolution of the state is understood in terms both of particular historical events and general sociocultural processes.

Models employing negative feedback need to be subject to empirical testing. Harris's (1966) theory concerning Indian sacred cattle was merely plausible until Odend'hal (1972) provided supporting evidence from a field study in Bengal. Rappaport's theory concerning the pig festivals of the Maring of New

Guinea (1968) has been criticized by studies showing that the Maring may not distribute pork principally to persons undergoing stress as is called for in the model (Buchbinder, 1973). Contrary to the expectation implied by some fundamentalist ecological models, some "traditional" societies do in fact degrade their environments (Sorensen, 1972; Martin, 1978). Still, virtually all systems exhibit some degree of stability, the conditions of which are worth investigating. Systems analysis encourages us to construct simulation models of system functioning (Dow, 1976; Johnson and Behrens, 1980). Such models, even where they fail to predict accurately the behavior of individuals and groups are potentially valuable because they lead us to ask new questions about the interrelationships among variables in a society and to attempt to build better models.

III. GROUP SELECTION

Some of the anthropological research of the 1960s was informed by the "group selection" models of animal behavior formalized by V. C. Wynne-Edwards in 1962. He suggested that certain aspects of social behavior, which had defied explanation in adaptive terms, serve to communicate information about local population density to the group as a whole, allowing the local population to adjust its numbers accordingly. The model suggested that certain members of a social group might reduce their individual fitness "altruistically" to enhance the overall survival of the deme, and that selection operated on entire demes according to their ability to regulate their densities. An example of this approach can be found in R. A. Rappaport's well-known study of warfare and ritual among the Tsembaga Maring of highland New Guinea (1968). Rappaport suggests that warfare and associated ritual practices serve as a homeostat sensitive to change in the state of the immediate environment by triggering events of ritual sacrifice and fighting at appropriate moments. The outcome of these events is to optimize the distribution of people and pigs with regard to resources, thereby avoiding degradation.

Recent work in population genetics questions the possibility of Darwinian selection operating above the level of the kin group. Sociobiologists have not denied the possibility of selection above the level of the individual and, indeed, the notion of kin selection based on the concept of inclusive fitness is widely accepted (Wilson, 1975).

According to sociobiological theory, most behavior patterns establish themselves in a population because they enhance the fitness (or reproductive effectiveness) of the individuals who carry genes for them. Interdemic or inter-population selection is unlikely, in this view, because it would require some individuals to sacrifice their own opportunity to pass along their genetic material to future generations. Altruistic individuals would tend to be eliminated from a population unless the extinction rate for entire populations was sufficiently high to offset the selective pressure on individuals. This line of reasoning casts doubt on the idea that social practices serve to limit population growth or otherwise maintain a population in check. Accordingly, proponents of sociobiology are looking at behavior not as it contributes to the adaptation of a population to its environment but as it serves to maximize the inclusive fitness of an individual (see Chagnon and Irons, 1979).

In my view, the minimum criteria for interdemic selection are in fact met in human populations. This is so because human groups are highly dependent upon learning rather than sexual reproduction as a means of transmitting behavior patterns. Thus the selective criterion for Homo sapiens is not always Darwinian fitness but rather successful adaptation to resource availability (Wilson, 1975, p. 560). The condition of high group extinction rates is met when we consider not only physical survival of genotypes but also the survival of culturally transmitted traits. I believe that natural selection occurs at a cultural level (cf. Ruyle, 1973; Pelto and Pelto, 1975; Richerson, 1977; Carneiro, 1981) such that behaviors can be acquired by a substantial number of individuals in a single generation. Traits, patterns or entire cultural designs can be extinguished by negative selection in a short period of time. Examples of such selection can be found in situations of rapid technological change, religious conversions, economic transitions and military conquests. The traits or patterns which undergo selection may be diffused from another society or they may already be present in the repertoire of a population. For example, the diffusion of the European plow did not have to await the effects of selection upon the genotypes of the groups who acquired and used it. This Lamarckian element makes sociocultural evolution much more rapid than biological evolution because it does not rely on the slow alteration of genotypes across generations. But the principle of selection is still highly relevant to understanding the process. In human groups, the range of cultural variability in a given social unit may serve in a fashion analogous to the allelic variants at a given locus on a chromosome. In other words, variant forms within a population represent a pool or storehouse of potential adaptive change. From the standpoint of selection, it makes little difference whether the variants arose as the consequence of accidents, deliberate inventions, or loans.

It may be helpful to exemplify what I am talking about. My example comes from changing patterns in agriculture in the U.S. Some accounts of farming in the U.S. suggest that the "mainstream" consists exclusively of commercial farmers who utilize machinery, chemical fertilizers, pesticides and herbicides, technical information and other inputs in order to maximize profits. Organic farmers are seen as radicals or "dropouts" who refuse to utilize modern inputs for ideological reasons.[3] Some recent research on organic corn (maize) farming shows that there is not such a great gulf between organic and nonorganic farmers. Lockeretz and others (1981) drew a sample of 174 organic farmers working farms of 100 acres (40 Ha.) or more. The results of their questionnaire showed that these farmers are motivated by a desire to lessen their dependence upon potentially hazardous chemicals. However, they tend to farm on a commercial scale for a definite market using as many modern inputs, aside from chemicals, as possible. They appear to be responsive to economic and technical information and they attempt to maximize the return on their investments. In other words, commercial organic farmers are not an isolated group totally at odds with other farmers, but rather a minority, standing at one end of a continuum defined in terms of degree of dependence on chemicals. The distribution of farming techniques is similar to an allelic distribution within a population known as balanced polymorphism, a situation which prevails when an otherwise maladaptive genotype is conserved in a population because it simultaneously confers some adaptive advantage on its carriers, e.g., the sickle-cell trait in human populations exposed to malaria.[4]

To carry the example further, consider the possibility that we are on the threshold of a major environmental change affecting the chemicals used in farming. The principal factor responsible for this change is the sudden rise in the price of petroleum and petroleum products precipitated by the "oil shock" of 1973. Nitrogenous fertilizers are derived from natural gas or other petroleum by-products as are other agricultural chemicals. The economic cost of using fertilizer has been rising very rapidly and the energetic cost has risen so much that the gross energetic efficiency of maize agriculture is less than 1.0 and declining steadily (Pimentel et al., 1973). Aside from their cost, other environmental pressures, particularly the tightening restrictions on the use of chemical pesticides and herbicides, are forcing farmers to reconsider their use. These developments constitute selective pressures favoring techniques requiring fewer chemical inputs. Organic farmers, while only a small part of the farming population, may be able to disseminate their experience to other farmers as the techniques used by the latter are subjected to increased negative selective pressure. If, as appears likely, American farmers are induced to adopt methods more nearly approximating organic techniques, I anticipate a concomitant development of an ideology, clothed perhaps in a religious or environmental idiom, which would help pave the way for acceptance of organic techniques and justify their use in terms of other already accepted social values. In other words, modern "high tech" farming in the U.S. may become so modified as to be considered "extinct" without any decline in the biological fitness of the majority of farmers who presently use the nonorganic techniques. The ability of the U.S. farming system to adapt to future changes may depend on the survival of various alternative farming strategies.

IV. THE INDIVIDUAL AND THE GROUP

With the advent of the sociobiological critique, an additional issue has come to the fore: the individual as the unit of analysis. There has been a convergence, as Orlove (1980) observed, on the individual actor as a unit of analysis in the social sciences (economics, anthropology, sociology) and in the bio-behavioral sciences (ethnology, ecology, psychology). This trend has an appealing "back-to-basics" flavor, and it is welcome because it forces us to reexamine the abstract concepts and models which may make good sense at the level of the group, but which may be absurd as accounts of what motivates individual action. Other sources of dissatisfaction with analysis above the level of the individual stem from discussions of group behavior as corporate behavior when it manifestly is not, or from the failure to recognize the scope of variation in individual behavior. There are approaches in both biology and economics in which individual variation plays a crucial role, e.g. in Darwinian selection and in theories of economic change that stress the unique roles of "entrepreneurs" or "risk takers."

It is useful to recall that, in scientific usage, the concept of the individual is no less an abstraction than the concept of the social group or breeding population. In most cases, the individual is picked out as a representative of a particular type from a limited set of such types, e.g. "risk averse" or homozygote. Even when a single individual is chosen from a study population for extended analysis, such as for a life history, he or she is an abstraction because of both observer bias and sampling error.

In the social sciences, the stress on the individual is sometimes accompanied by a concern with the "choices" made by an individual among alternatives or with the "decision-making" process. The idea that individuals choose among alternatives is attractive because it corresponds to our subjective view of how we decide to do things. But many of the contexts in which the term "decision" is used are not, strictly speaking, choice situations at all, i.e., situations in which an individual consciously weighs alternatives and selects the one most favorable to his or her goals. The idea of individual decision making is sometimes carried to an absurd level when actors are faced with a coercive situation as, for example, in the case of certain South American Indians who cannot receive medical care from missionaries unless they make a "choice" for Christ.

I support retaining the individual actor as a unit of analysis to serve as a model of the mechanism which accounts for the distribution of human behavioral outcomes. Sometimes we cannot do without it. We, however, should avoid making a religion of it. It makes little difference to say "ten million individual consumers chose to purchase beef last week," as opposed to, "demand for beef was high last week." In either case, the price of beef will rise. In many of the situations we are concerned with, particularly those in which there are interactions between the environment and a human population, it is the cumulative or aggregate effect of individual actions that counts. Benjamin Orlove, who makes a forceful argument for the individual as a unit of analysis, nevertheless, makes frequent reference to the "cumulative consequences of . . . choices" (Orlove, 1980, p. 257).

V. THE NEED FOR COMPARISON

I want to conclude by pointing out that ecological anthropology has strayed from its comparative and nomothetic roots by becoming increasingly particularistic. I have already referred to this tendency in the work of the structural Marxists, but it is also evident in many recent monographs written under the paradigmatic umbrella of ecological anthropology. Early studies in ecological anthropology addressed general problems in cultural evolution, such as the technoenvironmental conditions underlying the rise of the state (Steward, 1949; Childe, 1951; Meggers, 1954; Wittfogel, 1955; Carneiro, 1970). Their approach rested upon the explicit assumption that similar conditions produce similar effects on society. These studies were severely attacked on methodological and empirical grounds (e.g., Vayda and Rappaport, 1968; Adams, 1966). The severity of these criticisms was such that the next generation of ecological anthropologists all but completely avoided comparative studies. A concern with macroprocesses in culture change was replaced by a fascination with microprocess and the particular responses of single groups to specific environments.

As in earlier particularist reactions, too much may have been discarded. We now know that cultural evolution does not simply consist of invariant sequences in all cases. But too often, researchers have held up single exceptions to evolutionary sequences as conclusive disproof of a sequence (cf. Carneiro, 1973). The full methodological textbook on social evolution has yet to be written. The evidence is strong that societies change along convergent lines while it is also true that each particular social formation develops out of specific antecedent conditions. While this statement makes many anthropologists uncomfortable, most anthropologists appear, at least implicitly, to accept it. Many, if not most, anthropologists assume that there are broad processes of an evolutionary nature requiring a comparative perspective to be grasped and understood. For example, many investigators accept the general notions associated with dependency theory. This is a theory that explains underdevelopment as the outcome of a process involving asymmetric relations between a capital- and technology-rich core and a relatively defenseless periphery. Many individual case studies have been written from this point of view and there is invariably an explicit or implicit statement to the effect that the study exemplifies a more general world historical process. Nevertheless, very few anthropologists have conducted systematic comparative studies within this paradigm. The few comparisons done by sociocultural anthropologists are mainly of an ad hoc nature, carried out because the same researcher did field work in two places or because of a fortuitous association between two colleagues. Many anthropologists have paradoxically expressed open hostility towards systematic comparative studies while paying lip service to them on a theoretical level.

I believe that the time is ripe to return to a comparative mode, partly because an enormous wealth of data has been accumulated in the form of monographs, articles and theses. Ecological anthropology provides a valuable guide to such studies because it emphasizes systematic measurement utilizing categories which are cross-culturally comparable. I should stress that neither ideology, religion nor any other aspect of culture needs be slighted in such an endeavor. They can be and have been dealt with in an ecological context (e.g., Rappaport, 1968, on ritual; Moore, 1957, on divination; Harris, 1966, and Ross, 1980, on food taboos). But with its stress on the material causes and consequences of these aspects of culture, the ecological paradigm may provide a firmer basis for comparison than others.

Economic anthropologists, like their ecological confreres, are concerned with measurement, comparison and responsible theory building. Theoretically, there is much which unites them. While ecologists may not accept the universality of maximization in the same spirit as the economist, I have tried to show that they are forced to accept that people, like other organisms, economize in order to survive and

173

reproduce. Microeconomic approaches dealing with individual decision-making in a given cultural context are compatible with ecological frameworks which posit that individuals or groups optimize their access to nutrients or other resources. Some of the decision models used in microeconomic analysis are identical to those used in ecological analysis (see Ortiz's paper in this volume). Economic anthropologists may be suffering from the same reluctance to conduct comparative studies as the ecologists, but I believe they have the same vital interest in reviving them.

There are practical as well as theoretical reasons for combining the forces of ecological and economic anthropologists. Together we can attack some major issues in the areas of international development and social change: the production of biomass for nonfood energy, the expansion of export beef production in the third world, the destructive effects of forest clearance, and the influence of labor market development on indigenous minorities, the generation of toxic wastes by industry, the social consequence of land reform programs, and dozens of other major problems. The general area of economic development and change presents literally dozens of problems that ought to be tackled by ecologically and economically oriented anthropologists. For example, Xavier Totti (1980) recently suggested that the decline of schistosomiasis in Puerto Rico is more likely a result of behavioral changes induced by the changing economy than by public health measures. Billie DeWalt (1982) uses an ecological perspective to examine the consequences of the expansion of cattle raising in Central America. Catherine Dewey (1981) and Emilio Moran (1981) employ an ecological perspective to examine the consequences of colonization programs in Mexico and Brazil. Bodley (1981) proposes a new approach to the study of inequality in terms of energy flow patterns. All of these studies employ concepts and techniques that belong to both ecological and economic anthropology, e.g., Moran's discussion of peasant cropping techniques or DeWalt's consideration of the transition from subsistence crops to cattle. I am persuaded that there are many potentially fruitful areas of cross fertilization and collaboration between anthropologists economic and ecological, or more simply, research done by persons trained in both.

I am pleased to have been asked to discuss ecological anthropology with a group of economic anthropologists. So long as we continue to debate and redefine our interests in this fashion, our discipline will remain strong and relevant.

Acknowledgments

This paper was delivered orally at the Inaugural Conference of the Society for Anthropological Economics held at Indiana University on April 28, 1981. The author wishes to thank Silede Gross, Burton Pasternak and Frank Zimmerman for the timely and invaluable comments on the first and second drafts of this paper and Dr. Sutti Ortiz for her valuable suggestions. They saved me from many grievous errors. Those which remain are entirely my own responsibility. Support from the National Science Foundation (BNS 76-03378 and 78-25295) and the City University of New York (PSC/BHE Awards 11479E and 12182) for field research in central Brazil is gratefully acknowledged.

Notes

[1] The term "selection" may be a source of confusion because the discrimination that is made is not based on an actor's evaluation of the relative merits of different alternatives. Darwin's theory and most of the brands of economic theory are deterministic with regard to individual behavior.

[2] This observation bears directly upon a distinction that has been made in ecological anthropology between "possibilism" and "determinism" (Vayda and Rappaport, 1968). For example, Kroeber's (1939) delineation of the geographical limits of North American maize agriculture and the cultural complex dependent upon it is said to represent a possibilist approach. In contrast, Steward's theory of the patrilocal band (1949) is said to be deterministic because it does not simply specify a range of conditions within which a phenomenon may appear but specifically links a set of techno-environmental conditions to particular sociocultural practices. In these cases, both the possibilist and the determinist made allowances for the nonappearance of the sociocultural traits in question. Steward's theory is more articulated and specifies the conditions under which

particular socio-cultural phenomena can appear more precisely than Kroeber's. It would nevertheless be more accurate to describe both theories as "probabilistic," as are most empirical theories nowadays.

[3] The reader will note that neither my example nor the study cited purports to explain the motivations for all organic farming in the U.S.

[4] It is conceivable that a shift to organic farming might even increase the fertility of the farming population as a response to the greater labor demands of organic techniques and to the fact that organic techniques may require a reduction in the scale of the average farm establishment.

References

ADAMS, R. McC. 1966. The evolution of urban society. Chicago: Aldine.

BATES, D. G., and S. H. Lees. 1979. The myth of population regulation. In Evolutionary biology and human social behavior. N. A. Chagnon and W. Irons, eds. North Scituate, Mass.: Duxbury Press.

BODLEY, John. 1981. Inequality: an energetics approach. In Social inequality: comparative and developmental approaches. G. Berreman, ed. New York: Academic Press.

BUCHBINDER, G. 1973. Maring microadaptation: a study of demographic, nutritional and phenotypic variation in a highland New Guinea population. Ph.D. dissertation, Columbia University.

CARNEIRO, R. 1970. A theory of the origin of the state. Science 169:733-738.

CARNEIRO, Robert. 1977. The four faces of evolution: unilinear, universal, multilinear, and differential. In Handbook of social and cultural anthropology. J. J. Honigmann, ed. Skokie, Ill.: Rand McNally.

_____. 1981. The role of natural selection in the evolution of culture. Paper presented at meetings of the American Anthropological Association, 1982.

CHAGNON, N. A., and W. Irons, eds. 1979. Evolutionary biology and human social behavior. North Scituate, Mass.: Duxbury Press.

CHIBNIK, M. 1980. Working out or working in: the choice between wage labor and cash cropping in rural Belize. American Ethnologist 7:86-105.

CHILDE, V. G. 1951. Man makes himself. New York: New American Library.

DEWALT, Billie. 1982. The big macro connection: population, grain and cattle in southern Honduras. Culture and Agriculture: The Bulletin of the Anthropological Study Group on Agrarian Systems 14:1-11.

DEWEY, Katherine. 1981. Nutritional consequences of the transformation from subsistence to commercial agriculture in Tabasco, Mexico. Human Ecology 9:151-188.

DOW, J. 1976. Systems models of cultural ecology. Social Science Information 15:953-976.

ELDRIDGE, Niles, and Stephen J. Gould. 1972. Punctuated equilibria. In Models in paleobiology. T. J. M. Schoepf, ed. San Francisco: Freeman Cooper.

FOSTER, G. 1965. Peasant society and the image of limited good. American Anthropologist 67:293-315.

FRIEDMAN, J. 1974. Marxism, structuralism and vulgar materialism. Man 9:444-469.

GEERTZ, C. 1962. Agricultural involution. Berkeley: University of California Press.

GODELIER, M. 1977. Perspectives in Marxist anthropology. New York: Cambridge University Press.

GROSS, D. R. 1975. Protein capture and cultural development in the Amazon Basin. American Anthropologist 77:526-549.

_____. 1981. Consumo protéico en la cuenca Amazonica: una segunda revisión. Amazonia Peruana (Lima) vol. 6.

HARRIS, M. 1966. The cultural ecology of India's sacred cattle. Current Anthropology 7:51-60.

_____. 1968. The rise of anthropological theory. New York: Thomas Y. Crowell.

_____. 1975. Why a perfect knowledge of all the rules that one must know in order to act like a native cannot lead to a knowledge of how natives act. Journal of Anthropological Research 30:242-251.

JOHNSON, A. 1974. Ethnoecology and planting practices in a swidden agricultural system. American Ethnologist 1:87-101.

JOHNSON, A., and C. Behrens. 1980. Nutritional factors in Machiguenga food production decisions: a linear programming analysis. ms.

KEESING, R. 1972. Paradigms lost: the new ethnography and the new linguistics. Southwestern Journal of Anthropology 28:299-332.

KOTTAK, Conrad P. 1980. The living and the dead. Ann Arbor: University of Michigan Press.

KROEBER, A. L. 1939. Cultural and natural areas of native North America. Berkeley: University of California Publications in American Archeology and Ethnology, vol. 38.

LEE, Richard B. 1969. !Kung bushman subsistence: an input-output analysis. In Environment and cultural behavior. A. P. Vayda, ed. Garden City, New York: The Natural History Press.

LEWONTIN, R. C. 1978. Adaptation. Scientific American 239:212-230.

LEWIS, Oscar. 1966. La Vida: A Puerto Rican family in the culture of poverty. New York: Random House.

LOCKERETZ, W., G. Shearer, and D. H. Kohl. 1981. Organic farming in the corn belt. Science 211:540-547.

MARTIN, Calvin. 1978. Keepers of the game. Berkeley: University of California Press.

MEGGERS, B. J. 1954. Environmental limitations on the development of culture. American Anthropologist 56:301-324.

MOORE, O. K. 1957. Divination: a new perspective. American Anthropologist 59:69-74.

MORAN, Emilio. 1981. Developing the Amazon. Bloomington: Indiana University Press.

MURPHY, Robert F., and Julian H. Steward. 1956. Tappers and trappers: parallel process in acculturation. Economic Development and Cultural Change 4:335-355.

ODEND'HAL, S. 1972. Energetics of Indian cattle in their environment. Human Ecology 1:3-22.

ORLOVE, B. 1980. Ecological anthropology. Annual Review of Anthropology 9:235-273.

PELTO, P., and G. Pelto. 1975. Intra-cultural diversity: some theoretical issues. American Ethnologist 2:1-18.

PIMENTEL, D., et al. 1973. Food production and the energy crisis. Science 182:443-449.

RAPPAPORT, R. A. 1968. Pigs for the ancestors. New Haven: Yale University Press.

RICHERSON, P. J. 1977. Ecology and human ecology: a comparison of theories in the biological and social sciences. American Ethnologist 4:1-26.

ROSS, E. 1978. Food taboos, diet and hunting strategy: the adaptation to animals in Amazon cultural ecology. Current Anthropology 19:1-36.

_____. 1980. Patterns of diet and forces of production: an economic and ecological history of the ascendency of beef in the United States diet. In _Myths of culture: essays in cultural materialism_. E. B. Ross, ed. New York: Academic Press.

RUYLE, E. 1973. Genetic and cultural pools: some suggestions for a unified theory of biocultural evolution. _Human Ecology_ 1:201-216.

SAHLINS, M. 1976. _Culture and practical reason_. Chicago: University of Chicago Press.

SANJEK, R. 1971. Brazilian racial terms: some aspects of meaning and learning. _American Anthropologist_ 73:1126-1143.

SIH, A. 1980. Optimal behavior: can foragers balance two conflicting demands? _Science_ 210:1041-1043.

SORENSEN, E. R. 1972. Socio-ecological change among the Fore of New Guinea. _Current Anthropology_ 13:349-385.

STEWARD, J. H. 1949. Cultural causality and law: a trial formulation of the development of early civilizations. _American Anthropologist_ 51:1-27.

SUTTLES, W. 1960. Affinal ties, subsistence and prestige among the Coast Salish. _American Anthropologist_ 62:296-305.

TOTTI, Xavier. 1980. Economic transformation, behavioral change and the epidemiology of schistosomiasis mansoni (bilharzia) in Puerto Rico. M.A. thesis, Hunter College of the City University of New York.

VALENTINE, Charles A, et al. 1969. Culture and poverty: critique and counter proposals. _Current Anthropology_ 10:181-201.

VAYDA, A. P. 1961. Expansion and warfare among swidden agriculturalists. _American Anthropologist_ 63:346-358.

VAYDA, A. P., and R. A. Rappaport. 1968. Ecology: cultural and noncultural. In _Introduction to_ cultural anthropology: essays in the scope and methods of the science of man. J. A. Clifton, ed. Boston: Houghton Mifflin Company.

WILSON, E. O. 1975. Sociobiology: the new synthesis. Cambridge, Mass.: Harvard University Press.

WITTFOGEL, K. 1957. Oriental despotism. New Haven: Yale University Press.

WYNNE-EDWARDS, V. C. 1962. Animal dispersion in relation to social behavior. Edinburgh: Oliver and Boyd.

VIII. ENVIRONMENTAL HAZARDS AND DECISION MAKING: ANOTHER PERSPECTIVE FROM HUMAN ECOLOGY

Susan H. Lees

The central subject matter of ecological anthropology is the interaction between humans and their environments. But within this field, there are a number of different ways of understanding the nature of this interaction, each with significant implications for methodology and theory. In this sense, ecological anthropology is no more unified a discipline than is economic anthropology. In fact, the schism described as the substantivist-formalist controversy (perhaps an oversimplification) has its analog in ecological anthropology, though the dichotomy is not explicated in the literature on ecology as such (but see Orlove, 1980).

Differentiation within ecological anthropology can be traced to Vayda and Rappaport's call, in 1968, for a human rather than cultural ecology (Vayda and Rappaport, 1968). While Vayda and Rappaport's initial position has since undergone considerable evolution and change, their paradigm for ecological research (human ecology) as a whole can be contrasted with that whose articulation has best been expressed in the writings of Marvin Harris and labeled by him and his followers "cultural materialism" (Harris, 1979). Human ecology looks to human adaptation or response to environmental problems by whatever means, while cultural materialism looks to cultural adaptation instead. The former, whose approach is essentially behaviorist, bears some resemblance to formalist economics, while the latter is similar in many respects to substantivism. While both are fundamentally materialist in perspective, the units of study are different; it is this difference which accounts for their respective linkages and convergences with formalist and substantivist economic anthropology.

Human ecologists do not attempt to explain events or situations by resorting to culture, nor to explain culture itself. Therefore, the units under investigation are not cultures or culture traits. While initially, Vayda and Rappaport had proposed the "population" and the "ecosystem" as appropriate units, that approach has been superseded by one which substitutes the individual biological organism for "population" and "ecosystem" as the relevant adaptive unit (Vayda and McKay, 1975). This substitution has taken place in the context of developments within biology and ecological theory that have raised questions about the utility of the concepts of "population" and "ecosystem" for purposes of studying evolutionary adaptation and change. These developments, which I will not detail here, refer in part to the group selection controversy in evolutionary biology (Irons, 1979) and controversies about ecological diversity and stability (Holling, 1969). The outcome of the controversies has led human ecologists to focus upon the individual as a problem-solver, strategically responding to environmental perturbation.

Cultural materialism, by contrast, bears more continuity with the earlier approaches derived from Julian Steward's "cultural ecology" (Vayda and Rappaport, 1968). It has been concerned with explaining the persistence of cultural traits in terms of their ability to adjust to a more or less balanced (stable) environment and views imbalance as threatening the persistence of specific groups and cultures. Specific culture traits, including marital practices, food taboos, warfare and ceremonial rites, have been accounted for in terms of the role they play in maintaining ecological stability (Bates and Lees, 1979).

From a human ecology perspective, the persistence of a group or a culture trait is not as interesting as the observation that groups "ungroup," or that abandonment of a culture trait (its "extinction") may be necessary to prevent the extinction of its human carriers (Vayda and McKay, 1975). For this reason, it is inappropriate in a human ecology framework to apply Darwinian terms such as selection and adaptation to culture--though not to human organisms. Instead, it is more appropriate to look at models of decision-making to determine why people persist in certain behaviors and abandon others. Not everyone has a choice in making every change, and not everyone has the same types of choices to make, but this does not mean that choices, of an economic sort, are not being made. In this context, there are clear convergences between human ecology and formalist economic anthropology. Because Gross has already dealt extensively with the application of a cultural materialist approach to economic anthropology, I shall not attempt to explore that ground further in this paper. In what follows, I shall, instead, expand on the implications for research of convergences between decision theory and the human ecology perspective.

It is more useful to regard an environment as a series of events than as a set of conditions (static, or in dynamic equilibrium, or in the process of destruction). These events are best understood as a sequence of interactions between people and other variables, many of which are not subject to human control. An earthquake or a hurricane, for example, are environmental events which are neither generated nor controlled by humans. Humans must respond to them, and may do so by adjusting to them immediately or in the long run. Seasonal changes in weather conditions, or chronic environmental hazards (like frequent earthquakes, annual frosts, etc.) are types of events that tend to evoke systematic adaptive behaviors from human populations.

Other environmental events may be external in origin but are augmented or altered by human action. Floods and droughts, for example, may be precipitated by external conditions but are relieved or exacerbated by human agency. Human interference in such "natural" conditions involves a major component of the world's technology.

Finally, there are environmental events whose source is human technology itself. People seek to create environmental conditions favorable to their own ends, with the result that environmental events occur which would not have been generated without human interference. Sometimes these events are planned but other times they are the unintentional and often undesirable by-products of deliberate projects. Such events occur through human agency, but they involve characteristics of environmental factors not always controlled or understood by humans. One example is the proliferation of an animal pest population through the elimination of its predators or through the inadvertent introduction of a new species to an environment. The consequences of the use of DDT in many areas of the world illustrate this process (Holling and Goldberg, 1971).

To find explanations for historical events, it is useful to look at environmental events of all sorts.

Particular environmental events may kick off responses which later obscure the initial impetus. For example, a short-term drought may encourage the initial development of a simple irrigation system whose later growth and development has little to do with drought and more to do with the eventual dependence of the political and economic system on irrigation. Later environmental events may involve artificially created water shortages rather than natural shortages. Environmental events continue to be significant in the explanation of human activities and events but the nature and source of the events may change--always as a result of continuing human agency.

What has this to do with economics and decision theory? One problem with decision theory in economics has been the very abstractness of its application. There are so many decisions, for example, that farmers and livestock raisers have to make that it is hard to know what to focus on for comparative purposes. But if we turn our attention to environmental problems and disturbances that vary on scales of severity and duration--such as drought or even price fluctuations--we can compare strategic decision-making in a meaningful way, particularly to understand the influence of other variables (like poverty, or exposure to innovations) on decision-making. Certainly we gain a better understanding of particular cases when we examine how people's decisions change with changing environmental circumstances.

This was the perspective Dan Bates and I took when we attempted to provide a model for studying nomadic pastoralist specializations (Bates and Lees, 1977). Under what circumstances do livestock-raisers specialize in pastoral production, to the exclusion of other forms of production, and under what circumstances do they abandon such specialization? We tried to show that external influences, particularly those affecting the exchange value of herd products for other products, play a significant role that could only be understood in terms of the duration and intensity of change. For example, a small increase in the price of grain with respect to the price of wool, lasting for one season, could be expected to evoke a different strategic response than a gradual increase over a ten-year period. Furthermore, such changes affect members of a livestock-raising group differentially, according to their economic and social positions at the onset of the change. The decisions taken by a wealthy herder can be expected to be different from those taken by a poor one.

In that paper, we tried to show that to understand a classical ecological question, e.g. what is the "carrying capacity" of a specific environmental zone or region for humans, we may need to understand the market for their product. While this indicates the importance of economics for human ecology, it also indicates the complementarity of ecological studies for economics. The respective market prices of wheat and wool reflect changing environmental conditions, environmental events which make wheat and wool more or less costly to produce, hence more or less worthwhile investments for the farmer and the herder.

Choices made by farmers and herders are subject, obviously, to major constraints--social, technical, and environmental. It is possible, however, to overestimate the constraining role of environmental or institutional factors or to miscalculate their outcomes. National governments and international development agencies do it all the time. Miscalculations become very clear when we look at rural development policies and projects. There are many well documented cases of farmers and herders who refuse or are unable to follow development agency directives or incentives of one sort or another. The outcome of virtually all planned rural development is at variance with initial projections. The reasons for this are manifold, among them a misconception or miscalculation of the capacity of individual producers for following strategies which appear to them to be in their own interest. Another factor that should not be neglected is the self-interested decision-making strategies of development agents themselves.

It is in the context of environmental hazards that we most clearly see the utility of a convergence of formalist decision models and human ecology (Lees, 1980). This is because hazards present occasions for major order choices and strategies that have far-reaching consequences--which determine the evolutionary trajectories of both societies and ecosystems. Furthermore, the relevance of decision models is enhanced when they are brought to bear on people's real and pressing problems. Studying the ways that people solve or do not solve problems that are related to environmental events provides us with a critical key to the understanding of human evolution (Lees and Bates, 1983).

Generally speaking, natural environmental conditions are remarkably stable by comparison with human-affected environments. They fluctuate in various patterns, but restore themselves over the geological short-run. Thus, a natural disaster--flood, fire, volcanic eruption--may cause havoc for a time, but eventually an earlier set of conditions will reappear. People, however, often interrupt the process of environmental restoration. While initially they may be responding to one environmental event, in a short time they are obliged to respond to the cumulative effects of earlier responses.

George Morren's analysis of the British drought of 1975-76 provides a general model for looking at the positive feedback cycle of hazard, disaster, reaction, and increased vulnerability consequent to sequential responses (Morren, 1980). I have tried to show its cross-cultural applicability to cases from East Africa and Latin America (Lees, 1980). In all these cases, the sequence of events began with efforts directed toward the aversion of risks related to water shortage. Early strategies entailed decisions which eventually removed control over local decision-making by rural producers themselves, hence resulted in their becoming ever more dependent upon and vulnerable to non-local conditions and environmental events. Consequently, the nature of their own decision-making strategies was changed over time. For example, while farmers might initially be able to devise means of water conservation in response to a periodic rainfall shortage, such measures would become pointless at a later stage if the initial response involved linking their water supply system with others' not subject to the same constraints.

It seems to me that research on changes in decision-making by producers is, or ought to be, the most promising frontier of decision theory in economic anthropology, and that this research is crucial to, and reliant upon, developments in human ecology. The value of this research lies in its applicability to studies of economic development and underdevelopment, matters which are and always have been central to economic anthropology.

Of particular interest to ecologists has been the impact of shifts in the locus of certain types of decision making. At what level of a social structure are particular decisions concerning technological inputs, production levels and so forth being made, and to what extent does this affect the sensitivity and responsiveness of human activity to environmental conditions (Lees, 1974)? When this interest was phrased in systems theory terms, some types of shifts were seen as pathological in that they led a system away from homeostasis, thus appearing to reduce the system's ability to restore itself from perturbations (Flannery, 1972; Rappaport, 1969).

There has been less attention paid to the impact of shifts in locus of decision making on local-level producers: what decisions are left to them, and how do they respond to a loss of decision-making power by resorting to other types of strategies? For example, a central government might remove from a local area the power to decide how to allocate water in an irrigation canal, assuming control over quantity, timing, and distribution. Local farmers might then have a different array of strategies to meet their water needs: they might choose to "ignore" government directives, thereby taking on the new risk of getting caught; they might alter their crops and farming management practices to respond to an allocation system they cannot control. Bribery and theft are two of the most common reactions when water-allocation systems are non-locally controlled. The latter two strategies are not nearly as well documented in anthropological study as are the conflict and resistance responses (Hunt and Hunt, 1976). How do social and environmental events come together to create conditions in which one type of response (conflict) is more likely than another (bribery, theft, other extra-legal adjustments)? This is an example of the kind of questions that can be studied when we focus on shifts in decision-making loci and their impact on local-level producers' responses.

In sum, the value of a convergence between human ecology and economic decision theory may be in the insights it offers in the study of change. It suggests a focus on the role of environmental events and human response at the local level. It suggests a corrective to the sometimes too static perspective of decision-making studies, and to the view of some ecologists of humans as passive recipients of environmental influence.

References

BATES, D., and S. H. Lees. 1977. The role of exchange in productive specialization. American Anthropologist 79:824-841.

_____. 1979. The myth of population regulation. In Evolutionary biology and human social behavior. N. A. Chagnon and W. Irons, eds. North Scituate, Mass.: Duxbury Press.

FLANNERY, K. V. 1972. The cultural evolution of civilization. Annual Review of Ecology and Systematics 3:399-425.

HARRIS, M. 1979. Cultural materialism: the struggle for a science of culture. New York: Random House.

HOLLING, C. S. 1969. Stability in ecological and social systems. Brookhaven Symposia in Biology 22:128-141.

HOLLING, C. S., and M. A. Goldberg. 1971. Ecology and planning. Journal of the American Institute of Planners 37:221-230.

HUNT, R. C., and E. Hunt. 1976. Canal irrigation and local social organization. Current Anthropology 17:389-411.

IRONS, W. 1979. Natural selection, adaptation, and human social behavior. In Evolutionary biology and human social behavior. N. A. Chagnon and W. Irons, eds. North Scituate, Mass.: Duxbury Press.

LEES, S. 1974. Hydraulic development as a process of response. Human Ecology 2:159-176.

_____. 1980. The hazards approach to development research: recommendation for Latin American drylands. Human Organization 39:372-376.

LEES, S., and D. Bates. In press. Environmental events and the ecology of cumulative change. In The ecosystem concept in anthropology. E. Moran, ed. Boulder, Colorado: Westview Press, AAAS Selected Symposia Series.

MORREN, G. 1980. The rival ecology of the British drought 1975-76. Human Ecology 8:33-63.

ORLOVE, B. 1980. Ecological anthropology. Annual Review of Anthropology 9:235-273.

RAPPAPORT, R. 1969. Sanctity and adaptation. Prepared for Wenner-Gren Symposium The naval and esthetic structure of human adaptation. New York: Wenner-Gren Foundation.

VAYDA, A. P., and B. J. MacKay. 1975. New directions in ecology and ecological anthropology. Annual Review of Anthropology 4:293-306.

VAYDA, A. P., and R. A. Rappaport. 1968. Ecology: cultural and non-cultural. In Introduction to cultural anthropology: essays on the scope and methods of the science of man. J. A. Clifton, ed. Boston: Houghton Mifflin Co.

PART FOUR

ALLOCATION OF RESOURCES

Both the performance of an economic system and the impact of the environment can be examined from the microperspective of the behavior of producers, consumers and transactors. This perspective has a long tradition in economics. At the turn of the century Karl Menger was writing about the relationship between economic events and the activities of economizing individuals. Through logical reasoning he outlined possible solutions to the problem of how resources are likely to be allocated and the consequences implied by those solutions. A few years later, Olivier Leroy, a French contemporary of Marcel Mauss, argued that economic activities in "primitive" societies are likewise reasoned. In his book La Raison Primitive (1927) Leroy analyzed the various patterns of consumption, production and distribution from the perspective of familial units. These patterns, he believed, posed logical solutions to the problem of how to allocate resources, given the constraints, needs and dangers of environmental depletion. Unlike Menger, who did not use the concept of rationality, Leroy--perhaps because he was addressing himself to the writing of Bücher and Levi-Bruhl--made ample use of the term. His major contribution was not just to bring to anthropology some of the arguments of cartesian individualist economists, but also to remind students of primitive societies of two important concepts. First, it is just as important to pay attention to the mundane as to the exotic; and second, that individual economic activities have to be examined within the context of social organization (Gastellu, 1975).

The individual perspective became a natural approach for anthropologists interested in economic organization once they embarked on prolonged field work. Even Malinowski, who abhorred the notion of homo oeconomicus, explained many observations in terms of human needs and the indirect processes used to satisfy them. Raymond Firth (1939), in his early study on Tikopian economy, talked about want satisfaction in production and exchange, and discussed the constraints individuals face when they are allocating resources. Goodfellow (1939) wrote about principles of economic sociology from the perspective of individual economic units. The individualized choice format was used less to transpose economic theories than to reveal what factors affect allocations and what resolutions are most likely to be adopted. The term "rationality," in fact appears only in later editions of Firth's Primitive Polynesian Economy. On the other hand, rationality occupied a central place in Herskovits's book The Economic Life of Primitive Peoples (1940). The adoption of what has come to be known as formal models of rationality has become widespread in this country, thanks to Schneider's encouragement and his presentations of relevant economic principles and methods in his book Economic Man (1974). In Chapter IX Bennett and Kanel trace the two parallel traditions as well as the various meanings given to the terms "economizing" and producer's "rationality" in the anthropological and economic literature.

By the 1960s most economic anthropologists who continued to explore economic events from the perspective of the behavior of the producer turned from the study of the role of "things" and commodities to the study of the logic in resource allocation. Popper's teaching about the value of situational logic and the importance of formalizing observation and hypothesis had become influential. Furthermore, as economists became more interested in collaborating with anthropologists in identifying significant social variables, the search for a shared framework to evaluate relative significance brought economic anthropologists back to the concept of rationality. Now, the concept, having been battered about in the formalist-substantivist controversy, has lost its explanatory appeal (Cohen, 1967; Ortiz, 1973); but it could still be used to outline the economic conditions of a given situation (Nash, 1961).

The seventies were marked by further efforts to formalize models of rational choice. By now the concept no longer corresponded to what Menger, Leroy and Firth had envisaged. In Chapter X, Ortiz reviews the shifts in the concerns of economists and anthropologists when they began to use formal models as research tools as well as normative tools. She also examines the transformation of the models from tools used to think about organizing principles of economic systems or about the valuation of products, to tools used to clarify relationships and evaluate the impact of policies. In Chapter IX, Bennett and Kanel explain the difference between formal models of rational economic action and the economic behavior of producers. They warn us that only under certain conditions do the models portray and explain farming behavior and agrarian economic processes. They also make it quite clear that the intent of economist models is quite different from that of many anthropologists studying the behavior of producers.

In both chapters the authors raise a number of questions which must still be resolved if we are to model actual allocation processes in complex and uncertain environments. Bennett and Kanel point out that if we want to fully understand the behavior of farmers we must visualize them not only as reasoning allocators but also as men adapting to the constraints of their environments. Further, the manner of their adaptation and their choice of solutions will vary with management styles. These styles are subject to cultural constraints, the conditions affecting farming opportunities, and the stage in the reproductive cycle of the farm and the farm family. Ortiz discusses the importance of first determining the order and sequence of annual decisions and the factors that may alter them. Perception and evaluation of pay-off and costs are contextually determined; and the context differs both throughout the year and through the developmental cycle of the family farm. Only after we have achieved a sociological analysis of the decision process should we integrate some of the mathematical techniques developed by microeconomists. Scholars who are more interested in evaluating efficiency or in making normative suggestions may, on the other hand, find it appropriate to use the existing models. Gladwin's information processing model is perhaps the most useful of existing tools, but there is also a clear role for the efficiency models used by Plattner (see Chapter X).

Decision analysis is a useful tool for examining the allocation problem in depth, and thus for gaining a better understanding of the nature of the interrelationships among factors that affect resource allocation. It is also a necessary tool for development planners who must prescribe farm investment plans or evaluate the impact of policies on farm investments. Nevertheless, decision analysis has clear limitations. Its complexity forces economic anthropologists to be selective in the factors they consider. On occasion, what is left out from the analysis may be crucial for an understanding of macrodevelopment (Berry, 1980). Bennett and Kanel address this issue when contrasting the formal models with farming behavior.

Another set of limitations arises when economists attempt to aggregate the expected solutions and management decisions in order to make predictions about regional production patterns. The task of aggregation is feasible only when three conditions are met: 1) there is minimal interdependence and feedback among units of production; 2) the number of strategies likely to be adopted is not too large and can be simulated by the analyst (Ortiz, Chapter X); and 3) existing institutional arrangements force producers to favor certain solutions over others (Bennett and Kanel, Chapter IX). As Ortiz points out, an indeterminant economic and ecological environment may lead to multiplex sets of actual solutions to the allocation problem, regardless of whether or not there is a narrow set of stereotypic ideal solutions to the same problem. An understanding of an economic system thus cannot be gained only by focusing on the behavior of farmers. The institutional, or macro, approach discussed in other sections is just as important. Yet decision analysis has its own specific contribution to make, and should not be ignored.

References

BERRY, Sara S. 1980. Decision making and policy making in rural development. In Agricultural decision making, Peggy F. Barlett, ed. New York: Academic Press.

COHEN, Percy. 1967. Economic analysis and economic man: some comments on a controversy. In Themes in economic anthropology. Raymond Firth, ed. London: Tavistock.

FIRTH, Raymond. 1939. Primitive polynesian economy. London: George Routledge and Sons.

GASTELLU, Jean Marc. 1975. Un économiste fourvoyé en anthropologie: Olivier Leroy. Cahier Internationale de Sociologie 49:315-336.

GOODFELLOW, D. M. 1939. Principles of economic sociology. London: George Routledge and Sons.

HERSKOVITS, Melville. 1940. The economic life of primitive peoples. New York: Knopf.

LEROY, Olivier. 1927. La raison primitive. Paris: P. Geuthner.

NASH, Manning. 1961. The social context of economic choice in a small society. Man 61:186-91.

ORTIZ, Sutti. 1973. Uncertainties in peasant farming. London: Athlone Press.

SCHNEIDER, Harold K. 1974. Economic man. New York: The Free Press.

IX. AGRICULTURAL ECONOMICS AND ECONOMIC ANTHROPOLOGY: CONFRONTATION AND ACCOMMODATION*

John W. Bennett and Don Kanel

I. PROLOGUE

We attempt in this paper to describe the relation between the two fields--agricultural economics and economic anthropology--and to suggest bases for fruitful collaboration between them.

The two fields have different objectives. With respect to agriculture, the anthropologists have been concerned mainly with the informal, personalistic, community centered activities of people who must produce to stay alive, and who must honor their complex social obligations in order to produce. Agricultural economists, on the whole, have studied farmer-producers who must adhere to a set of impersonal standards in order to survive economically in the setting of large-scale market agrarian systems. Agricultural economists, therefore, must be as aware of and concerned with these external system imperatives as they are with the farmer and his problems.

Despite these different orientations, the anthropologist and the agricultural economist have a number of points of convergence. Most of these derive from the fact that farmers in modern agrarian systems retain some of the social and behavioral characteristics of tribal-peasant peoples. These points of similarity derive from the fact that most farming and livestock production, whether it is done for subsistence or for markets, is largely controlled by family-operated enterprises, that is, by people whose social organization tends to be dominated by kin ties and local community relations. We should hasten to acknowledge substantial trends toward agribusiness and factory farming, and with these forms of production we are not concerned in this paper. However, the fact remains that the world over, including North America, the majority of agricultural producers form local groups whose social life as well as economic livelihood is tied up with agricultural activities. This fact has led to a number of differences in the outlook and approach of agricultural economists and those economists who specialize in industrial systems and business organization. These differences provide some points of contact and cooperation with anthropologists.

The need for greater collaboration has emerged especially in the past two and one-half decades of agrarian development and change in the third world. Many early attempts to persuade peasant cultivators to shift to commercial regimes or otherwise adopt the technology and strategies of market agriculture failed for a variety of reasons: some were simply the result of failures on the part of the development programs to provide the kind of backup needed to reduce the uncertainty and risk associated with change. Other failures were the result of the inability of economists to grasp the fact that production may have a variety of aims other than the purely quantitative-economic. The failures and difficulties also were in part the expected consequence of a transitional order: it takes time for such shifts in human institutions to occur and, during the period that the change is occurring, the record is marked by confusion and contradiction. At any rate, as development efforts directed at agrarian sectors began to shift toward social objectives of alleviating poverty and improving the bargaining position of indigenous agriculturalists--"people oriented" development--the need for anthropological analyses of the social conditions of production--the "soft" factors--began to be appreciated. Anthropologists have been appearing in increasing numbers in the field of agrarian development. This also means that partnerships are being struck between economists and the anthropologists who find common ground in the empirical work required for better design of development programs.

II. AGRICULTURAL ECONOMICS AND ANTHROPOLOGICAL ECONOMICS

Most of the history of agricultural economics in North America took place in the land grant universities and the U.S. and Canadian Departments of Agriculture. The field represented the coalescence of several interest groups which became active at the turn of the century. George F. Warren of Cornell University was the outstanding figure in the farm management group of scientists in agricultural colleges whose attention shifted from biological sciences to the economic problems of farmers. This group was particularly interested in farm costs and improvement in the economic performance of farmers. Henry C. Taylor of the University of Wisconsin became interested in agricultural issues as a graduate student in economics, and he represented a group of economists and sociologists interested in tenancy, attainment of ownership of land, land use, and conservation. In 1919 the two groups joined to form the American Farm Economic Association, later becoming the American Agricultural Economics Association (Salter, 1967; Case and Williams, 1957).

The activities of departments of agricultural economics in land grant colleges from the beginning included research and extension as well as teaching. Agricultural colleges used county extension agents as links to farmers; county agents were assisted by extension specialists on college faculties, and these in turn kept in close contact with the research of their faculty colleagues; often the same faculty member would do both research and extension as well as some teaching. Through these links, ideas flowed in both directions. Farm problems generated inquiries to extension and these in turn could become applied research problems. In the other direction, research results were disseminated to farmers through the extension service.

At an early point agricultural economists became concerned with policy issues as well as with economic problems of individual farm families. These included the great national issues of farm surpluses, depressed farm prices, incomes, farm tenancy and credit, as well as state and local issues of local taxation and government services, land use zoning, conflicts over land and water use, urban sprawl, pollution, and other environmental problems. After World War II, many agricultural economists became involved with agricultural development in the third world. In all of these issues, agricultural economists were involved in "system maintenance"--not just theory and pure research. That is, they were directly concerned with the welfare of their subjects of research and, on occasion, were involved in efforts of "soft compulsion," i.e., in persuading the subjects to modify their procedures in order to better survive and prosper, for the good of the nation and the agricultural establishment.

Another important influence on the development of
agricultural economics came from formal economics.
John D. Black of Harvard University and Theodore W.
Schultz at the University of Chicago played major
roles in reformulating the interests of agricultural
economists in terms of economic theory and in
promoting increasing attention to economic theory in
graduate studies in agricultural economics.

As a result of these influences agricultural
economics includes persons with varieties of functions
and intellectual approaches. At the practical end of
the spectrum are people with an intimate knowledge of
farming and others who may assist farmers to organize
cooperatives or advise state legislatures on
preservation of farmland; these activities include
problem-solving applied research and an attention to
empirical matters[2]. At the other end of the spectrum
are persons working at the frontiers of economic
theory and econometric methodology.

As a result of the prestigious influence of
economic theory, the availability of computers, and
the increasingly theoretically sophisticated graduate
training of agricultural economists, professional
research publications have become predominantly
quantitative and related to formal theory; they have
tended to neglect social and institutional aspects of
agriculture and the contextual, empirical generalizing
theory appropriate to them. However, intermittent
studies of this kind have continued in agricultural
economics and can be of considerable value to an
anthropologically oriented approach.[1]

There is awareness among many agricultural
economists that analysis of agricultural development
in the third world requires a broader approach and
probably a greater attention to interdisciplinary
design of research problems than has been achieved to
this point. There is appreciation, though not well
defined, that anthropological research would be
relevant to these problems. But at the time of
writing, agricultural economists are largely unaware
of the recent work of anthropological students of
decision making and reciprocal sharing among peasant
agriculturalists[2] --perhaps partly because this work
is new and not widely disseminated.

Anthropology's concern for economic phenomena was
labeled "primitive economics" in the 1920s,with a

number of outstanding ethnologists involved in the effort. Bronislaw Malinowski's studies of the kula exchange system (Malinowski, 1922) and yam production and distribution systems of Melanesian tribes (Malinowski, 1935) were among the outstanding publications--the latter remains the most intensive study of tribal-level subsistence agricultural activities ever made. Richard Thurnwald's (1932) general treatise on primitive economics was an important source of theory, but the field was usually associated in the United States with the name of Melville Herskovits, who published his Economic Life of Primitive Peoples in 1940. The latter book was the first attempt to explore the relevance of ethnological findings for standard neoclassical economic concepts like scarcity and efficiency. Herskovits emphasized the socio-cultural context of economic behavior in tribal societies, and how this departed from the rationalistic and profit-oriented models of economic theory. A different version of this tradition was elaborated in Karl Polanyi's work, developed in anthropological literature by George Dalton and others. Polanyi's studies (e.g., Polanyi, 1957) struck an important historical note that Herskovits had neglected: Polanyi saw economic institutions as an historical phenomenon, a civilizational emergent, which contributed to the revival of cultural evolutionary theories in anthropology in the 1950s.

Malinowski helped to train a number of anthropologists who continued in his tradition of detailed case studies of economic activities among tribal people (e.g., Raymond Firth; Audrey Richards), a tradition that went into the third generation with people like Scarlett Epstein and Richard Salisbury. However, the North American tradition followed Herskovits and the culturalogical approach generally, focusing on ethnographic descriptions of technology and social organizations, and less on the production process as an activity in its own right.

The American tradition of cultural analysis of economic activity received its ultimate theoretical expression in the work of Julian Steward. Economics, for him, represented a "core" of activities which, along with physical resources, helped to shape the direction of cultural effort and social organization. INdeed, the objective of Steward's work was really to shed light on the nature of cultural evolution and

human ecology, rather than economics per se (see
Steward, 1955, for a definitive collection of his
early theoretical papers). Steward's students, like
those of Malinowski, followed in their teacher's
footsteps, performing a series of studies of tribal,
peasant, and, in Puerto Rico, market agricultural
communities (Steward, 1956), but these were concerned
with the social concomitants and consequences of
economic behavior and the use of resources, rather
than with production and management of agricultural
enterprises. Horace Miner's (1949) study of an
American entrepreneurial farming community also
focused on the socio-cultural basis of farming.
Walter Goldschmidt's (1947) study of California
agricultural communities was concerned with problems
of social equity and the social impact of external
control of the economic process. Thus the several
strains of American anthropological economic inquiry
led away from the dominant interest in management,
production, and marketing exhibited by the
professional agricultural economist. It was not until
the 1960s that serious effort was made by
anthropologists to deal with professional economic
concepts and theories; Harold Schneider's introduction
to Economic Man (1974) and the symposium volume he
edited with Edward LeClair (1968) are the milestones.
These works helped to set the stage for a renewed
interest in production and management. Bennett's
(1969-77) earlier study of a Canadian agricultural
region represented this concern: recognizing the
central importance of farming in an entrepreneurial
national economic system, he tended to see
socio-cultural factors as necessary elements in the
managerial process, and how the needs of farmers to
deal with external agencies shaped their thought and
behavior. He, therefore, emphasized that the economic
position of the family farmer required an extension of
economic thinking to the family and domicile--a theme
more completely developed in his book on farm
management as an adaptive process (Bennett 1982a).
This approach, featuring a concern for agricultural
production, has recently become a focus of research by
several anthropologists, notably James Acheson's study
of small-scale New England fishermen (Acheson and
Wilson, 1981) and Christina Gladwin's (an agricultural
economist with anthropological training) study of
small farmers in Florida (Gladwin, 1980).

Much of this recent research focuses on the
decision-making process (as illustrated in the

symposium volume edited by Barlett, 1980b). The subject of research is the thought and behavior of the individual producer, and while milieu factors like social organization and the community are considered, they are visualized as influences on the cognitive process of decision. Bennett's view, on the other hand, is to see the entire process as a social system, and decision more as an outcome of various institutions and events and less as an individual cognitive act. He felt that most decisions of agricultural operators are stretched out over relatively long periods of time, and emerge as vectors of management rather than as discrete behavioral acts. Nevertheless, these newer studies of decision offer an important empirical approach to production from the behavioral standpoint.

Whatever the emphasis, the anthropological approach to agricultural production is <u>not</u> primarily concerned with what LeClair and Schneider in their introduction call "economizing," i.e., seeking the maximum gain with the greatest economy of means. The standard view of the anthropologist is simply that while "economizing" behavior certainly exists, it is not acceptable as a surrogate for all behavior, i.e., that the application of utility theory to noninstrumental forms of behavior is dubious and potentially misleading since it ignores a whole range of motives and social pressures not found in ordinary economic contexts.

On his part, the anthropologist perhaps can be advised to make the most of his empirical contact with the data of real life situations and go easy on theoretical criticism of economics. Some anthropologists struggling with the issues often pitch their arguments on the same lofty plane as economists; i.e., they claim that "economizing" is a "wrong" theory of human behavior, and that their theory of symbolic or affectual causation of behavior is the "right" one. In such arguments, the anthropologists discourage the real need for concentrated empirical study of how economic institutions--especially in the modern world--do in fact come to shape human behavior and motives. The real issue, to which both economists and anthropologists need to pay attention, is that human behavior is multidimensional and multicausational, and that every disciplinary view of this complex phenomenon has grasped some element of the truth.

When the agricultural economist focuses on the way economic forces shape the production and marketing decisions of farmers, he is not, in the usual sense, enunciating a general theory of behavior, but simply functioning in his role as an agent in the general system-maintenance activities of a great social institution. Practical economists seek to help farmers change their product and improve their credit position and, in order to help them do this, it is necessary to teach them the principles of our pervasive market system. Anthropologists need to better understand this practical role of the economist. As the anthropologists working with North American, European, and Oriental farmers become engaged with the development process, this realization comes as a matter of course, and their associations with practical economics and agricultural colleges and agencies help them to understand the dynamics of the larger system. They may, of course, come to reject this system on ideological grounds, but this is another issue entirely.

III. THE SMALL SCALE AGRICULTURAL PRODUCER AS A UNIT OF ANALYSIS

Thus far we have suggested that agricultural economics and anthropological economics concerned with agriculture find their most significant common ground in the study of the producer as an economic agent and as a participant in social systems. Let us discuss this in greater detail.

First, most agricultural production the world over is in the hands of relatively small social units, commonly based on blood and affinal kinship ties, which are assembled into sets of spacial groupings with social and political functions and linkages that we call communities, tribes, districts, neighborhoods, counties, etc. In the course of economic growth and development, often these social and spacial units come under external control and are required to accept institutional forms of organization and interchange-- cooperatives, communes, corporate farms, state farms, etc. These latter forms can modify the older social ties, but the fact remains that perhaps the most successful--economically successful--forms of agricultural production remain in the care of relatively small, kin- and community-based producer units. The reasons for this persisting tendency will be noted later.

Second, these production units--whether tribal, peasant, or farmer--are located on the scene of their productive activity, not at some remove, for the reason that agricultural production is based on physical resources which must be manipulated. This activity is always in some sense labor intensive; that is, regardless of the extent of mechanization, the people engaged in production must be in close contact with resources and must exert themselves on a variety of tasks requiring some physical labor. Thus the majority of agricultural producers the world over are in more intimate contact with nature, and with the human effort that producing requires, than are people engaged in many other economic activities. The historic political resentments of agricultural producers are influenced by their distrust of people and institutions that manipulate resources and products as pure commodities in which labor is not involved. This resentment has been as pronounced in the market agrarian systems of modern North America as it has been for peasant revolutionaries of Europe, Latin America or Asia in past epochs, although the social responses vary.

Third, agricultural producers, no matter how deeply enmeshed in market systems, have some contact with the ideals of self-sufficiency and production for home use. In North America, farm gardens, home canning, and diversion of some stock animals to the home diet remain a significant feature of local economy, despite the basic reliance on a cash income. This feature may, of course, be of minimal importance for economic survival in market agrarian systems, but even in such cases, the symbolic value of the possession of land and labor, the capability to raise one's own food is of great significance. It is a factor which accounts for at least part of the staying power of the family farm when its commercial position may be vulnerable and weak. In the developing world, the security of home production and relative self-sufficiency is a feature that accounts for much of the resistance that peasant producers have shown to agrarian schemes which may weaken this capacity. In many cases this wisdom of the producers has often been shown to exceed that of the planners, when the commercializing schemes have failed to provide adequate markets, prices, credit, or transportation (Galaty, Aronson and Salzman, 1981; Hoben, 1979).

Fourth, agricultural producers of the majority type examined here have a perennial problem of economic scale. This problem is, of course, a function of their involvement in market systems, but these are becoming universal. While some degree of self-sufficiency may continue to characterize producers everywhere, the spread of market agrarian systems is rapid and pervasive, as developing countries become evermore integrated into the world economy. To the extent that such producers do produce for commercial sale, they experience problems of costs, labor, equipment maintenance, and credit. As already noted, developing countries--like our own economy at intervals in the recent past--have found it difficult to supply the small producer with the inputs he needs to function at the levels of production and efficiency he must have in order to achieve his required income, or even to survive. This in turn sets up forces which lead to increases of scale--the purchase of more land or more machinery, and the securing of more bank or government loan money. These moves in turn can increase costs of production, setting up another round of scale increases. While the process of commercialization has some limits and controls, in North America it has led to an accelerated loss of farm units and a steady increase in acreage and capitalization of the remaining firms. The process is associated in many cases with increasing specialization of production, i.e., increasing reliance on a single or a very few cash crops. As these trends develop in the third world, one can expect the same scale problems to appear, and can expect the same economic difficulties and associated political unrest in the rural population.

Fifth, and really a corollary of the foregoing, the relatively small-scale agricultural producer operates in a decision milieu of considerable uncertainty and risk. Whether this is an intolerable situation or not depends on its degree, and also on the adaptive strategies that may have evolved to cope with it. Farmer-ranchers in the North American West, Australia, and similar countries with market agriculture carried on in dryland regions, are used to a much higher level of uncertainty and unpredictability of climate, costs, and prices than those in humid regions. In a culture devoted to security and high levels of consumption, such uncertainty has contributed to outmigration and the turnover of much land to corporate interests. It has also led everywhere in the developed world to producer collective action designed to obtain protection against price fluctuation, gouging, foreclosures, and erratic farm policies, and these movements are appearing as well in the developing countries. John R. Commons, the distinguished founder of "institutional economics," was particularly concerned with such combinations (Commons, 1961, esp. vol. 1).

These remarks have, of course, singled out the entrepreneurial form of agricultural production as the dominant type, and this needs qualification. The cooperative, whether local, sectional, producer-corporative, or government-sponsored, has been reasonably successful in many countries at various levels of market development, as a means to shield the farmer against uncertainty, to help him spread risks, and in general to increase scale at least with reference to the control of input costs or marketing facilities and prices.[3] Agriculture extensively organized in producer and marketing cooperatives, as, for example in Japan, blurs the outline of the entrepreneurial procedure, although it by no means eliminates all of its features. Moreover, if cooperatives become a vehicle of dominant government control, as they have in Egypt, the results can be a rise in costs and a diminishing of production incentives for many reasons. Egypt is now experimenting with a partial return to a freer entrepreneurial situation both at the level of farmer decisions and in the production of vital inputs like fertilizer.

The foregoing is a description of the main structural features of the relatively small scale mode of agricultural production. It must be supplemented by acknowledgment of the fact that, structural similarities aside, the world's farmers and peasants are also bearers of cultural styles and traditions of great variety and distinctiveness. While they all share something by virtue of the structural imperatives and the way these have created problems for producers from the Bronze Age to the present, the symbolic content of thought and behavior and the styles of adaptation differ considerably. To generalize broadly, the agricultural economist is dominantly concerned with structure; the anthropologist has, at least until recently, been mainly preoccupied with style and content.

Perhaps the key variable is the degree of exposure to market systems. The economist tends to assume that market systems are pervasive and can influence everyone equally and at the same rate; the anthropologist can correct this assumption. The anthropologist tends to overvalue cultural style and symbol and assume it has causal significance over and above structural imperatives; here the economist can help him see the woods for the trees.

Lost somewhere in the disciplinary specializations and the theoretical debates is the important problem of whether the persistence of small-scale production units, usually under the control of kin, on a worldwide basis is simply the result of historical lag, or whether there are important functionalities in this system which make it relatively resistant to takeover by larger organizations. There is no definite answer to this question at the moment. Most certainly some of the features of the entrepreneurial system described previously offer persuasive arguments for its functionality despite its problems of scale. The important symbolic values of country life and control of land and water, the opportunity of being one's own boss regardless of how much attention must be paid to external forces, are all important. Even more important is the fact that the symbolic satisfactions help to provide incentive and motivation to work hard and take risks at levels unacceptable to urban workers. This willingness to furnish labor and attentiveness at relatively low personal returns may well be the key factor in the persistence of small scale agricultural production.

IV. THE SMALL SCALE AGRICULTURAL PRODUCER: AN INTRODUCTION TO MODELS OF ANALYSIS

In the preceding section we have proposed that the most significant common subject matter for both agricultural economists and economic anthropologists--at least in the context of their collaboration for research and practical effort--is the relatively small scale entrepreneurial production unit wherever this may be found. The general type described is broadly cross-cultural in its structure, and this creates a number of similarities in resource allocation; decision making, the handling of uncertainty and risk, and the relationships of the producer and his community to the external forces of national governments and economic markets. Beyond these comparabilities, there are many differences in cultural style. Moreover, these stylistic differences can result in modifications of the behavioral patterns produced by structural forces.

This suggests that, by and large, the economist can provide detailed information on the structural comparabilities, while the anthropologist can furnish detailed accounts of how cultural styles and social organizational peculiarities influence adaptive responses to these forces.

These conclusions, however appropriate, do not dispose of the problem of disciplinary differences in basic concepts and approaches to the common subject matter. That is, neither anthropology nor economics starts from scratch; both are heirs to intellectual styles and traditions of considerable historical depth, and these must be coped with. Both disciplines follow, in large part, the tenets of scientific method and objective analysis of data objectively gathered. Yet, in the social realm, it is not possible to attain total neutrality or objectivity for many reasons, not the least of which is the intellectual tradition and rhetoric of the discipline itself.

Currently most scholarly fields in the social science mode accept the notion of a model as the most useful way of conceptualizing basic subject matter and processes of function and change. Such models can be at many levels of abstraction and can contain varying amounts of traditional disciplinary content and language. We shall attempt in this section to discuss the intellectual basis of potential models of the small agricultural production unit. The section is an introduction to more detailed treatment of the models in the two sections to follow.

First, some general considerations. Most obvious is the fact that the small family farm--this is one familiar term for the "relatively small-scale kin-based agricultural producer"--is not equivalent to large corporations, industrial plants, or plantations. That is, its economics as well as its social life differ from these other instrumental entities in many significant ways. Small family farms are owned or rented by their producers, not by stockholders, although for convenience many family farms in recent years have used the corporate form of organization.

213

However, in such cases most of the stock is held within the matrix of kin or local control, and the use of the corporate form does not materially modify the basic features of the family farm as described in the previous section. The same may hold for the close relation of family farms to cooperatives and other institutions of joint action. Such accommodation may belong more properly in the domain of empirical analysis of adaptive strategies and does not destroy the utility of the basic models.

In any case, the fact that the small farm is not equivalent to larger, hierarchical, and more diffuse economic organizations means that the tools for economic analysis as well as the theories that were developed to assist in the understanding of the larger forms are less appropriate for the description of the small farm unit. This issue, of course, is a familiar one in anthropological economics. Here we are making a simple empirical point, really: that the small family farm is a distinct class of phenomena and should be treated as such, at least for most or many research purposes.

However, while distinct from large corporations, from the analytical perspective of agricultural economists the small farm is a firm--or at least a relatively small firm with distinct problems of information gathering and uncertainty. That is, when the economist views a small family farm, he is likely to perceive a firm rather than an interacting social group. This concern for the firm is derived from the traditions of the economic discipline, which is concerned primarily with a particular sector of behavior--on the whole, the sector labeled "economizing" by LeClair and Schneider. But there is more. Economizing, in a fully developed market economy, is expected to take place in a particular organization which is beholden to the laws and rules of the market economy and its legislative dimensions. Hence, the firm is taken as the central organizational format. This means that farmers are, for the purposes of the standard agricultural economics model, businessmen, or at least members of firms. And of course they are--at least with respect to one role or aspect of their activities.

The study by economists of the activities of firms is generally called microeconomics (Henderson and Quandt, 1971). It concerns the way firms survive by coping with the economic forces of their time: how they get capital, cover costs, attain efficient standards of performance, and so on. All of these are perfectly valid and legitimate topics, and their analysis is nothing more than a recognition that microsocial agents are required to perform at certain levels and styles by the larger institutional and organizational imperatives of developed economies. There are no theoretical arguments here; it is simply a matter of applying familiar measuring rods to economic performance and observing who stays, who goes.

The study by anthropologists of the family farm (and all approximations and simulations thereof) has been accomplished without any one major model like the firm. As a matter of fact, the relative recency of anthropological interest in the agricultural market and production process has prevented the emergence of any dominant approach or model. There are, as we have already suggested, several models: the kinship or social-organizational, the ecological or econological, the behavioral or decision making, and the symbolic-ceremonial. Arguments range among anthropologists themselves on this question of whether or not to standardize approaches. However, among those anthropologists concerned with production, and especially those concerned with agriculture in North America, Europe, and East Asia, there may be a growing consensus on a general approach which is sketched out in the last section of this paper.

If one conceptualizes the family farm as a firm, and others model it as a kin group or cultural system, there is really very little possibility of collaborative research, because the categories of data collection are fundamentally different and reflect different empirical interests and, worse, very different disciplinary theories of behavior. One way out is to attempt to combine the different sets of data and interests and attempt to discover some sort of interaction or causal feedback. This approach recognizes that the aim of understanding the entity as a functioning system is not served by simply adding up different facts, but rather by attempting to view these facts in a concurrent, interacting system model. Such a concurrent-interactive model provides concrete hypotheses about interrelations of phenomena. These are very abstract terms, however. More important is the conception of just how the system works. We

215

believe it works as all social systems work: ultimately by individual decisions and actions, based on available information. That is, the model ultimately must be based on behavior and not on abstractions like "culture" or "maximization." One must be concerned over goals, needs, decisions, compromises, constraints, and opportunities. Such behavioral vectors are important because we are dealing, on the whole, with an _instrumental_ system--not an aesthetic or religious one. Production is the main goal--production to stay alive, launch a family, maintain a household, make profits, improve technology, and so on.

What is ideally needed, then, is a model which combines both the economic and the social components of the farm enterprise and its social group, while providing some way of transforming the data from one part of the system to the other. One way to do this is to view the individual members of the farm household as people who make decisions and act in both economic and social contexts; e.g., when it is necessary to invest in new machines, this must be weighed against the cost of a college education for the successor son. The decision-maker must play two roles here: that of a business manager and that of a father. The decisions are not ready-made, because, depending on the strength of current economic and social forces, certain decisions may be more predictable than others. It should be the task of both the economist and the anthropologist as behavioral scientists to work together to assess the strength of these forces and to try to understand the direction of outcome, and how that direction may change with changing social, economic, and political factors.

To summarize: We have said that the interface between agricultural economics and anthropology is an empirical, not a theoretical one; or rather, that theoretical arguments often reinforce the tendencies of the two disciplines to head in different directions. The empirical target is a relatively small production unit which is operated by a consuming labor force obtaining part of its sustenance from activities associated with production. The labor is generally derived from family members, relatives, neighbors, and hired employees. The relatively low cost of the labor is one reason why the entity has persisted in the face of problems of scale that might have rendered a small city business undertaking unviable. Characteristically, returns to labor on the part of the family and kin participating are relatively low, but this is a trade-off for the advantages of self-direction and country living. The social aspects of the system are characterized by a pressure toward cooperation and collaboration on important tasks within the unit, and also by a mixture of roles and perspectives, so that decision making is a complex process of compromise and trade-off. Strategies designed to cope with relatively high uncertainty and risk must be developed in situ, although information inputs from farm extension services--now increasing rapidly in developing countries as well--can assist in this process.

V. THE MICROECONOMICS OF THE FARM FIRM AND THE "FARMING NICHE"

A. Introduction

It is time now to describe some parameters of the standard economic model of entrepreneurial production, with special reference to farming. This is not a formal or mathematical model, but a discussion of the basic concepts used by agricultural economists for the construction of a quantitative model. We do not do the latter because it would be necessary to have more specific types of production in mind. For example, important qualifications of the model would be needed for farming in different parts of North America, where conditions of uncertainty and risk vary greatly.

This microeconomic prolegomenon also is not, of course, the synthetic model we advocated in the closing paragraphs of the last section, though it takes some modest steps in that direction. The task of constructing a synthetic model, in which economic and social elements can be transposed, is for the future; we can only suggest some of its properties in this and the following section. It should be noted that an attempt at a more detailed, book-length modeling of the microeconomics of the small firm has been presented by economist James A. Wilson of the University of Maine, supplemented by anthropological considerations by James M. Acheson, of the same institution (Acheson and Wilson, 1981). The project concerned small New England fishermen, however, and not farming. There is no doubt that many of the factors and processes discussed in our paper are echoed in the Wilson and Acheson effort, and an interesting task for the future would be to examine the differences and similarities of small-scale fishing and agriculture. This type of effort, with empirical rather than theoretical relevance as the major objective, is precisely the kind of project the present authors recommend as one frontier of collaboration between economists and anthropologists.

The microeconomic mode of analysis is in essence an attempt at systematic explanation of the interdependencies and constraints created by the way markets serve to integrate the decisions of the managers of firms and of consumers, workers, and investors. We assume that a market economy is a collection of firms and households. Households are defined as consuming units and the homes of workers and owners of capital and resources needed for production. The production task itself is organized by firms that hire workers from the households in exchange for income payments (an exchange taking place in factor markets), and then utilize these resources to produce goods and commodities which the households purchase from the firms. By contrast, the small farm is itself a combination of a household and a firm in the same framework. In this small, kin-controlled, agricultural firm, the household provides labor to and receives cash income and food-in-kind from its own firm, so to speak, without the interventions of markets. However, farm households also buy goods from outside firms both for consumption purposes a well as for various production needs.

B. Microeconomic Analysis of Firm and Household Behavior

For the purposes of building their theory, economists assume that firms hire all the factors of production from households; under this assumption only the entrepreneur himself is self-employed, and all production is for the market and not for subsistence. Such a situation could be achieved in the real world if households owned all the factory buildings, machines, and other productive facilities, and the firms had to rent or hire them on short-term contracts. In actual fact, households provide financial capital to firms as investors and creditors, through stocks, bonds, and other credit instruments, and they may be linked to production firms either directly or through financial institutions. The firms in turn use the capital obtained to acquire buildings and machines and to carry inventory. Thus, in analyzing the dependence of firms on factor markets through which resources are secured from the households, economists distinguish between the "short run" in which firms need only to hire workers and maintain their inventories of raw materials and intermediate products, and the "long run" in which firms need to both physically replace their durable capital goods and refinance their credits and investments. (For the purpose of this discussion we will not concern ourselves with the fact that stock investments do not have to be refinanced and that depreciation reserves belong to firms and not to households.) The point is that from the perspective of microeconomic analysis, <u>the firm and its entrepreneur do not own anything; the firm organizes production with resources it has to obtain at market prices.</u>

This assumption, of course, is often difficult for noneconomists to grasp. The anthropologist, doing field work with small farms and their managers, assumes offhand that these units do in fact "own" their land, buildings, machines, etc. While this may be correct in a legal sense--they have "title" to them--in an economic sense these facilities have been purchased from suppliers, and in part with funds derived from banks, government loan programs, and other sources which charge a price, e.g., interest, for the resources. In contemporary farming, it is commonly found that farmers are often in the position of renters rather than owners. They may be operating on the basis of a rotating indebtedness so that their "ownership" of the resources is really shared with other agencies of the market system. In contract farming, for example, the entrepreneur accepts money and sometimes equipment with which to produce a crop for a company, and in this sense he is operating in a manner economically identical to a small manufacturer accepting subcontracts for parts from a larger company. With the increasing price of agricultural land, many farmers have found it makes more sense financially simply to rent the land from people who have title to it than to attempt to buy it outright. A large proportion of Western cattle ranching in North America is done on government land that is made available on the basis of grazing fees. Such patterns tend to make the agricultural system conform, at least in part, to the microeconomics model of the production system, rather than to the model of the isolated, wholly owned, and self-financing pioneer or tribal establishment. This is a worldwide trend.

Given these assumptions, and the economic realities, the firm is a vulnerable enterprise constrained by competitive pressures. These pressures include prices generated in markets in which the firm buys inputs and raw materials and sells its products, as well as potential entry of new firms into industries in which existing firms are making above-normal profits. ("Normal profits" are defined as returns to entrepreneurship just sufficient to attract the entrepreneurial effort to organize a firm.) With prices generated by markets, survival of a firm depends on organizing production in such a manner that income will cover costs and yield normal profit; inability to cover costs means that the firm cannot continue hiring factors of production and thus cannot continue producing. Under long-term competitive conditions, all firms need to be as efficient as possible. If this is not the case, the most efficient firms will be earning extra profits, and this will attract new firms to the industry, increasing production and lowering product prices. The end result would be the survival of those firms with the most efficient production, the elimination of other firms, and price levels generating normal profits only for the efficient firms.

The economists use the profit-maximization assumption along with assumptions about household behavior to trace results of interactions operating through markets. The conclusion they reach is that firms have no choice if they are to survive: competitive pressures force them to be efficient. Under such competitive pressures, profit maximization yields only "normal" profits; anything less than profit maximization means sustaining losses and bankruptcy.

It should be clear from the above that profit maximization is used here not as a theory of human behavior, but simply as an analysis of conditions for survival. That is, if the processes move as defined, then those firms that survive will be those that have operated as efficiently as possible, i.e., have sought out the profits needed to survive. The economist, of course, is fully aware that the conditions that affect firm survival are constantly changing as the result of technological advances, inflation, and other forces. Such changes may create opportunities for increased efficiency and higher profits while at the same time making previous technologies uneconomic. Some firms are likely to utilize these opportunities for competitive advantage, but, in turn, their innovation attracts new firms, increases production, and lowers prices consistent with increases in efficiency. Such innovations, through competitive market pressures, are sufficient to compel all other firms to adopt the new strategies. In the case of the other firms, however, the motive is to survive in the presence of changed prices rather than to increase profits.

Once again, we see that profit maximization, when visualized in terms of its competitive consequences in a market system, is not a <u>motive</u> in the behavior of entrepreneurs or firms, but is a set of conditions that firms need to observe in order to survive; they need to maintain a competitive position--or to be fiscally solvent. Actually, entrepreneurial activity includes attention to many functions utilizing many skills: managing personnel, community relations, applying engineering, evaluating market opportunities, maintaining contacts with suppliers and buyers, providing technical advice and services to users of the firm's products, etc. All kinds of motives arise in the context of carrying out these activities, depending on technical, economic, or interpersonal problems that arise. However, one of the tasks of top management in all firms is to make sure that the net result of all of these activities is fiscal solvency of the firm.[4]

The market interactions described above are of the long-run mode, and take place in the presence of competitive markets. But conclusions might differ if we look at short-run phenomena, and if we considered that competitive forces were more limited, allowing more discretion to decision-making units. Also, attention would need to be paid to household behavior. Such considerations are particularly relevant for small scale farming.

Without entering into the many complications, several modifications of the argument are particularly relevant. <u>Short-term</u> is defined primarily to mean that firms operate with capital assets acquired sometime in the past, but are not fully depreciated and are still usable. In effect that means that the

array of firms differ in the kind of equipment they
use and that therefore they differ in their
efficiency. Survival (fiscal solvency) in the short
run requires that only currently variable costs be
covered by receipts, and not necessarily the costs of
depreciation. Or, put differently, it takes time for
competitive pressures to force firms into bankruptcy
and out of the industry.

Large firms, whose very size as well as
competitive policies create barriers to entry of new
firms, gain considerable autonomy though not complete
immunity from market forces. Such firms represent
great aggregations of power in relation to workers,
suppliers, retail dealers, financial institutions, and
government agencies managing economic policy.
Managers of these firms are in control of large
investable funds which give them options in research
and development strategies, development of new lines
of activity, access to new markets, etc. Market
constraints on freedom of action can appear from
various directions, such as the emergence of
substitute products, the entry of large firms into the
sphere from other industries, and changes in demand.

In particular, the model needs to take account of
the impact of market conditions on self-employed
persons, a condition characteristic of family-farm
agriculture. For a farmer, a decreased margin between
gross income and cost does not mean unemploying
himself, but accepting lower income from his farm.
Such a reduction in income may lead him to consider
alternatives, but availing himself of alternative
employment means considering not only what he could
earn elsewhere, but also what he could obtain from
renting or selling his farm, from selling livestock
and machinery inventory. He will also consider
possible changes in social status and working
conditions attendant on a shift to wage or salary
employment, travel to work, and change of residence
("opportunity costs"). For many farmers it is easier
to shift to part-time farming than to completely move
out of agriculture. Especially for older farmers,
alternative employment options and costs of
disinvestment may be less attractive than remaining in
farming at levels of income lower than available
elsewhere in the economy. In many cases the shift is
made by the younger generation of farm people who will
not remain in farming if they do not have the
prospects of entering into or building up a farm

enterprise capable of generating attractive incomes.
This is the economic underpinning of the sociological
process of succession of sons to family-farm headship.
Thus, competitive pressures generated through markets
leave greater leeway for enterprises to survive than
would follow from strict application of the
maximization criterion to the decision-making behavior
of participants in market transactions.

At this point in the discussion we will describe
the way microeconomic analysis treats the behavior of
household members. In an earlier section we noted
that utility-maximization theory is often used to
describe the behavior of households as consumers, a
practice that raises hackles among social scientists
who prefer to use nonquantitative motivation theory to
explain various actions. However, as in the
profit-maximization issue, economic analysis is really
quite specific and limited: it simply assumes that
consumers make choices in using their income for
expenditures on different goods and services as well
as for savings. Utility maximization means that the
actual or observed pattern of consumption is preferred
to other combinations of goods that could have been
purchased with the same income. From these
assumptions are derived the indifference curves and
from these, in turn, the demand curves for the
products that the firms produce.

With respect to labor and employment, microeconomic theory generally uses income maximization as its
prime analytical tool. Maximization of income by
workers implies mobility to more remunerative
employment opportunities in different firms. Movement
would theoretically continue until wages would be
equalized throughout the labor market for workers with
the same level of skills. Movement for some workers
affects wages for all, given the additional condition
that firms compete for workers. The importance of
these assumptions is that they provide a basis for
deriving supply curves of labor. Similar arguments
are used to obtain supply curves for the other factors
of production: capital and natural resources.

The economists need the various behavioral
assumptions to derive the demand and supply curves
that generate market prices, which in turn create the
competitive pressures on the firms. These pressures
come from product and factor markets. In the product
markets, demand curves originate from consumer

behavior and supply curves from the behavior of firms. In the factor markets, the firms are the demanders, while supplies come from workers and households as owners of the factors of production.

While demand and supply curves are generated from assumptions about human behavior that often make other social scientists uncomfortable, their meaning can be stated more directly. Thus, in the product markets, the negatively sloping demand schedule states that any lower prices would attract consumers to divert their income toward purchasing this commodity rather than other commodities, while the positively sloping supply schedule indicates that only high prices would make it possible for firms to produce more by bidding away factors of production from other industries. In the factor markets, the negatively sloping demand schedule states that firms could produce and sell more products only if prices of factors or production were lower; the positively sloping supply schedule reflects the higher factor payments needed to shift workers and other resources from other industries, which are able to resist such shifts because their product prices would rise and they could afford to pay the higher prices for factors of production if their production were to increase.

All of the above statements can be reduced to the economist's concept of opportunity cost. From the consumer point of view, the opportunity cost of buying an automobile is the foregone opportunity of purchasing an equivalent value of alternative products. From the producer point of view, the opportunity cost of producing wheat is the foregone production of other products which could have been obtained had the necessary land, labor, and other resources not been diverted to wheat production. Thus the analytical apparatus of the economist is a way of showing how competition and mobility of resources compel the complex, interdependent market economy to honor opportunity costs in using factors of production to satisfy consumer wants.

But there is another implication in this analytical approach. The essence of a market economy is indeed the individualism of consumers, workers, and entrepreneurs making independent decisions. The other side of the coin is that, under competitive conditions, all these actors become helpless individual pawns of their own mass decisions.

Consumers, as a mass, get the products they want; if they were to change their buying patterns, resources would be reallocated and the product mix of the economy would change. But as individual consumers face the prices generated by their mass behavior, firms as described above are narrowly constrained by product and factors prices, and resource owners face factor prices and changing employment opportunities, again as generated by the mass behavior of households. Analytically, it turns out that human behavior translated into market pressures is only a means whereby the factor endowment of the economy and the available technologies interact with consumer choices to generate the equilibrium output of the economy. Only consumer behavior constitutes significant decision making (at least in the sense that economists take wants as given and do not inquire into their formation). All other human behavior is influenced by competitive pressures to keep the wheels of the economy turning.

C. Microeconomics and Behavior: Economic
Opportunities as Niches

This kind of analysis is significant in increasing our understanding of the economic results of individualization and interdependence in modern market societies. These, however, are insights about the restraints on and opportunities for human behavior, rather than about behavior as an autonomous process. These opportunities and restraints could be thought of as economic niches: firms, jobs, investment opportunities. Economic analysis is most relevant for explaining the number of such niches in various industries, the level of income generated by them, and the reasons why such niches are increasing or decreasing.[5]

This conception of "niches" is particularly useful, since it makes it possible to separate the economic analysis of niche creation from the application of other social science approaches to the study of human behavior with respect to niches. So viewed, human behavior includes movement between niches as well as varieties of behavior within a niche. This conceptualization of economic analysis as dealing with niche creation--an instructional or social process--may free the study of human behavior from controversies about behavioral assumptions made primarily for the sake of constructing economic theory.

D. Opportunities to Farm and Behavior of Farm
    Families

The following illustration describes how technological change modified the niches of workers in lettuce harvest for the early 1960s. It compares machine harvest with two nonmechanized approaches (the shed-pack system and the field-pack system) utilizing the work of Mexican braceros:

Agricultural engineers give $35,000 as a rough estimate of the original cost on the first two-row lettuce harvesters now under development. This price would include service and repairs for the first year while the "bugs" were being worked out of the machine. If we assume that the machine is completely depreciated in three years, one year's depreciation would be $11,667. Interest on the average value of the investment would be $875 per year using five percent as the interest rate. Therefore, fixed costs total $12,542 per year. Repairs may be neglected because they are included in the purchase price. Operating costs for the machine would be similar to those of the field trucks and drivers necessary under the other system.

It is estimated that this two-row machine will cut 400 cartons of lettuce per hour if a 50 percent cut is available. This cutting rate would require about 22 men cutting under the shed-pack system and about 40 men cutting and trimming under the field-pack system. If cutters can be hired for one dollar per hour the shed-pack system would cost $22 per hour for cutter labor alone. In addition, foremen and pusher labor would be required. A harvesting machine would have to work only 570 hours per year to reduce its fixed cost to $22 per hour. Operating costs may be neglected since they are comparable to the operating costs of the trucks and conveyers. At eight hours per day, 570 hours is only 71 days work per year. If the machine could be kept at work for 300 eight-hour days, the comparable cost is only $5.22 per hour.

Obviously tremendous savings are possible even if the price of labor is not higher than $1.00 per hour--the present guaranteed wage for the Mexican Nationals. Further, no camp costs nor compliance with government regulations are necessary with the machines. The conclusion is obvious. Machines will replace cutter labor as soon as the machines become available whether braceros are available or not. (Padfield and Martin, 1965:122-23)**

The quotation clearly, though not explicitly, assumes causation through competitive pressures. It anticipates that at least some farms will be attracted by the economies of machine harvesting, and that their attempts to market more lettuce at a lower price will bring price pressure on other lettuce-growing farms to adopt machine harvesting or shift to other crops. Adoption in turn will decrease the number of harvest jobs for seasonal workers.

Throughout U.S. agriculture the structure of a farm as a niche in terms of the amount of combined labor, land, and various forms of capital changed gradually as tractors replaced horses, and in turn as larger tractors replaced smaller ones. Tractors increased the capacity of the farm family to operate more land, and average size of the farm increased. In terms of agriculture as a whole, tractor mechanization was a substitution of capital for labor, and total employment in agriculture and the number of farms decreased. But the technological change had an underlying economic logic: the greater productivity of farm labor and higher farm incomes that it created were consistent with rising levels of income in the rest of the economy; if technology to increase labor productivity in agriculture were not available, farm product prices would have had to increase to achieve increases in incomes of farmers.

Tractor adoption affected almost all farms in North American agriculture, and was a major factor in a decrease in the number of farms, from a peak of almost 7 million in the United States in the mid-1930s to 2.7 million in 1978, and a corresponding increase in the average size of farms. Much more drastic changes occurred in some specific types of farming. Thus the making of cheese and butter shifted from farms to off-farm processing plants and disappeared as a farm activity by the 1930s. A more recent rapid change occurred in the production of eggs and poultry. As recently as 1950, three-quarters of all U.S. farms had flocks of chickens, mostly small in number. By 1970 chickens were found on only fifteen percent of U.S. farms, and only 5,000 of these farms, with over 20,000 laying hens each and constituting only one percent of all farms with chickens, accounted for over fifty percent of the production of eggs (Schertz, et al. 1979:155). This change in egg production involved changes in technology, in market channels, in specialization in farm production, in regional location, and in autonomy of farmer decision making. The farm chicken flock was typically a sideline enterprise of the farm housewife, utilizing in part feeds and scraps produced on the farm, with surplus production marketed directly by the farm family or sold through various local buyers and assembled for distribution in consuming centers. The shift to large scale egg-and-broiler production was based on the greatly improved efficiency of converting feed into meat and eggs that could be obtained by a technological package of improved poultry breeds, appropriate feed mixes, and measures for control of disease in confined housing. To achieve these innovations, feed and other companies contracted with poultry farmers to produce eggs or meat according to specifications, with farmers obligated to purchase feeds and medicines from and sell broilers or eggs to the contracting company.

The above illustrations describe changes in farms as economic niches. Mechanization of lettuce harvesting changes the number of hired workers per farm. Introduction of tractors changed the size of farms in all U.S. agricultural regions and increased cash expenditures for machinery, fuel, and repair. The disappearance of farm production of cheese and butter released family labor for other activities and changed market outlets for milk. The revolution in egg-and-poultry production removed that enterprise from most farms, created a specialized type of farming for a small number of farmers, and changed both market outlets and farmer relations to such outlets.

If we now turn attention to the behavior of people interacting with the changing niches in farming, we will find the market-created constraints and opportunities, but also many other patterns of behavior. For one thing, the life histories of people encompass movement between farming niches and other

228

economic opportunities, sometimes for economic reasons such as low farm prices or attractive nonfarm jobs, or for noneconomic reasons as accidents or ill health, divorce, death of family members, or personal preferences for occupations or ways of life. Other behavior is directly concerned with survival and success in the changing farm niche. For example, the introduction of tractors requires investment in their purchase and levels of production high enough to cover costs of depreciation and eventual replacement. But there are various ways of accomplishing this task, such as the riskier approach of borrowing to purchase machinery, borrowing to buy land, and repaying the resulting debts from increased production, or the risk-avoiding way of belt-tightening to save out of current income and expand as savings allow. These and yet other alternatives depend not only on general economic conditions and the financial position of individual farmers, but also on personal and social conditions such as patterns of family assistance, age of farmer and stage of family life cycle, changing role of women in the household, and the personalities of the members of the farm family (all topics of anthropological concern).

Because of their close interaction with farmers, agricultural economists have conducted considerable research dealing with behavior of farm people in coping with changing conditions. Some of this research was concerned with evaluation of alternatives in order to assist farmers in making their decisions; in such cases, research was often followed up with extension publications. Other investigations attempted to analyze how farmers actually adjusted to change. In the latter, economists would typically analyze average behavior with respect to several conditioning variables, both economic and noneconomic. A typical example is a study of capital accumulation of a group of Colorado tenant farmers. A regression analysis measured the dollar amount of capital accumulation in relation to such economic variables as number of livestock, size of farm, crop yields, economic conditions during the period each farmer had operated his farm, the amount of beginning capital, and the type of lease under which the farm was rented. The following noneconomic variables were also considered: the number of years the respondent was a farm operator, his age and education. The first four of the six economic variables and the first of the three noneconomic variables were significantly related to capital accumulation (Crecink, 1956:39-51).

Such studies, concerned with average or typical behavior, are informative about what the farmer did, but not usually about how decisions were made nor about the struggles to survive and to seize opportunities. A fuller understanding of the processes of change and the social and cultural content of coping with changing circumstances can be gained with the assistance of other social sciences, including such anthropological approaches as adaptive strategies and management styles, which are discussed in the next section.

Agricultural economists have not confined themselves to issues that could be analyzed using the concepts of maximization. For example, in the context of working with problems of farmers and with such policy issues as increased rate of tenancy, agricultural economists have undertaken to study the so-called agricultural ladder (Spillman, 1919). As originally formulated, the agricultural ladder is a conception that a farmer typically progresses through the stages of being an unpaid worker on the home farm, a paid hired worker, a tenant, and finally an owner-operator. This conception can be linked to anthropological and sociological studies of family structure and life cycles of individuals, issues that are also mentioned in the next section.

The agricultural ladder is also important in analyzing a farm as an economic niche. From a microeconomic perspective, a farm is a combination of land, labor, buildings, machinery, livestock, and operating expenses. But these factors of production have to be brought together under the control of the farm family by purchase, rental, credit, or assistance from the extended family, in other words, by a combination of own and outside resources. The traditional agricultural ladder reflects the methods for achieving control over resources at different stages of the life cycle of farmers. Young people who lack ownership of financial or physical assets earn income by working for others; savings from such work, as well as family assistance and credit, are used to acquire machinery which makes it possible to rent a farm; and, later still, an even larger accumulation of savings and access to credit can allow the purchase of a farm. The ladder can also accommodate retirement, whereby a farmer retires by becoming a landlord with an income obtained from the ownership of land rather than from labor.

Thus the agricultural ladder can be the means of accomplishing the transmission of farm operatorship between generations, with the older generation of farmers acting as employers and landlords, and the younger, as workers and tenants. The ladder can take many alternate forms depending on whether the resources to younger people are provided primarily within or outside of the extended family, whether nonfarmers are actively competing with farmers for the ownership of farmland; movement up the ladder can be slowed up under adverse economic conditions, etc.

A final implication of this discussion is that farm families as individual units must accommodate to changing economic conditions as given to them by market forces if they want to survive in farming. Attempts to modify the dictates of the market can be obtainable only by group activity or political action, and then only within limits. Cooperatives, government-sponsored credit programs, price-support legislation are examples of what farmers have achieved by organized efforts. These modify the alternatives open to farm families, but do not fully remove restraints originating from market forces. In this context economic analysis becomes relevant in understanding intended and unintended consequences of programs and policies.

VI.   THE ANTHROPOLOGICAL APPROACH TO FARM FAMILY,
      FIRM, AND PRODUCTION PROCESS

We turn now to an examination of the anthropological approach to the small entrepreneurial farm. As in the microeconomics section, we do not construct a formal model, but rather describe the conditions of such construction and important dimensions of the model. This is not equivalent to the ideal "synthetic" model in which data and concepts can be transformed, but we believe that some of the parameters of such a model may be visible here.

We shall deal with four major topics: 1) the influence of the macroeconomic system on the microsocial base of farming; 2) the nature of adaptive coping with respect to these influences; 3) the nature of management behavior of "style" of the farm operator and how this emerges from the socioeconomic matrix of the farming occupation; and 4) the interaction and conflict of cycles of the farm family or household, and the economic cycles of the economy and the firm.

A.   Macrosystems and Microsystems

Perhaps the most important social change in modern national societies is the breakdown of local isolation, self-sufficiency, and the freedom of people to make decisions based solely on personal, familial, or community interests. This process in the agrarian field can be viewed from three perspectives: first, as a set of constraints on behavior which tend to erase local cultural and behavioral styles of management of society and enterprise, and make them conform to universal patterns. Second, the process can be seen as a set of opportunities for local agriculturalists to make a living and even improve their lot. Third, these developments can be viewed as a political process of exploitation or oppression of the many by national and international economic elites.

The first of these views is held by ethnologists who regret the passing of the distinctive cultures of tribal and peasant peoples, or even of the local flavor of regional styles in a country like the United States. The second is the perspective of the development specialist who seeks to improve the lot of rural populations in a world of change. The third is the view of leftist intellectuals who consider that the development process is in effect a continuation of colonialism and imperialism.

The anthropologist's view of these processes of change should be sensitive to all possibilities, although special difficulties arise when particular ideological points are introduced. Regardless of one's ideological pessimism or optimism, the incorporation of local communities into larger frames of reference is a fact, and must be dealt with on its own terms. Rural populations everywhere are learning that they no longer can enjoy complete self-determination or subsistence. Although some may choose to move toward revolt, the majority accept a mixed strategy in which they seek to exploit opportunities, as well as develop forms of resistance and manipulation to mitigate the perceived ill effects of incorporation. This process needs understanding and exploration; the anthropological analysis of modernization and agrarian change has already made salient contributions.[6]

In the context of this paper, the key issue is the commercialization of the farm or herding production unit. Its activities must be devoted increasingly to production for the market, and this has meant less emphasis on production standards based on a mix of subsistence and symbolic components designed to further a social system. This is not only true for third world situations, but also for transition periods faced by relatively isolated family ranches in the North American West when they become vertically-integrated livestock producing units for supermarket chains and packing companies. As commercialization proceeds, cultural changes do likewise, although every agricultural community manages to preserve or synthesize many of its traditional values and activities with the externally oriented modes of economic function.

B. Adaptation and Coping

With these cultural and behavioral processes we engage the heart of the anthropological model of small scale agricultural production in the contemporary world. This sphere of analysis focuses on what may be the most salient contributions of the anthropologist to agricultural effort; it is the domain in which we may discover what difference the anthropological approach can make in the economic study of farming.

The concept of adaptation is central (Bennett, 1976; 1982a, Chapt. 1): it refers to the way people respond to both constraints and opportunities in order to survive in a particular physical and socioeconomic environment. Adaptation can mean, among other things, departure, flight, ingenuity, innovation, conformity, or playing it safe. All of these are behavioral vectors of management or the conduct of the enterprise through any period of time. The farther one descends into the community and into individual firms and their personnel, the more variation in adaptive style is found. Aggregated economic statistics tend to average out these approaches; the economist relies on this patterning in order to make his generalizations. However, these adaptive patterns of behavior frequently develop rapidly and divergently, and the economist may need studies of local innovations and of departures from the norm. This is particularly the case in developing countries, where the agrarian system is still in process of change and farmers are in the midst of a stage of adaptation and adjustment prior to full acceptance of market mechanisms and commercial production.

Studies of adaptive strategies at the microsocial level are also relevant for special programs designed to assist farmers to finance expansion and improvement of management techniques, organize cooperatives, participate in marketing schemes, or shift to new crops. Frequently these programs have failed or have achieved unexpected results due to the lack of information available to the specialist on how production is geared to distinctive patterns of social and economic behavior. Anthropological studies of pastoralist livestock producers in Africa in recent years have revealed the causes of failure of many programs designed to convert pastoralists to commercial ranching and other forms of livestock production for domestic and export markets--a matter of considerable importance in many countries with a need for increased protein supplies and export earnings. These studies show that the ecology of transient pastoralism requires a different animal sex ratio and use of forage than is required for commercial beef production. Equally significant are studies of the management techniques for raising and owning animals that rely on distributing animals through networks of herd owners as a way of coping with variable climatic and pasture resources--all techniques resistant to Western-type commercial ranching regimes. On the basis of these studies of micro-level strategies, foreign aid agencies engaged in livestock projects have been in the process of revising the scope and format of programs to deal with these factors and also to permit the pastoralists to preserve many of their traditional strategies.[7]

Bennett's studies of adaptive strategies among Great Plains farmers and ranchers yield a description of how farmers cope with the changing requirements of agriculture in a dynamic market system--as well as the impact of such changes on the family and community. Similar studies by anthropologists are under way in other parts of North America (e.g., Salomon and O'Reilly, 1979). This mode of research focuses, among other things, on how farmers view their social and economic position and make assessments of risk and how to deal with it. These studies really analyze the way farmers enter the "niche" of production, and how they cope with the changes in resource packages needed to define the niche. They also deal with the way social status in farming communities is related to the style of management and general response to needs for change in individual farmers. For example, very energetic maximizing behavior in many North American communities is frowned on, as a case of "going too much after the dollar," and studies have shown that this fear definitely may slow the pace of farmers who do not wish to risk a negative social evaluation.

This type of research finding is, of course, an empirical datum; the relationship could in other communities be just the opposite. It is the existence of multiple possibilities in micro-level adaptive behavior that leads many agricultural economists to operate on the basis of an averaging assumption. However, while this may be correct in large aggregate studies, it can lead to erroneous predictions and outcomes of statistical studies for particular regions, or for particular kinds of programs. In such cases, empirical information about the details of management strategies are vital, both in developed and developing agrarian populations.

The implicit model of adaptation developed by agricultural anthropologists contains a series of flexible, heuristic concepts which can be summarized. Adaptation as a form of behavior is based on anticipatory thought or planning; that is, the agriculturalist looks ahead to anticipate outcomes and adjusts his current strategies accordingly. Adaptation therefore has a time dimension: projects are undertaken in a sequence of steps, each planned in terms of the behavioral, social, and financial costs--either implicitly or explicitly. Decision making in this approach is viewed as a temporal phenomenon, not as a timeless, one-shot act. As in the classic microeconomics of the firm, there are short- and long-term modes of adaptive behavior: frequently farmers will forego short-run returns in order to achieve better results at some future date, and, of course, vice versa. Such patterns vary greatly among different farmers and different communities and societies. In some lexicons, the short-term responses are called "adjustment"; the long-term, planned operations, "adaptation."

Finally, there is a distinction to be made between adaptive strategy and adaptive process: the former are the actions taken by the agriculturalist; the latter are the general vectors and outcomes of strategies as constructed and observed by the researcher--and also by the farmer, when he has made similar objective analyses of his operations. Often the processes are not the same as the strategies; i.e., outcomes are often unanticipated due to lack of full information. As with the economist, the anthropologist is aware that the world is an imperfect one; complete symmetry and predictability is a will-o'-the wisp.

C. Management Style

Another heuristic construct available for use by the anthropologist is what can be called "management style," or the general characterological pattern of decisions and strategic actions undertaken over a period of time. The term "management style," is Bennett's, as he has used it in his book (Bennett, 1982a, Part 5), so it should not be thought as having general currency in the field. However, anthropologists doing studies of management use similar approaches, with different methodological nuances. The point is that since the anthropologist is interested in behavior, he will be inclined to view management not as the permutations of production factors, but as the behavior of people in time and culture. In such research, the economic results or output are not the sole or main target of analysis, but rather the methods employed to reach these ends. Local communities establish their own labels and conceptions of management style; some familiar terms in use among Western agricultural operators are: "scrambler," to refer to a small, undercapitalized operation in which frantic production activity is not such as to provide any guarantee of financial or social establishment (the two go hand-in-hand); "sitter," referring to a manager who "sits" on an enterprise with good resources but does nothing to improve it (his income satisfaction level may be low); or "a man doing a real good job," to refer to a manager who innovates and responds to change carefully and cautiously. These conceptions define real empirical cases, and in Bennett's research he has been able to validate and refine them by making detailed behavioral and economic studies of sample cases.

Management style is the cultural and behavioral analogue to the economist's measurement of the firm's performance. Instead of using the firm as the unit, the anthropologist focuses on the operating manager or staff, and analyzes their behavior through time. Management style is not a fixed pattern, but is subject to change as the manager himself changes, or as the conditions affecting farming opportunities alter. Management style must be based initially on the community's characterizations of its members' behavior; therefore, like other aspects of the anthropological model, it is especially useful in analyzing the responses of producers in particular localities and types of farming, where such knowledge may be of importance in designing programs. In any event, the stylistic characterizations of the managerial behavior of farmers always need to be examined against the background of hard economic data, and thus partnership with the economist is a desideratum.

The anthropological analysis of management style further illustrates the differences between the economics and sociocultural approaches to the production process. Recalling the discussions of maximization and other economics concepts, it was apparent that the chief anthropological criticism concerns the value of such concepts for describing behavior. We noted that this is, at least in part, a misunderstanding of how the concept is used by economists--not for analyzing actual behavior, but for sorting out firms that do what is required to survive from those that do not. However this may be, the anthropologist has a point insofar as he is concerned with the behavior of real people in real situations, and the economist's ideal types do not adequately convey the complexity of this behavior.

When the anthropologist views the typical farm operator, he is concerned with the differences in observed behavior: no operator does the absolute most for his enterprise, since he has other interests as well, and since his own energy and informational level are variables. Hence the maximization and utility functions raise interesting questions and can provide standards, but the more important issue for the anthropologist is the observed variability, and the causes of this variability. The anthropological approach to management phrases the question of how and why a manager does what he does to his farm in terms of the entire milieu: the family interests and needs; community pressures and standards; agronomic factors; and of course financial and economic matters. When all these influences are observed and considered, the analysis becomes a matter of viewing decision-making behavior in a social as well as in an economic context; it is a study of human behavior, and not of the behavior of an abstract entity, the firm. The economic data on the firm and its operations are, however, vital information against which to view the behavioral and social data, and the anthropologist is remiss if he does not collect them. Again, we find a need for scholarly partnership.

It is apparent that in the design of agrarian development projects--as well as in farm programs in developed countries--the economic factors form the basis of planning and action in the great majority of cases. Social, cultural, and behavioral elements are rarely if ever effectively built into these projects, and this is one reason so many have failed or achieved unexpected and sometimes undesirable results. The group ranches instituted for pastoral populations in several African countries were planned on the assumption that the pastoralists would manage them as commercial livestock enterprises. However, these expectations have been met only rarely. The Maasai in both Kenya and Tanzania, for example, have considered ranches (to which they were given a kind of title) as more secure rights to land, not primarily as opportunities for improved management (Galaty, 1980). They continue to move their herds outside of the ranch properties in order to follow the ecological and economic pattern of management they know best. They perceive the ranchland as a device to make political demands, or possibly as property to dispose of in some fashion that will benefit them later--a pattern familiar enough to students of American Indian reservation societies over the past century. The ranch projects might have been better planned if investigations into the sociocultural aspects of Maasai management practices and property institutions had been made earlier, or had at least been considered.

The anthropologist in effect is free to measure production performance against whatever standards he deems relevant. In pure anthropological research these standards are derived from the population under study, as well as from independent sources like books

238

on economics, management, or general social and cultural theory. This willingness to use more than one model, and to include conceptions derived from the ideas of the research population itself, is perhaps the key underlying difference in methodology between the two fields. In general, it is the anthropologist's aim to establish <u>relative</u> standards of performance, "substantive" rationality as against "formal," in the language of Max Weber. If maximization and other concepts are used in the analysis, this will be done in order to determine whether or not, or to what extent, the people under study have learned such concepts and act on them. The economic theories have become part of the cognitive map of many farmers, especially since college education is now a norm in many districts. The farmer is as likely to know all about these ideal types as the economist, and may guide his actions with them. As noted earlier, however, the farmer is no slave to these standards, and the anthropologist will be interested in the extent to which he may follow them, or precisely how he manipulates or changes them in actual managerial behavior.

This view of managerial behavior differs from that developed by decision theory specialists, as previously noted. Decision making as an approach is closer to the economic conception of farm management than to standard anthropological conceptions of economic activities. In particular, it is based on the theory of rational choice: decisions are made after comparison of several desired ends, or of several means to a particular end. The ultimate decision to follow a particular course is thus a trade-off between two or more alternatives. The rational-choice approach has been explored by sociologists and political scientists, but anthropologists have not found it easy to use it except heuristically. The issue of rationality as a standard or as a behavioral vector has been a source of continual controversy in anthropological economics (e.g., Cancian, 1974; Godelier, 1972; and, with respect to rational choice, see Heath, 1976).

D. Cycles of Family and Enterprise

Entry into the farming niche, and the continuity of the farm firm, is importantly directed by the life cycles of farming populations. These social cycles are intersected by cycles or movements in the farm firm as conditioned by national economic trends. The art of management of the relatively small, family-operated agricultural enterprise includes the need to plan so that these social and economic cycles do not conflict; e.g., so that family labor is available when economic opportunities arise that may require additional effort at low cost.

The family or social cycles are really a nest of several cycles. First, there is the biological cycle of the reproductive unit and its kin group, constructed of births and deaths. The order of birth and the ages of children and adults have an important relationship to labor needs, physical vigor, and educational capacity of members at particular points in the development trajectory of the enterprise. Second, there is the process of transmission of the headship of the enterprise and/or family household from a senior to a junior member. In a majority of agricultural societies the world over, this headship role is usually vested in one person, but this formal assignment does not necessarily conform to the actual give-and-take of family governance or enterprise movement, which may be shared among several persons of both sexes.

A third cycle concerns the changes in ownership of resources and in the social status of the family and its members in the community. Here the concept of the "agricultural ladder," described in the previous section, becomes relevant.

Access to resources may also be obtained through family ties, which can be used to obtain gifts and loans of resources to young starters, or the renting of land to relatives at low rates. Anthropological studies of farmers in many societies have shown that the economic value of these informal means of assembling resources are extremely important, and can be missed by conventional economic analysis.

Off-farm agricultural employment has been a source of cash savings toward capital accumulation almost everywhere in the developed countries, and to an increasing extent in the developing countries. Part-time farming has become more widespread as costs have risen and as savings or help from relatives have not been sufficient to provide money for the purchase of a farm. Such employment in business or industry has also provided funds for maintaining consumption levels, and supplementing income from farming.

As size of farm and competition for agricultural land grew apace in North America (especially since 1950), entry into farming by young people has become more difficult. Family assistance has become a more crucial factor that it was before World War II, since in many regions the only secure way to enter farming is through partnership arrangements between parents and children. The common pattern has meant that the farm enterprise must be enlarged to provide employment and income for two or more families--leading to larger and fewer enterprises in the district.

Accompanying the social and economic ladder progressions are cycles of consumption standards and other cultural values which affect farming strategies. As farming becomes integrated into national economic and cultural currents, the attitudes and preferences of the farm families change accordingly. The process is standard in the developed countries; it is known as the "revolution of rising expectations" in the Third World. In the recent history of North American farming communities, a rapid rise after World War II in consumption levels, especially among farm women and children, exerted powerful effects on income demands placed on the enterprise. Similar developments have occurred in Europe. On the production side, the use of agricultural machinery and chemicals has important symbolic value to the operator in addition to whatever its economic benefits may be.

To Summarize: The anthropologist, working with farming as a social system, is concerned with two main levels of analysis: first, he works with the microsocial level, which is concerned with the way the farm firm and family are related to the local community, and to the network of friends and relatives which help supply the unit with labor, capital, and encouragement. This level is also concerned with the cycles of the family and the firm, and how these cycles, operating on different temporal rhythms, may coincide or conflict, creating both opportunities and constraints. Descending to the farm operator, the anthropologist works with a concept like "management style," which refers to the habit patterns and definitions of the situation used by individual managers to maintain the unit and ensure its efficient survival.

The second level of analysis, the macrosocial, is concerned with the institutions and organizations of the national society and economy that impinge on the farming operation. These are, in general, located outside the local community, although to an increasing extent their representatives may be found in offices in the community, where the farmer has access to them. These agencies supply information, capital, and material inputs to the farm firm; the farmer, and his family, must acquire whatever he needs from these sources, in order to maintain the unit in efficient condition. However, the standards here are not absolute, and the farm family can choose whatever level of efficiency, or profitability, it desires or needs. This flexible relationship between the individual producers, and the larger institutions on the outside, like the market, leads to a dynamic situation which is often difficult to predict. Economists attempt their predictions with aggregated data on the whole; these are frequently off the mark because of the selective variation at the microsocial levels. It is this nexus of interplay that constitutes the basic frontier of collaboration between economist and anthropologist.

Acknowledgments

[*] This is a revision of a paper presented at the First Annual Conference of the Society for Anthropological Economics, held at Indiana University-Bloomington, April, 1981.

[**] By permission from Farmers, Workers and Machines: Technological and Social Change in Farm Industries of Arizona, by Harland Padfield and William E. Martin, Tucson: University of Arizona Press, Copyright 1965.

Notes

[1] For examples of research by agricultural economists exploring social and behavioral factors in management from varying points of view and for different periods, see the following: Barkley, 1976; Coughenour, 1976; Brunthaver, 1975; Gilbert, 1971; Mumey, 1967; Pond and Wilcox, 1932.

[2] For a conspectus of anthropological work on agricultural decision making see the recent

symposium volume edited by Barlett (1980b) and her view of recent studies (Barlett, 1980a).

[3] For a review of the role of cooperatives in agricultural development in third world countries, see Bennett, 1983.

[4] Parenthetically, we should note that this argument--that the crucial features in the behavior of firms are competitive pressures transmitted through markets, rather than profit-maximization as a motive--has relevance to Polanyi's argument about the inapplicability of neoclassical theory to nonmarket societies. His theory is grounded primarily on the absence of markets as transmitters of competitive pressures rather than depending on a theoretical statement about human behavior.

[5] We realize that the economy is not as competitive as postulated in introductory economic analysis. But even so, the analysis of market forces is likely to indicate the direction of change in such economic variables as employment opportunities and numbers of farms, even if it cannot establish the exact level of these variables.

Economists are well aware of limits of the competitive model and have a number of concepts to deal with industrial organization under different degrees of competition. Human attempts to increase their autonomy from market forces have taken the form of both deviations from competition and various forms of collective action.

[6] There exist a number of symposium volumes on the contributions of anthropologists to development, but the field at the time of writing has yet to achieve a theoretical or conceptual synthesis. One of the more useful volumes, though now somewhat out-of-date, is Poggie and Lynch, 1974. The volumes of studies of economic anthropology edited by George Dalton also contain numerous examples of both empirical and theoretical materials.

[7] A good introduction to this newer type of anthropological research on pastoralism is provided by Galaty, Aronson and Salzman, 1981.

References

ACHESON, James, and J. Wilson. 1981. A model of adaptive behavior in the New England fishing industry. Report to the National Science Foundation, vol. 3. University of Rhode Island-University of Maine Study of Social and Cultural Aspects of Fisheries Management in New England under Extended Jurisdiction. Washington.

BARKLEY, Paul. 1976. A contemporary political economy of family farming. American Journal of Agricultural Economics 58:812-819.

BARLETT, Peggy F. 1980a. Adaptive strategies in peasant agricultural production. Annual Review of Anthropology 9:545-604.

_____. 1980b. Agricultural decision making: anthropological contributions to rural development. New York: Academic Press.

BENNETT, John W. 1969-77. Northern Plainsmen. Chicago: Aldine.

_____. 1976. Anticipation, adaptation, and the concept of culture in anthropology. Science 192:847-893.

_____. 1982a. Of time and the enterprise: North American family farm management in a context of resource marginality. Minneapolis: University of Minnesota Press.

_____. 1982b. Agricultural cooperatives in the development process. In Comparative studies in international development. Forthcoming.

BRUNTHAVER, Carroll. 1975. Agricultural economics as an aid in management decision making. American Journal of Agricultural Economics 57:889-891.

CANCIAN, Frank. 1974. Economic man and economic development. In Rethinking modernization: anthropological perspectives. John J. Poggie, Jr., and Robert N. Lynch, eds. Westport, CT: Greenwood Press.

CASE, Harold C. M., and D. B. Williams. 1957. Fifty years of farm management. Urbana: University of Illinois Press.

COMMONS, John R. 1961. Institutional economics. 2 vols. Madison: University of Wisconsin Press. First published by Macmillan Co., 1934.

COUGHENOUR, C. Milton. 1976. A theory of instrumental activity and farm enterprise commitment applied to wool growing in Australia. Rural Sociology 41:76-98.

CRECINK, John C. 1956. Tenant farmers, South Platte Valley, Colorado. How they get farms and accumulate capital. ARS-43-18. Washington: Agricultural Research Service, U.S. Department of Agriculture.

GALATY, John. 1980. The Maasai group ranch: politics and development in an African tribal society. In When nomads settle. P. Salzman, ed. New York: Praeger Special Studies, J. F. Bergin Publishers.

_____, Dan Aronson, and Philip Salzman. 1981. The future of pastoral peoples. Ottawa: Commission on Nomadic Peoples; University of Nairobi, Institute for Development Studies; and the International Development Research Centre of Canada.

GILBERT, Howard, et al. 1971. Recognizing personality characteristics related to managerial potential in agriculture. Agricultural Experiment Station Bulletin No. 584. Brookings: South Dakota State University.

GLADWIN, Christina H. 1980. A theory of real-life choice: applications to agricultural decisions. In Agricultural decision making. P. Barlett, ed. New York: Academic Press.

GODELIER, Maurice. 1972. Rationality and irrationality in economics. London: New Left Books.

GOLDSCHMIDT, Walter. 1947. As you sow. New York: Harcourt Brace.

245

HEATH, Anthony. 1976. Rational choice and social exchange. New York and London: Cambridge University Press.

HENDERSON, James, and Richard Quandt. 1971. Microeconomic theory. 2nd ed. New York: McGraw-Hill Book Co.

HERSKOVITS, Melville J. 1940. The economic life of primitive peoples. New York and London: A. A. Knopf.

HOBEN, Allen. 1979. Lessons from a critical examination of livestock projects in Africa. AID Program Evaluation Workshop no. 26. Washington: Studies Division, Office of Evaluation, Bureau of Program and Policy Coordination, U.S. Agency for International Development.

MALINOWSKI, Bronislaw. 1922. Argonauts of the Western Pacific. New York: E. P. Dutton.

_____. 1935. Coral gardens and their magic. 2 vols. London: Allen and Unwin.

MINER, Horace. 1949. Culture and agriculture: an anthropological study of a corn belt county. Ann Arbor: University of Michigan Press.

MUMEY, G. A. 1967. Comparative investment behavior of United States and Canadian farmers. Canadian Journal of Agricultural Economics 15:21-27.

PADFIELD, Harland, and William E. Martin. 1965. Farmers, workers and machines. Tucson: University of Arizona Press.

POGGIE, John, and Robert N. Lynch. 1974. Rethinking modernization. Anthropology perspectives. Westport, Conn.: Greenwood Press.

POLANYI, Karl. 1957. The great transformation. Boston: Beacon Press.

POND, G. A., and W. W. Wilcox. 1932. A study of the human factor in farm management. Journal of Farm Economics 14:470-479.

SALOMON, Sonya, and S. M. O'Reilly. 1979. Family land and developmental cycles among Illinois farmers. Rural Sociology 44:524-542.

SALTER, Leonard A. 1967. A critical review of research in land economics. Madison: University of Wisconsin Press. First published by University of Minnesota Press, 1948.

SCHERTZ, Lyle P., et al. 1979. Another revolution in U.S. farming? Washington: USDA Economics, Statistics, and Cooperative Services, Agricultural Economic Report no. 441.

SCHNEIDER, Harold. 1974. Economic man: the anthropology of economics. New York: Free Press.

_____, and Edward E. LeClair. 1968. Economic anthropology: readings in theory and analysis. New York: Holt Rinehart and Winston.

SPILLMAN, W. J. 1919. The agricultural ladder. American Economic Review 9(supplement no. 1):29-38.

STEWARD, Julian S. 1955. The theory of culture change. Urbana: University of Illinois Press.

_____, et al. 1956. The people of Puerto Rico. Urbana: University of Illinois Press.

THURNWALD, Richard. 1932. Economics in primitive communities. Oxford: International Institute of African Languages and Literatures, Oxford University Press, by Humphrey Milford.

X. WHAT IS DECISION ANALYSIS ABOUT?
THE PROBLEMS OF FORMAL REPRESENTATIONS

Sutti Ortiz

Thanks to careful accounting, exploitation of resources and diligence, Robinson Crusoe's despair eventually was to yield happiness with the harvest of grain and peace with the knowledge that his desires had been met. His production plans were in equilibrium, and he could rest. This story should have been of very little interest to economists because Defoe did not populate his island with other consumers and producers. After all, Robinson Crusoe talked more about God than about his production plans.

Nevertheless, many creative thinkers, enchanted by the fairy tale analogy, attempted to order premises and build arguments about the essential determinants of production on this simplistic foundation. Not surprisingly, their arguments often suffered the same fate as did <u>Robinson Crusoe</u>. Yet other early economists and philosophers did successfully build on the analogy because they perceived what Robbins (1932) was much later to point out--that the basic elements of Robinson Crusoe's economic problem was that he had assumed norms, ambitions and expectations while having to cope with his own limitations and nature's parsimony.

For years, homo oeconomicus remained a very unappealing construct for many sociologists and anthropologists. They remained doubtful or disdainful of the theoretical contributions by cartesian economists and the followers of the Vienna school. Malinowski attacked homo oeconomicus' cousin, Primitive Economic Man, as a fanciful creature "whose shadow haunts even the minds of competent anthropologists, blighting their outlook with a preconceived idea . . ." (Malinowski, 1964, p. 60). Mauss saw Economic Man as a recent ominous creation: "The mere pursuit of individual ends is harmful to the ends and the peace of the whole, to the rhythm of his work and pleasures, and hence in the end to the individual" (Mauss, 1964, p. 75). Such views on morality and anthropologists' predilection for yet another analogy kept them from examining the value of the individualistic perspective. Quesnay's use of the human circulatory system as an analogy for economic

249

systems had a greater appeal. The physiocrats' focus on flows and exchanges (Gudeman, 1980) was a more comfortable perspective for Durkheim, Mauss and their followers--a heritage finally fully acknowledged by Dumont (1977).

I agree that to understand individualized solutions to economic problems one has to have an understanding of the impact of aggregate events and social norms. But I strongly object to Godelier's contention that such an understanding can be gained only through studying the laws of the functioning and evolution of economic or social systems (Godelier, 1972, p. 24). Although some relations and dynamics are best revealed at the macro level, for others one should focus on the individual and model economic relations on a typical producer or consumer.

One need assume neither free will nor that all actions result from conscious evaluation of strategies to adopt an individualist perspective (Bourdieu, 1977; Elster, 1979). One need make only two assumptions: first, that certain regularities and macrostructures will be revealed in the actions and reactions of prototypic individuals, and second, that the state of the world (ecological conditions, political and social institutions, norms, obligations, etc.) does not entirely structure one's actions, though it does define options, interests and preferences. Individual behavior cannot, after all, always be regulated. The total integration of nature and culture is simply an illusion. In fact, the complexity of social institutions, differential articulation of various sectors, and multiplex interrelations of economic and political factors engender unpredictable events. Indeterminacy and complexity not only leave room for individual initiative but force individuals to resolve conflicting demands and to adjust constantly to changing conditions. Decisions and manipulations are unavoidable; by studying them we can more fully understand macroprocesses. Because anthropologists have often minimized the relevance of this perspective, they have tended to overstructure formal descriptions of socioeconomic processes. Decision analysis is a good antidote for this tendency. It can be used to elucidate: 1) the constraints and conflicts of the microenvironment; 2) the type of adjustments likely to be made; and 3) the cyclical nature of some adjustments.

One can elucidate the norms and constraints that affect decisions by analyzing statistically the incidence of each type of solution. Studies on residence rules and options are good examples of this approach.[1] But production problems are more complex, requiring a priori assumptions about the principles that guide the choices among options. Economists and psychologists have made assumptions about the logic of not only the situation but also the decision process. Two types of models have been developed outlining the elements that are likely to be considered and the conditions affecting the consideration and evaluation of elements: 1) rationality models and 2) information processing models. The first conceptualizes the decision maker as a pondering evaluator of options. The second conceptualizes the decision maker as a programmed allocator who processes information and chooses an option that matches goals and expectations.

Neither approach pretends to explain social or psychological phenomena. They simply assume that allocation is a problem to be resolved and that the resolution of this problem is constrained by a number of social and ecological events and by the nature of mental processes. If we can determine the impact of such constraints, we can estimate the range of likely solutions. Decision analysis does not always assume that there are single or optimal solutions to allocation problems.

I. RATIONALITY APPROACH TO DECISION ANALYSIS

The introduction of the cartesian reasoning ego allowed economists to develop integrated arguments about production and exchange, and thus rescue some of the atheoretical observations of mercantilists (Mini, 1974). As an a priori assumption, rational man was entirely dependent on the imagination of his creators. In its original guise the cartesian ego was not a cold maximizing calculator, as described (with the help of lags and coefficients) in contemporary economic literature, but an actor with wants. For Karl Menger it was wants, rather than insatiable desires or calculating abilities, that drove economic man to find solutions to the problems of production and valuation of goods. In his book Grundsätze, published in 1871, he discussed "wirtschaftlender Mensch"--economizing, managing man, not maximizing man. To meet their needs, economizing men transformed

251

seeds into goods, and then determined their value. Judgments about the quantities of goods available to meet requirements determined the relationships among goods; misjudgments caused relative scarcity. Misjudgments are inevitable in a complex environment; fluctuations of resources are a state of nature. Thus man is forced to economize, Menger (1950) argued because of economic or ecological scarcity.

By defining the value of an economic good as the significance "that command of each concrete unit of the available quantities (my emphasis) of these goods has for our lives and well being" (Menger, 1950, p. 116), Menger provided us with a decision rule: Options are ranked and chosen according to their value. Menger's discourses on valuation of goods stemmed partly from his interest in operationalizing his model of economic man, but also from his disagreements with other theories on the subject. He opposed both the labor theory of value and the concept of "use value." Goods acquire value when their intrinsic characteristics are related to needs, he asserted. But the relationship is not direct; it is mediated by choice and shaped by the conditions that make choice necessary. To determine a good's value to the producer, we must relate its need satisfaction to its availability. Thus value, for Menger, was a judgment that, made by well-informed individuals, leads to congruency and harmony: each individual demands what he needs and produces to satisfy the demands of other individuals. As judgments and relationships change, new values arise and previous ones disappear (Menger, 1950).

Menger's theory that the value of a good fluctuates according to need satisfaction and availability led him to formulate the concept of marginal value. Because value is related to satisfaction, an increment in the quantity of a good will not always have the same value; the value of the increment will decrease as quantity increases until an extra unit no longer has any value to the consumer or producer. At this point economic man stops producing any more extra units; his production plans are in equilibrium (Menger, 1950, p. 127).

Menger's argument--shared with and elaborated by other economists of his time--was intriguing and has been retained in a different guise in most mathematical decision models. It does present some yet unresolved problems:

1) It is easy to express the relative value of a good when value depends on the ratio between availability and need, and when all goods are produced with the same limited inputs. For example, we can compare the value of varying quantities of maize and sugarcane when we must allocate limited land and labor to them. But when the land used for maize is different from that for sugarcane, we have to be able to equate one to the other. This is easiest when there is a market for land or when maize and sugarcane are exchanged. Economists resolve the problem by equating value with price. Anthropologists have translated value of output into quantity of labor required to produce each good.[2] Psychologists and sociologists have suggested that we determine relative preferences for goods empirically (see IA). None of these solutions is, however, entirely satisfactory.

2) The value of a good is more difficult to determine when the same good satisfies different wants. Maize, for example, can be used to feed pigs, grow more maize, feed humans, pay tribute, and serve as an offering to the gods. Thus its value varies because in different contexts only one of its several attributes is of significance. Menger simplified the issue by saying that the value of a good is determined first by how it satisfies the most important want, and subsequently by how it satisfies other lower ranking wants.

3) Menger talked about the relative value of an increment but never specified either its significant magnitude or how we are to determine it (Stigler, 1960). The issue is often bypassed through a variety of measures, which we conceptualize as sets of units: Economists use monetary increments in profit; anthropologists use numbers of days of labor inputs or labor values.

Menger's attempt to reformulate how goods acquire value and how value does and must fluctuate, was intriguing, though problematic. His decision format proved seminal, but anthropologists still search for solutions to the riddle of how to measure value without measuring it. The issue may be easier to resolve if we mind Menger's suggestion that valuation arises in the process of allocation and if we realize

253

that allocation decisions are in fact a series of sequential decisions. We can then account for changes of value by specifying the relationship between each decision step and the context in which it is made.

An alternative decision rule that contrasts dramatically with Menger's approach is labor accounting, or the labor theory of value. Such an approach is worth considering. We must keep in mind that there is a fundamental difference between the assumption that what gives value to a commodity is how it relates to the individual and symbolizes social obligations, and the assumption that what gives value to the commodity is how labor transforms nature and commodities into other commodities (Ortiz, 1979c; Firth, 1979). This issue is presently being examined by Cook (1982).

Mary Douglas suggests an entirely different approach to understanding the value of goods. She suggests that instead of looking at production and how goods relate to the producer, we should examine consumption and how the goods serve to mediate the relationship between the consumer and his social world. In other words, the value of goods is in their meaning as part of an information system (Douglas, 1979, p. 10).

The question is, can we, after reading Menger, divorce exchange values from the relationship of output to means of production? Value remains an enigmatic and elusive concept. It is no wonder that decision models confine themselves to profit, costs, concrete quantities, and relative preference. Anthropologists should reexamine this issue, relating the ideas of Menger to those suggested by Douglas.

As I have said, Menger's contribution was to point to the significance of homo oeconomicus as a construct capable of engendering hypotheses about the interrelationships of variables and the dynamics of economic behavior. Furthermore, he provided us with a set of concepts which, though problematic, allowed us to pursue arguments logically. Homo oeconomicus, not surprisingly, became a symbol of certain schools of thought. As such it was an easy target. But in one form or another homo oeconomicus was necessary for microanalysis and for anthropologists interested in the adaptations and adjustments that marginal farmers and peasant farmers must make. Like Robinson

Crusoe's, homo oeconomicus' island was soon peopled by other homo and men (Machlup, 1967).

Likewise, Menger's concepts had to be transformed. In order to operationalize the rationality model, economists had to translate concepts into mathematical formulations and in the process some concepts were altered. For example: 1) arguments about value have been replaced by arguments about utility and preference; 2) the value of inputs has changed to the cost of inputs, and the value of outputs has become a price; and 3) marginal utility has lost its cardinal value having become the slope of a curve or an ordinal measure. The more ambitious aspects of Menger's work have been totally neglected. He had hoped to outline the logical implications of a system of producers with given tastes, needs, and perfect knowledge who must confront scarcity and versatility of resources. Menger was not interested just in production strategies but also in how these strategies related to the choice to transact and to favor certain exchange rates. The obstacles were insurmountable--as I review in the Introduction to Part Four--so Menger did not go beyond a discussion of bilateral exchange (Abele, 1977). He was, of course, aware that homo oeconomicus would not help us understand the totality of events in the real world. As Shackle (1966) was to point out, homo oeconomicus failed to deal with both general uncertainty and the specific uncertainties of how much to produce and at the prices at which goods would have to be purchased or sold.

A. Utility Models

The shortcoming in Menger's formulations had to be resolved; the arguments against homo oeconomicus, economic man, and rational man had to be countered. Subjective reasoning had been helpful in clarifying many problems, but economists now had to observe the behavior of managers, farmers, and investors. They also had to make use of the experimental results of some psychologists who were gathering information on responses to gaming situations. Rather slowly, some of the utility models presently in use began to emerge.

These models had to incorporate three variables: the value of payoffs, the value of production requirements, and the uncertain realization of each (that is, the likelihood that inputs would be available and the particular values would be realized). The relation among these variables had to be integrated into a relatively simple model. A mathematical expression had to be found so that specific predictions could be made and other axiomatic relations deduced.

Not surprisingly, some economists chose to ignore the philosophical foundations of homo oeconomicus while retaining the trappings of the rationality model; the decision rule was consequently transformed from a choice according to value to a choice according to profits. Although this simplification seemed to open the door to the development of neat normative and predictive models, instead it ushered in a number of debates. Objections were raised on both pragmatic and logical grounds. It was pointed out that the rule of thumb used by most firms when making production decisions is not the maximization of profit but the attainment of some reasonable profit level (Baumol, 1963). Secondly, firms cannot maximize actual profits but only expected profits, as they have no certain knowledge of what the demand for their products will be. Thirdly, money itself has utility, and its marginal utility is not linear (Stigler, 1960). Finally, firms and farmers are not just producers but also consumers; hence, no simplified rule could encompass the object of their various strategies. At least the concept of value, problematic though it was, could integrate a number of characteristics of goods: their ability to satisfy capital wants, and consumption, security, and communication needs.

Another alternative still used for modeling economic decisions is to assume that one need not value prospects in order to choose among them. A decision maker needs only to rank options according to their utility, not to determine the utility of each; in the language of economics textbooks, he has only to determine ordinal utility. This solution has a certain appeal because it retains the fundamental theoretical purpose of decision analysis. If ranked utilities reflect value scales, then one should be able to deduce the logical consequences of the allocation process for production and exchange.

It is often possible to rank goods in this way, as long as the ranking is based on a sound questionnaire and one does not assume that it represents a universal scale. There is always room for generalizations of personal utility rankings. The matter becomes more complex when ranking involves not just contrasting one good against another but comparing specific amounts of each good, as marginal value analysis intended to do. The solution is to confront individuals with sets of paired options which contain different quantities of each good, and then to note when the subject expresses indifference between the two options. Indifference curves, as they were to be labeled, could be taken as reflections of utility ranking.[3] The problem becomes still more complicated when each item to be contrasted has more than one use for the consumer. Nevertheless, economists and psychologists have attempted to devise yet more complex questions and contrasts to allow for the determination of multiattribute utilities (Keeney, 1972; Anderson, 1979).

Determining the relative preference for a specific income is just as problematic. Ramsey (1931) and von Neumann and Morgenstern (1947) suggested a practice that could be used to arrive at ordinal utility or preference of monetary returns. The practice consisted of asking the subject to choose between two investments, one of which brings in a sure but lower return and the other a higher return with a specified probability. The researcher then repeats the question, varying either the probability or the return and noting the points where the subject indicates indifference between the two. At this point the sum of the utilities must be equal to one.[4] To avoid the tedious exercise of determining utility curves empirically when the possible outcomes are multiple, the researcher notes only a few points. He can then derive other points by making assumptions about the properties of preferences or the shape of utility curves.[5]

In my discussion of utilities I have indicated that rank depends on preference not only for an outcome but also for the likelihood of that outcome. So intertwined have these two concepts become that current definitions of utility come close to being a preference for a probability distribution of outcomes than a preference for an outcome. Elicitation formats seldom separate one from the other, and mathematical derivations consider both at the same time. The theoretical consequences of merging the concepts of preference and incidence under the rubric of utility

257

is that decision models can no longer elucidate how goods acquire value in the course of allocation and exchange. A different research strategy has now to be devised, one that relies much more on techniques familiar to anthropologists: participant observation, elicitation of judgments through open-ended questionnaires, and the use of descriptive behavioral models simulating actual decision processes.

The merging of preference and incidence was not just a consequence of the difficulty of determining ordinary utility measures--for example, money--but also of the impossibility of assuming that the expectation of an outcome would coincide with the probability of that outcome. The world is complex; knowledge is limited; and decision makers hardly can be expected to have enough information to determine the probability of each event (Shackle, 1949). Hence, models must use subjective probability measures elicited from the subjects. But eliciting subjective probabilities is even more problematic than eliciting preferences. There are no distribution weightings on people's heads. At best they are formulated in response to prodding by a researcher--therefore, the methods used to elicit probabilities may have a direct impact on the responses obtained.[6]

By allowing the concept of utility to subsume both preference and expectation of outcomes, we may seem to resolve the measurements problem. But this only clouds the significance of the shape of utility curves. It has become impossible to determine whether slopes, discontinuities, or incongruities reflect complexities in preference ranking, difficulties of elicitation procedures, or the unsuitability of the statistical framework. Not surprisingly, these partly deductive, partly empirically derived models do not always perform well. Agricultural economists, who are involved in field observations, have introduced a correcting device to their models. Noticing that farmers are unlikely to court disaster, they assume that farmers will not only display a preference for a certain probability distribution of outcomes, but also avoid options that may lead to starvation, indebtedness, or high incidence of very low incomes. The observation is no doubt correct, and the resulting generalization--for example, in statements of safety-first behavior--are eminently sensible.[7] The difficulty is that one cannot know whether a choice of strategy is due to risk avoidance, to an erroneous elicitation of preference and expectations, or to a mathematical framework that can only inadequately represent continuous values (Ortiz, 1980). Much more research is needed on how farmers rank prospects, formulate outcome expectations, and simplify the evaluation process.

Anthropologists have expressed yet another concern about these models. Rationality models also assume another rule: maximization of utility. If the model is used normatively to advise on a best strategy, the assumption may be valid; but if it is used to simulate the behavior of farmers, the assumption will have to be altered. An alternative has been suggested to substitute bounded rationality for maximization (Simon, 1957; Georgescu-Roegen, 1958). Maximization has great appeal because it generates neat solutions and unique answers, which are useful for an analyst who wants to use decision outcomes as clauses for other arguments or as data for policy recommendations. As a compromise, Roumasset has suggested the application of lexicographic safety-first models to simulate farmers' decisions. In this model farmers' "first screen out all acts which are not viable in the sense of satisfying the risk constraint and then use the criterion of expected profits to choose the best of viable acts" (Roumasset, 1979, p. 99).

Alternative models have been suggested--for example, the "satisficing models" proposed by Simon (1957) and by Georgescu-Roegen (1958)--but they are not favored by most agricultural economists, and hence have not received the attention they deserve. Although the solutions offered by these models are interesting, more research is required to systematize the definition of the satisfactory level that farmers aim to attain, and to determine how prospects and information are examined and evaluated. Furthermore, an allowance has to be made for more than one possible solution to the allocation problems under uncertainty. The analyst has to be able to evaluate the possible distribution of various outcomes and the possibility that the choice of strategies in the long run would cluster along a given dimension.

Most allocation problems are not resolved through a single complex decision. A sequence of decisions is often required. The sequence has been described as a tree with a decision at each branching point. The utility model thus does not have to incorporate all relevant prospects and all aspects of the strategy, but only those crucial to that particular decision point. Decisions can, of course, be very complex, and the tree, as Raiffa (1968) warns us, can easily become a bush in need of trimming. Three simplifications may relieve the overburdened analyst: 1) delete branches when choices are not problematic; 2) assume that the significant outcome is a short-term outcome--that most decisions have short planning horizons; and 3) design decision trees for a single product whenever possible.

These simplifications are warranted when decision makers themselves must simplify the process. They are not warranted if the simplification process is derived solely from mathematical requirements or from scattered empirical observations. Anthropologists should look more closely at decision processes to determine what constraints determine decision points (Ortiz, 1973); what constraints determine planning horizons; what determines whether a decision is focused on one, two, or more products; and what goals are kept in mind at a particular decision point (Ortiz, 1979b). Only then can we derive a set of modeling rules that are congruent with both the behavior of the farmers and the theoretical concern of the models.

Despite their inherent difficulties, utility models have attracted the attention of some anthropologists and like-minded colleagues. Kozelka (1969) reanalyzed Davenport's model of fishing strategies in Jamaica using a very simple utility model.[8] However, the information available does not allow either of the authors to explore the model's capabilities in any depth.

Aubey, Kyle and Strickon (1971) use portfolio theory to explore the implications of information and the indirect costs of gathering it on strategies that are used (as measured by the standard deviations from those that are expected). This study's relevant contribution is its illustration of how a particular decision analysis model can be used to evaluate the significance of social channels and organizational arrangements in the economic behavior of producers. There is a considerable amount of information related to this argument in agricultural economists' literature on innovation.[9]

Because agricultural economists also have been attracted by these models,[10] anthropologists cannot ignore them. Part of the attraction of utility models is that compared to other, more realistic models, they are structured around the assumed logic of economic dynamics: rational adjustments to uncertain prospects, to complex environments, and to interrelated units. Utility models allow for some alteration of the meaning of rationality and for the intellectual integration of conclusions about microdynamics into a macrodynamic framework. But at the moment these conclusions are far from satisfactory, for the models incorporate some unwarranted assumptions.

B. Game Theory

Utility decision models transform the uncertainties in the world into a set of weighted prospects. In planning his strategy, the decision maker takes into account the probability distribution of winnings. His choice is not considered to affect the world, which is conceived by the analyst as a neutral environment.

The world, of course, is not always neutral. Sometimes it seems to contend with the decision maker, as happens when one is playing chess, when other boats are competing for fish in the same ocean, or when other producers are trying to command the largest possible share of the market.

If the relationship among producers is akin to that of competitive players, then a decision process can be depicted as a series of moves to outwit one's opponent and obtain maximum gain at minimum cost. For example, assume two players are betting against each other, independently, on the outcome of a coin toss. For one player to win the prize, not only must he guess correctly but the other player's strategy must fail. In this case, it is not enough for our decision maker to know that the probability of his guess is 0.5. He must also guess what the other player will bet.

Game analysis shares some of the formal attributes of utility analysis: Probabilities and payoff are subsumed under the concept of utility; formal elicitation procedures are similar; and in both, the solution can be set up in matrix form.

Barth (1959) introduced the rudiments of game theory analysis to anthropology; later, Salisbury (1969) used it to explain borrowing and lending strategies of shell money in Rossel Island. But neither author goes further than suggesting formal arguments; neither explores the gaming strategies mathematically.

The application of game theory is more problematic when nature is the assumed contender. This was the case in Davenport's early study of Jamaican fishermen's strategies with changes of weather and season. But Davenport's study is only a superficial illustration of game analysis, not an explanation of fishermen's choices. Other anthropologists qualified Davenport's findings by mentioning other factors that the fishermen must have been taking into account at the time of decision (Read and Read, 1970; Kozelka, 1969; Williams, 1977). And a more serious objection has also been raised: that nature cannot be considered a contender.[11] Weather does not play against a fisherman or a farmer.

Besides being complex, game theory analysis is weakened by other restrictions:

1) The competitive relationship has to be conceptualized as a game in which all players know the rules, options, and payoffs. The only uncertainty is the strategy (sequence of moves or bids) of the other players.

2) Preference ranking of payoff must remain constant through the game.

3) The analyst must be able to elicit utility functions, which are a combination of payoffs and probabilities.

4) Game theory can portray the uncertainties of competitive gaming, in which the number of possible outcomes is limited and one can determine the probability of prospects. But it cannot capture the uncertainty faced by farmers.

C. Linear Programming Models

During the 1950s anthropologists were introduced to another mathematical mode of programming logical problems. At first linear programming was applied to military problems; later it began to be used for other managerial tasks. In 1963 Len Joy introduced this model to a conference of British social anthropologists (Firth, 1967). But his attempt did not meet with success. Part of the difficulty was that sophisticated models require sophisticated data. Furthermore, the interdisciplinary cooperation required for data processing is not always forthcoming.

Although the model's formal characteristics are narrow, it can incorporate a large number of complex constraints found in real decision situations. For example, the model assumes the simple rule that a quantity is to be maximized. But it can make that rule more complex and realistic by conditioning it to a number of constraints: the labor input required by each crop per unit of land, the availability of land specifically suitable for that crop, the consumption requirements of the household, social obligations expressed as labor or goods requirements, etc. These constraints must be expressed as a sequence of additive equations; in other words, the absence of a resource or constraint cannot be crucial, or it must never approach zero.

Linear programming has, of course, its limitations, as do all other models. However, I doubt this has been the reason for its lack of popularity among anthropologists. One of the model's major theoretical limitations is that it initially conceives relations between variables to be linear; that is, the model does not think in terms of sloping marginal utility curves. At the practical level this is not serious, because it does not hinder the incorporation of variables that are nonlinearly related. It is feasible, though cumbersome, to transform nonlinear equations into linear equations (see Menges, 1973, pp. 107-124). Furthermore, it is possible to describe the nonlinear qualities of a relationship in linear terms by adding a set of constraints that add linearity (price fluctuation constraints, cost constraints, etc.).

As I have pointed out, one can most easily solve the allocation problem by making a maximization assumption. Nevertheless, the linear programming format allows for more freedom than do utility models. Boussard and Petit (1967), for example, assume that the French farmers of their study maximize normal or mean revenue (an empirically derived expectation). Other objective functions that can be and have been considered as maximizing rules are: net value of farm at the end of the planning horizon, discounted consumption, actual output for single-crop models or for monocrop farms. Whether there are other, more suitable rules should be the subject of anthropological research. Those who are interested in this problem should keep in mind that whatever objective the farmer is to maximize, the analyst must have a suitable rule to reduce all outcomes to a single one. Otherwise the model will not encompass all of the farmer's producing strategies. In other words, the model can program for only a single objective function.

Alternatively, each crop can be treated as a discrete decision related to or dependent on other decisions. Under this alternative one uses a decision tree format (i.e., dynamic programming). Each program incorporates the previous programmed solutions in the form of available funds for investments, stock of stored grain for consumption or sale, etc. If the farmer's goal is a long-range investment (for example, permanent crops, cattle), then one should use dynamic programming with a maximizing rule representing the value of the farm; this would take into account long-range investments in fencing and pasture that the farmers are likely to consider.

Until recently the major objection to the use of linear programming was that outputs were expressed as sure prospects. Recently there have been several attempts to adapt the model so that it can take into account that farmers are aware of output variations and that they make their plans accordingly. One such technique has been to assume that the decision maker maximizes expected value, given a risk aversion coefficient. This solution, which Freund originally proposed in 1956, has received considerable attention. It requires complex quadratic programming (Hazell, 1971), which assumes that farmers keep in mind the variance of their possible income and that one can determine their risk aversion coefficient (a thorny problem already discussed). A more palatable solution is to assume that farmers will want to avoid the possibility of failure, and therefore they will avoid any maximizing strategy that can bring them below a certain output or income level. This solution, known

FORMAL REPRESENTATIONS

as the safety first constraint (Day, 1963), does not imply that farmers consistently avoid risks, as some anthropological writings have assumed. The safety first constraint implies that farmers will prefer strategies under which a mix of crops will ensure a minimum level of income or a minimum level of food output.

Safety first is only a constraint in a model that otherwise assumes maximization of some objective or other, and a considerable amount of risk taking (Scandizzo and Dillon, 1979). To my mind a more intriguing solution has been Boussard and Petit's attempt to incorporate Shackle's notion that when evaluating options investors keep in mind the likelihood of lowest possible return and the most familiar highest return. Boussard and Petit operationalized these "focus gain" and "focus loss" points by redefining them. Focus gain is redefined as normal mean revenue and focus loss as the difference between the revenue expected in an average year and the minimum subsistence income. The redefinitions are most applicable to commercial farmers or relatively affluent peasant farmers; they also relate to capital/labor ratio of enterprise and the significance of crops in farmers' total managerial strategy (Ortiz, 1979a). This subject would profit from further anthropological research.

The greater the number of constraints and specifications the more complex the derivation of unknown quantities of the model (the amount of resources to be used for each crop, the viable expenditure on improved technology, etc.). The development of computer technology has made linear programming attractive to agricultural economists, who must predict changes in output, evaluate changes when constraints are lifted, and design more profitable investment plans for small farmers. Linear programming has been used, for example, to examine some empirical allocation problems that bear on the acceptance of innovation (Etuk, 1979); the relative use of available resources (Biserra, 1981); the interrelation between consumption patterns and capital formation (Langham, 1968); the interrelation among family labor, consumption pattern and output (Chayanov's concern); and the minimum resource requirements for a specified set of income ranges. It has also helped economists to study the amount of labor a given farm can profitably absorb, and thus the

265

need for off-farm employment in particular regions (Sektheera, 1979); the advisability of sustaining sharecropping contracts (Soares, 1977); and production implications of policy alternatives (Dechates, 1978).

Linear programming should interest anthropologists because this model allows them to specify factors of production in a familiar manner (acreage of land, available family labor, hired labor, exchange labor, etc.) and to use these categories to consider likely constraints to the decision rules implied by the model. Consumption requirements (consumption of food in storage, food to be purchased) can also be included in the model as constraints. The format of linear programming allows anthropologists to express variables in concrete form, which fit better with the reality of the farming unit and can mirror seasonal requirements and cash flows. Thus linear programming makes it easier to integrate the type of data obtained from intensive field experiences. Anthropologists are likely to value this quality and not to mind a concomitant condition: that the number of activities and resources encompassed by the models are given in the situation. In other words, what the model specifies is the allocation of land, labor and capital among different crops. Ideally, a separate program should be set up for each producing unit, as each represents a unique situation. However, as such an exercise would be impractical, the analyst has to stratify his population and select one or more representative units. The process of selection can vary and is not defined by the format of the model.

The application of the model has contributed to an awareness that there is a range of possible solutions. In fact, some of the favored solutions may be nonmaximizing strategies. Furthermore, the use of linear programming models has dramatized the disparity between simulated solutions and the observed range of solutions. This disparity is due to: farmers' differential managerial abilities; the model's incompleteness; a contrast between the farmers' goals and model's maximization function; the difference between the algorithms used by the farmer and the model; and/or the fact that models are designed to predict long-range adjustments after a period of trial and error. The disparity between model and reality makes it very difficult, if not impossible, to test the models. At the same time, the disparity should help the anthropologist to frame relevant research questions about the information used by farmers, the conceptual frameworks used by them to evaluate options and outputs and the reasons for their choice of a strategy.

II.   INFORMATION PROCESSING MODELS

With the previous models the decision maker is expected to gather information until it becomes too costly and then to evaluate each prospect according to preference and likelihood. If the decisions are mapped as a tree and if we are careful to take into account the effect of the environment on the options, then the decision maker will face only a limited set of options and simple short-term goals. Nevertheless, we still picture him as an evaluator of options.

Alternatively, a decision maker can be described as an information processor. We may assume that he has a stock of well-integrated knowledge and that as he perceives new options he will sort them out and choose accordingly. Or we may assume that he has the options clearly in mind and that what he processes is information about them. In this description, the decision maker resembles a computer rather than a pondering, doubt-ridden Robinson Crusoe. This is not an idle analogy. In fact, an information processing decision tree is a sequence of judgments to accept or reject an option or a prospect: Each step is a dyadic confrontation for the decision maker. If a given option passes all steps, then it is judged appropriate and is assumed to be chosen.

I want to make quite clear that these models do not intend to describe the actual steps decision makers take. Like rationality models, they are "as if" models. Individuals are not neatly programmed; they may muddle through, back and forth, and around options. The only necessity is that in the end, after some trial and error, the decision arrived at should be congruent with the one elicited by the information processing models.

Several theorists have attempted to formalize this approach. I mention only one such attempt here because Gladwin uses a variant of it to examine allocation decisions by small farmers. It has become known in the literature as elimination by aspects.

A. Elimination by Aspects: Hierarchical Trees

In this model, options are first identified and then characterized by a set of discrete aspects (for example, maize as food for the family, as fodder, as food for chickens, as a cash return; fertilizers as a cost, as an amount of labor required, as a gain in yield, etc.). These aspects are not fixed natural characteristics of options (maize, fertilizer, etc.); their value, cost, and probability must be elicited from the decision maker. Each option is considered separately, each aspect of the option evaluated sequentially. For example, the decision maker considering a particular variety of maize first judges whether it is good for eating, then whether it is good for fodder, whether it has higher yields than other varieties, whether growth requirements fit available resources, etc. If at every step the judgment is positive, that variety of maize is planted.[12] The example I use above illustrates three limitations of all elimination by aspects models: 1) only one option (in this case maize variety) is considered at the time; 2) the main decision goal must be very specific and must remain constant for each particular tree (either maize for food or maize for fodder);[13] 3) at each step a yes or no answer has to be possible; the models do not allow for uncertain judgments.

This format is most useful for modeling discrete decisions about short-term investments. It has not yet been adapted to decisions under uncertainty. Furthermore, since each option has to be considered singly and since the goal of each decision tree has to be specific (maize for food or maize for fodder), the integration of all decisions into annual or long-range strategies is somewhat problematic and may, at times, be arbitrary. Gladwin attempts to predict annual cropping strategies by assuming that if farmers have enough land they will plant all crops that pass the constraints. If they do not have enough land for all crops, they will give first priority to crops that are at least <u>twice as profitable</u> as subsistence crops, then plant as much food crop as they need to feed the family, and only later plant other crops. These last crops must be at least as profitable as corn. If cash crops and corn compete for land, then a separate tree must be designed to resolve the conflicting options. Gladwin's solution to the problem of how to integrate decisions into annual or long-range strategies hinges on her use of empirically derived rules of thumb;

anthropologists should now examine the theoretical foundations of such rules. But eventually she must make use of the concept of relative value (at least twice as profitable) which, as we have seen, is not always easy to determine.

A more serious objection was raised, and partly resolved, by Tversky (1972). He pointed out that whether an option passes all steps may depend on the ordering of the aspects. He suggested that aspects should be ranked according to their importance, so that the tree becomes a hierarchical tree. He did not, however, specify by what criteria we are to rank the aspects.

B.   Elimination by Aspects: Nonhierarchical Trees

C. Gladwin not only offers us alternative solutions to those suggested by Tversky, but has elaborated a simple and interesting model. She has adapted the existing information processing models, incorporating some of Tversky's suggestions, Lancaster's ideas based on his analysis of consumer demand, and H. Gladwin and Murtaugh's elaboration of purchasing decisions. Her nonhierarchical elimination by aspect model has two advantages: It is operationally simple, and the simplifying procedures do not violate those used by decision makers themselves. Because the details of her modeling procedure are described in the literature (Gladwin, 1975, 1976, 1979a, 1979b, and 1980), only its main characteristics and some of its strengths and limitations are outlined here.

Gladwin elicits the aspects of each option during in-depth interviews with farmers, using ethnoscientific eliciting techniques.[14] But as the farmers' lists of aspects may be very large and may include post-decision criteria, she suggests the following procedure for discarding irrelevant or redundant aspects: 1) Retain only those that are mentioned when the decision is discussed.   2) Eliminate aspects that are not relevant distinguishing characteristics of the option (for example, labor requirements if they are similar for the options).   3) Eliminate aspects that are of equal importance to other aspects.   4) Eliminate aspects that affect choice through another aspect. Because the adequacy of this first step in the modeling of decisions is crucial to the adequacy of the model, it should receive more attention.

Gladwin is careful to check the validity of the aspect selection by testing the model's predictive ability with a second sample of informants. Thus when using this model we must be cautious with sample size and statistical significance, for both the premises and the results are being tested. It is also important to note here that the model attempts to identify and sort the choice criteria farmers use in specific situations; it does not identify likely outcomes. If the model is going to be used to predict choice outcome in other situations, we have to assume constancy of choice criteria.

Once the sets of aspects are selected, Gladwin orders them but does not rank them. She does not fully specify the ordering procedure analysts should use to simulate the farmers' decisions. At times it is not clear whether the ordering specified is that of the decision maker or the analyst. This is an area that requires further consideration; the trial and error procedure Gladwin uses is feasible for the types of decisions she analyzes but may not be for arriving at an appropriate ordering in more complex decisions. Nor does this method consider problems that arise when the number of aspects, even after reduction, is large (see Kronenfeld, 1977). We need to develop precise criteria for determining the number of aspects and their ordering in the decision tree. Furthermore, if decisions are to be made about allocation of resources, the criteria to order and to limit the set should relate to economic goals and relevant economic relations.

If the decision tree is correctly specified--that is, if appropriate aspects are selected--and if the ordering does not violate the logic of the decision problem, the options should either pass through the decision tree or be eliminated. If an option gets stuck with a "maybe" at any step, the model does not work. This may signal an inadequate selection of aspects, but it may also mean that farmers are unable to accept or reject the aspect with certainty. It is possible, of course, to rephrase the aspect and thereby make a dyadic choice possible. But before doing so, one should examine whether farmers have enough information to judge an option positively or negatively with respect to that aspect.[15] When prospects are uncertain or knowledge is limited, such a judgment may be impossible. Gladwin's decision tree, for example contains questions that in some

situations (though not in her case study) may elicit
indeterminate answers: "Do you have the time or labor
for a second application of fertilizer?" "Do you have
the capital or credit to apply the fertilizer?" "Is
urea too risky to apply?" "Is it more profitable?"
"Is it twice as profitable?"[16] In such cases the
analyst must take into account that indeterminate
judgments may represent uncertain prospects, and that
one should eliminate aspects only after ascertaining
that they are not of crucial importance.

Another important limitation is that each option
is evaluated separately from the others. This implies
that they are not interrelated. Farmers may plant a
low-yielding cash crop because wages are low or
because they are unable to find employment during
their own slack farming season. One can make a
correction by carefully phrasing the aspects so as to
encompass the interrelation. In other words, the
aspects can never be limited to those elicited from
the decision maker, because he may consider only the
characteristics for each option and not the whole
long-range scheme of his farm planning.

Another limitation is that the model does not
allow for tradeoff among aspects. For example, it may
discount a high yield in beans, which would bring a
good income, because the beans use land that otherwise
would be planted with maize for consumption. To
disregard this aspect is unwise, because a farmer may
prefer to have cash so he can purchase maize and other
items rather than a crop of maize to consume.

Nevertheless, the procedure is very attractive
because it is relatively simple, direct, and adaptable
to specific situations. Furthermore, one avoids
having to deal with subjective or a posteriori
probabilities or utility judgments. It should be
particularly useful for examining some of the
obstacles to the incorporation of new practices and to
experimentation. At the same time, the model cannot
handle uncertain answers, so it is not the best tool
for predicting adoption rates. Other, more esoteric
economic problems, many which are still part of the
literature of expected utility models, cannot be
adequately researched using elimination by aspect
models. But that, of course, was not their intent;
and we would be wise to use them for their intended
purposes--to examine the behavioral decision process,
to postulate how decision rules may be generated and

what types of decision rules are used, and to examine the elements that are considered in decisions with short-term planning horizons.

III. DECISIONS AS A MECHANICAL RELATION BETWEEN INPUTS AND OUTPUTS

There is a considerable amount of research that directly or indirectly implies a decision even when the analysis is not set out as a decision problem. Both regression paradigms using variance and covariance, and multiple regression techniques to sort out conditions and relevant relations, have been used to examine a range of outcomes.[17] Sometimes these techniques are also used to elicit rules, as represented by patterns of outcomes.[18]

There is another body of research that regards production not so much as an allocation problem as a transformation problem. This approach, which has a considerable history in the economic literature, has for some time also been used by anthropologists. It is known as production function, and is now being used to evaluate the "rationality" of certain decisions and the economic consequences of the efficient or inefficient use of resources. I consider production function here because the arguments that emerge from its calculations are used in discussions about the allocative behavior of farmers.

The production function is the specification of a rule that defines output given a set of inputs and a known way of organizing production. Many are the functional relations described in the literature; most are variants of a basic set of proposed mathematical rules. The one anthropologists use is the Cobb-Douglas production function. But this is not always the most suitable function. The selection of a function should depend on several issues: the nature of the problem, the type of relationship which seems to exist between input and output (linear, concave, discontinuous, etc.), the adequacy of the constraints, and the assumption of each function.

The Cobb-Douglas function allows for a concave function; that is, a situation in which there is a demonstrable decrease in the marginal utility of output. The other advantage of this function is that it can relate a number of inputs to an output, in a simple manner:

$$\text{Output} = \text{Constant} \cdot \text{Input A}^{\alpha} \cdot \text{Input B}^{\alpha}$$

This expression is useful because it allows us to consider the effect of one extra unit of any input or output, but only when all other inputs are held constant. In other words, it cannot be used when inputs are strongly interdependent. For example, tractors and labor cannot be considered separate variables, nor can water and fertilizer, because one directly affects the output effect of the other. The expression also assumes that a change of inputs will affect outputs but not the organization of the enterprise--in other words, that the sum of the elasticities of all inputs will not be greater than one. Greater simplicity can be achieved by limiting the application of the formula to cases where the goal is to maximize an output.

Ever since Cobb and Douglas formulated the function in 1928, economists have attempted to extend its use to situations where the Cobb-Douglas assumption does not hold. The CES production function was developed to take into account situations in which elasticity of substitution was not unitary. It has also been corrected to take into account profit levels rather than profit maximization (Zellner, Kurenta and Dreze). Furthermore, the factors that initially could not be taken into account have been introduced as disturbance (Just and Pope, 1979; Dillon and Anderson, 1971). Each of these additions adds greater mathematical complexity, which may or may not be warranted.

Once it is clear that the function is applicable to the situation under analysis, one can proceed with the selection and specification of variables. Variables that are interrelated must either be aggregated or not considered in the equation, except as conditions or disturbances. If the function is to represent a relation between inputs and all outputs, the latter must be aggregated as profit or revenue or expected value. Using regression analysis, one can then estimate the coefficients by determining elasticity of production over a given population of producing units. The elasticities for each input are considered separately and should all add up to one.

To determine whether allocation is efficient or not, one compares the marginal value of production to the marginal cost of factors of production. If the relationship is less than one, the resource is inefficiently underused; if it is greater than one, the resource is inefficiently overused. Unfortunately, these results do not say much about whether a farmer is efficient or not, as the equation is based on an average farm (Gladwin, 1979b). If the farmer is inefficient, the function throws little light on the reason (Mijindadi, 1981).

Production function can also be used to elucidate the returns to input in the average farm of the sample and the effect of changes of input combination. Agricultural economists have used it to evaluate the economic--rather than just the technical--impact of new factors like pesticides (Carlson, 1979), fertilizer (de Janvry, 1972), and new practices (Pachico, 1980; Gladwin, 1979b). It has been used to determine key factors affecting the existing level of production (Mijindadi, 1980). It can also be used to select or reject issues for further analysis.

Plattner (1975) used production function to evaluate the relevant contribution of factors suspected to affect the income of itinerant traders in Mexico. In an ongoing study of marketing behavior in an urban marketplace, Plattner (1981) uses production function to evaluate short-run efficiency of factors as well as to ponder the conditional assumptions about the efficiency of labor input.

Finkler (1978) uses production function to estimate the marginal value product of each input and to determine whether the percentage that each input makes towards marginal output relates to the share received by the providers. The lack of congruency, however, does not provide her with an alternative explanation.

IV. SOCIAL STUDIES OF DECISION PROCESS

Despite his dismissal of economic man, Malinowski's early study on exchange and production set the pace for later consideration of how obligations and relations give meaning to wants--which, in turn, define patterns of action. Firth further developed this concept by talking about choices involved in all sorts of acts. Since then, descriptive and discursive decision analysis has been part of the literature in economic anthropology. We have a considerable amount of sensitive information on the effect on production of: access to resources, composition of household, incentives to produce, social mobility, innovation, savings, etc. In recent years the discursive style has been narrowed, and now adheres to a more rigorous format. Regression analysis has been used to evaluate the effect of a variety of social factors on the results of production (Chibnik, 1980; Shapiro, 1975; DeWalt, 1979; Cancian, 1979).

The impact of managerial style on economic behavior has a long history in sociological and anthropological literature. It was forcefully brought to our attention by Max Weber when he categorized types of economic action and linked them to the meanings attached to them by the actors themselves. This approach yielded a considerable amount of information on the sociological definition of managerial styles and the impact of the styles on production. Until recently, however, the variables were not often integrated into a decision process format; they were used only to explain ranges of outcome. In an effort to bring the analysis of value and cultural patterns of management to the context of decision making, Firth (1965) suggested that we categorize types of management decisions and responsibility for them. Belshaw (1964), following the same line of thought, examined the likelihood that individuals with the required management abilities will be placed in the appropriate niche and will be able to foresee the minutiae of costs and opportunities that ensure the success of the enterprise.

In 1967 Glade--according to Greenfield (Greenfield et al., 1979)--wrote an influential article on management, ideology and situational constraints. Bennett (1969) related management styles to modes of adaptation, a theme that he has since explored in greater detail and with clear reference to decision process. Many other writers have since attempted to relate decision outcomes to management and allocation constraints.[19] The final step will have been taken when the determinants of managerial style are fully incorporated into decision trees, affecting either the definition of decision points, the perception of options, or the evaluations of returns and prospects. Only then will we keep sight of one of the major purposes of using the decision perspective: determining how the logic of the situation and of decision making in it affects actions.

Variations in output cannot be entirely explained by differential access to resources or managerial experience. We also have to analyze the range of strategies used by farmers who may otherwise be equally endowed. Most farmers have to rely on subjective estimates when selecting a strategy, and these estimates can vary considerably (although they may cluster around certain objective figures). Expectations are derived from experience and are summarized as the most familiar outcome or set of outcomes (Ortiz, 1979b); but they also vary with ideas of what is sufficient, desirable and necessary (Michie, 1976). It is in the areas of how expectations are formed and prospects evaluated that work needs to be done by anthropologists, not just by psychologists experimenting with game situations. Some of the problems Gladwin encountered in her models will be solved or at least mitigated when we are able to answer these questions: By what rules are marginal values measured? How much more of a yield, or a cost, makes a difference to the decision maker's accounting procedures? What rules are used as choice criteria? Moerman (1968), Geoghegan (1969), and Quinn (1975) discuss some of these questions.

No decision analysis is possible unless the goal of the decision is clearly outlined. This goes beyond arguments as to whether informants maximize profit or revenue, satisfy well-being (Williams, 1977), or safety (Cancian, 1979). In most decision analysis one has to define the decision's planning horizon in very specific terms. This implies that one must define both the decision maker's goal and his time frame. Few studies are specific on this subject. Williams (1977) is one of the few anthropologists who considers this point when he indicates that his Welsh farmers' strategy was to maximize income per unit of time rather than income per unit of land. (See Chapter IX for further discussion of this point.)

Thus, three questions must be asked: What defines the planning horizon or set of hierarchical planning horizons? What experiences and social constraints mold the perception of the decision goal? To what extent does the decision process affect the intended objective function? This last question requires particular attention, not because it is especially important but because it tends to be disregarded. One hopes that the attention now given

to information processing models will alert scholars
to the limitations of some of existing decision-making
models.

Anthropologists have long been aware that to
understand patterns of production one must also
understand patterns of consumption. In 1939, Audrey
Richards published a study of Bemba households:
Land, Labour and Diet in North Rhodesia. Still
regarded as a major study in that field, her book
discusses patterns of cooking, measuring, and storage
and how they relate to what is consumed and produced.
Her sensitive flow chart could easily have been
translated into a decision tree format had she not
generalized and aggregated her data. In the years
since her book was published, many anthropologists
have added information about how social obligation
affects consumption and acts as a motivating force in
production. I mention her work here not just because
it is one of the early detailed studies on the
subject, but because her use of the choice and
decision format can provide guidance on how to
integrate consumption decisions with production. When
she discusses the amount of grain used in cooking and
in brewing beer, she is also talking about how the
grain is measured and the stock in store evaluated.
Savings and fields are depleted as a consequence of
decisions to consume. But the act of consuming is
seldom determined by fixed factors. For instance,
consider the simple example in Figure 1.

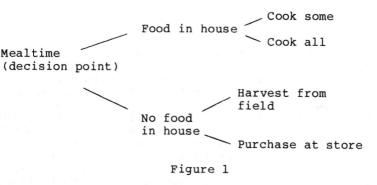

Figure 1

The choice will depend not just on preferences and
prices but on who does the cooking, the social
significance of the food prepared, who plants the

277

fields, who has the rights to the crops in the field, who controls the cash resources in the family, etc. The incentives to maintain a subsistence field of a particular design will depend on the flow of consumption decisions and not on a measure of minimal subsistence requirements, which economists and many anthropologists (including myself) are tempted to use. An alternative is to approximate amounts likely to be consumed by simulating consumption decisions with decision trees.[20]

Decision trees or flow charts are useful constructs for graphically simulating the complex process of decision making. They are implied in the writings of many anthropologists and discussed specifically by Gladwin and Ortiz. Yet these two authors use very different tree formats and illustrate widely divergent processes. Gladwin uses the tree format to simplify complex evaluations and transform them into dyadic judgments. Ortiz uses it to convey the sequential nature of decisions. In Gladwin's tree, time is of no consequence; in Ortiz's the length of the branches corresponds to the time between decisions which is determined by degree of uncertainty and by ecological and technological requirements. Gladwin's format is direct and simple, and is most useful for the study of ongoing decisions with determinable outcomes. On the other hand, when the subject is long-range strategies or the development of an enterprise, Ortiz's format is more appropriate, as long as the ordering and timing of decision points is carefully determined.

Decisions about what to plant, invest, and consume are not always made by the same individual. Many decisions are made by a group after various options have been discussed. Problems of consensus and methods of arriving at joint evaluations are covered in some detail in both psychological and anthropological literature. But even when the final responsibility falls on an individual,[21] seldom is the same person responsible for a whole series of linked decisions. In Latin America, for example, the husband may decide how much maize to plant and how big the manioc field should be. But it is often the wife who decides how many pigs to buy with the proceeds of last year's sales and at what weight the pigs, which are fattened on maize and manioc, should be slaughtered. The husband may be the one to decide on investments; but the wife, by choosing the staples to be purchased, determines how much money is available to invest. Thus it is not enough to outline the shape of the trees; one must also determine who is responsible for a decision at each branch. Only then can we assume that our models simulate decision processes, and that we can predict the range of likely outcomes. It is also important to specify the degree of control that a decision maker has over available resources (capital, labor, land, etc.), as that will affect his or her evaluation of options. Individual decision trees need not be large. A tree can encompass short sequences but be linked to previous and subsequent trees, thus forming interdependent sets: one set providing funds for investments, to subsequent sets of decisions thus setting limits on future actions.

In summary, I propose that in most cases we construct decision trees to simulate the actual time sequence of decisions and the time lapse between decision and action. We must determine who is responsible for each decision, and how values, role, and status may affect the decision maker's choice. The choice itself is a judgment by the decision maker that one of two or more options has more "value" for reaching particular criteria or goal. But the criteria used to judge the options may be different for each decision point; the use of a tree does not imply single or consistent goals, as do "elimination by aspect" models and "utility" models. Yet goals or criteria cannot change arbitrarily; they must be predictable and contingent on certain factors (uncertainty, technological requirements, changes in composition of unit of production, life cycle status of production unit, household consumption patterns, financial flows, availability of labor).[22]

More research is needed to determine how goals and criteria change through the annual and long-range cycles of producing units, and to determine the maximal and minimal output levels desired. The number of options to be evaluated at each decision point is unlikely to be very large, as it is determined by what is perceived as most relevant at that time. Only the most obvious constraints and returns are likely to be in the mind of the decision maker at a choice point. Furthermore, he is unlikely to evaluate a return with high uncertainty, as he will not be able to conceptualize it clearly enough to use it as a decision element.

The simplification of decision procedures thus emerges from the decision process itself, and can be predicted by the analyst. At most decision points the evaluations may be simple and predominantly technical in nature: Does one variety imply more labor than another? Do extra yields warrant higher labor inputs? Yet at other points the farmer will have to decide whether he prefers corn to beans, cash to food. In a complex environment, the only tool available to the analyst to determine the outcome of such judgments is a system of preference curves that must be elicited from informants. Although this procedure can be empirically accurate, it is also cumbersome. Anthropologists should thoroughly investigate evaluative processes so they can develop simulation procedures that are both theoretically sound and easy to operationalize. Once the tree has been diagrammed and the responsibility problem and mode of resolution have been clarified for each decision, one can transform the tree into a matrix.

CONCLUSION

Initially the cartesian homo oeconomicus may have seemed a neat construct for working out the logic of economic actions. But after Menger, he suffered the fate of many of the characters in Lewis Carroll's Tangled Tales--to find him we have sometimes to go "Straight down the crooked lane / And all around the square" (p. 4). Though camouflaged with logarithms and probabilities, he is still alive in utility models. If you can master the technical language you can use him to think about relations and fluctuations. But he is not an easy companion in a fieldwork exercise. Farmers do not think in terms of probabilities, and their preferences are so complex that it takes more than one Tangled Tale to turn them into neat mathematical problems.

Yet there is still a clear role for homo oeconomicus, and that role could expand if social sciences can manage to clarify the principles that are used to rank preferences and to estimate outcomes of the evaluative processes. This is a task that should not be left entirely to psychologists. It entails more than mental processes; as Marx, Menger and Mauss suggested, it also involves social processes. Values are an expression of a relationship between people and commodities that are being produced or transacted.

With linear programming homo oeconomicus becomes
Economic Man. He loses many of his relationships but
can program his allocations. His maximizing foresight
is finite; it can be set where he wants with as many
conditions as necessary. His calculations are based
on the limited set of assets he has or knows he can
acquire. He offers us a closed model in which we can
work out how planning ought to or might change if his
asset structure changes, or his mode of production is
altered. Although the rule assumed to solve the
allocation problem is some variant of rationality
(satisfying, bounded, etc.), it should be possible to
alter the rule as long as we can translate the
alterations into constraints. As Day and Singh (1975)
point out, linear programming is a neat model to
represent a decentralized decision-making sector in
which farmers operate in an environment (market,
government, and nature) which they do not fully
control. In such an environment, Economic Man alters
his allocation plans (consciously or automatically) in
response to changes in resources and returns (see
Chapter IX). The linear programming model does not
focus on external relationships, and neither does
Economic Man in an agricultural sector like the one
Day and Singh described. Consequently, each set of
farmers with different asset structures or modes of
production requires a different model. When Robinson
Crusoe moved to another island he had to rethink how
to allocate resources; when we move to a new level we
have to do likewise. Alteration of strategies and
range of possible strategies adds to the
indeterminateness of the economic environment of
farmers and in turn compounds the task of economists
interested in aggregating microprocesses.

Theoretically, linear programming models are less
interesting than some others. We cannot use them to
think about a system, about relationships within a
system (except to describe the input-output
relationships among units), or about the dynamic of
valuation. On the other hand, they are easily adapted
to practical planning problems, and they allow us to
incorporate variables that concern anthropologists.

With information processing models the
intellectual landscape is entirely different. We are
no longer pondering Robinson Crusoe's doubts and the
intellectual boundaries of his problem. We are no
longer using complete analytical models that can be
made more complex by deducing yet other relational

propositions.[23] But we are still using subjective, imperfect, and problematic constructs. One of these problematic constructs is the assumption that choice is always reduced to a dyadic problem--that an answer is always possible if we specify the correct set of alternatives. The model's way of incorporating uncertainty is to become more and more specific. Furthermore, to build this type of model we must still rely on subjective criteria that characterize and order decision points. These models will become more convincing once we learn more about how decision rules emerge, and how to select ranking criteria. It may very well be that we can use the models themselves to research the subject. They have certainly brought us to the level of the farmer, who, instead of pondering, spins endless solutions, each one suggesting another.

Menger had hoped that by understanding patterns of allocation he could outline the foundation of the theory of exchange, of price, of production. He believed economic events reflect the action of individual producers and consumers: "A social economy is made up of individual economies" (Menger, 1950, p. 187). The difficulty is that the individual portrayed in a decision model is only a stereotypic construct; it cannot capture the range of behavior of real producers and consumers. Because the actions of consumers and producers depend on the reactions of all others, each one of them has to make constant adjustments and readjustments. It may well be that in an equilibrating world, if such a world exists, the adjustments and readjustments would eventually cluster around a mode (see Chapter IX). In such a world the stereotypic decision models may portray trends. Nevertheless, they cannot predict the next set of decisions. Decision models can be used to predict with great accuracy only when equilibrium is a state of nature or when the producers are not totally dependent on their immediate economic environment (see IIC). Ironically, these models are probably most applicable to peasant production problems.

Economic events are also affected by institutional arrangements that integrate units of production. The locus of these arrangements is often in the polity. One cannot discover the dynamics of such institutional arrangements by focusing solely on behavior of the units it integrates. Therefore, microdecision analysis can never reach the grand goal Menger envisioned. It can, nevertheless, be very useful for determining the aggregate output and aggregate response of a sector that is relatively homogeneous and that produces a surplus that is controlled by external forces. In other words, it can help determine the contribution of a particular peasant sector and evaluate the extent of exploitation. Decision analysis is also a valuable tool for planners and project evaluaters to examine the relative impact of variables at a micro level. Decision analysis may never reach the theoretical heights that Menger and the marginalists foresaw, but this is no good reason for discarding the approach.

Nevertheless, the models used until now need further refinement and transformations, a task that anthropologists should undertake. Timeless models should probably give way to sequential models, diagrammed as trees; and judgment procedures should be more carefully examined before we allow ourselves to be trapped by computer systems. Once again, we should examine behavior before further formalizing our argument. The paradoxes that squares can be rounded, that rationality is sometimes irrational, and that a yes sometimes signifies a no are, after all, products of our intellect. Reality may help us disentangle the tale, and once we feel clearheaded we may no longer mind conceiving crooked lanes as straight lines.

Notes

[1] Geoghegan (1969) elicited rules of choice in residence from patterns, and Fjellman (quoted in Quinn, 1975b) did likewise from incidence and problem solving exercises given to informants. The approach is possible when the options and conditions affecting choice are deterministic.

[2] Salisbury (1962) and Gudeman (1978). Firth, however, reminded us that arguments about cost accounting are not arguments about value of products (1967, p. 21).

[3] Schneider (1975) and Salisbury (1976) have suggested the use of indifference curves in anthropology. They have been used in Aubey, Kyle and Strickon (1974).

[4] See Hull, et al. (1973), Coombs (1975), and Shanteau (1975) on utility and its measurements.

[5] The assumptions about the characteristics of preferences are linearity, additiveness, and dominance. It cannot be assumed that preferences are consistent through time; instead one has to deal with distribution of preference ranking. See Edwards and Tversky (1967), Hull, et al. (1973), Raiffa (1968), Restle (1971), Officer and Halter (1968), Kozelka (1969), Masson (1975) for the implications of utility determinations.

[6] For a description of methods used to elicit subjective probabilities from farmers, see Anderson et al. (1977) and Binswanger (1978, 1980). For a discussion of errors incurred when attempting to elicit probability constructs that are not present prior to elicitation, see Estes (1976), Kahneman and Tversky (1972), Hogarth (1975). See Quinn (1978) and Ortiz (1979b) for the problem of assuming that fishermen and farmers describe probability distributions.

[7] See Moscardi and de Janvry (1977), Dillon and Scandizzo (1978), Binswanger (1978), Young (1979) on the importance of attitude toward risk in management as well as the implication of risk preferences.

[8] See Davenport (1960) for the initial exposition using game theory. See Walker (1977) for a correction of Kozelka's model.

[9] This lengthy literature tries to incorporate the effect of imperfect information.

[10] See Anderson et al. (1977), Officer and Halter (1968).

[11] See Calavan (1977) and Roumasset (1979) for similar objections to the application of game theory to farm planning.

[12] There is considerable argument among psychologists as to whether this is a good representation of judgment process. See Hillel and Hogarth (1981), Slovic et al. (1977) for a review of the literature. But I am concerned here not with accuracy of the mental process, but with a model describing possible selection that

produces results congruent with outcomes of farmers' decisions.

[13] This is clearly illustrated in Randall's (1977) study of sequence of actions involved in fishing.

[14] Plummer (1980) relies first on his general knowledge of maize and oil palm agriculture in the area, then assesses relevance using variance analysis of suspected criteria.

[15] Gladwin avoids indeterminate answers by eliciting the payoffs of new yields that would entice farmers. Another technique is to ask questions about planting X acreage with a crop then planting another lot with the same or another crop.

[16] I am not arguing with her specific model, merely using her questions as illustrations.

[17] See Chibinik (1980), DeWalt (1979), and Calavan (1977).

[18] See Quinn (1975a) for an attempt to model such decisions. There is, of course, a large number of studies in the psychological literature.

[19] There are many studies; I shall cite only a few examples: Long (1970), Coughenour (1980), Moran (1979), Ortiz (1973), Cancian (1979), Moerman (1968).

[20] Barnum and Lynn (1979a,b) have integrated consumption decision with production decisions by using a set of interrelated linear utility models. See the above authors for other references to this approach. This is of course implied in Farm System Approach (Norman, 1980).

[21] Two examples where there are extreme cases of discrete allocation of responsibility for interdependent tasks are Barth (1967) and Berleant Schiller (1977). Many other cases must be familiar to readers.

[22] Calavan (1979) examines how production targets define labor input. Barlett (1980a) examines returns to labor using Chayanov's model.

23 See Fusfeld (1980) for a discussion of the use of the axiomatic method in economics and a review of Gödel's, Popper's, and Kuhn's argument about incompleteness, inconsistency, and falsification.

References

ABELE, Hanns. 1977. Towards a neo-austrian theory of exchange. In Equilibrium and disequilibrium in economic theory. G. Schwödiauer, ed. Dordrecht, Holland: D. Reidel Publishing Company.

ANDERSON, J., J. C. Dillon, and J. B. Hardaker. 1977. Agricultural decision analysis. Ames: Iowa University Press.

ANDERSON, Jock. 1979. Perspective on models of uncertain decisions. In Risk, uncertainty and agricultural development. J. A. Roumasset, et al., eds. New York: Agricultural Development Council.

AUBEY, Robert, John Kyle, and Arnold Strickon. 1974. Investment behavior and elite social structures in Latin America. Journal of Interamerican Studies and World Affairs 16:71-95.

BARLETT, Peggy F. 1977. Labor efficiency and the mechanism of agricultural evolution. Journal of Anthropological Research 32:124-140.

_____. 1980a. Cost-benefit: a test of alternative methodologies. In Agricultural decision making. P. Barlett, ed. New York: Academic Press.

_____. 1980b. Adaptive strategies in peasant agricultural production. Annual Review of Anthropology 9:545-573.

BARNUM, Howard N., and Lyn Squire. 1979a. A model of an agricultural household. World Bank Staff Occasional Papers no. 27. Baltimore: Johns Hopkins University Press.

_____. 1979b. An econometric application of the theory of the farm-household. Journal of Development Economics 6:79-102.

BARTH, Fredrick. 1959. Segmentary opposition and the theory of games. Journal of the Royal Anthropological Institute 89:5-21.

_____. 1967. Economic spheres in Darfur. In Themes in economic anthropology. Raymond Firth, ed. London: Tavistock.

BAUMOL, William J. 1963. Toward the construction of more useful models. In Models of market. Alfred Oxenfeldt, ed. New York: Columbia University Press.

BELSHAW, Cyril. 1964. Under the ivy tree. London: Routledge and Kegan Paul.

BENNETT, John W. 1969. Northern plainsmen. Chicago: Aldine.

BERLEANT, Schiller Riva. 1977. Production and division of labor in a West Indian peasant community. American Ethnologist 4:253-273.

BILMES, Jack M. 1979. The evolution of decisions in a Thai village: a quasi-experimental study. Human Organization 38:169-178.

BINSWANGER, Hans. 1978. Attitudes towards risk: implications for economic and psychological theories of an experiment in rural India. Economic Growth Center Discussion Paper no. 286. New Haven: Yale University.

_____. 1980. Attitudes towards risk: experimental measurements in rural India. Journal of Agricultural Economics 62:395-407.

BISERRA, Jose Valdeci. 1980. Uncertainty and decision analysis on large sharecropped farms in Northern Brazil. Ph.D. Thesis, Ohio State University.

BOURDIEU, Pierre. 1977. Outline of a theory of practice. London: Cambridge University Press.

BOUSSARD, J. M. and M. Petit. 1967. Representation of farmers' behavior and uncertainty with focus-loss constraint. Journal of Farm Economics 49:869-880.

BURKE, Robert. 1979. Screen revolution technology and farm class in Mexico. Economic Development and Cultural Change 28:135-152.

CALAVAN, Michael M. 1977. Decisions against nature: an anthropological study of agriculture in northern Thailand. Northern Illinois University: Center for South East Asian Studies, Report no. 15.

_____. 1979. Prospect for probabilistic re-interpretation of Chayanovian theory: an exploration discussion. Paper presented at Central States Anthropological Society. Milwaukee, Wisconsin.

CARLSON, Gerald A. 1979. Pest control risk in agriculture. In Risk, uncertainty and agricultural development. J. A. Roumasset, et al., eds. New York: Agricultural Development Council.

CARROLL, Lewis. 1958. Pillow problems and a tangled tale. New York: Dover.

CANCIAN, Frank. 1979. The innovator's situation. Stanford: Stanford University Press.

CHIBNIK, M. 1980. Working out and working in: the choice between labor and cash cropping in Belize. American Ethnologist 7:86-105.

COOK, Scott. 1982. Zapotec stoneworkers. Washington, D.C.: University Press of America.

COOMBS, Clyde H. 1975. Portfolio theory and measurement of risk. In Human judgement and decision process. Martin F. Kaplan and Steven Schwartz, eds. New York: Academic Press.

COUGHENOUR, C. Milton. 1980. Farmers, location and the differentiation of crops from livestock in farming. Rural Sociology 45:569-590.

DAY, Richard. 1963. Recursive programming and production response. Amsterdam: North Holland Publishing Company.

DAY, Richard and Inderjit Singh. 1975. A dynamic model of regional agricultural development. International Regional Science Review 1:27-49.

DAVENPORT, W. 1960. Jamaica fishing: a game theory analysis. In Yale University Papers on Caribbean Anthropology 59:3-11.

DECHATES, Supote. 1978. On farm impacts of economic policy choices in Thailand. Ph.D. Thesis, Washington State University.

DE JANVRY, Alain. 1972. The generalized power production function. American Journal of Agricultural Economics 54:234-237.

DEWALT, Billie. 1979. Modernization in a Mexican ejido. London: Cambridge University Press.

DILLON, John L. and Jock Anderson. 1971. Allocative efficiency, traditional agriculture and risk. American Journal of Agricultural Economics 53:26-35.

DILLON, John L., and Pasquale C. Scandizzo. 1978. Risk attitudes of subsistence farmers in North East Brazil: a sampling approach. American Journal of Agricultural Economics 60:425-435.

DOUGLAS, Mary and Banu Isherwood. 1979. The world of goods. New York: Basic Books.

DUMONT, Louis. 1977. From Mandeville to Marx. Chicago: University of Chicago Press.

EDWARDS, Ward and Amos Tversky, eds. 1967. Decision making. London: Penguin.

EINHORN, Hillel J. and Robin M. Hogarth. 1981. Behavioral decision theory: processes of judgement and choice. Annual Review of Psychology 32:53-88.

ELSTER, John. 1979. Ulysses and the sirens. London: Cambridge University Press.

ESTES, William K. 1976. The cognitive side of probability learning. Psychological Review 83:37-64.

ETUK, Enefiok. 1979. Microeconomic effects of technological change on small holder agriculture in Northern Nigeria: a linear programming analysis. Ph.D. Thesis, Michigan State University.

FINKLER, Kaja. 1978. From sharecroppers to entrepreneurs: peasant household production strategies under the ejido system of Mexico. Economic Development and Cultural Change 27:103-120.

FIRTH, Raymond. 1965. Primitive Polynesian economy. London: Routledge and Kegan Paul.

_____. 1967. Introduction. In Themes in economic anthropology. Raymond Firth, ed. London: Tavistock Publications.

_____. 1979. Work and value. In Social anthropology of work. Sandra Wallman, ed. London: Academic Press.

FREUND, R. J. 1956. The introduction of risk into a programming model. Econometrica 24:253-263.

FUSFELD, Daniel B. 1980. The conceptual framework of modern economics. Journal of Economic Issues 14:1-51.

GAFSI, Salem, and Terry Roe. 1979. Adaptation of unlike high-yielding wheat varieties in Tunisia. Economic Development and Cultural Change 28:119-135.

GEOGHEGAN, William. 1969. Decision-making and residence on Tagtabou Island. Working Paper no. 17. Language and Behavior Research Laboratory, University of California, Berkeley.

GEORGESCU-ROEGEN, N. 1958. The nature of expectations and uncertainty. In Expectation, uncertainty and business behavior. J. Bowman, ed. New York: Social Science Research Council.

GLADWIN, Christina. 1975. A model of the supply of smoked fish from Cape Coast to Kumasi. In Formal methods in economic anthropology. Stuart Plattner, ed. Washington, D.C.: Special Publications of the American Anthropological Association.

_____. 1976. A view of the Plan Puebla: a hierarchical decision model. American Journal of Agricultural Economics 58:881-887.

_____. 1979a. Cognitive strategies and adoption decision: a case study of nonadoption of an agronomic recommendation. Economic Development and Cultural Change 28:155-173.

_____. 1979b. Production functions and decision models: complementary models. American Ethnologist 6:653-674.

_____. 1980. A theory of real life choice: applications to agricultural decisions. In Agricultural decision making. P. Barlett, ed. New York: Academic Press.

GLADWIN, Hugh, and Michael Murtaugh. 1980. The attentive/pre-attentive distinction in agricultural decisions. In Agricultural decision making. P. Barlett, ed. New York: Academic Press.

GODELIER, Maurice. 1972. Rationality and irrationality in economics. London: New Left Books.

GREENFIELD, Sidney, Arnold Strickon, and Robert T. Aubey. 1979. Entrepreneurs in cultural context. Albuquerque: University of New Mexico Press.

GUDEMAN, Stephen. 1978. The demise of a rural economy. London: Routledge and Kegan Paul.

_____. Physiocracy: a natural economics. American Ethnologist 7:240-258.

HAZEL, Peter B. R. 1971. A linear alternative to quadratic and semivariance programming for farm planning under uncertainty. American Journal of Agricultural Economics 53:53-62.

HILLEL, J. E., and R. M. Hogarth. 1981. Behavioral decision theory. Annual Review of Psychology 32:53-88.

HOGARTH, R. M. 1975. Cognitive processes and the assessment of subjective probability distributions. Journal of the American Statistical Association 70:271-294.

HULL, J. C., P. G. Moore, and H. Thomas. 1973. Utility and its measurement. Journal of Royal Statistical Society 136:226-247.

JUST, Richard E., and Rulon D. Pope. 1979. On the relationship of input decisions and risk. In Risk, uncertainty and agricultural development. J. A. Roumasset, et al., eds. New York: Agricultural Development Council.

KAHNEMAN, Daniel, and Amos Tversky. 1972. Subjective probability: a judgement of representativeness. Cognitive Psychology 3:430-454.

KENNEY, R. L. 1972. Utility functions for multi-attribute consequences. Management Science 18:276-287.

KOZELKA, R. 1969. A Bayesian approach to Jamaica fishing. In Game theory in the behavioral sciences. J. R. Buchler and H. G. Nutini, eds. Pittsburg: University of Pittsburg Press.

KRONENFELD, David B. 1977. Information processing constraints on culturally standardized cognitive systems. Paper presented to the Annual Meeting of the American Anthropological Association.

LANGHAM, Max R. 1968. A dynamic linear programming model for development planning. In Economic development of tropical agriculture. W. W. McPherson, ed. Gainesville: University of Florida Press.

LAU, L. J., and P. A. Yotopoulos. 1971. A test of relative efficiency and application to Indian agriculture. American Economic Review 61:94-109.

LIN, William, G. W. Dean, and C. V. Moore. 1974. The empirical test of utility vs. profit maximization in agricultural production. American Journal of Agricultural Economics 56:497-508.

LONG, Norman. 1970. Rural entrepreneurship and religious commitment in Zambia. Internationales Yahrbuch für Religionssoziologie 6:142-157.

MACHLUP, Fritz. 1967. L'homo oeconomicus et ses collègues. In Les fondements philosophiques des systemes economiques. M. Classen, ed. Paris: Payot.

MALINOWSKI, B. 1964. Argonauts of the Western Pacific. London: Routledge and Kegan Paul.

MASSON, Robert T. 1975. Utility function with jump discontinuities: some evidence and implications from peasant agriculture. Economic Inquiry 12:559-566.

MAUSS, Marcel. 1954. The gift. London: Cohen and West.

MENGER, Karl. 1950. Principles of economics. Glencoe, Illinois: Free Press.

MENGES, Günter. 1973. Economic decision making. London: Longmans.

MICHIE, Barry Harwell. 1976. Structure in diversity: variations in productivity and efficiency in Indian agricultural. Ph.D. Thesis, Michigan State University.

MIJINDADI, Ndanusa B. 1980. Production efficiency on farms in Northern Nigeria. Ph.D. Thesis, Cornell University.

MINI, Pierro. 1974. Philosophy and economics. Gainesville: University of Florida Press.

MOERMAN, Michael. 1968. Agricultural change and peasant choice in a Thai village. Berkeley: University of California Press.

MORAN, Emilio F. 1979. Criteria for choosing homesteaders in Brazil. Research in Economic Anthropology 2:339-359.

MOSCARDI, Edgardo, and Alain de Janvry. 1977. Attitudes toward risk among peasants: an econometric approach. American Journal of Agricultural Economics 59:710-716.

MURTAUGH, Michael, and Hugh Gladwin. 1979. A hierarchical decision-process model for forecasting auto-type choices. ms. School of Social Sciences, University of California, Irvine.

NORMAN, David W. 1980. The farming systems approach: relevancy for the small farmer. Michigan State University Rural Development Paper no. 5.

OFFICER, R. R., and A. N. Halter. 1968. Utility analysis in a practical setting. American Journal of Agricultural Economics 50:257-277.

ORTIZ, Sutti. 1973. Uncertainties in peasant farming. Monograph in Social Anthropology, London School of Economics. London: Athlone Press. New York: Humanities Press.

_____. 1979a. The effect of risk aversion on subsistence and cash crop decisions. In Risk, uncertainty and agricultural development. J. A. Roumasset, et al., eds. New York: Agricultural Development Council.

_____. 1979b. Expectations and forecasts in the face of uncertainty. Man 14:64-80.

_____. 1979c. The estimation of work. In Social anthropology of work. Sandra Wallman, ed. London: Academic Press.

_____. 1980. Forecasts, decisions and the farmer's response to uncertain environments. In Agricultural decision making. Peggy Barlett, ed. New York: Academic Press.

PACHICO, Douglas H. 1980. Small farmers' decision making: an economic analysis of three farming systems in the hills of Nepal. Ph.D. Thesis, Cornell University.

PLATTNER, Stuart. 1975. The economics of peddling. In Formal methods in economic anthropology. Stuart Plattner, ed. American Anthropological Association Special Publication no. 4.

_____. 1981. Economic decision making in a public place. Center for International Studies, Occasional Papers.

PLUMMER, Orlay. 1980. Economic strategies of Mfantse farmers' decision making: land access and oil palms. Ph.D. Thesis, University of California, Riverside.

QUINN, Naomi. 1975a. A natural system used in Mfantse litigation settlement. American Ethnologist 3:331-351.

_____. 1975b. Decision models of social structure. American Ethnologist 2:19-47.

_____. 1978. Do Mfantse fish sellers estimate probabilities in their heads? American Ethnology 5:206-227.

RAIFFA, Howard. 1968. Decision analysis: introductory lecture on choice under uncertainty. Reading, Mass.: Addison-Wesley.

RAMSEY, F. P. 1930. The foundations of mathematics and other logical essays. New York: Harcourt.

RANDALL, Robert. 1977. Change and variation in Samal fishing. Ph.D. Thesis. University of California, Berkeley.

READ, D. W., and C. E. Read. 1970. A critique of Davenport's game theory analysis. American Anthropologist 72:351-355.

RESTLE, Frank. 1971. Mathematical models in psychology. London: Penguin.

RICHARDS, Audrey. 1939. Land, labour and diet in Northern Rhodesia. London: Oxford University Press.

ROBBINS, Lionel. 1932. An essay on the nature and significance of economic science. New York: St. Martin's Press.

ROUMASSET, James A. 1979. Introduction and state of the arts. In Risk, uncertainty and agricultural development. J. A. Roumasset, et al., eds. New York: Agricultural Development Council.

SALISBURY, Richard F. 1962. From stone to steel. London and New York: Cambridge University Press.

_____. 1969. Formal analysis in anthropological economics: the Rossel Island case. In Game theory in the behavioral sciences. Ira Buchler and Hugo Nutini, eds. Pittsburg: University of Pittsburg Press.

_____. 1976. Transactions or transactors? an economic anthropologist's view. In Transaction and meaning. Bruce Kapferer, ed. Philadelphia: ISHI.

SCANDIZZO, Pasquale. 1979. Peasant agricultural and risk preference in Northeast Brazil. In Risk, uncertainty and agricultural development. J. A. Roumasset, et al., eds. New York: Agricultural Development Council.

SCHNEIDER, Harold K. 1974. Economic man. Chicago: Free Press.

SEKTHEERA, Rapeepun. 1979. The allocation of family resources to farm and non-farm activities in a village in Northern Thailand. Ph.D. Thesis, Michigan State University.

SHACKLE, G. L. 1949. Expectations in economics. London: Cambridge University Press.

_____. 1966. The nature of economic thought. London: Cambridge University Press.

SHANTEAU, James. 1975. An information integration analysis of risky decision making. In Human judgement and decision process. Martin Kaplan and Steven Schwartz, eds. New York: Academic Press.

SHAPIRO, Kenneth H. 1975. Measuring modernization among Tanzanian farmers. In Formal methods in economic anthropology. Stuart Plattner, ed. American Anthropological Association Special Publication no. 4.

SIMON, Herbert A. 1956. Models of man, social and rational. New York: Wiley.

SLOVIC, Paul, Baruch Fischhoff, Sarah Lichtenstein. 1977. Behavioral decision theory. Annual Review of Psychology 28:1-39.

SOARES, Augusto Cesar. 1977. Resource allocation and choice of enterprise under risk on cotton farms in Northeast Brazil. Ph.D. Thesis. Ohio State University.

STIGLER, George. 1960. The development of utility theory. In Essays in economic thought. J. J. Spengler and W. Allen, eds. Chicago: Rand McNally.

TVERSKY, Amos. 1972. Elimination by aspects: a theory of choice. Psychological Review 79:281-299.

VON NEUMANN, John, and Oscar Morgenstern. 1947. Theory of games and economic behavior. Princeton: Princeton University Press.

WALKER, Michael. 1977. Jamaica fishing study re-interpreted. Theory and Decision 8:265-272.

WILLIAMS, G. 1977. Differential risk strategies as cultural styles among farmers in the lower Chubut Valley, Patagonia. American Ethnology 4:65-83.

YOUNG, Douglas C. 1979. Risk preferences of agricultural producers: their use in extension and research. American Journal of Agricultural Economics 61:1064-1070.

ZELLNER, A. J., J. Kurenta, and J. Dreze. 1966. Specification and extension of Cobb-Douglas production function models. Econometrica 34:784-795.

PART FIVE

DEVELOPMENT: THEORY AND PRACTICE

The transformation of economic systems to more efficient, more production and equitable systems, has not been the central concern of most anthropologists interested in general theory. Instead, since Thurnwald (1932), they have argued about the evolution of primitive systems, paying more attention to the economic requirements for the emergence and restructuring of political institutions than to the economic institutions themselves. In Part One of this book, Blanton, Carrasco, and Berdan, following this tradition, review the arguments that link political development, fluctuations in population, and change in resource use and technology as factors that determine the growth in productivity and the increased complexity and autonomy of distributive systems.

Evolutionary economic anthropologists have not made further use of their historical insights--with the notable exceptions of Geertz (1971) and some ecologists. It has been left to Marxist anthropologists to examine present-day economic transformations by thinking dialectically about the ability or inability of systems to reproduce themselves. In Part Two Hart examines, historically, Marx's and Marxists' concerns about such processes in precapitalist systems, reviewing some of the propositions that have emerged from this approach.

A system's inability to regenerate its mode of production may stem from the way resources are appropriated in the distributive process. As Becker (1977) has pointed out, the historical origin and transformation of the capitalist system are a consequence of the way surplus products are exchanged. Thus this process cannot be ignored, nor can it be reduced to exchange imbalances generated by modes of production. Marketing studies by anthropologists, geographers, and economist reenforce the argument that to understand imbalances, flow irregularities, and instability of modes of production, one must also understand modes of distribution. But they also specifically suggest the demographic and production patterns, as well as the administrative arrangements, that are responsible for particular regional imbalances. Although these studies have not made use

301

of a Marxist perspective, they have shed a considerable light on the reproductive ability of some sectors, as Smith demonstrates in Chapter XI.

Economic systems have never existed in total isolation. Trade in slaves and luxuries among nations has always been important for political and economic reasons (see Part One). It was not, however, until the twentieth century that industrial expansion led to regional and national interdependence. As world theorists have made eminently clear, even precapitalist and peasant systems are influenced by extra-regional relationships. In fact, their survival or transformation depends on events and relationships outside their own regional niche. Thus, we can no longer study them in isolation. At the same time, Smith argues in Chapter XI, we cannot oversimplify the impact of external systems on regional developments. We must examine, as well, interregional dynamics as reflected in modes of production and distribution. Regional analysis will inform large-scale world theorists about the nature of imbalances and the likelihood that they will lead to sociopolitical and economic differentiation.

Smith examines dependency theories from her vantage point as an anthropologist concerned with regional analysis and systems of distribution. Her reviews are therefore somewhat polemical. One hopes her critique will encourage more regional case studies and give them direction. But both she and world theorists must still translate abstract theories about relationships among ideal types into theories about relations among sets of producers. This requires attention to their activities or their regional coexistence. At the macrolevel, theorists simplify their arguments by using homogeneous categories. But at the regional or microlevel (as Smith illustrates with her case study), we cannot allow ourselves this luxury. No doubt the dialogue between world theorist and regional analyst will be stimulating and informative, but their differences are likely to remain as insoluble as those between macro and micro economists (Trager, conference comments). Nevertheless, regional analysis will help to clarify the nature of interdependence and source of imbalances.

The theoretical foundation of arguments about imbalances between producers or producing sectors is the assumption that under certain conditions prices of production fall above or below exchange value. Marx arrived at this proposition through an analysis of the systemic competitive interrelationships of producing units. Although he concluded that exchange value is unlikely to equal production costs, he implied that an equilibrating relationship between them is logically possible. The concept of equilibrium, which has been central to all arguments about growth and development since Adam Smith, thus also shadows the disequilibrating, nonregenerating arguments proposed by Marxists.

Bates (Chapter XII) makes a convincing case for reexamining the concept of equilibrium before we theorize further about development. And he argues that two other basic concepts must also be reexamined: rationality and efficiency. Many policy propositions rest on efficiency arguments: the importance of industrialization for development when the country holds a comparative advantage; the contribution of the agricultural sector to the national economy; the advisability of government intervention on marketing policies or farm investment. Yet the assumptions implied in these concepts are shaky; they are weak foundations for the construction of development theory or policy formulation. Bates urges anthropologists to reexamine these concepts and directs us to look not only at their meaning but also to determine whether the goals of individual rational action compliment those of group action. He also urges us to look at the morality of arguments about development, welfare and equity.

In a different guise the issues surface again in Chapter XIII. As anthropologists become active participants in the development process as consultants to governments or agencies, they must familiarize themselves with the tools used by technical experts. Salisbury urges us to examine the sociological validity of impact analysis procedures, and reviews some of the implications in the erroneous use of one such procedure: cost-benefit accounting. The errors and biases are understandable; they are partly due to difficulties in measuring changes and estimating returns. But they are also caused by an inability to clearly identify the sector or region that is to benefit from the project. As Bledsoe (conference comments) points out, if the cost-benefit analyst does not first determine the target population--to highlight the worth of the project--he may be tempted to exclude some population sectors that receive no clear immediate benefits.

Cost-benefit analysis is not, of course, the only evaluative tool used. Existing manuals on project analysis (Cernea, 1979; Perrett, 1980; Daines, 1979) suggest that one should also use qualitative logical arguments to evaluate project impact. In fact, the difficulty of gathering the complex data required for cost-benefit analysis often renders this technique useless. Furthermore, evaluation of a project should not rest simply on a measure of its expected impacts, which may be hard to determine when prospects are uncertain, but also on the feasibility of the project itself. Despite their limitations, cost-benefit analysis, and other similar accounting techniques are very useful, particularly when planners must chose among several investment options for one of the aspects of a project (for example, a type of road surface, a type of irrigation system, a farm investment strategy, a specific set of services to target populations). Salisbury's cautionary remarks must thus be read carefully.

Some anthropologists, however, would rather discourage the use of accounting tools and even their academic examination for fear of introducing irreparable biases. Scudder (conference comments) and others are concerned that an encouragement to use accounting evaluative techniques will foster the adoption of projects that lend themselves to such technical evaluations. He wonders whether such techniques are not responsible for a perceived preference for projects with short time planning horizons, few multiplier effects, and strategies that focus on a small number of export crops rather than complex farming systems with off-farm components. The message conveyed in Chapter XIII is that anthropologists must be careful when walking the cost accounting tightrope. They should familiarize themselves with the procedures because cost accounting is the language of communication within certain teams, but also because it signals the issue that anthropologists must analyze and the information they must gather to ensure even coverage of all relevant issues. As cost-benefit analysis may be a critical decision tool, anthropologists should also contribute to an improved formulation of accounting procedures.

References

BECKER, James F. 1977. _Marxian political economy_. London: Cambridge University Press.

CERNEA, Michael. 1979. Measuring project impact: monitoring and evaluation in PIDER rural development project--Mexico. World Bank Staff working paper No. 332. Washington, D.C.: World Bank.

DAINES, Samuel R. 1979. Agribusiness and rural enterprise, project analysis manual. Agency for International Development. Washington, D.C.

GEERTZ, Clifford. 1971. _Agricultural involution_. Berkeley: University of California Press.

PERRETT, Helie. 1980. Social and behavioral factors in project work. World Bank Staff working paper. Washington, D.C.: World Bank.

THURNWALD, Richard. 1932. _Economics in primitive communities_. Oxford: International Institute of African Languages and Literature, Oxford University Press.

XI. REGIONAL ANALYSIS IN WORLD-SYSTEM PERSPECTIVE: A CRITIQUE OF THREE STRUCTURAL THEORIES OF UNEVEN DEVELOPMENT

Carol A. Smith

Regional analysis is rooted in the conviction that a different approach from anthropology's traditional one is called for in the study of complex societies (those social systems differentiated by hierarchically organized classes and settlements). My argument is, essentially, that the whole is more than the sum of its parts and that one can never fully understand economic systems by concentrating only on their various components: individuals, communities, cities, sectors. One must, rather, examine the relationships among the different elements of a differentiated system and consider how the functioning of the parts is conditioned by their place within the whole.[1]

Recently, a very persuasive argument has been put forward by Immanuel Wallerstein (1974, 1979) to the effect that regions and nations are themselves too small to be units of analysis because they form incomplete parts of an even larger whole. He identified this larger socioeconomic unit as the modern world system, a system that came into being in the "long" sixteenth century as part and parcel of a new economic order, capitalism. The world system, which was created by a single world market articulating an international division of labor, presently incorporates all corners of the earth and thus affects all of the places traditionally isolated by the economic anthropologist. In Wallerstein's view, even if anthropologists raise their sights to the regional level they will continue to misinterpret the basic economic, social, and political dynamics of the people and groups they study in this century. For until they see the position of these people and groups in the larger whole, they will falsely motivate the dynamics they perceive--dynamics fundamentally conditioned by the workings of the world capitalist system. This assertion challenges all of us, regional analysts and anthropological traditionalists alike, to either defend or abandon our historic mission.

I take up Wallerstein's challenge in this essay by defending the approach of regional analysis, attempting to show how it can inform a major debate presently engaging world-system theorists, Marxist opponents, and other students of global economic development and underdevelopment. The major question in this debate: why has capitalism unfolded in a dynamic fashion in some parts of the world while it has been deformed, mutilated, or simply unrealized in other parts of the world? asks one to consider the process of capitalist development on a world scale. Anthropologists do not look at anything on a world scale, not even practitioners of regional analysis do so. But they can evaluate general processes in smaller focus. So to bring this global debate down to a more manageable level I will ask whether any of the general theories of world differentiation and inequality can account for the pattern of regional differentiation and inequality I have encountered in western Guatemala.

I address the global issue of underdevelopment on a regional scale for three other reasons. First, regions are arenas from which one can consider both local class relations and global conditions as they are realized in particular historical contexts. The particular debate I consider here concerns precisely the weight of these two factors: the degree to which global conditions create local class relations or vice versa. Hence, a regional analysis is especially useful for considering this question. Second, I believe it is time to confront the abstract claims of the people arguing for or against the global view with some relevant case histories and specific data. I do not assume that "the facts" will resolve issues of interpretation. But I do contend that interpretive stances must be informed by the facts--i.e., particular cases such as the one I will treat here. And third, the regional level is probably the highest level at which one can attempt to examine systemic transformations in the holistic tradition of anthropology. If anthropologists can contribute anything to world-system theory, they can do so only if they demonstrate that processes occurring in smaller systems, especially regional systems, are relevant to scholars focusing on the world system. The reverse is also true: if world system theory can contribute anything to anthropology, it is likely to be through the vehicle of regional analysis.

I.   THREE STRUCTURAL THEORIES OF UNEVEN DEVELOPMENT

A basic dynamic of the capitalist world economy, according to Wallerstein, is zonal or spatial differentiation in the division of labor. Through world differentiation, the transfer of surplus and other forms of primitive accumulation, the wealth from peripheral regions funded the economic differentiation of a core region, leading to unequal market expansion, unequal growth of technology, and unequal development of free labor. The structural relationships between core, periphery, and semiperiphery, once established, became necessary elements to the functioning of the whole. While the economic roles of the different parts have changed as the whole system has evolved, and while different parts of the system have shifted from core to periphery or vice versa, the division between core and periphery has not been and can never be eradicated so long as the basic economic relation upon which the world economy is based is retained: commodity production for a world market by private owners of capital and labor--i.e., capitalism. The economic relations producing development, then, are assumed to be tied to those producing underdevelopment.

The mechanisms by which the economic inequality of core and periphery are maintained have been variously identified by the globalists.

1)   Baran (1957) and Frank (1966) argue that impoverishment of the periphery occurred through direct surplus extraction based on political coercion and economic (market) monopoly.

2)   Emmanuel (1972) presents a theory of unequal exchange in which unequal wage rates between core and periphery drain surpluses without requiring coercion or monopoly.

3)   A number of structural Marxists (LaClau, 1971; Meillassoux, 1972; Rey, 1973; Wolpe, 1975) point to the maintenance of precapitalist relations of production under the dominance or control of world capitalism, a phenomenon that while cheapening the labor power available to peripheral capitalist enterprises creates contradictions between different branches of production and thus instability and crises in the periphery (see also Amin 1974, 1976).

C. A. SMITH

It is not at all difficult to find all of these
factors at play in the underdevelopment of particular
places, as for example in a country like Guatemala or
a regional system like western Guatemala. But it is
much more difficult to determine whether the presence
of these factors is an historical accident or the
necessary or sufficient cause of underdevelopment.
This problem has plagued the globalists from the
beginning, so that even as they draw more support from
the ranks of traditional modernization theorists, they
are racked by increasing dissension among themselves.[2]
The disagreement, even rancor, is especially strong
between neo-Marxists (most of the world system school)
and orthodox Marxists. Differences between the two
groups center on the adequacy of standard Marxist
theories of development and underdevelopment. Those
who proffer classical Marxist explanations for
underdevelopment reject the basic neo-Marxist premise
of "world" capitalism. Orthodox Marxists claim not
only that the periphery retains precapitalist
relations of production and is fueled by dynamics
other than the imposed needs of capitalism, but they
also contend that the periphery has been little
exploited by capitalism, or at least, that it has "not
been exploited enough" (Kay, 1975:x). They locate
their disagreement with neo-Marxists, then, in the
relative autonomy of local class relations (see Rey,
1973; Brenner, 1977) and suggest that political and
historical barriers to the development of free labor
have maintained the underdevelopment of the periphery.

Two intermediate positions exist on these issues
as well. Some who accept the necessity of a global
perspective (e.g., Frank, 1966; Hecter, 1974; Gonzales
Casanova, 1969) suggest that world-scale processes are
replicated at smaller, regional scale. They take
the position that while it may be necessary to
consider world events and dynamics to situate the
"needs" of world capitalism at any particular moment,
one can come to grips with the actual processes of
world capitalism by examining closely the economic and
social relations existing in each of its smaller
constituent parts. Others who wish to consider
world-capitalist expansion at both global and local
levels find the replication position too mechanical.
Its neglect of specific local history and class
relations, they argue, not only fails to account for
the diversity of developments in the world periphery
but also falsely explains the dynamics of world
capitalism itself. An otherwise divergent group

310

(Cardosos and Faletto, 1971; LaClau, 1971; Amin, 1976; Wolf, 1980; Kahn, 1980; and Verdery, 1981) unites on this issue, all recommending that we combine consideration of global economic processes only within locally specified systems of class interaction. This, in their view, is the corrective to narrow parochialism on the one hand and functionalist teleology on the other hand. This latter view is one that I share and shall defend in this paper.

But unlike most of the scholars noted above, I will direct my attention to the specific problem at issue in world-system theory: the mechanisms responsible for core-periphery differentiation (development and underdevelopment) within the modern world system (surplus extraction, unequal exchange, or the maintenance of precapitalist relations of production). I shall take each of these mechanisms in turn, considering both the world-system view of the matter and the orthodox Marxist critique, asking if and how these mechanisms operated in the process of regional differentiation that took place in western Guatemala in this century. First, however, I briefly describe the regional division of labor in western Guatemala, noting both its similarity and its dissimilarity to the world division of labor discussed by Wallerstein for the sixteenth century when capitalism was in its earliest stages of development.[3]

A.   Western Guatemala's Regional Division of Labor

Western Guatemala consists of the nine departments in the far west of Guatemala, which hold some forty percent of the country's population. This region is of interest because it is differentiated into various spatial interrelated parts of unequal wealth and unequal wage rates. The spatial parts or zones can be divided into the classic world-system trinity: 1) a more developed core, in which capitalist (plantation) agriculture predominates; 2) a less developed semiperiphery, whose role involves regional trade and the production of middle-level goods for regional consumption; and 3) an underdeveloped periphery, made up of peasant farmers who also provide a labor reserve to the capitalist sector.[4]   In terms of territory, the periphery includes half the region, whereas the other half is divided equally between the core and semiperiphery. In terms of population, the periphery holds one quarter of the region's people, the core holds one

311

third, and the semiperiphery holds slightly less than one-half.

   In the developed core of the region, which is paradoxically a plantation area producing low-level goods (mainly coffee) for world trade, capitalist relations of production predominate. That is, wage labor predominates, hence, the level of production is higher, the forces of production more developed, and the organization of the labor force more efficient than in any other part of the region. The core area offers people in the regional system temporary wage labor;[5] it also consumes staples produced in other parts of the region under less developed systems of production. I contend that this zone extracts labor much as the world system extracted lower-order goods in the sixteenth century; I investigate the mechanisms that are most important in this process; and I also show how these mechanisms develop over time.

   The region's semiperiphery[6] is the area with the most developed domestic marketing network, a network peopled by petty merchants and provisioned by small-scale producers of food staples and other household goods. The wage rate is highest in this zone and wage relations commonplace.[7] Most producers in the semiperiphery are "free" peasants who own their means of production and who fully depend upon the market for consumption goods and for some capital goods. The semiperiphery not only provides the region with market middlemen and other middlemen functions (labor trafficker, owners and organizers of the region's transportation system, creditors) but it also acts as a political buffer between the plantation area and the seasonal-worker area. A conservative, administrative elite, who reside in the small urban centers of the semiperiphery, has done much to create the political and ethnic relations extant between the region's workers and its nascent (core) bourgeoisie. For through the exercise of political might in many guises, this commercial elite has maintained and can still activate a noncapitalist form of domination over many peasants in the region.[8]

   The periphery of the region produces some low-order goods for the regional market, but mainly exports its labor. Between sixty and ninety percent of the active work force of the area spends between three and six months annually working on the southern plantations. At the same time, these workers try to eke out as much of a livelihood as they can from marginal farming operations in their own zone. The wage rate is lowest in this zone and wage relations common only in agriculture, not in other enterprises. Local class relations in the periphery take the form of relations between slightly differentiated peasantry whose corporate communities have long been destroyed, and a Ladino elite.[9]

Explaining why capitalism developed most strongly in the plantation area does not appear to require much imagination nor does it seem to depend upon the mechanisms discussed by either world-system theorists or more orthodox Marxists. All students of Guatemala agree that the plantation system was implanted by the state in western Guatemala's lowland area because it was most receptive (in both ecological and social terms) to this form of production; the state, moreover, originally directed the extraction of labor from the adjacent peasant highlands. But the implanted plantation system depended upon forced labor levies rather than upon free wage labor and thus was no more developed or capitalist than were the peasant areas. Later, however, capitalist relations of production (use of free wage labor) took over on the plantations. What I shall try to explain, then, is how the transition from coerced to free labor took place.

I cannot contend that the transition took place in an arena of competition between numerous states in a single supranational economic system (a key element in Wallerstein's world system model); but I can argue that neither the transition from coerced to free labor in the plantation core nor the rearrangement of economic functions that took place in the periphery and semiperiphery was directed by the state. The state did not care which peasants became wage laborers; and it seemed to worry very little about how everyone was to be fed in this new specialized order. Thus I assert that the producers and takers of regional commodities operated in a relatively "free" political environment, and that market forces rather than political forces determined how different communities responded to capitalist production in one part of the system. It is the operation of these particular forces, as they affected and were affected by transformations in the regional organization of production, that I wish to investigate here.

313

My main focus is upon the differentiation of the semiperiphery from the periphery of western Guatemala, rather than upon the dynamic of the region's core. The development of (and impact of) surplus extraction, market monopoly, unequal exchange through unequal wage rates, and changes in precapitalist relations of production can be seen and assessed most fully by examining the transformations taking place in a periphery. And, according to Wallerstein, the semiperiphery played a crucial role in the creation of a periphery. He contends that agents of the semiperiphery helped carry out much of the primitive accumulation that reorganized local institutions in the periphery and created the dependency of the periphery on the core. (Even orthodox Marxists agree that merchant capitalists played a major role in the underdevelopment of the periphery.) It seems plausible that producers and traders in western Guatemala's semiperiphery played a similar role in the differentiation that occurred in the regional system, assisting both the transition from coerced to free labor in the core and in the underdevelopment of production and exchange systems in the periphery. This, at least, is the major question I ask in my critique of the three structural theories of uneven development.

It should be obvious from the above description that the differentiation that took place in western Guatemala does not directly parallel the differentiation of the modern world system in either the sixteenth century or the present. Western Guatemala's core area is hardly "autocentric" inasmuch as it exports coffee to the world market and obtains much of its capital from abroad. The periphery exports labor rather than the usual low-order goods and has been directed in this at various times by a single state. Thus I cannot hope to test propositions about the functioning of the modern world system with this particular case study. But my aim is not to discover the cause of differentiation and uneven development within the modern world economy so much as to discover the processes responsible for differentiation and uneven development within a particular modern regional economy. I show that only some of the mechanisms supposedly at play in the world system are relevant to a regional system while others are not; and I sometimes argue by extension that some of these mechanisms seem able to account for world patterns while others are not able to do so. But my main contention is that the world system view of the dynamic <u>within</u> regional systems is by itself quite inadequate--and until this view is altered, world system theory is itself inadequate.

B.   Thesis 1:   Surplus Extraction and Market Monopoly

The theory of surplus extraction has two parts: 1) coercive political mechanisms were utilized during colonialism to extract a surplus from and impoverish the periphery;   2) market monopolies that were established during the coercive era are still present and continue to maintain the underdevelopment of the periphery.

The first part of the theory has been widely applied, both at a world-system level (Baran, 1957; Frank, 1966; Wallerstein, 1974) and at a regional level (for Central America see Beltran, 1967; Stavenhagen, 1969; and Rivas, 1971).   In conjunction with market monopoly it is certainly the most popular explanation of how patterned inequality came to be and it is often invoked rather loosely by anthropologists as relevant to a wide variety of economic issues (e.g., W. Smith, 1975; Collier, 1975; Diener, 1978). It is, however, the most frequently attacked thesis of the neo-Marxists and has few serious defenders at present, given its poor performance in dealing with recent developments in the periphery (Sunkel, 1973; Roberts, 1978).   I have already critiqued this theory as regards its application to Guatemala (Smith, 1978), hence I only briefly review it here, paying greater attention to the market monopoly part of the argument.

The difficulty with the original surplus extraction argument--which proposes that the most "developed" part of the colonial world becomes the most "underdeveloped" part of the postcolonial world--is that too many contrary cases exist.   In the case of Central America, for example, one is hard pressed to demonstrate that Mexico, heavily exploited during the colonial era, is now more underdeveloped than neglected Honduras.   And in the case of western Guatemala, we find the most oppressed peasant sector in an area almost ignored during the colonial period.

It seems clear that the particular pattern of regional inequality one finds in western Guatemala today is primarily a consequence of coffee agriculture, a postcolonial system of production for export thrust upon the region following Barrios's reforms of 1871. Before the coffee economy, western Guatemala consisted of a relatively undifferentiated mass of peasants controlled and exploited by an urban elite who used the powers of the state to exact tribute and taxes from them. Little nonpeasant production took place in the region as the hacienda developed very late in highland Guatemala;[10] in fact, the hacienda developed to displace highland labor for lowland planatation use (McCreery, 1976). Even then, hacienda production in the region was extremely limited in scale and importance. Tribute and repartimiento levies were especially heavy on the central Indian communities that were later to form the regional semiperiphery, for several interrelated reasons. Population density was greater, urban concentrations more numerous, and specialized rural production more developed. But where surplus extraction was most fully implemented, one finds today one of the most vital and autonomous systems of peasant commodity production and merchant capitalism extant in all of Latin America.

Carmack (1981) documents that by the end of the colonial era the precolonial and early colonial patterns of differentiation had largely disappeared, all of the native areas having become less differentiated and specialized than formerly. The coffee economy, therefore, began the present process of differentiation, developing the Pacific lowlands that had been neglected in the colonial era, and underdeveloping the northern peasant communities of the region that had been equally neglected in the colonial era. Thus, colonial surplus extraction per se seems entirely inadequate to account for the system of patterned inequality presently extant in western Guatemala. It is basically too "primitive" a theory to account for variations in the pattern of underdevelopment, nor does it pinpoint the mechanisms through which underdevelopment is maintained.

The imposition of merchant monopolies seems a much more promising avenue to explore, one that seems applicable to western Guatemala and that seems relevant to world-scale processes as well. The globalists, however, have done little to develop this thesis very far, merely asserting that monopoly played a significant role at various periods but failing to explain how competition among merchants in the core areas allowed imposition of monopolies in the periphery. The form of market monopoly posited by Frank (1966), for example, is a system of metropole-satellite domination that has the whole world system structured into levels of dependency with local cores and peripheries replicating the structure of the world-system core and periphery. When applied to a concrete case Frank's theory posits a system of administrative control working throughout the world system, with major cities in dependent nations linked to even larger and more powerful cities in the core, each major city controlling its own hinterlands through provincial cities that in turn control rural areas. In this theory merchants are considered managers of monopolies that are granted to them by the state, but the state retains control of the market operations of these monopolies. Hence, this theory of market monopoly gives life to structures rather than to merchant gamblers who are so prominent a feature of Wallerstein's exciting sixteenth century.

Metropole monopoly may have existed widely as a system of exploitation in the colonial period of Latin America (and in other colonial regimes), but it never formed the <u>basic</u> system of monopoly exploitation in the capitalist world system. It is, in fact, a system of surplus extraction characteristic of precapitalist rather than capitalist systems (Smith, 1978). In capitalist economies, by contrast, merchants are relatively free to move into any market and are under intense competitive pressure. In order to develop a specific theory of merchant monopoly under capitalism, then, we must consider other forms and mechanisms of merchant domination. The theory of dendritic marketing systems, developed in a regional framework (see Johnson, 1970; Kelley, 1976; Appleby, 1978), has already clarified some world-system features of market monopoly (Smith, 1978), and can probably be developed further.

My work on dendritic marketing systems emphasizes the way in which the growth of competition within a marketing system leads to concentration and monopoly in spatial terms within a larger system (Smith, 1975). This argument assumes that a competitive marketing system that can come into existence for any number of reasons, always tends to expand spatially as well as to proliferate internally. That is, merchants will seek new markets both at home (by trying to meet needs previously met outside the commodity economy) and abroad (by finding new areas and people willing to

317

engage in exchange). Whereas internal expansion (creating and meeting new needs) tends to intensify local competition, external expansion (finding new market areas) tends to take a monopoly form. For as merchants go out seeking new markets, they open up channels to those areas that are linked only to the merchants' source of supply and that do not interconnect to other new areas--thus the branching feature of dendritic systems. A classic example is that of the Central American republics at the turn of the century: the trade relations that these republics had with Europe far outweighed local trade (both within and among the Central American republics). The same pattern has been identified at a regional scale in a variety of places.[11]

Turning to western Guatemala to show how the system works, we find that by the turn of the century the major marketplaces existing outside of the major administrative centers were located in the area I term the semiperiphery. As the commodity economy of the region geared up in response to the plantation economy and the communities in the central highlands were favorably located for provisioning the towns and plantations with domestic goods that were then needed in far greater quantity than they had been during the precoffee era. Both commodity production and local trade thus expanded in the central highlands in the two directions posited: 1) marketplace trade expanded to meet the consumer needs of those peasants who, with the growth of the plantation economy, were specializing in commodity production rather than in subsistence production; 2) traders from the central area developed regular peddling routes outside their zone, moving into the plantation area and the periphery. The artisan-merchants, especially those from the department of Totonicapan, later helped found markets in both the plantation area and the peasant periphery. Since these merchants founded markets that would meet their own needs--in order to sell commodities produced in their communities--the marketing system that emerged in the periphery was classically dendritic: its several branches had no local points of connection (the exclusive aspect of the dendritic system), and its market centers decreased in importance and differentiation as distance from the major market centers increased (the dependent aspect of the dendritic system).

Now obviously I have just described a simple growth pattern, and one that might be expected to correct itself as the commodity economy expands. That is, so far I have not suggested the mechanisms by which this kind of market organization, that gives advantage to the center over the periphery, would harden into a permanent state. It hardens and becomes permanent, I argue, because of the way in which competitive forces are played out. The system I have just described (unlike the metropole-satellite pattern) is one that puts intense competitive pressure on the center. Merchants in the center compete strongly with each other in their local, central system and even in the dendritic extensions. In so doing, they drive down the cost of commodities everywhere in the system and a competitive price is achieved throughout. This is what happened in western Guatemala. That is, insofar as I could determine, no "monopoly" price is presently charged in the periphery by the market agents from the semiperiphery, though it may have been charged in the past. Moreover, commodities produced in the semiperiphery are much cheaper than similar commodities produced in the periphery, and thus semiperipheral production fosters the commodity dependence of peripheral areas. Competitive pressure in the semiperipheral center has entailed a major reorganization of production and distribution there in which the capital/labor ratio is much higher and the organization of production is much more complex than elsewhere in the "peasant" economy. In consequence, the producers of the periphery are unable to compete with producers of the semiperiphery unless they develop protected industries.

The most important consequence of the dendritic marketing system, from the perspective of the regional division of labor, is that the system helped in the transition from a system of coerced labor to a system of free wage labor. Whereas through 1945 the plantations had to use various systems of corvee (which paid workers only token wages) to bring peasant laborers, labor could be found by the mere offering of a market-determined wage after that date. The immediate cause of the change from coerced to free labor was a change in political administration that outlawed systems of coercion. But the new political order could be effected without destroying the plantation economy only because peasants in western Guatemala's periphery had become so dependent upon wages for meeting basic subsistence needs that laborers came to plantations <u>without</u> coercion. The traders and commodity producers of the semiperiphery played a major role in the increased dependency of the peripheral peasants. By producing commodities much more cheaply (in labor time) than peripheral peasants could produce them on their own, they had destroyed most production for exchange in the periphery and thus made wage labor the only· alternative available to many peripheral peasants.

The institutionalization of full wage labor on the plantations was a gradual rather than sudden change. Wages had been paid to workers all along and at no point had wages become sufficient for the peasants to reproduce themselves without their own subsistence production. But the change was an important one for the regional economy. Plantation owners were forced to become more cost-effective in their use of labor than they had been earlier, which spurred some mechanization and some rationalization of production—though, as I discuss later, not as much as an orthodox Marxist might suppose. More important, the plantation economy (and the peasant economies in the rest of the region) had to begin to function without the intervention of the state. In the periphery, this led to a proletarianization of the peasantry, "free" to work on plantations. In the semiperiphery, wage labor allowed peasants to specialize even more in petty commodity production and trade, without having to worry that the rather blind hand of state corvee would fall upon them.[12]

It is important to note that in the regional system I have described, rural merchants from the communities of the central area had never had protected monopolies, nor had they benefitted from any actions of the state. The protected monopolies granted by the colonial Spanish Consulado during the preplantation period (Woodward, 1966) created a system of <u>urban</u> or <u>metropole</u> satellite markets that were based on the forced deliveries of peasant goods. This earlier system prevented the participation of rural peasants in the marketing system except as forced producers or bearers. The <u>rural</u> marketing system that grew up <u>with</u> the plantation economy was ignored rather than guided by the state and allowed the active participation of peasant producers and merchants (see Smith, 1978). These new rural merchants operated in as close to a situation of "pure" competition as one could find.

But it is also important to remember that pure competition leads to concentration and monopoly. The producers and traders who can achieve lower prices through economies of scale, or returns to capital, or whatever, expand and enlarge at the expense of producers who have higher costs, making it increasingly difficult for new producers to enter the field. This "natural" tendency of capital (Levine, 1975)--especially in the context of a dendritic marketing system which fosters exchange between zones of unequal development rather than among areas of equal endowment--maintains and even increases the development of a center at the expense of the development of the periphery. The only "natural" advantage of the periphery, cheap labor, is no advantage at all, as the following section shows in some detail. Here I merely point out that within Guatemala's regional system one already has all the conditions, due to the operation of the dendritic marketing system, necessary for the distorted development of the periphery as dependent region opposed to the development of an "autocentric" center as suggested by Amin (1976). I see no difficulty at all in grafting this regional model onto the world system, using the regional model to understand some of the dynamics of the world-systems model.

The major objection to this kind of argument is that it fails to locate causality in production, where it "belongs" (Kay, 1975). The charge of circulationism can properly be made against Frank's market model, but I do not think it applies to the dendritic market model I outlined above. In Frank's formulation, surplus is extracted through merchant monopoly per se (charging prices above "value" by putting blocks between direct producers and consumers). But this is not the crucial feature in the operation of dendritic marketing systems (though I may have been guilty of so implying in my earlier work). Surplus is extracted in dendritic marketing systems because these systems foster differential growth in productive capacity. That is, the monopolies held by merchants at the center are monopolies rooted in their capacity to increase production at the expense of producers in the periphery who are blocked from finding more profitable market options in production.

321

The point that should be made about circulationism, however, is not that relations of production should always take precedence in one's analysis of local, regional, or world economies. But that as relations of production and relations of exchange are so intimately connected in all economic systems, one must always consider their mutual interactions. In the regional example discussed above, it is clear that changes in the organization of production (the emergence of large-scale coffee plantations) created changes in the organization of exchanges (the development of the dendritic marketing system), which in turn brought about further changes in the organization of production (the utilization of free rather than coerced labor). The series of changes, however, did not necessarily begin with changes in production. To neglect either of these factors in the explanation of regional inequality in western Guatemala, would then, fracture the dialectic of historical determination.

C. Thesis 2: Unequal Exchange and Wage Differentials

Arghiri Emmanuel's (1972) theory of unequal exchange is invoked by many others (e.g., Wallerstein, 1974; Amin, 1976, de Janvry and Garramon, 1977), though frequently without an explanation of how they think the theory works. Such an explanation is needed because in its present state the theory of unequal exchange is quite incomprehensible. If I make no other contribution to it, I hope to make the theory more widely understood. Considerable controversy surrounds the theory, especially Emmanuel's use of the Marxian "law of value." Some do not think it is appropriate to apply this law cross-nationally, because it assumes that capital is mobile and labor immobile.[13] To do justice to this controversy would take me far beyond the bounds of this paper. Thus, I will consider the theory in what I take to be its "simple" form, ignoring insofar as possible the law of value and thus making no claim to be treating the argument as fully meant by Emmanuel.

There are two parts to the unequal exchange thesis: the less controversial "general" part and the more controversial "strict" part. The first part is a rather unexceptional critique of the Ricardian theory of trade, important mainly because that theory is so wholeheartedly endorsed by neoclassical economists. Ricardo argued that specialization and trade between

two countries with different levels of productivity
would benefit both countries, even if one country had
a higher level of productivity in all branches of
production and thus had to import goods that were
produced less efficiently (at higher cost) than it
could produce them itself. By concentrating on the
commodities in which they had the greatest
comparative advantage, all countries would reap the
benefit of higher overall levels of productivity.
Emmanuel's challenge to this thesis is that it
maintains the lower organic composition of capital and
thus lower productivity in the less developed trading
countries.

Emmanuel's challenge is based on the following
argument. Increases in productivity come about in the
main from capital investment and most capital must
ultimately be paid for in labor (is congealed
labor). If one accepts this proposition, one must
concede that any country specializing in branches of
low productivity (low organic composition of capital)
for international trade foregoes increasing its
overall labor productivity to the degree that it
produces trade goods rather than its own capital
goods. Should it produce labor-intensive sugar, for
example, in order to import capital-intensive
automobiles, it will squander the labor that could
have allowed an increase in the overall capital/labor
ratio in its own systems of production. Moreover, it
would import goods costing its developed trade partner
a lower percentage of its available labor, allowing
the developed country to gain a higher percentage of
the less developed country's labor--and through this
exchange gain an overall trade advantage. The more
developed country has the ability to capitalize at the
expense of the less developed country; and this
ability to capitalize will intensify over time.

This noncontroversial part of Emmanuel's thesis
deserves much more attention than it gets because it
is a factor of obvious importance in the increasing
gap between the developed world and underdeveloped
world and a good explanation for why those countries
that "withdraw" from the world system for a time are
more likely to develop than those fully engaged in
world trade. It also helps explain the trade
advantage of western Guatemala's central-area
producers over the peripheral-area producers.

Textile producers in the central highlands of western Guatemala can make cloth of equal quality in ten hours whereas it takes thirty hours for producers in the periphery to make the same cloth because of better capital/labor ratios and better labor organization. Thus textile producers in the center have driven out most cloth production in the periphery. Merchants from the central area now trade their textiles against peripheral goods that are produced with little or no capital (e.g., baskets, rope). The cost of this exchange to the periphery can be seen in the following hypothetical example: a semiperipheral community, Totonicapan, of one hundred weavers produces enough cloth to exchange against the baskets and rope produced by a peripheral community, Huehuetenango, of two hundred producers. In other words, if we value all goods by the days of labor required to produce them (or to obtain the cash needed to purchase capital inputs), one hundred days of labor in Totonicapan can purchase two hundred days of labor in Huehuetenango—holding wage levels constant.

It is clear that if the Totonicapan producers expend less labor producing cloth but more producing baskets than Huehuetenango producers, the latter can gain some of Totonicapan's labor by making basket full time and importing cloth, even if Totonicapan gains more labor in the deal. (This is the basic Ricardian "free" trade argument.) The problem with the argument, however, is that it is static and does not take into account the development consequences of trade. In fact as Emmanuel remarks, trade is not even the optimal static solution; the best solution is for Totonicapan weavers to bring their capital to Huehuetenango and produce both baskets and cloth there, an alternative course of action that "core" countries are increasingly taking. The point is, one must take a long-run view of the situation and realize that Huehuetenango will always be less productive than Totonicapan if it does not invest in capital. And it can invest in capital only by taking some labor out of production for trade and putting it into production for capital goods, foregoing an immediate trade income that will be most costly in the long run (see Amin, 1976, pp. 134-135).[14] The problem for Huehuetenango, pressed as it is to the subsistence minimum, is that is can no longer forego its trade income.

It is precisely this kind of advantage, I argued above, that the dendritic marketing system gives to

the central area communities. Peripheral producers
cannot afford to capitalize their industries because
their existing incomes are so low, a situation
perpetuated by the "unequal exchange"--that is in turn
perpetuated by the dendritic marketing system.
Furthermore, producers in the periphery of dendritic
marketing system have no choice but to trade with
producers of the semiperiphery, because of the way in
which their markets are organized, and thus are forced
to produce for the world market (coffee plantations)
rather than for their own needs. Local specialization
for exchange with regional producers, who utilize
similar levels of capital, is possible only when the
marketing system is oriented toward local needs and
local distribution. The actual organization of the
marketing system, however, does not give the
peripheral producers this option because it ties them
more closely to the more developed zones of the region
than to the different parts of their own zone. Thus
peripheral producers engage in unequal exchange for
commodities with the semiperiphery and unequal
exchange for wages with the plantation core.

The controversial part of Emmanuel's thesis has
to do with wage rates. He argues that when two
countries with equivalent productivity of labor (equal
organic composition of capital) and equivalent rates
of profit enter into an exchange, the country with the
higher wage rate will exploit the country with the
lower wage rate. The logic of the second argument is
similar to that for the first. If we assume that in
Huehuetenango, in western Guatemala's periphery, labor
is the only input in corn production and that it costs
ten days to produce a quintal (hundredweight) of corn,
as the labor is priced at ten cents a day, the price
of corn will be set at one quetzal per quintal. Let
us assume that the same quintal of corn costs only
five days to produce in Totonicapan, in western
Guatemala's semiperiphery, where the wage rate is
twenty cents a day, because land is more fertile in
Totonicapan. It too will cost one peso per quintal.
If the two quintals of corn are exchanged, Totonicapan
gains in the deal, even though the price is the same,
because Totonicapan needs to spend the value of only
five labor days to purchase the corn, whereas
Huehuetenango must spend the value of ten labor days
to purchase the corn. The same would be true for any
exchange between Huehuetenango and Totonicapan, even
holding labor productivity constant. Let us say
Totonicapan produces wheat and Huehuetenango produces

325

corn, both with labor as the only factor of
production. If the prevailing wage rate is higher in
Totonicapan than it is in Huehuetenango, Totonicapan
will gain in the exchange of corn and wheat, even
though the <u>same</u> number of labor days are needed to
produce the quantities exchanged, because the
Huehuetenango wage buys less Totonicapan labor and
vice versa.[15]

Following an argument similar to the one
presented above but on a world scale, Emmanuel argues
that core countries can exploit peripheral countries
because differing wage rates lead to an unequal
exchange, thus exploitation can be explained
considering only the sphere of circulation. Various
criticisms have been made of this argument. First,
Emmanuel assumes that the rate of profit has been
equalized in the world market without affecting or
equalizing wage rates, a fact and a possibility that
some people question.[16] Second, Emmanuel does not
bring in class interests to explain the maintenance of
wage differences and, in fact, has no explanation for
the <u>maintenance</u> of unequal exchange at all. And
third, Emmanuel does not explain <u>why</u> wage rates are
different between core and periphery, treating the
wage rate as an independent variable and finding it
the <u>cause</u> of differential growth in the world system
rather than a type of world system <u>development</u> that
calls for explanation. I shall treat these criticisms
below, after describing the operation of "unequal
exchange" in the regional system of western Guatemala.

Now, what is the concrete context of wage
differences in western Guatemala's periphery,
semiperiphery, and plantation area? The first point
is that wage rate differences between the periphery
and semiperiphery have been roughly two to one as far
back as 1930. In 1970, for example, unskilled
agricultural labor cost 75 cents per day in the
periphery and 1.50 quetzales in the semiperiphery,
without food, for a day of about nine hours. The
plantation wage rate at this time was uniformly 1.25
quetzales per day, without food.[17] Second, while
peasant labor does flow to the plantation area, it
does not flow from one community to another <u>within</u>
the periphery and semiperiphery: in the context I
treat it, then, labor is relatively immobile. Third,
the organic composition of capital in the two zones is
quite different in some branches of production
(textiles), but not in others (agriculture); since I

consider here only the differential pay in agriculture, I do not have to worry about the effect of different levels of capital investment on other economic activities. And fourth, the rate of profit is the same in both semiperiphery and periphery because there is no monopoly profit to be made by merchants who take goods produced in the central area to the periphery or vice versa. Thus, while the general situation of labor and capital in western Guatemala is quite different from what it is at the international level, for the particular exchange that I consider here (that between periphery and semiperiphery), the regional conditions approximate fairly closely the world conditions posited by Emmanuel.

Three additional questions must be asked of the regional data before we can assess Emmanuel's argument in the regional context. First, we must ask whether the two wage rates have similar acquisitive power. For if the regional commodity market is very imperfect, differences in the cost of living could explain differences in the regional labor market (and we could not assume equilization of the rate of profit). If the "real" wage rates are different, we must then determine whether differential wage rates can be explained by differential labor productivity or labor scarcity. These are the two explanations for differences in wage levels usually given by neoclassical economists and though Emmanuel's attack on them is telling, we should not dismiss them out of hand. Finally, if the neoclassical explanations are not relevant, we must ask what sets the regional wages rates and why they are not equalized in the region, given that the plantation wage rate seems to generally activate a flow of labor.

The answer to the first question is that the real wage is different because the market cost of subsistance is about the same throughout the region. The regional market in staples is fairly well integrated (Church, 1970; Smith, 1972), so peasants in central and peripheral areas pay about the same for food. Housing and clothing are much fancier in the central area than in the periphery, but this seems a result rather than a cause of wage differences: most peasants in the central area pay more for housing and clothing, but if they are poor they can live for about the same amount of money in roughly the same conditions. On the same grounds--the small price variations in the regional commodity market--I also take it as demonstrated that the rate of profit in commodity distribution is more or less equal throughout the region.

Is labor more productive or more scarce in any of the three zones? Labor productivity in agriculture (and we are discussing only wages for agricultural labor now) is almost certainly higher in the plantation area than elsewhere, but wages are even higher in the semiperiphery than in the plantation area, though labor productivity is lower. In the periphery and semiperiphery, the productivity of labor is about the same. (Agricultural productivity is higher per unit area rather than per unit labor in the semiperiphery because more labor rather than more capital is invested in food production.) Labor for agricultural production maybe slightly scarcer in the central area than in the periphery, considering the two zones as a whole, but I do not find this significant overall because some peripheral communities suffer from extreme labor scarcity while some semiperipheral communities have surplus labor. This does not cause the wages offered in the two zones to vary, the zonal levels being quite standard across communities.

Nor do other neoclassical explanations work well in this context. Scholars who have worked in the periphery of western Guatemala have usually assumed that local wage rates are much lower than plantation wage rates because of peasant preferences: people would rather work at home than on plantations, so it takes a higher wage to pull people out of local employment (Tax, 1952). But this explanation fails to account for the even higher wage rates in the semiperiphery. Are we to suppose that people in Totonicapan, a department in the semiperiphery, would rather work in core area plantations than at home? Those who work in the central highlands (semiperiphery) assume that the local wage rate is higher than the plantation wage rate because the skill rate (and thus marginal productivity) is higher. But it is striking that specialized or skilled labor earns little more in the central highlands than does unspecialized agricultural labor: a highly-trained operario (wage laborer) who weaves a length of local textiles and makes a much higher return for an hour of labor than a fieldhand, earns about he same as the fieldhand clearing the weaver's cornfield.[18]

Since neither the productivity, nor the skill rate, nor the abundance of labor determine the compensation received by a worker, neoclassical explanation of wage rates in western Guatemala must be abandoned. That is, Emmanuel is probably correct when he says that wage rates are not determined by factor scarcities or the marginal returns to production, an argument that has never satisfactorily explained wage rates anywhere (see Robinson and Eatwell, 1973). In short, the classic "historical and moral" determination of wage rates, invoked as explanation by Emmanuel, is more powerful. But this is not to say, as Emmanuel suggests, that the wage rate is set independently of other factors that create cores and peripheries.

Many people, who accept the rest of Emmanuel's argument, have difficulty with his proposition that there is no prior link between the development of a country's industry and the level of its wages, i.e., that wage rates are truly "independent" variables.[19] Emmanuel himself observes that wage rates were similar worldwide until the modern world system developed because originally wages were determined more or less by estimates of subsistence requirements. Thus it appears that many of the factors differentiating the core from the periphery in the sixteenth century might also have influenced the core wage rate. Yet Emmanuel sees no link between the above arguments and continues to assert that core wages diverged from the subsistence minima for different (cultural) reasons in different places. He observes that wages became higher not only in the European core of the world system, but also in the white settler colonies that were later to become part of the core (e.g., the U.S., Canada, Australia). Since the higher wage rate alone, in his view, caused the differential development of core and periphery, he can go on to assert that a country can change its position in the world system by raising its basic wage rate.

Emmanuel is one of the few dependency theorists to directly confront the cultural differences between core and peripheral countries and to find an economic explanation for how culture works in the favor of the core. He does not explain, however, how the cultural differences emerge: are the nascent capitalists of the periphery simply more brutal than their counterparts of the core, or their workers more docile? Kahn (1973) finds Emmanuel unconvincing on

329

this point and has suggested an alternative explanation for lower wages in the periphery: workers' wages in the periphery are lower because they are supplemented with subsistence activity, but this does not happen in the core. Is Kahn's explanation suitable to account for the difference in wage rates in western Guatemala?

I have no data on wage rates for the preplantation period on the region.[20] But the data I have on the present period suggest that the degree of self-sufficiency in the periphery is not greater than in the semiperiphery. Market dependence is quite high in both zones and variation by family and community is greater than variation by zone. Each household strives to meet as many of its own needs as possible in both semiperiphery and periphery and in both zones the household seems about equally successful--which is to say, not very successful. Thus Kahn's suggestion that lower wage rates may exist in peripheries because they are subsidized by noncommodity production does not apply to the Guatemalan case. His suggestion, may be too functionalist anyway. Do the real reproduction costs or "needs" of labor determine the wage rates anywhere?

Like Kahn, however, I reject the idea that wage rates are entirely unrelated to the other factors that determine the status of core and the periphery. Too many other differences characterize the cores and peripheries of the modern world system as well as the sixteenth century world system. And these differences do not follow from differences in wages, a proposition that requires an underconsumptionist explanation[21] for differences in levels of investment. On the other hand, I do accept Emmanuel's and Marx's views that a "historical and moral" element enters into the determination of wage levels. My own explanation for the "historical and moral" determination of wage rates in western Guatemala is the following.

When wage labor was first institutionalized in peasant agricultural production in western Guatemala, probably at the same time plantations were established, the peasant communities in the central area were much more involved in a commodity economy than were those in the peripheral area. This, in itself, did not set the wage rates. That is, it was not that peasants in the periphery could afford a lower wage rate than peasants in the semiperiphery and therefore accepted a lower rate. They received a lower rate because they were in a poorer bargaining position. People in the peripheral communities could forcibly be taken out of their communities as vagrants and made to work on plantations for virtually nothing (less than the cost of reproducing their households), as hardly any wage labor opportunities existed in the periphery. The few employers in peripheral areas were consequently in an excellent position to offer a very tiny wage, and that is what they did. Thus the peripheral wage-rate was not set by the "needs" of the laborers, nor by the marginal return to labor, nor even by the rates established by plantations; it was set by the poor bargaining position of peripheral labor with capital and the peasants' lack of alternatives.

Developments in the central communities (semiperipheral area) were quite different. First, as the local demand for laborers was high relatively few people had to seek work. Furthermore, as occupational mobility rates in the center were relatively high, and wage laborers eventually could become either traders or employers. Thus individuals frequently had the option of seeking alternative sources of income, which gave them a bargaining advantage over employers. Moreover, because of the high mobility rates between employees and employers, the perceived cultural gap between labor and capital was not important. This may explain why many employers in the central area told me that they paid a certain (high) wage not only to avoid a rapid turnover in their labor force but also because they thought it was what labor was "worth." (Employers in the periphery never suggested that argument.)

The wage paid for plantation work also can be explained in terms of class power. A wage rate sufficient to call forth "free" labor was not established on the plantations until 1945, when the various forced systems of labor control were abolished. (Wages, of course, were paid before 1946, although the company store retained most of the wage payments.) Wages were minimal and totally arbitrary before 1945, whereas in 1945 the rate seems to have been set in relation to the wages paid to agricultural laborers in the peasant areas. Plantation wage rates were thus the contingent rather than the determinant rate in the region. Plantations, in fact, continue to offer a uniform wage slightly above the wage level

331

prevailing in the periphery, but below the wage
offered in the semiperiphery as this rate brings them
labor in sufficient quantity. The planation wage rate
has not become general in the region because labor is
not mobile throughout the peasant area, and because of
the limited availability and seasonal nature of
plantation employment. Needless to remark, the poor
bargaining position of part-time peasant labor in this
system has kept the wage rate very low--below even the
cost of reproducing peasant labor power. That this
leads to a very narrow and limited domestic market for
commodities is of little moment to capitalists
producing for an external market.[22]

Generalizing from this case, I think one could
make an argument about the determination of wage rates
in the world's periphery following Marx's line of
argument about the determination of the length of the
working day in early capitalism (Marx, 1976, Chapter
10).[23] Marx suggested that during the period of
"primitive accumulation" wage labor is more vulnerable
than it typically is at any other time in its
history--because it has been forcibly deprived of
means of subsistence (usually suddenly), it is
completely disorganized, employment opportunities are
limited and at first there is more labor available
than capital (this is certainly the case in western
Guatemala's periphery). The above reasons suggest a
"pattern" in the historical determination of wage
rates.

In the early periods of capitalist accumulation,
wages are set very low (and the length of the working
day is set very long) because of the poor bargaining
position of labor versus capital. Laborers are paid
so little and work so long that if the situation is
left unchanged it would destroy the labor force.
Wages are driven up over time for the following three
reasons (following Marx's line of argument about the
working day): laborers increase their bargaining
position when they organize; capitalists begin to
compete for labor as capitalist production expands and
deepens; and the state intervenes to preserve the
labor force--to keep it from actual destruction.[24]
Although the above factors have affected wages in the
world core they have not affected wages in the world
periphery, where very low wages persist. We also see
how different historical circumstances in Guatemala's
semiperiphery (which may be similar to the way in
which wage rates were established in various part of

the **world's** semiperiphery) allowed wages there to be set well above the regional minimum.

The explanation for differential wage rates I develop in my discussion of western Guatemala regional wage rates, provides an answer to those critics of Emmanuel who wonder why wage rates are invariably lower in the periphery--sometimes Emmanuel does not explain. It also places the unequal exchange theory in its proper perspective. While unequal exchange clearly operates in western Guatemala, especially between periphery and semiperiphery, it is not the only determination of inequality in the region, nor is it an accidental fact maintaining the advantage of the center over the periphery. Rather, it is an historical fact rooted in the operation of many particular mechanisms causing inequality (the initial level of commodity production, the dendritic marketing system, the narrowness of an oligopsonist "capital" concentrated in a single branch of production, occupational mobility or lack thereof, and so forth), all of which are given concrete expression in particular "class struggles."

The other major argument made against Emmanuel is that he ignores the role of local class relations. What has been a red flag to many Marxists, in fact, is the political implication of Emmanuel's argument: that exploitation in the capitalist world economy is not of labor by capital but of periphery by core. Since this appears to pit country against country rather than class against class, it offers ideological support to bourgeois nationalism.

Kay (1975), for example, wonders why unequal exchange is not eradicated by peripheral capital (bourgeois nationalists) by merely paying higher wages to labor, if that is all it takes. But this seems a formalist absurdity. We begin the whole exchange operation with many different employers of labor (capitalist fractions) trying to obtain a profit through the exploitation of labor power. Peripheral capitalists do not ask how they can keep their social formation from being exploited. They ask how they can make a profit. And the answer, clearly, is to pay the lowest possible wages in producing goods for the market. Core capitalists, too, try to pay the lowest possible wages, but cannot pay wages as low as those prevailing in the periphery because of the greater bargaining power of labor. So when producing for

333

exchange the two different groups of capitalists must produce goods in which they have a comparative advantage. The peripheral capitalists have an advantage in cheap labor and the core capitalist have an advantage in labor that can be more intensively employed. In maintaining their relative advantages in the world (or regional) market, then, the peripheral capitalists maintain a low organic composition of capital and cheap labor (augmenting unequal exchange) and the core capitalists constantly improve their labor/capital ratio because they must pay a higher wage rate (also augmenting unequal exchange). The upshot is greater inequality in production. There is no question in this formulation that it is capital exploiting labor in both core and periphery. The issue addressed by unequal exchange is why capitalism takes different forms in core and periphery, but this issue cannot be explained by reducing all capital and all labor to undifferentiated abstractions.[25]

Emmanuel invites the kind of criticism made by Kay, however, because Emmanuel does not look at how unequal exchange is played out through the determination of core and peripheral production strategies in general (as does Amin, for example) or through particular class struggles. He seems more interested in the arcane possibility that goods that have an equal organic composition may be exchanged between core and periphery and that this exchange leads to inequality in circulation alone. Actually such exchange is possible, in a very limited way, because capital-intensive production is not unknown to the periphery. But this kind of production is rarely for export, more frequently resulting from the periphery's attempt to produce their own luxury goods in protected industries (import substitution industrialization). The major exchanges between core and periphery continue to be between branches of industry that have very different composition. A partial explanation for why that is so, is embedded in the unequal wage rate phenomenon. Only by taking this element into account and by considering the local determination of wage rates (through class struggle) is the import of unequal exchange seen.

It is not entirely clear to me how widely the unequal exchange argument (as developed by Emmanuel, Amin, or me) can be applied to explain regional systems of inequality.

Many will object that it does not even apply to western Guatemala because capitalist development in the two parts of the region I consider is far too weakly developed. But I think the answer to this will be forthcoming (and kinks in the argument worked out) only if more attempts are made to employ the theory in the consideration of systems whose "real" wage rates can be determined and history of wage-level development can be reconstructed.

D. Thesis 3: Retention of Precapitalist Modes of Production

As I noted in the introduction to this essay, Kay's rejoinder (1975) to scholars utilizing a dependency or world-system framework is that underdevelopment is caused not by the fact that peripheral areas are exploited too much, but by the fact that they are not exploited enough. Behind the provocative rhetoric, Kay takes a more conventional position: that underdevelopment is the result of the retention of precapitalist relations of production in conjunction with dominant capitalism. What Kay offers to that argument, developed by Meillassoux (1972), Wolpe (1975), Rey (1973) and others; is an explanation for how the conjunction developed and was maintained unequally. Merchant capitalism, which he sharply distinguished from capitalism proper, is his villain. To dissect these ideas, I will consider their two parts separately: 1) the retention of precapitalist modes; 2) the operation of merchant capital. Later I will consider Brenner's (1977) variant of this thesis.

At the empirical level it is clear enough that those third world economies that have maintained large peasant sectors (e.g., Guatemala, Ecuador, Peru) are in general less developed than those economies that have not (e.g., the U.S., Canada, Argentina). The problem with this empirical observation, however, is that it makes no distinction between undeveloped and underdeveloped economies, thus rendering the explanation tautological: i.e., a statement merely that where precapitalist economies are concentrated, one finds a lesser development of capitalism. Furthermore, this observation, in and of itself, does not explain why precapitalist systems are retained in some places and not in others, nor why it is that one finds heavy concentrations of peasants where no precapitalist economy existed (or where existing systems were destroyed). This second point has been made forcefully by Mintz (1973, 1977), who has described the devolution of Caribbean peasantries from capitalist economies founded and sustained by the world market.

The data from western Guatemala make a slightly different though related point: that variation in the strength of underdevelopment can not be explained by variation in the strength of the retained precapitalist modes of production. The peripheral part of western Guatemala is no more precapitalist than is the semiperipheral part. Both areas were at one time similar, then as a result of contact with capitalism each evolved in very different directions. People in the more developed semiperiphery presently engage more in petty commodity production than do people in the less developed periphery, but petty commodity production is itself a noncapitalist form of production. And if we consider the degree to which earlier relations of production have been retained (use of communal land, of family rather than wage labor, of nonwage labor exchange, and so forth) we find little difference between the two zones. Even when it comes to dependence on the market for subsistence goods, we find the periphery as dependent as the semiperiphery. The retention of precapitalist relations of production simply cannot explain the differentiation between the more and less developed parts of the region.

Leaving aside the empirical considerations, I now outline the theoretical elements of Kay's argument. In particular, I consider his explanation of how the operation of merchant capital slows the development of capitalist relations of production thus preserving existing precapitalist relations. Kay contends that the mission of merchant capital is to find super profits through monopoly exchange with relatively unconnected parts of the world system. Merchant capital sets up blocks to free trade and these blocks prevent the transformation of existing relations of production in the periphery even as the periphery is drawn into the world market.[26] Kay argues that merchant capital has a different motivational force than industrial capital, the former using systems as it finds them and the latter always tending to destroy and transform the systems it contacts. He believes that merchant capital initially was an independent agent within the world economic system, later becoming the agent of industrial capital as it eventually undermined its own existence through the growth of the commodity economy it sponsored. Kay's underdevelopment thesis is, simply, that the long period of merchant-capital dominance in the periphery maintains precapitalist systems longer than would have been the case had precapitalist economies come into direct contact with industrial capital (as it happened in the core). Presumably, when capitalists need raw materials or markets, they utilize merchant capital, but when capitalists need labor or investment opportunity they destroy both merchant capital and precapitalist systems.

Kay's formulation, unlike most others of this genre, has the virtue of setting up a variety of class fractions with a variety of motives vis-a-vis the precapitalist systems. We can accept that merchant capitalists might have certain motives that lead to certain ends that are not "functional" either for them, or for industrial capitalists, or for the exploited classes in the long run, though perfectly understandable motives in the short run. Most other writers (e.g., Meillassoux) talk in terms of a general capitalist rationality that imposes its own logic everywhere in order to function better (whether to expand its markets, find investments for surplus profits, or keep the rate of profit from falling). A number of people by now have pointed out the functionalist absurdity of such a position (Foster-Carter, 1978; Kahn, 1980; Mouzelis, 1980).

Kay's formulation, however, is not completely satisfactory because it fails to show how the operation of capital is itself constrained by the conditions (and resistance) it faces. Let us examine this problem with our case study. The questions we must ask are the following: 1) Did the merchants of the pre-coffee era set up the conditions for the later pattern of underdevelopment in the region? 2) Do the petty merchants of the semiperiphery now attempt to block the transformation of the precapitalist systems of the periphery? 3) Do the capitalist plantation owners do so? 4) Are the peasants of the periphery and semiperiphery at the mercy of capitalists (of whatever variety)?

I argued earlier that merchants, who were clearly dominant in western Guatemala throughout the colonial period up to the development of the coffee economy, did not so much underdevelop the region as leave it

337

undeveloped. They did, certainly, help transform the pre-existing noncapitalist systems of production to another kind, but they did not cause the periphery to differentiate from the semiperiphery. What they created was a _less_ diversified commodity economy than the one that existed in the precolonial period, a more dualistic and less autocentric one. But I think it can be shown that this was not the result of the "will" of merchant capitalists trying to impose monopoly control over the region but rather a result of the "will" of a highly resistant peasantry.[27] The colonial merchants tried valiantly but in vain to sustain the commodity economy of the peasantry, which increasingly withdrew into self-sufficiency (Woodward, 1966). Why this is not difficult to imagine: in its monopoly form, merchant capital inevitably come into conflict with producers and imposes a no-win solution to increased commodity production. To the extent that peasant producers increase production, merchants extract larger profits; by maintaining a lower level of production peasants retain the meagre subsistence level that merchants leave them anyway, but at least manage to work less.

But, this is not what Kay argues. Kay argues that merchant capital deforms precapitalist economies by successfully imposing its will. "Initially it sponsored an increase in productivity by encouraging commodity production, and with it an extension of the division of labor; but subsequently it was unable from its situation in the sphere of circulation to increase it any further" (Kay, 1975, p. 124). Thus, according to Kay, merchant capitalists strengthened rather than undermined precapitalist relations of production, making it all the more difficult to reorganize production along capitalist lines.

The commodity economy of western Guatemala, however, boomed _after_ the demise of externally-imposed merchant capital--a demise brought about by the coffee economy, but _before_ capitalist relations of production developed in the coffee economy. When hundreds of new marketplaces blossomed all over the region and the rate of profit was equalized in regional trade (because the petty traders of the semiperiphery took over the marketing system) the no-win situation for _some_ peasants was changed. Central area peasants were able to improve their livelihoods (subsistence levels) by deepening their market dependence. This improvement was possible because profit levels were determined by market forces rather than market monopolists. Peasants responded strongly to increased profits by increasing production and trade. At this point we find the periphery and semiperiphery diverging in their roles within the regional division of labor.

We must next consider the likelihood that the petty merchant-capitalists of the semiperiphery (or even the planter capitalists of the core) imposed their will on the periphery and thus sustained precapitalist relations there. The reality of the situation seems much more complicated. Plantation owners wanted to obtain the cheapest and most docile labor force; petty merchants of the semiperiphery wanted to deepen and expand their own commodity economy; "industrial" capitalists wanted to destroy the petty commodity economy, substituting their own products; and peripheral peasants wanted to hang on to their peasant communities. That the interests of plantation owners and local merchant capitalists coincided was quite accidental. The merchants, in fact, would have preferred a completely proletarianized peasantry and thus were in partial conflict with both plantation owners and the peripheral peasants. Thus, the interests of plantation owners and peripheral peasants partially coincided, <u>contra</u> the interests of the merchants: both wanted <u>part</u> rather than full proletarianization. At the same time, the plantation owners did not care <u>how</u> the peripheral peasants sustained themselves, they only wanted cheap and docile labor. And peripheral peasants would have preferred options other than plantation work, but had none. They certainly did not resist full proletarianization because it was in the interest of plantation capitalists, but because of their own interests. In short, many different interests were involved and produced a <u>historically contingent</u> rather the <u>logically necessary</u> outcome.

Notably, the same inadequate market for labor in eastern Guatemala did <u>not</u> sustain precapitalist (peasant) economies but destroyed them. Many people in this area became free, willing, mobile, permanent members of the proletariat (or the reserve army of unemployed), migrating to the cities for "informal" employment when left unsustained by the plantation economy.[28] To explain the retention of precapitalist economies, then, one has to consider both (or all) sides of the equation. Not only the perceived benefits to capital (or merchant capital), but also the perceived benefits to labor--and its own historically determined ability to resist.

This argument is not original with me, but part of the arsenal used by Robert Brenner (1977) to attack the whole edifice of world-system theory. Brenner is concerned with two of the problems in the framework put forward by Wallerstein and his supporters: the lack of appreciation for the dynamic of capitalism other than its relations with the periphery and the lack of attention given to local class struggle. I consider each of these problems in both world system and regional contexts.

Brenner strongly objects to the dependency thesis that capitalism is dependent upon underdevelopment for its basic dynamic. He argues that it is a system with its own internal dynamic which _may_ have certain effects on noncapitalist systems, but which _can_ operate as a system independent of other systems. In a sense, he brings capitalism down from a world scale to a "firm" scale, observing that where the crucial capitalist relation of production (wage labor) exists, there is an inherent accumulation dynamic that governs capitalist behavior, forcing capitalists to expand, concentrate, and accumulate. Capitalists who do not behave in this fashion will be taken over by others; the search for relative surplus value rather than absolute surplus value continually compels the surviving capitalist to revolutionize the forces of production (technological development and capital accumulation) regardless of the world in which this development takes place. What creates the conditions for accumulation is the concentration of privately owned means of production and disposable labor power in the hands of various capitalists. No other form of labor control is so efficient as capitalism because no other form can treat labor as a mere (disembodied) quantity that can be put to production in any fashion and in any relative quantity deemed or found profitable by capital. All other forms of production must use labor as it finds it, and controlling _labor_ rather than _labor power_, will tend toward the absolute exploitation of it (as Chayanov's family farm) rather than the most efficient use of it. (This argument is taken directly from Marx's _Capital_, Volume 1, Chapter 12.)

After soundly rebuking Wallerstein and others for their failure to understand this dynamic of capitalism, Brenner attempts to account for underdevelopment along the lines explicated above. That is, he explains the underdevelopment of the world periphery on the grounds that noncapitalist relations of production predominate and that these relations either overexploit or underexploit labor, thus undermining overall productivity and growth. I argue, contra Brenner, that retention of precapitalist relations alone cannot explain the process of underdevelopment in the periphery. First, variation in underdevelopment does not seem to correspond to variation in the dissolution of precapitalist relations of production; and second, the institutionalization of wage labor does not seem a sufficient condition for creating the dynamic of autocentric capital as opposed to outward directed capital. In other words, the formation of class relations themselves seems to require consideration of the world scale of capitalism. Different kinds of capital and capitalism exist and their relations to one another is a relevant factor in the process of underdevelopment, just as the relations of local capital to local forms of labor.[29] Let us consider this notion on our regional scale, looking in detail for the first time at developments in the region's core.

As noted earlier, coffee is produced in Guatemala by both "free" wage labor and "partially free" wage labor. The seasonal, migrant labor force is only partially free because it is not totally reproduced by wages (it is partially reproduced by the workers in their part-time role as peasants). It is, however, relatively free to the _employers_ of labor, in that they can employ the exact quantity of labor they need for any particular harvest season, paying only for that quantity of labor needed at the moment. If peasant labor is in short supply in the periphery, plantations can still attract laborers by paying a slightly higher than average wage; but capitalist coffee growers are not concerned if there is a surplus of peasant labor in the periphery. They are under no compulsion (or traditional sense of obligation) to use the same amount of labor season after season. Thus the conditions that Brenner sees as both necessary and sufficient for the dynamic of capitalism--the continuous revolution of the forces of production--are extant in the core area of Guatemala.[30] But are these conditions sufficient to revolutionize coffee production in Guatemala--or the production of other commodities such as those produced by wage labor in the semiperiphery--and to insure constant capital accumulation?

To help answer this question, let us examine whether coffee production in Guatemala is now, during the era of free wage labor, more or less technologically dynamic than it was during the era of coerced labor control. Good data on this question are hard to find, but the prevailing opinion among students of the region is that coffee production is no more dynamic now than it was earlier. Before World War II, German planters were quite innovative and tended to plow profits back into the acquisition of equipment as well as into the expansion of coffee production (McCreery, 1976; Falcon, 1970). In recent years coffee production has been capitalized further, but much less than one would guess if the institutionalization of wage labor were the main significant variable. Studies of coffee production efficiency in Guatemala show two other unexpected patterns. First, the industry is undercapitalized and has relatively low productivity vis-a-vis other coffee growing regions of the world (where holdings are _less concentrated_); and second, the large enterprises, more heavily dependent upon wage labor, are much less productive than the small ones, that depend more heavily on _family labor_ (Villacorta, 1976). Planters tend to invest in enterprises other than coffee production or simply consume their profits. But in any event, they have not been greatly spurred to invest capital in coffee by the institutionalization of free as opposed to coerced (or family) labor.

Many plausible explanations exist for the present technological stagnation in coffee production: capital is flowing from this less dynamic branch into more dynamic branches of Guatemalan production (such as the more mechanized urban industries); capital is flowing from production into consumption and the retention of a luxuriant planter lifestyle; capital is flowing from the less politically stable periphery to the world core; the "cheapness" of the labor force available for coffee production and the high cost of technology (imported from the core) delay mechanization; the position of coffee plants vis-a-vis the labor market (and the coffee market) is such that they face little competitive pressure. But to pick among these "plausible" explanations requires us to look beyond the abstract "tendencies" of capital in general to the particular historical circumstance in which a particular capitalist class finds itself. And in order to see that circumstance, one must take into account the entire world system of capitalism at the time.

The other difficulty with Brenner's position is that it fails to appreciate the dynamic that existed in places like Guatemala during coercive eras. The forced-labor system that supplied Guatemala's plantations did not prevent technological investment nor did it fail to break down the noncapitalist systems of production extant before plantations. Plantations not only recklessly used peasant labor during the coercive period, but in the process plantations also destroyed a large portion of the peasant economy. This destruction of peasant economy made it later possible for plantations to institutionalize free wage labor. The plantation economy also created a very dynamic form of petty commodity production in the region's semiperiphery, one that came to depend upon wage labor in its own systems of production. The failure of wage labor to breathe real life into the petty commodity economy of the semiperiphery, moreover, cannot be explained by some failure of its own noncapitalist dynamic; rather it must be explained by the position of western Guatemala's semiperiphery in the world system, facing competition from more efficient Guatemalan producers in the world economy (Smith, 1978).

My arguments here do not invalidate Brenner's basic criticism of world-system theorists. Brenner is quite right to note that they ignore a major economic dimension of capitalism giving it only the ability to underdevelop the rest of the world--a dynamic which if carried out to its logical conclusion would merely redistribute surplus value rather than produce more of it. But when Brenner moves to the abstract level of his analysis he abandons the most useful part of his own argument and becomes as "economistic" as those he critiques, if not more so. For while Brenner argues for a historically specific determination of the origins of capitalism--showing it to be a system of class relations that is never automatically called forth by the "needs" of anyone or anything (certainly not by an expanded market)--he motivates capitalism, once it has come into existence,

343

with only abstract rather than historically specific tendencies, an error we cannot accuse the world-system scholars of making.

The main point I make contra Brenner, then, is that classes are never "pure," and never "expressions" of some principle unleashed by various material circumstances in the word. Rather, classes are relational and take on definitions, even purpose, in relation to other classes. If we consider the national bourgeoisie of Guatemala, for example, we must consider their historical origin, their relation to capitalists in the same and other branches of production, their relations to finance or raw materials, and their relations with labor in the region in order to understand their particular capitalist rationality. The "law of value" does not stop history, and the tendencies of capitalism as a system are only tendencies, the laws of which are logically rather than historically necessary. In short, the historical specificity of the world system itself becomes as relevant to any analysis as the historical specificity of local class relations.

CONCLUSION

None of the three structural theories of underdevelopment I examined here withstood the close scrutiny of a regional study. The surplus extraction thesis in its general form is not only too general but simply wrong. Regions of the world heavily exploited by capitalism in earlier centuries are not "doomed to the underdevelopment they now live," all other things being equal. Some neglected places remain undeveloped, some pits of surplus extraction later thrive. But the surplus extraction thesis can be amended to help explain the more usual cases as well as the exceptional ones. I show how a more closely specified dendritic market model, for example, can describe a structural arrangement that keeps some parts of the periphery from developing. To make this point, I had to consider how the organization of production was affected by the organization of exchange. Nonetheless, I could argue, contra certain orthodox Marxists, that a particular form of marketing system does, ipso facto, prevent capital accumulation in a periphery. At the same time, I could show, contra certain dependency theorists, that new commercial forces generated outside an area could reorient a previously extractive marketing system in

such a way that its future dynamic was positive and
was not predetermined by its past. An important part
of the general argument has been that no structural
tendencies are immutable: to explain the situation of
any place requires us to look at numerous factors,
some global and some local, all of which can affect
the outcome in distinctive ways.

Emmanuel's unequal exchange thesis fared better
than the others, but not in its pure form. I was not
able to demonstrate that the differentiation of
western Guatemala's periphery and semiperiphery took
place only because their wage rates diverged. The
wage rates did diverge, however, and the higher
wages of the semiperiphery may have been a key factor
in its commercial and productive growth. Certainly
the semiperiphery's higher organic composition of
capital in production was crucial to the trade
advantage it enjoyed over the periphery. But that is
the rub. So many factors were involved in the
differentiation of core, periphery, and semiperiphery
in the region that it becomes impossible to assign
causality to any one of them (such as wage rates).
And this, I think, would always be the case. I have
argued, then, contra Emmanuel, that the changes in
wage rates that he considers to be the independent
variable of the world-system pattern of
differentiation is more likely to be a related
variable. And I have tried to show how the rise of
wage rates in a core (or semiperiphery) is related to
other developments, especially the position of labor
in an expanding capitalist system.

I also found the maintenance of precapitalist
relations of production thesis faulty. On the one
hand it is sometimes tautological--of course
capitalism is less developed where precapitalist
relations are maintained. And on the other hand, it
often begs the issue--it does not explain why
precapitalist relations are maintained. When an
explanation is proffered, it is usually a
functionalist explanation, such as capitalism needs
cheap labor. Capitalism may need cheap labor--doesn't
it always?--but it also needs expanding markets and
other things requiring the destruction of
precapitalist relations of production. So the outcome
in any particular case is never a predetermined one.
My major contention against this position (a position
shared by some neo-Marxists as well as some orthodox
Marxists) is that capitalism is not a unitary force,

but rather a contradictory force. Capitalism per se does not want anything. Some capitalists want cheap labor, some capitalists need expanding markets, some capitalists want the state out of their affairs, and other capitalists want the state to help them. I will not even go into the issue of how well capitalists perceive their own interests. (Many plantation owners in Guatemala today would like to see the whole native labor force destroyed--for political and ideological reasons.)

There _is_ a logic to capitalist accumulation, a logic fully described in Marx's Capital, Volume 1. This logic would ultimately destroy all precapitalist forms. But this logic requires certain actors-- capitalists, workers, and the state--to be persuaded of the logic. And some people do not let the logic of Capital mow them down without a struggle. Thus, to understand the retention of precapitalist forms or relations of production, we have to understand what gives some people the desire and ability to face the onslaught of capitalism with some resistance. Brenner recognizes this issue in his discussion of the origins of capitalist relations of production, but forgets it once capitalism exists in the world. Thus his approach to understanding the retention of precapitalist relations of production in western Guatemala's periphery and semiperiphery is a very helpful one: we must look to local class relations in their particular historical context. But, his approach to understanding the dynamic of capitalism in the periphery is absolutely wrong headed. Capitalism in the periphery is not like capitalism in the core, and to understand its own perverse dynamic we must consider the world system of capitalism that provides the relevant environment.

I conclude this essay by reaffirming the importance of a world-system perspective, after having critiqued some of its particular theories with considerable vigor. My point is not to attack all general theories on the grounds that if they cannot explain events in that center of the universe, western Guatemala, they cannot explain anything. Rather, my point is to argue that both perspectives (neo-Marxist and orthodox Marxist) are helpful, but not exclusively so. Each gives us a point of departure that can illuminate local as well as world dynamics, specific histories as well as the abstract tendencies of systems. Both err to the extent that they emphasize only one or the other or claim that their own explanation cannot include the other.

The final point I wish to make is that while we anthropologists must concern ourselves with world system processes, world-system theorists need to concern themselves with particular regional histories. To treat the problems of underdevelopment and inequality, therefore, anthropologists do not have to abandon their rootedness in the culturally particular, their strength in understanding the interaction of social, cultural, and economic forces. They need only to raise their sights from the community to the region, where the pattern of class, political, and economic differentiation caused by the growth of the capitalist world economy can be seen in microcosm. I conclude by defending a "regional analysis," when it gives attention to the organizations and relations of production as well as exchange and when it considers world and national class dynamics as well as regional ones.

Acknowledgments

I would like to thank Keith Hart, Paul Krause, Stuart Plattner, Bill Roseberry, Lillian Trager, and Katherine Verdery for very gentle critiques of the first version of this essay; Sutti Ortiz offered a more robust critique and many editorial suggestions, for which I am grateful. None of the above can be held accountable for the final version, for I did not always take up their suggestions. I would also like to thank Tom Wartenberg, Paul Krause, Janet Seiz, Chuck Bergquist, and Mary Rayner for the discussions which helped me think through some of these issues. Finally, I would like to acknowledge those people and institutions that helped me gather the data on which this essay was based—data that are embedded in the analysis, even though not entirely visible. I was supported in fieldwork by NSF Grant BNS 77-08179 and by many Guatemalan field assistants I will not name individually but to whom I am profoundly grateful. I have also been very ably assisted in my analysis by Ruth Nix and Robert Jackson.

Notes

[1] The framework of regional analysis is presented in a two-volume work that I edited (Smith, 1976).

[2] An excellent critique of modernization theory can be found in a work edited by Oxaal, Barnett, and Booth (1975).

[3] I use Wallerstein's (1979, p. 1-36) distinctions of core, periphery, and semiperiphery as well as his discussion of these divisions for the sixteenth century rather than for later periods because the sixteenth century was the period of expanding capitalist relations of production in agriculture for the modern world system, just as the twentieth century is the period of expanding capitalist relations of production in agriculture in western Guatemala.

[4] In earlier publications (Smith, 1975, 1977), I divided western Guatemala into three zones from the perspective of market organization. Here I divide the region into three zones from the perspective of production and the spatial division of labor. Thus my "central" marketing zone (which included the highland departments of Totonicapan, Quezaltenango, Solola, Chimaltenango, and the southern half of El Quiche) is now the semiperiphery of the region because of its "middle" role in the division of labor. And the southern lowlands (Suchitepequez, Retalhuleu, and southern San Marcos) is no longer the plantation "periphery" but rather the production "core." The northern marketing periphery (Huehuetenango, northern San Marcos and northern El Quiche) remains "the" periphery in the present discussion. The "new" division of the region proposed here does not so much abandon my previous system of classification and its methodological rationale as amend it slightly by giving as much weight to relations of production as to relations of exchange.

[5] The importance of migratory labor to the plantations should not be underestimated. The bulk of the plantation workforce is made up of migratory laborers from the periphery of the region and the percentage of workers who are seasonal as opposed to permanent has increased rather than decreased over time (Schmid, 1967).

[6] Wallerstein is not entirely clear on the role of the semiperiphery, noting mainly that it

carries out middleman functions similar to those merchant groups in world empires and that it acts as political buffer between core and periphery. Verdery (1981) helps further define the semiperipheral role in her discussion of the Hapsburg empire in the eighteenth and nineteenth centuries. My semiperiphery does appear to carry out the economic role of a semiperiphery if not the political role. But it is interesting to consider the political role carried out by the traditional elites of my semiperiphery in buffering relations between the plantation bourgeoisie and the peasants of the area.

[7] In Smith (1981) I discuss the position of wage labor in petty commodity production in greater detail, noting that wage labor does not reproduce itself as a class under the conditions of production extant in western Guatemala.

[8] No class analysis of western Guatemala can ignore the overriding importance of ethnicity in the region (the division between Indians and Ladinos). Indians are the cultural descendants of the native population of Guatemala, Ladinos are the cultural descendants of the Spanish conquerors. The urban administrative elite of the region, still supported by special market prerogatives and political office, is exclusively Ladino. The political power of the traditional Ladino elite, resident in the semiperiphery, has played a major role in the formation of core, periphery, and semiperiphery in the region, although the power of this group has declined significantly in recent years. I give less attention than I should to political and ethnic relations involved in the formation of my regional division of labor because of the limits of space. I acknowledge here their importance.

[9] Shelton Davis (1970) provides the most useful discussion of the disintegration of the closed corporate community in the periphery of western Guatemala and the kinds of social relations that remain in it.

[10] Histories of the spread of haciendas in western Guatemala are presented by Carmack (1981) for the Quichean area of western Guatemala and by Davis (1970) for northern Huehuetenango. Carmack

shows that some haciendas were developed in the early colonial period, largely by the Church, but they were not oriented to commercial production.

[11] The best regional studies of dendritic marketing systems are those of Kelley (1976) and Appleby (1976, 1978), who worked on the Navajo reservation in the U.S. and Puno, Peru, respectively. Less detailed work has been done in Haiti (Johnson, 1970).

[12] In the first period of labor drafts (1860-1878), the old colonial system of mandamiento was utilized; this system seems to have fallen as heavily on the communities of the semiperiphery as on those of the periphery. When the system changed to one of wage contracts, which became a form of debt peonage (1878-1934), semiperipheral communities were not as heavily affected, nor were they called on as much under the vagrancy law system (1934-1945). But only with the complete abolition of forced labor laws did many communities of the semiperiphery become altogether free of arbitrary labor drafts (Jones, 1940).

[13] It has been argued that if labor is not freely mobile, one does not have the conditions under which the law of value, invoked by Emmanuel, should operate and thus the whole argument he has developed for world dynamics (assuming labor immobility) is wrong headed. (See Kay, 1975, and Pilling, 1973; see also Bettelheim's review of Emmanuel included in Emmanuel, 1972). But this seems far too demanding a condition for the law of value. It took centuries for "free" labor to emerge in Europe and it has never been completely mobile. One could argue, in fact, that until World War II labor was not fully mobile in the U.S. because a majority of the potential work force (females) was still blocked from free participation in the labor market and commodity economy. Yet few would argue that the U.S. did not have an economy in which the law of value operated. I would argue that one has to look at labor mobility from the perspective of capital. In western Guatemala, for example, labor is freely available in the quantity and quality needed to capital, even though it is not fully "free" of its own means of production.

14 Amin used Ricardo's example (wine and wheat production by England and Portugal) to demonstrate numerically how trade between two countries with unequal compositions of capital acquires more labor of the less developed country.

15 Emmanuel allows that trade takes place only if some "unequal" benefit is to be realized (Totonicapan and Huehuetenango would never exchange corn, for example). This is why he puts so much emphasis on the "strict" part of his argument, that involving unequal wage rates.

16 My case study cannot deal with whether or not profit rates have been equalized in world trade; but it does show that profit rates can be equalized in a region where labor is not a mobile factor of production and is not equally rewarded.

17 The particular wages paid by plantations are variable depending on whether the plantation produces coffee, cotton, or sugar. But the cash wage differential seems balanced by the amount of food offered in addition to cash and by the living conditions offered at the plantation.

18 I explain the compression in wage rates between agricultural and nonagricultural labor (unskilled and skilled) as follows. Employers in the area pay almost all labor the same locally determined subsistence wage because hope for mobility supplies sufficient labor to the skilled trades. Wage labor in handicraft production is perceived by employers and employees alike to be a kind of apprenticeship system. Though craftsmen today seem to have less chance of becoming owners or capitalists than they did in the past, most still expect to be able to do so at some point and are willing to receive relatively low wages in order to learn the ropes. One could argue, in fact, that learning the ropes is part of their wage.

19 Wallerstein, for example, frequently invokes Emmanuel's theory of unequal exchange, but his own explanation for the origins of the world differentiation into core, periphery, and semiperiphery (Wallerstein, 1974) calls upon many other factors, most notably the freedom of labor.

[20] Travellers' accounts indicate that wage rates varied quite widely by community in nineteenth century Central America, but given the scattered nature of the data it is difficult to establish any patterns. It is probably pointless to worry about what established wage rates in that period anyway, because the commodity market for staples was not regionally integrated in the preplantation period.

[21] Emmanuel must explain the relatively low rates of capital investment in peripheral formations, given cheaper costs of production there, by the argument that capital invests where the market is best developed rather than where costs of production are low. I do not take up the pros and cons of this underconsumption view here.

[22] The depressed market conditions resulting from low wages probably motivates the actions of few core capitalists producing for an internal market as well; while they might like all of their competitors and fellow class members to pay higher wages, most capitalists in a competitive market must try to keep their costs as low as possible, including their wage bill.

[23] As Emmanuel frequently points out, Marx never completed the chapter on wages that he planned but Marx does indicate here and there what the content of that chapter might have been. I think Marx's chapter on the length of the working day (an obvious element in a wage) gives the clearest view of the many factors that would be involved. This chapter does not support Emmanuel's contention that Marx assumed wage rates to be set by local social standards alone, but shows instead how Marx considered many factors, including local culture, class organization, and the state.

[24] This argument follows Marx's line of thought on the lengthening of the working day. Marx argues that though individual capitalists resisted a reduction in the length of the working day, capital as a whole saw its interests furthered by its reduction and the latter was represented by the state. How the interest of capital as a whole is seen, understood, and carried out by groups whose own interests must be

more specific than that has never been fully elucidated in Marx or Marxian theories, a problem that crops up again and again in my own discussion. It seems clear that we need a better theory of class, class consciousness, and ideology before we will make any headway on this issue (see Clarke, 1981).

[25] Kay also charges that unequal exchange as described by Emmanuel affects the relationship between different capitals but not that between capital and labor, because it has no necessary effect on the rate of labor exploitation in either developed or underdeveloped parts of the region. I have begged that issue by ignoring the various arguments about the law of value. But I think Kay confuses the issue by insisting that the same mechanism which maintains an unequal exchange relation must be implicated in the origins of the unequal situation. I think the two elements must be separated and that unequal exchange assumes an already extant inequality in the rate of exploitation and asks if relations in circulation can help perpetuate that inequality.

[26] Kahn (1979) has made an argument about merchant capital that appears similar to that of Kay's, but that is very different because of the attention he gives to local resistance and variable outcomes of the struggle between precapitalist labor and merchant capital.

[27] Rey, unlike Meillassoux, for example, recognizes that the resistance of people in precapitalist economies to capitalism is a major dynamic in the lack of development in the third world. He, in fact, argues that underdevelopment in the third world can be seen as the more successful resistance of nonfeudal forms of precapitalism to capitalism than of feudalism, which protected rather than resisted it. In his view, the violence of colonïalism was necessary to successfully break down the resistant systems. This formulation, attractive as it is in some ways, may reverse causality. It seems equally plausible to argue that third world precapitalist systems resisted capitalism because it was associated with colonialism and violent coercion. In the Guatemalan example, for instance, it would appear that peripheral peasants are loathe to give

up their traditional economy because their alternatives are not equally attractive; semiperipheral peasants, however, more readily abandon tradition (wage relations in local production are much more prevalent) because they are in a much more advantageous position when changing.

[28] In Smith (1980) I document the changing labor market with urban growth in Guatemala, showing that a free labor market was not extant until 1950 anywhere in the economy and arguing that the free labor market took its initial form through a proliferation of the informal sector.

[29] Clarke (1981) provides an especially pointed critique of the "capital in general" school, arguing that this classic position provides no adequate theory of transition for any mode of production.

[30] An even more convincing argument along these lines could be made about El Salvador, where the coffee plantation economy is equally stagnant, technologically, but healthy in terms of sustained levels of production and where a fully proletarianized labor force has been extant since about 1930 (Cardoso, 1975).

References

AGUIRRE BELTRAN, Gonzalo. 1967. Regiones de refugio. Mexico City: Instituto Indigenista Interamericano, Ediciones Especiales, No. 46.

AMIN, Samir. 1974. Accumulation on a world scale. New York: Monthly Review Press.

_____. 1976. Unequal development. New York: Monthly Review Press.

APPLEBY, Gordon. 1976. Export monoculture and regional social structure in Puno, Peru. In Regional analysis Vol. II. C. A. Smith, ed. New York: Academic Press.

_____. 1978. Exportation and its aftermath: the spatioeconomic evolution of the regional marketing system in Highland Puno, Peru. Unpublished Ph.D. dissertation, Stanford University.

BARAN, Paul. 1957_. The political economy of growth. New York: Monthly Review Press.

BRENNER, Robert. 1977. The origins of capitalist development: a critique of neo-Smithian Marxism. New Left Review 104:25-93.

CARDOSO, C. F. S. 1975. Historia economica del café en Centroamerica. Estudios Sociales Centroamericanos 10:9-55.

CARDOSO, F. H., and Enzo Faletto. 1971. Dependencia y desarrollo en America Latina. Mexico: Siglo Veintinuno Editores, S. A.

CARMACK, Robert. 1981. The Quiche Mayas of Utatlan. Norman: University of Oklahoma Press.

CHURCH, Phillip. 1970. Traditional agricultural markets in Guatemala. Unpublished Ph.D. dissertation, University of Oregon.

CLARKE, Julian. 1981. 'Capital in general' and non-capitalist formations. Critique of Anthropology 16:31-42.

COLLIER, George. 1975. Fields of the Tzotzil. Austin: University of Texas Press.

DAVIS, Shelton. 1970. Land of our ancestors: a study of land tenure and inheritance in the Highlands of Guatemala. Unpublished Ph.D. dissertation, Harvard University.

DE JANVRY, Alain and Carlos Garramon. 1977. The dynamics of rural poverty in Latin America. The Journal of Peasant Studies 4:206-216.

DIENER, Paul. 1978. The tears of St. Anthony: ritual and revolution in Eastern Guatemala. Latin American Perspectives 3:92-116.

EMMANUEL, Arghiri. 1972. Unequal exchange: a study of the imperialism of trade. New York: Monthly Review Press.

FALCON, Guillermo. 1970. Erwin Paul Dieseldorff, German entrepreneur in the Alta Verapaz of

Guatemala, 1889-1937. Ann Arbor: University of Michigan Microfilms International.

FOSTER-CARTER, Aidan. 1978. The modes of production controversy. New Left Review 107:47-77.

FRANK, Andre Gunder. 1966. Capitalism and underdevelopment in Latin America: historical studies of Chile and Brazil. New York: Monthly Review press.

GONZALES CASANOVA, P. 1969. Internal colonialism and national development. In Latin American Radicalism. I. L. Horowitz, et al., eds. New York: Random House.

HECHTER, Michael. 1974. Internal colonialism. Berkeley: University of California Press.

JOHNSON, E. A. J. 1970. The organization of space in developing countries. Cambridge, Mass.: Harvard University Press.

JONES, Chester Lloyd. 1940. Guatemala, past and present. Minneapolis: The University of Minnesota Press.

KAHN, Joel. 1973. Imperialism and the reproduction of capitalism. Critique of Anthropology 2:1-35.

_____. 1979. Mercantilism and the emergence of servile labor in colonial Indonesia. Unpublished ms.

_____. 1980. Minangkabau social formations. London: University of Cambridge Press.

KAY, Geoffrey. 1975. Development and underdevelopment: a Marxist analysis. London and New York: St. Martin's Press.

KELLEY, Klara B. 1976. Dendritic central-place systems and the regional organization of Navajo trading posts. In Regional analysis, Vol. I. C. A. Smith, ed. New York: Academic Press.

LACLAU, Ernesto. 1971. Feudalism and capitalism in Latin America. New Left Review 67:19-38.

LEVINE, David. 1975. The theory of the growth of the capitalist economy. Economic Development and Cultural Change 24:47-74.

MARX, Karl. 1976. Capital, Volume 1. Middlesex: Penguin Books.

MCCREERY, David. 1976. Coffee and class: the structure of development in liberal Guatemala. Hispanic American Historical Review 56:438-460.

MEILLASSOUX, Claude. 1972. From reproduction to production. Economy and Society 1:93-105.

MINTZ, Sidney. 1973. A note on the definition of peasantries. The Journal of Peasant Studies 1:91-106.

_____. 1977. The so-called world system: local initiative and local response. Dialectical Anthropology 2:253-270.

MOUZELIS, Nicos. 1980. Modernisation, underdevelopment, uneven development: prospects for a theory of third world formations. Journal of Peasant Studies 7:353-374.

OXAAL, I., T. Barnett, and D. Booth. 1975. Beyond the sociology of development: economy and society in Latin American and Africa. London: Routledge and Kegan Paul.

PILLING, Geoffrey. 1973. Imperialism, trade and 'unequal exchange': the world of Aghiri (sic) Emmanuel. Economy and Society 2:164-185.

REY, Pierre-Phillipe. 1973. Les alliances de classes. Paris: Maspero.

ROBERTS, Bryan. 1978. Cities of peasants: the political economy of urbanization in the third world. Beverly Hills: Sage Publications.

ROBINSON, Joan and Joan Eatwell. 1973. An introduction to modern economics. London: McGraw Hill.

SCHMID, Lester. 1967. The role of migratory labor in the economic development of Guatemala. Unpublished Ph.D. dissertation, University of Wisconsin.

SMITH, Carol A., Ed. 1976. Regional Analysis, Volumes I and II. New York: Academic Press.

_____. 1972. An analysis of price correlations for selected commodities in Guatemala. Unpublished ms.

_____. 1975. Examining stratification systems through peasant marketing arrangements. Man, N.S. 10:95-122.

_____. 1977. How marketing systems affect economic opportunity in agrarian societies. In Peasant livelihood. R. Halperin and J. Dow, eds. New York: St. Martin's Press.

_____. 1978. Beyond dependency theory: national and regional patterns of underdevelopment in Guatemala. American Ethnologist 5:574-617.

_____. 1980. On urban primacy, export dependency, and class struggle in peripheral regions of world capitalism. Unpublished ms.

_____. 1981. What is the 'informal sector' and how does it affect peripheral capitalism? Unpublished ms.

SMITH, Waldemar. 1975. Beyond the plural society: economics and ethnicity in middle American towns. Ethnology 14:225-244.

STAVENHAGEN, Rodolfo. 1969. Social classes in agrarian societies. Garden City, NY: Doubleday.

SUNKEL, Osvaldo. 1973. Transitional capitalism and national disintegration in Latin America. Social and Economic Studies 22:132-176.

TAX, Sol. 1952. Economy and technology. In Heritage of conquest. Sol Tax, ed. Chicago: Free Press.

TORRES RIVAS, E. 1971. Interpretacion del Desarrollo Social Centroamericano. San Jose, Costa Rica: EDUCA.

VERDERY, Katherine. 1981. The social history of a Transylvanian village. Unpublished ms.

VILLACORTA, Manuel E. 1976. Recursos economicos de Guatemala. Guatemala: Editorial Universitaria.

WALLERSTEIN, Immanuel. 1974. The modern world system: capitalistic agriculture and the origins of the European world economy in the sixteenth century. New York: Academic Press.

_____. 1979. The capitalist world economy. London: Cambridge University Press.

WOLF, Eric. 1980. Convergence and differentiation in world capitalism. Unpublished ms.

WOLPE, Harold. 1975. The theory of internal colonialism: the South African case. In Beyond the sociology of development. Oxaal, Barnett, and Booth, eds. London: Routledge and Kegan Paul.

WOODWARD, R. L. 1966. Class privilege and economic development: the Consulado de Comercio of Guatemala, 1793-1871. Chapel Hill: University of North Carolina Press.

XII. SOME CORE ASSUMPTIONS IN DEVELOPMENT ECONOMICS

Robert H. Bates

The purpose of this paper is three-fold. It seeks to outline "conventional" development economics. It criticizes the field. And it indicates what should be salvaged from it for social analysis.

The principal argument of the paper is that development economics offers a weak foundation for social analysis. One road to such a critique has already been well traversed and will not be taken here: to move outside the economic paradigm, to indicate the range of critical variables that have been omitted by development economists, and to note how their conclusions are vitiated by the exclusion of these factors. Anthropologists have participated vigorously in this form of criticism and it would add little were I to recapitulate their contribution. An alternative and more powerful tactic, however, is available: to criticize development economics from within its own paradigm. The attraction of this approach is that it is more fundamental. For if development economics can be shown to be "bad economics," then it is in difficulty even before being falsified on other grounds.

Contemporary development economics spans an enormous range of topics and perspectives. Any attempt to critique the field is, therefore, open to a persuasive rejoinder: that the critic is attacking an inaccurate characterization. To finesse this counter, I confine myself, in part I of this paper, to what I consider to be the minimal agenda of the field. The various approaches taken in development economics and the different applications of it can then be seen as variations on the themes which I explore. And insofar as the field does make core assumptions, they will be evident in the manner in which it handles this minimum agenda. My criticisms should thus be well directed.

I. THE AGENDA OF THE FIELD

Like economics in general, development economics focuses on the efficient allocation of resources. It is concerned with efficiency at particular points in time. But what principally differentiates it from other branches of economics is its concern with the efficiency of allocations over time. In particular, the field has a central and distinctive concern with economic dynamics: with changes in per capita incomes and with the changes in productive activities and their interrelations which make these changes possible.

No less than their cohorts in other fields of economics, development economists are concerned with static efficiency. They criticize trade policies, for example, in terms of the excessive costs that they engender. A common criticism is that poor countries employ too many resources in the production of manufactured commodities which they formerly imported from abroad. Such resources could more productively be spent, it is argued, in promoting the export of goods in which the country holds a comparative advantage; for through such specialization the country could both finance needed imports and still have resources left over with which to undertake further productive activities. The classic criticism of import substituting industrialization has been mounted by Little, Scitovsky and Scott (1970). It has been extended and deepened in the volumes produced by the National Bureau of Economic Research under the editorship of Krueger and Baghwati.[1]

Particularly notable is the relevance of this literature to the study of rural societies. For a major theme is that the trade policies adopted as part of the effort to promote domestic industrialization impose, in effect, a tax on agriculture. The overvaluation of domestic currencies that serves to cheapen capital imports for industry serves as well to penalize export agriculture; and the protection of domestic industries raises the price of manufactured consumer items, thus shifting the terms of trade against the rural sector.[2] One consequence is an undermining of the incentives to farmers and a contraction of the agricultural economy. Another consequence rapidly follows. In efforts to counteract the decline in agriculture, governments create new production incentives in the form of subsidies for farm inputs; and an important effect of such policies is the promotion of large-scale, mechanized production. Thus, not only do the trade regimes tend to weaken the agricultural sector, but they also tend to lead to the adoption of policies that transform the structure of rural society.[3]

The concern of development economists with efficiency also marks their evaluation of marketing policies in third world countries. They criticize these policies for the economic distortions which they create. A common charge, for example, is that governments intervene in markets and impose uniform prices and that they thereby waste resources. Because prices are uniform over space, regions of the country which would have stayed out of production, had prices reflected real transport costs, enter production. Furthermore, because prices are uniform over time, governments fail to reduce prices when goods are no longer scarce; instead they devote resources to holding large inventories that could more profitably be spent in other activities.[4]

Jones (1975), Dodge (1977), and others, for example, have noted that the spread of maize monocropping agriculture in Zambia is due at least in part to the government's attempts to establish a uniform maize price throughout the nation. Places far distant from urban markets had once specialized in the production of high value crops, such as tobacco, coffee and groundnuts; with the rise in maize prices in distant locations, however, farmers stopped producing such cash crops and began to produce maize. Zambia therefore experienced shortfalls in the production of high valued crops. Ironically, despite the movement into maize brought on by the uniform pricing policy, there was no concommitant increase in deliveries of maize to the urban areas. The costs of the policy of uniform pricing--higher prices and declines in the production of other crops--were not balanced by the expected increase in the supply of grains. For uniform pricing policies disregarded the costs of transport and so provided no incentives for persons to move maize from one location to another.

Uniform prices over space thus lead to failures to allocate resources in a way that conserve for the costs of distance; they lead to inappropriate production decisions and to failures in transport. Similarly, uniform prices over time lead to failures to cut back on production when costs are low and failures to increase production when costs are high; they therefore exacerbate periods of glut and famine and require unnecessary expenditures in storage. An illustration of this phenomenon is provided by the Kenyan dairy industry (Hopcraft, 1976). By not allowing prices to fall during the rainy season, when pasturage was ample and milk production inexpensive, the Kenyan policy of uniform prices led to over production and necessitated costly programs of milk storage and disposal. Conversely, by failing to increase prices in the dry season, the policy failed to provide incentives for farmers to spend resources on supplemental feeding so as to promote off-season milk production. The result was seasonal shortages--shortages that were invariably attributed by the public to drought rather than pricing policies.

These examples illustrate the emphasis on static efficiency that characterizes the literature on economic development. This emphasis is reflected as well in the tool kit of the development practitioner. Development specialists use, for example, econometric methods to measure the technical efficiency of firms, i.e. to determine whether, given their resources, firms are utilizing a technology which enables them to produce the maximal output. And they have developed as well econometric models to test the price efficiency of firms, i.e. methods of determining whether at the margin producers are selecting imputs and producing outputs in proportion to their relative prices, thereby maximizing profits.[5] Moreover, development economists repeatedly utilize one of the most basic tools of applied economics: the methods of project appraisal. Correcting for the distortions in prices that lead to an inappropriate assessment of true scarcity, they seek to determine whether the proposed use of resources is efficient, i.e. whether resources are being used to the point where the costs equal the benefits at the margin and whether the net benefits are greater than those generated by alternative uses of scarce resources.[6]

This concern with efficiency should not be surprising. Development economics is, after all, but a branch of economics. Moreover, the field is concerned with countries in which scarcity is a particularly dramatic fact of life. In areas where productive resources are extraordinarily scarce, misallocations are likely to have larger than average consequences. Particular care, then, should be paid to their efficient utilization. The emphasis is thus appropriate and unsurprising.

The concern with static efficiency is a characteristic that development economics shares with other branches of economics. What distinguishes development economics is its concern with the temporal property of economies. Development economists argue not only that the quantity and quality of productive factors is a function of time; but that their production interrelations alter with time.

The emphasis upon the temporal property of economies is most clearly seen in the stress placed upon capital. Capital is considered as inherently intertemporal; it takes resources out of consumption in one period so as to increase consumption in another. Moreover, the productive possibilities of any group at any point in time are determined by the capital stock at its command; to increase per capita incomes one must therefore increase the ratio of capital to labor. Given the importance of increasing the per capita consumption which lies at the heart of development economics, it is therefore natural that persons in the field would place primary emphasis upon capital formation.

This emphasis characterized much of the early work in the field; many of the early growth models--such as those of Harrod (1952) and Domar (1946)--were driven by the process of capital formation. The later "stage theories" rested upon the assumption that growth results from savings and capital investment; these later theories are still best represented by Rostow's (1961) seminal contribution. More recent contributions (Schultz, 1964) have altered the materialistic bias inherent in these earlier works and affirmed instead the central role of people. These recent contributions emphasize the formation of "human capital" and stress the importance of investing in training the present generation to promote future economic growth. This general emphasis on capital formation has been criticized by some; but many who dissent from it do so only because they believe that the quality of capital is at least as important as the quantity, that is, that it must be of the "appropriate" kind in order to be productive (see Schumacher, 1975).

An analysis of capital quite naturally dominates a field which is so centrally concerned with the temporal property of economies. The concern is reflected as well in the emphasis given to how other factors of production alter as a function of time. Labor and land are modelled as a function time in

population studies and in ecological analysis. But
development economics stresses as well changes in the
nature of production functions, i.e. changes in the
way in which productive factors are combined.
Inquiries into the dynamics of technical change and
investigations of the determinants of innovative
capabilities--both naturally belong in a field
concerned with the dynamic as well as the static
properties of economies.[7]

As in the study of allocations made at single
points in time, development economics stresses the
analysis of the efficiency of allocations that are
made over time. It is concerned in particular with
the selection of optimal investment programs--programs
which withdraw resources from present consumption so
as to enhance future consumption possibilities. The
analysis of optimal growth strategies is central to
this field.

It should be noted that in elaborating on the
central themes of their discipline, development
economists have long engaged in a vigorous interchange
with anthropology. The importance of this interchange
is marked, for example, by the fact that
anthropologists no longer can pretend that local
communities stand in isolation from the economic
forces generated by government policies. The
significance of these policies for economic behavior
has been underscored by development economists; and
under the tutelage of those in development economics,
anthropologists have come to appreciate the importance
of government policies.

The interchange between economists and
anthropologists, however, has not been one sided.
Anthropologists have bolstered the foundations of the
development economists' critique of government
programs, for example, by demonstrating the
rationality of peasant behavior and thus the
susceptibility of peasants to the distortion of
incentives induced by public policies. The works
surveyed in the chapter by Ortiz illustrate this
contribution. Other anthropologists have taken the
opposite tack and underscored the limited
applicability of the assumptions of development
economics. Some, for example, have shown that
economic considerations are not the sole forces
driving decision making by peasants; problems of risk
and risk management are also critical in peasant

decision.[8] In these and other ways anthropologists have challenged some of the major premises underlying the analysis of static efficiency by development economists.

The contributions of anthropology have been more marked in the analysis of economic dynamics. Anthropologists were among the first to examine the factors which promoted the degradation of soils and the growth of populations; Boserup's (1965) seminal work addressed both land use management and population growth and did so within a single framework. The work of Allan (1965) on the carrying capacity of land, of Ruthenberg (1976) on rotational practices, and of Jacobs and others (1980) on the use of land by pastoralists, illustrate the continued interest in this area. Anthropological studies have also scrutinized the role of capital and the way in which it can change with time; in particular, they have examined the ways in which capital is located, mobilized, and invested in societies lacking formal markets for this resource. Hill (1963) and Berry (1975), for example, analyzed capital formation in the tree crop economies of West Africa, a theme I have followed up on in my studies of human capital formation among families in the Laupula region of Zambia (Bates, 1976).

Anthropologists have also contributed to the study of the ways in which productive factors have been recombined so as to enhance the value of the output that they generate. Hill (1963), Berry (1975), and Epstein (1962) have examined the role of innovators and entrepreneurs in the economies of developing societies; Boserup (1965), Geertz (1963), Ruthenberg (1976) and others have studied the dynamic properties of production functions, particularly in peasant agriculture.

In this dialogue, there remains much for anthropologists to learn from their colleagues in development economics. Changes in peasant production functions have been modeled, for example, by Gotsch (1975); and the work of Hyami and Ruttan (1971) on induced innovations is insufficiently known. Both studies emphasize the role of prices in inducing technological change--something that anthropologists tend to underplay, placing as they do greater emphasis on the role of the physical factor proportions.

Development economics is thus concerned with static efficiency. It is distinguished by its concern with the intertemporal property of economies. There is another distinctive characteristic, however, that deserves to be mentioned. As a branch of "conventional" economics, development economics places an inordinate stress on the role of governments.

Development economists remain deeply skeptical as to whether private, decentralized decision makers can make efficient intertemporal choices. Economists contend that private decision makers may discount the future at too high a rate; governments, as custodians of the interests of all generations, may therefore be better suited to choosing an appropriate level of savings. Moreover, economists believe that optimal levels of capital formation entail savings decisions made under conditions of imperfect markets; for there is a public goods property to intergenerational transfers.[9] Human capital formation is also subject to market failure; as investments in human capital generate external benefits, too little is likely to take place if left to private choice (Schultz, 1964). In addition, much of the capital required for the execution of optimal intertemporal programs is for roads, communication systems and other infrastructures; hence it has inherent public goods properties. It is argued that even when investment decisions involve purely private goods, these investments, to be productive, must be centrally coordinated and require firm mutual assurances, for, failing these, no decisions may be made at all.[10]

The inference drawn from all these lines of reasoning is that governments have a major role to play in the development process. Indeed, in no other field of "conventional" economics is government intervention so freely prescribed. As a consequence, as a technical field, development economics often becomes public sector economics; it becomes an exercise in planning. Rather than the private market, the government becomes the central mover in the creation and implementation of intertemporal programs.

II. DEFICIENT ASSUMPTIONS

A. Individual Rationality Equals Social Rationality

I have argued that the basic commitment of development economics is to the efficient allocation of resources, both at a given point in time and intertemporally. Few would contest this central premise. Efficiency, after all, is a necessary condition for the maximization of almost any conception of the social welfare; whatever one's normative commitments, these values will best be realized when society's resources are allocated in the most productive manner. It is not as an ethical standard, then, that this premise is deficient; rather, it is deficient as a guide to positive analysis.

The criterion is misapplied in at least two ways. In both instances, the inferential process begins by noting that resources have been inefficiently employed and ends by deriving conclusions concerning the rationality of individuals. Social irrationality-- i.e., the inefficient use of resources--is cited as sufficient reason for inferring the irrationality of individual decision makers. Noting the widespread inefficiency of resource use in the developing areas, particularly as a consequence of governmental policy choices, economic analysts frequently infer that people (especially policy makers) are engaged in irrational choice making.[11]

B. Misconceiving Rationality

As ex-post evaluations of rationality are used to criticize decisions made ex-ante, such an inference is in error. Rationality requires that individual decision makers choose their "top" or most preferred alternative. These alternatives will be ranked in terms of their value to enable the individual to secure his or her preferences. Rationality says nothing about the content of these preferences. Some models of rational choice, for example, posit preferences which imply an aversion to risk while others do not; minimax models of rational choice require that alternatives be ranked in terms of their least favorable possible outcomes, clearly implying an extreme form of risk aversion and, for many purposes, a bizarre form of preference. Equally as important, rationality does not require perfect information. Quite the contrary; most models of rational behavior allow for imperfect estimates of outcomes and, granting that information is costly, many allow for the acquiring of "optimal" levels of information. The implication is clear: behaving rationally, people may well choose to remain ignorant. This accords with every day experience, for many of us cheerfully and profitably remain ignorant of forces that are too weak to affect us strongly or too impenetrable to be understood without an exorbitant expenditure of effort. And, when forces do make a difference, we often acquire information in its least expensive and often imperfect form, e.g. by talking to a family member, coworker, or friend, rather than by becoming a well informed specialist on the subject.[12]

The concept of individual rationality is thus a narrow one. It does not impose conditions on the content of preferences. Nor does it require perfect information. It requires only that choice makers order alternative courses of action in terms of their estimates of the consequences for the values they seek to attain and that they choose the alternative which they expect will yield the most favorable outcome. Were the individual to systematically choose an alternative at the "bottom" of his or her ranking--i.e., one that would secure the least preferred result--then that person would be behaving irrationally. The systematic choice of such self-defeating alternatives lies outside the realm of rational choice analysis; its analysis lies within the special domain of those sciences that study irrational behavior.

Perfect knowledge, then, is not required as a condition of rationality. But when development economists review the past experiences of developing societies, they appraise project choices, compare retrospectively the performance of various economies and analyse the success of alternative development strategies. Evaluating choices retrospectively, development economists possess "perfect" information: they know how decisions worked out. When they employ that knowledge to criticize the supposed rationality of the makers of the decisions, they are implicitly assuming that the decision makers themselves possessed such a "full information" vantage point. The decision makers, of course, did not. And when they make decisions which proved socially irrational, that does not then necessarily mean that the decision makers were themselves behaving irrationally. They may have been overtaken by unforeseen events or simply have been mistaken.

In no other social science discipline is the concept of rational choice so deeply embedded as it is in economics. It is particularly disturbing, therefore, that development economists should misuse this concept.

C. Social Rationality Implies Individual Rationality

Confusing "ex-post" and "ex-ante" decision making is thus one way in which the efficiency criterion is mistakenly employed when drawing inferences. Another source of error is the apparent belief that individual rationality is a necessary condition for the attainment of socially rational outcomes.

Observing the inefficient use of society's resources, development economists often infer that persons make irrational choices. This inference is not warranted, for, <u>individual choices, even when rational, do not necessarily lead to socially rational outcomes.</u> This point is fundamental. It goes to the core of much of contemporary economics. And it is of great significance for other social sciences as well. It therefore warrants elaboration.

Since Adam Smith, the market has been analyzed as a mechanism for aggregating individual wants into social outcomes and has been extolled for its ability to do so in a highly desirable manner. The benevolent operation of the "hidden hand" is, of course, a well known construct. The market is expected to secure efficiency in the allocation of scarce resources. But in the early 1950s a reanalysis of the properties of market economies generated deep skepticism concerning the ability of markets to secure efficient outcomes. So basic were these results that they are referred to as the fundamental theorems of welfare economics (Quirk and Saposnik, 1969). A major finding was that the "hidden hand" could operate beneficently only under an extraordinarily restrictive set of assumptions. <u>Rational actors, operating in market settings, would make choices which produce socially rational, i.e. efficient, outcomes only under the most exceptional circumstances.</u> The obvious inference to be drawn is that there is little reason to expect that individually rational behavior, even by all members of society, will induce the efficient use of society's scarce resources.

The conditions under which individually rational choices aggregate into socially irrational outcomes have proven to be very general.[13] And many of the

371

most interesting areas of contemporary economic research have focused on the conditions that lead to socially irrational outcomes. One common condition is the direct physical linkages among producers unmediated by any market. Such a condition is referred to as a production externality. When no market-like institution spans an externality, then economic incentives fail to induce rational actors to operate at levels of production that support a socially desirable use of society's resources. For example, a profit maximizing firm may use resources in a way that produces too much pollution (a "negative" externality) or a labor force with limited skills (a "positive" externality). In the presence of externalities, too few resources go into activities that produce beneficial external effects and too many into the activities that produce harmful ones. Innovating market-like incentive policies--e.g. imposing fines for pollution or selling "licenses to pollute"--correct the problem by making producers take into account the social costs or benefits of their production decisions. These policies thereby induce rational actors to make private choices that lead to the efficient use of society's resources.

Another common condition involves the interdependence of utility functions of individual actors. Such a condition arises when the consumption choices of one person directly affect the utility function of another. This situation commonly occurs when the choice is about public goods. The provision of security is a classic public good; if, for example, one person safeguards a village from attack by building a wall around it, then the action of that person enhances the security of all other villagers. Other examples would be the provisions of clean water, the building of roads or a market place. In the above examples the benefits of a service provided to one person in a given locale becomes available to everyone.

The reason that markets fail to lead rational individuals to supply a socially desirable level of public goods is that public goods generate perverse incentives. Because any individual can "free ride" on the efforts of others, no one has a particularly compelling individual incentive unilaterally to supply the public good. Each individual can credibly believe that he does better waiting for another to furnish the good and then consuming the benefits for free.

Choosing rationally, individuals will, therefore, behave in a way that undersupplies public goods.

Noncompetitive markets constitute a third condition under which individual rationality leads to socially undesirable outcomes. When there are but a few large actors in a market, then each actor knows that his or her choice "makes a difference"; that is as their choices will represent a large proportion of the transactions in the market, they will affect market conditions in general. Large scale decision makers will therefore make choices with a regard for the effect of these choices on other actors and for their expectations concerning the responses of these other actors. Acting rationally they therefore will act strategically, and their strategic behavior thus is likely to lead to socially harmful decisions--decisions, for example, to collude, to form oligopolies, or to engage in restraining trade.

The study of production externalities, public goods, and imperfect competition has generated interest in economics precisely because these conditions constitute areas in which markets fail to lead individually rational choice makers into the making of socially rational decisions. From the point of view of economic theory, these are compelling conditions for they represent counter examples to one of the basic presuppositions in the field. They are also significant because they point out those areas where forms of social intervention may be required to correct the deficient operations of the market. These conditions are thus "basic fare" in the economics of policy analysis. The study of these problems has inspired some of the most important methodological advances in contemporary economics, advances in game theory being a case in point. And yet the significance of these creative areas of contemporary economics appears to have been lost on those development economists who see the inefficient use of resources as prima facia evidence of irrational individual decision making. This fallacy of aggregation-disaggregation is startling and depressing, given the state of the economic arts.

It should be noted that just as development economists fail fully to appreciate the importance of problems of aggregation, so too do anthropologists. Frequently, for example, the properties of social allocations--their equity, their fairness, or the

373

recognition they extend to certain values: age, wealth, scholarship, or courage--are attributed to the values held by individual members of a society. The reasoning that undercuts the inference of individual irrationality from social irrationality extends to this case as well: choices made by individuals out of a regard for the values they hold do not in general aggregate into allocations that support the attainment of these values. This is the lesson of much contemporary research in economics. And the clear implication is that any literature in anthropology which explores the "value basis of societies" must be treated with the utmost suspicion.

Any literature, moreover, that explains institutions and social practices in terms of their "rationality" also rests on faulty underpinnings. Explaining social practices by "rationalizing" them-- i.e. by discovering the sense in which they would be chosen by rational individuals--merely recapitulates the basic fallacy of aggregation. An example is provided by Posner (1980), who in a recent article examines the ways in which kinship and lineage systems serve as mechanisms for social insurance. When Posner and others who have pursued this line of analysis imply that kinship institutions exist because they efficiently fulfill the needs for security against random losses, they then commit the fallacy of aggregation. Precisely because everyone would be better off in a society that provides such insurance, it is in no one's particular interest to organize it; for the benefits would then be reaped by all members of society and each member would therefore do better letting someone else meet the costs of organizing and then enjoying the benefits for free. The equilibrium result is thus nonexistence of the institution; and the source of this inefficient outcome is the public goods problem--the existence of perverse incentives which lead rational individuals to make socially undesirable decisions.[14] Posner's argument is thus undercut. So too are the arguments of a host of others: the anthropological ecologists who explain the behavior of hunters and gathers or pastoralist peoples in terms of the "rationality" of their practices, those who examine the relations between patrons and clients as a form of insurance, or those who account for the formation of state systems in terms of the superior prosperity that centralized political institutions can provide.

Rational individual choices do not in general lead to socially rational outcomes. Outside of economics, the importance of this fundamental result has been explored most actively in political science. Legislatures and electoral systems, like markets, serve as means for aggregating individual preferences into social outcomes, and the implications of these systems for the use of society's scarce resources have been explored by a host of scholars in the discipline.[15] Some, like Popkin (1979) and myself (Bates, 1983), have extended this research by examining the importance of aggregation procedures in the study of agrarian societies. But no one to my knowledge has fully explored the implications of the aggregation problem for anthropology in general.

This is regrettable, for it is anthropology, of all the social sciences, which insists on the interdependence of human agents. And the basic factor that generates the problem of aggregation is the interdependence of rational actors, be it in their utility functions, as in the case of public goods; their production functions, as in the case of externalities; or in their interactions in the market place, as in the case of imperfectly competitive markets. The lesson from contemporary economics, in short, is that it is precisely when people are interdependent that individually rational behavior is likely to produce socially irrational outcomes. And anthropology, of all the social sciences, is therefore most strategically poised to reap the intellectual rewards posed by the paradox of aggregation.

In any case, the importance of the aggregation problem was first recognized in economics and it has provided the basis for much of the recent creative work in that field. Development economists, however, often reason in ways that suggest a failure to understand its significance. This is disturbing.

D. Income as a Welfare Measure

Another set of problems derives not only from an implicit maximand of development economics, but also from the measure of valuation employed. This measure is often a function of the gross national product: GNP itself, the per capita value of GNP, or changes in the real value (or real per capita value) of GNP. Policies that do better as measured by the criteria of GNP maximization are commonly designated "successful" development strategies. However, the measures used to choose among public policies rest on extraordinarily shaky foundations.

To employ any measure based on the value of the gross national product as a welfare measure is to employ a criterion based on the sum of the incomes of all members of society. Such usage makes a variety of critical assumptions. One assumption is that a person's income is an adequate measure of the individual's welfare. Naturally, this is not the case. It is certainly not the case in societies where goods and services are exchanged through channels other than markets; the welfare of people in subsistence economies or in economies where social reciprocity is of great significance would not be adequately measured by this criterion. Nor is it the case in developed societies, where such factors as physical externalities—air and water pollution, the spread of carcinogens, noise pollution, etc.—make a significant impact upon people's welfare but cannot be bought or sold in the market place and thus cannot be corrected through the expenditure of income. Moreover, in every society, there are critical noneconomic values. Where these are significant to people, choices which increase people's incomes but reduce the extent to which they share in these other values can make people worse off. But this fact would not be captured when people's income are taken as the measure of their welfare.

Even allowing income to be a measure of individual welfare—and I make that allowance only for purposes of further argument—a second problem rises: that of aggregation. GNP refers to the summation of all individual incomes. But incomes can be added into a composite welfare measure only if an additional unit of income generates the same satisfaction for each person; failing that, one is, in effect, adding "apples" and "oranges." Summation thus requires that, at the margin, a unit increment of income be valued the same by all persons. Such an assumption must of course be rejected. It is particularly untenable in situations where there are disparities in income, for it may well be the case that additional income is valued more by poor persons than by rich ones. As a composite welfare measure, then, GNP is particularly inappropriate in the context of developing societies. Given the extent to which this index is employed in development studies, it is even more startling to realize that the use of GNP as a welfare measure requires that in adding the welfare of individuals into a single composite measure, the welfare of each individual must be weighted in <u>proportion</u> to his or her income. A ten percent gain in the welfare of a very rich person, after all, represents a larger change in the gross national product than does a ten percent gain in the welfare of the poorest person; and development economists often select as best those policies which lead to the greatest gain in the gross national product.

At minimum, this critique suggests that development economics would do well to avoid the confusion of income with welfare. Indeed, most branches of economics do not subscribe to that equation; people are assumed to maximize utility rather than income. Fortunately, contemporary development economics has tended to move away from this restrictive viewpoint and to recognize the importance of other values. Nevertheless, significant problems remain.

Scholars now acknowledge that people have preferences not only with regard to their incomes but also over the distribution of income; they recognize as well that people have preferences over the certainty and reliability of their incomes as well as with respect to their magnitude. The growing emphasis on policies which would secure a more equitable income distribution, even at the cost of growth, and the wider acceptance of the need to diversify and to reduce dependency upon particular markets--both signify this shift in perspective (Chenery et al., 1974).

There is thus a movement from income to utility as the relevant value to be maximized in development economics, a move that is certainly welcome. Nevertheless, the problem of aggregation remains. It does little good to join the ranks of scholars such as Goulet (1971) who unblushingly expand the range of "core" values to include "life-sustenance," "self-esteem" and "freedom." For some people may disagree with the relative weights he assigns to different values and with the trade offs he is willing to make among them. Having dethroned GNP as a measure of the best policies for society, what value system are we to put in its place? And, in the face of

differences among individuals' values, how are we to
know what is socially best?

E. The Values of Government Equal the Values of
Society

Confronting such questions, development
economists make two heroic assumptions: that the
concept of society's "welfare" or "best interests"
exists and that the values of society will be those
values articulated by its government. An illustration
is offered by a development economist with whom,
otherwise, I am in great sympathy. Michael Todaro
(1977) writes "Economics cannot be 'value free' . . .
Once . . . subjective values have been agreed upon by
a nation or, more specifically, by those charged with
the responsibility for national decision making, then
specific . . . public policies can be pursued." The
assumption, in short, is that something called the
values of society can be distilled from the values of
its members and that the values of the government
reflect this composite called the social welfare.

Common sense tells us such assumptions are not
valid. For those working in the developing areas, the
experiences of Vietnam, Iran, or Chile suggest the
magnitude of the separation between popular aspira-
tions and government policy. And Watergate brings the
lesson even closer to home. The equations of the
government's values with those of society thus makes
little sense; indeed, in the light of recent history,
it violates good taste. And insofar as development
economists generate planning models to more
efficiently implement the objective functions posited
for them by third world governments, there should
remain grave doubt as to whether these economists are
in fact helping to maximize the social welfare.

More relevant to the theme of this essay,
however, is a second ground for criticizing the
tendency to equate governmental policies with the
social welfare. There exists in economics a
fundamental theorem, one which was cited by the
selection committee when they conferred the Nobel
Prize upon Kenneth Arrow. Arrow's theorem states that
one may be able to derive a social welfare function
for a society; that is, one may in fact be able to
distill from the preferences of individuals an
ordering of alternatives for society such that one
alternative can unambiguously be revealed as socially

best. But, the theorem also states: <u>if this is</u>
<u>true, then there is for sure a dictator</u>, a member of
society who can secure his wishes as the social choice
even when his preferences are unanimously opposed by
all other members of society.[16] The convergence of
the lessons drawn by common sense and the results of
formal theory is startling. Inferring what is
socially best from the preferences of governments is
only "safe" when the governments are dictatorships.

Anthropologists are not, of course, immune to
this critique. They too advise governments; and they
too take reassurance from the conviction that
governments articulate the social welfare.
Particularly when governments are democratic
governments, anthropologists are tempted to believe
that the policies they implement are in the best
interests of society. But the obverse of the Arrow
theorem undercuts the foundations of this belief. If
the achievement of a social ordering is possible only
given the existence of a dictatorship, then it is
impossible when no dictator exists--i.e., when there
is a democracy. Under a democracy there is, in
general, no way to determine what is "socially best."
It is possible only in nondemocratic systems; but
then, of course, the determination of what is socially
best reflects not the preferences of society's members
but of a small subset of them: a dictator, an
oligarchic elite, or the bureaucracy itself. The
dilemma is basic and profound.

As with the development economists,
anthropologists should have learned from recent
history that there is no necessary relation between
the preferences of governments and the welfare of
societies. Unlike the anthropologists, however,
development economists have little reason to be
forgiven for having ignored Arrow's theorem one of the
most important theoretical statements in contemporary
social science--as it originated in their own
discipline. The theorem undercuts the rationale for
much of what development economics attempts to do, but
it is rarely cited in the development literature.
That development economists ignore it suggests a
measure of isolation from what has been one of the
creative and important currents in contemporary
economics--a level of isolation that deeply troubles
those who turn to economics for insight into the
development process.

F. Social Equilibria are Not Economic Equilibria

We have already noted that there is a pervasive tendency among development economists to regard efficiency as a natural end state, as an allocation of resources that characterizes the interaction of rational human beings. Closely linked with this tendency is a second: the tendency to presume that economic equilibria determines social outcomes.

In general, there is no reason to believe that economic equilibria are efficient; as we have seen, one of the major lessons of contemporary economics is that only in special cases is that true. Furthermore, there is certainly no general reason to believe that economic equilibria will correspond to social or political equilibria.

The problems with this approach are strikingly illustrated in the analysis of policy formation. That this is so is troublesome, for it is precisely at the level of policy analysis that development economics strives to make its major contribution.

Public policy in developing areas leads governments to intervene in markets. Yet governments in developing countries do not intervene in ways that increase efficiency; indeed, they often prefer forms of public intervention that are inefficient, for inefficiency can be politically useful. Moreover, the techniques they employ often involve disequilibrium prices. The behavior of governments in policy formation thus violates two of the premises that characterize attempts to explain their behavior in terms of economic analysis.[17]

To illustrate these arguments, consider the interventions of governments in developing areas in, say, the markets for foreign exchange or for credit. In these markets, governments commonly set disequilibrium prices, ones which create excess demand; they over value their currencies, for example, or subsidize rates of interest. Such policies are inefficient. Nonetheless, from a political point of view, such policies are expedient. They are perfectly rational.

The political, as opposed to the economic, rationality of these forms of intervention is suggested by the nature of the political resources generated by the disequilibrium pricing policies. Governments lower prices below their equilibrium level; the result is excess demand. At such prices, markets do not clear and some other means of allocating the goods in question--be they foreign exchange, credit, or what not--must be employed. Most commonly the form employed is rationing. In the face of artificially induced shortages, public authorities confer access to the scarce resource upon those whose political support they seek to attain or to reward. They thereby build a coalition of political followers who owe their privileged standing to the policies of the regime in power.

Typically, many such measures have concentrated benefits; they are reaped by the few who gain special access to the regulated market. The costs, however, tend to be diffuse. In the case of foreign exchange, for example, the costs are spread across all who seek to consume imports or local goods made with imported materials. Those individuals who are tied to the government in power through their dependence on rationed access to the scarce resources, become a group supportive of the regime in power. But those who bear the costs of the policy remain a diffuse and disorganized collection of interests, aggrieved but politically in disarray. The policy choices are therefore politically stable.

Such forms of government intervention are common place. They take place not only in the markets for credit and foreign exchange but also in agriculture markets, markets for land and housing, and markets for subsidized inputs and technologies. The policies are not economically efficient; and they do not employ an equilibrium set of prices. But such policies are politically expedient; they are politically rational. And, at least in the short run, they have proven to be politically stable as well. Despite their obvious economic costs, they continue to be chosen by governments and the pattern of relative privilege which they sustain remains firmly in place in many developing nations.

III. QUO VADIMUS EX HOC?

Development economics, then, makes a variety of assumptions that weaken it at a very fundamental level. These assumptions include:

1) That inefficiency implies irrationality.

2) That the notion of the social welfare is a meaningful concept; that it can provide a guide to public policy; that it can be measured in economic terms; and that it is embodied in the choices of governments.

3) That rational people will make choices that lead to efficient outcomes and that these outcomes will be stable.

The primary argument of this paper is that these assumptions are wrong and that development economics, therefore, is a disappointing source for a social scientific theory which can be used to explain what we commonly observed in the developing areas.

Viewed from a more distant perspective, it is possible to see the problems of development economics as stemming from a confusion of normative and positive analysis. Economics analysis does indeed provide a fairly powerful set of theories to guide the selection of choices that will best attain desired values. Moreover, it provides a criterion--that of efficiency--for criticizing and evaluating proposals for their attainment. This normative role for development economics remains intact, even granting the criticisms put foreward in this paper.

Nevertheless, as presently constituted, development economics provides little insight into how people actually behave or how collective allocations actually get chosen. There are certain premises which should, however, be salvaged for use in efforts to develop such theories. In this section I isolate these premises and attempt to illustrate their usefulness.

One premise is the presumption that people are maximizing agents. Our critique suggests not that we abandon this premise but that we expand our notion of what is being maximized to include more than the narrow set of values represented by monetary income. One of the most important lessons of anthropology, certainly, is the realization of the diversity and richness of human values. This insight should not be lost.

Another premise is that of equilibrum analysis. Although it would be wrong to abandon the use of equilibrium analysis, three important points must be made. One is that equilibrium analysis <u>does not</u> assume the existence of an equilibrium, much less the uniqueness of an equilibrium. Indeed, efforts to analyze the outcome of social processes--i.e., to solve for their equilibrium--will commonly yield a proof of the nonexistence of an equilibrium; alternatively, even when existence is proven, it may be impossible to prove uniqueness. In other words, the use of equilibrium analysis does not imply a conviction that the world is "in equilibrium"; nor does it imply an adherence to a belief that the world is "static" or determinate. To equate the use of equilibrium analysis with subscription to one or the other of these positions is simply to raise a false issue.

A second point is that I am not advocating the use of equilibrium analysis at the macro level. I am advocating its use in the analysis of particular, micro-level problems. By an equilibrium I mean a situation in which no party has an incentive unilaterally to alter its behavior. The patterns we observe in developing areas and that we seek to explain represent, after all, regularities in choice making. And it is the lack of incentives to depart form prevailing patterns of choice that defines an equilibrium.

Lastly, I am not advocating the use of equilibrium analysis in a purely economic fashion. Rather, I feel that the notion of what determines an equilibrium should be expanded to include social and political institutions and not merely markets. Such institutions are part of the settings within which maximizing choices are made. They offer to decision makers other values in addition to economic values: membership, office, prestige, etc. Social and political institutions also provide decision makers with access to resources other than income or productive technologies: access to power, to followers, to networks, or to systems of rights and obligations. And these institutions provide frameworks within which bargaining takes place and strategies are developed; they define, in short, the "rules of the game" which determine the values of outcomes which can be sought by alternative courses of action.

I shall illustrate these points with two examples. One example arises in the literature on West Africa at the time of the impact of colonialism. Contemporary scholars, while sometimes romanticizing the facts, nonetheless have credibly argued that precolonial chieftancies were "democratic," in the sense that within the ruling lineages there existed a variety of "candidates" for chiefly office and that their capacity to gain popular support was often decisive in gaining succession to the throne. They have also argued that it was the colonial powers--particularly the British--who instituted rigid codes of geneological succession and that their reasons for doing so included not only their failure to understand the nature of African societies but also their desire for predictability in the public affairs of the traditional kingdoms (Barrows, 1976). It was left to Ferguson and Wilks (1970) to see the ironic property of the British "solution"; that it increased, rather than decreased, unpredictability in public affairs. The detection of this irony represents an implicit use of the maximization postulate and equilibrium analysis in a noneconomic setting.

The underlying model that explains the ironic properties of the British solution is that of Anthony Downs (1957). Downs's model rests on the premise that both citizens and aspiring politicians are maximizers; all make choices so as to fulfill their objectives. People have their own preferences over public policies and they seek to secure policy stands by public officials that are in accord with their preferences. To do this, they support those candidates whose policies are closest to their own most preferred position. Candidates seek office; to attain office, they take stands on issues so as to secure the support of a majority of the citizenry. Maximizing citizens and candidates are the basic actors in Downs's model.

Figure 1 illustrates a three person citizenry. Policy stands are represented along the horizontal axis; they can be thought of as falling, say, along a "radical-conservative" direction. And people's preferences are represented as smooth, single-peaked curves which take on greater value as they reach higher levels along the vertical axis. To illustrate the concept of equilibrium, assume that there are two candidates, one of the left (candidate A) and one of the right (candidate B). Clearly the candidates for office have strong incentives to adopt policy positions that lie at the middle of the horizontal axis. Say, for example, that A were to remain at the left and B were to take a middle position, as in figure 1. Candidate A's stand lies at person one's most preferred position; hence A gets person one's support. Candidate B is at person two's most preferred position; hence B gets person two's supports. But candidate B also gets person three's support vote, for person three prefers B's position to A's. B is closer to person three's position and B's policy stand therefore lies at a higher level of B's utility curve than does the policy stand of A.

Utility

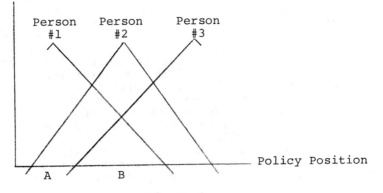

Person #1   Person #2   Person #3

A   B

Policy Position

Figure 3.
A Representation of Preferences in a Single Division

The lesson is obvious. Candidate A does not want to lose. Therefore A, in response to B's choice of strategy, does best by moving to the center in an effort to attract the support of a second person. Insofar as people choose candidates, and the latter seek to attain office by winning majority support, there is thus a predictable, equilibrium outcome: the candidates will move to the center. The candidates who gain the support of a majority will therefore be those who adopt as their policies the position of the "median voter."[18]

The historical lesson is clear. When the British constrained competition and created a geneologically determinate order to succession, the incentives creating predictable policy outcomes were destroyed.

Who succeeded to office was determined; but the public policies endorsed by the holders of office were not. An element of randomness was therefore introduced into public affairs and the objectives of the British "reforms" were defeated by the measures which they chose to secure them. The assumption of maximization and the methods of equilibrium analysis can thus give insight into micro-level problems.

A second example, using the work of Evans-Pritchard (1940), supplemented by the work of Howell (1973), it is possible to reconceptualize one of the basic problems in social anthropology: the sources of order in societies without states.

Among the Nuer, cattle are the basic form of property. To secure wealth, the Nuer invest resources in breeding and raising cattle. Another way of acquiring wealth would be theft. Every indication is that the Nuer are tempted to steal, and Evans-Pritchard states "cattle are their dearest possession and [the Nuer] gladly risk their lives to pillage those of their neighbors" (Evans-Pritchard, 1940, p. 16). The strength of their desire to steal is further suggested by Evans-Pritchard when he recounts: "As my Nuer servant once said to me: you can trust a Nuer with any amount of money, pounds and pounds and pounds, and go away for years and return and he will not have stolen it; but a single cow--that is a different matter" (Evans-Pritchard, 1940, p. 49).

The puzzle, from Evans-Pritchard's point of view, was that despite the potential for theft and disorder, the Nuer in fact tended to live in relative harmony. Insofar as the Nuer raided cattle, they tended to raid the cattle of others; raids within the tribe were a relatively rare phenomenon (Howell, 1973, pp. 200-201). Somehow the Nuer appear to have avoided the potentially harmful effects arising from the unbridled pursuit of self-interest. And they appear to have done so even while lacking those formal institutions so common in Western societies which specialize in preserving the peace and forestalling violence: the courts, the police, and so on.

In discussing Evans-Pritchard's analysis of the problem of social order, we can credibly abstract his account in a number of forms. In this essay, I will portray it in the form of a two-person non-cooperative variable-sum game, traditionally known as the prisoners' dilemma (Luce and Raiffa, 1957).

All that I have said thus far suggests that such an abstraction does little violence to Evans-Pritchard's analysis. All that is required is that we conceive of the situation as involving two property-holding units, each of which desires to increase the number of its cattle, and that we consider the incentives that motivate each unit. Call the units families I and II, and assume that both hold ten cattle. Each family can choose between two alternatives: to use force or to remain passive and nonviolent. Each knows that the other family faces a similar choice. And each knows what the results of their choice will be.

Both families know that should both adjure the use of force, each will continue to enjoy the possession of ten cattle. But both also know that raiding is profitable. Should family I raid family II's herd while family II failed to resist, it could appropriate eight of family II's cattle, we shall assume; similarly, should family II raid family I and family I not forcibly resist, family II could gain eight cattle at family I's expense. Both also know that in the face of a raid from each other, there are gains to those who resist, even though they may pay a price in physical suffering. For purposes of argument, assume that during the course of battle, a family loses six cattle due to property damage and in the breakdown of herding. In any case, this outcome is to be preferred to not using force to protect one's herds, for then eight cattle are lost to the predatory party.

The situation is summarized in Figure 2 below. The choices for family I are listed on the left: F designates the choice of force and F̄ designates the renunciation of force. The choices for family II are similar and are listed at the top of the figure. The entries refer to the outcomes for the paired choices of families I and II, the value of the outcomes being expressed in terms of numbers of cattle, the value to family I being listed first and the value to family II being listed second.[19]

II

	F	F̄
F	4,4	18,2
F̄	2,18	10,10

(left label: I)

Figure 2

The nature of the dilemma is clear. It is rational for each family to choose to use force; as can be seen from Figure 2, each does best employing force <u>no matter what</u> the choice of the other. Moreover, it is also clear that the use of force by both families represents an equilibrium and that this equilibrium is unique. When both use force, it is in neither's interest to renounce it; were family I unilaterally to abjure the use of force, then its holdings would drop from four cattle to two; and the same is true for family II. No other pair of strategies is in equilibrium; in all other cases, one or the other family does better by unilaterally changing its choice of strategy. The equilibrium is thus unique. What is peculiar and compelling, however, is the nature of this equilibrium: under it, <u>both families are worse off</u>. Had they renounced the use of force, they could each have ten cattle but they now get only four. Individual rationality thus leads to a socially irrational outcome, an outcome under which all persons suffer. Put another way, <u>all would be better off living peacefully, but none can afford to live that way</u>. The structure of the prisoners' dilemma thus captures the fragility of social order.

In analyzing the origins of order in decentralized societies, Evans-Pritchard pursued two lines of inquiry. One was to look at the role of mechanisms for conflict resolution and dispute settlement; these mechanisms, in effect, were employed by the Nuer to curtail the natural tendencies set in motion by the incentive structure characteristic of the prisoners' dilemma. The second was to conjecture about the more basic and fundamental institutions that did not control socially dangerous behavior but rather operated at a deeper level and altered, in effect, the very structure of incentives which so threatened the cohesion of Nuer society. The "deeper" institutions arose at the level of religion and the moral order. Elsewhere (Bates, 1983) I have analyzed both kinds of social controls and shown how they alter the nature of the payoff matrix that captures the incentives leading to the prisoners' dilemma.

This example illustrates the use of the assumption of maximization and the tool of equilibrium analysis in non-market settings. It also illustrates an earlier point: that rational choice by individuals can aggregate into socially irrational outcomes--outcomes which no one prefers. In defiance of the hypothesis of the "hidden hand," equilibria, when they exist, can correspond to outcomes that are abhorrent to all members of society.

IV. A RESEARCH AGENDA

There are a multitude of other potential applications of "economic" analysis, and these stand as candidates for a research agenda that could generate increased interaction between economics and anthropology.

One controversial and therefore interesting application would be the development of rational-choice models for non-market economies. As the Polanyi school points out, there are many societies in which markets are not complete. In such societies, certain goods or services can not be traded or exchanged through the market. Alternatively, factors may be exchanged but at prices that are set outside the market, i.e. either by political fiat or by custom; as a consequence, the prices are invariant. It may also be true, the Polanyi school points out, that prices, when they exist, are not uniform; they vary according to the social category of the parties to the exchange.

These characteristic patterns are well known by anthropologists. Less well known is that these patterns correspond closely to those observed in regulated industries in advanced industrial economies. The study of industrial regulation is a well developed branch of applied microeconomics.[20] In regulated industries, certain factors may not be exchanged--e.g. atomic fuels in the nuclear energy industry or air routes in commercial aviation. Prices are set and maintained at fixed levels for long periods of time and are subject to change through political, rather than market, mechanisms. Frequently, different prices are set for different categories of consumers; home owners, for example, are charged different rates than industries for the use of telephone or electrical services. The models that have been developed by economists for the analysis of the behavior of regulated industries should be explored by anthropologists seeking to analyze the implications of the "Polanyi type" restrictions upon economies.

Another area ripe for analysis is the study of the formation of institutions. In fulfilling human wants, people sometimes use markets. They more commonly use organizations. When it is that they employ the one instead of the other is a question that is sporadically explored in economics; and it is one that should inspire a fruitful interchange between economics and anthropology. An area in which this question is examined by economists is in the study of the firm. Firms represent means of combining productive factors through organizations rather than markets, and it is an interesting problem in economic analysis as to why firms arise.[21] Another area is in the study of incentive systems. Economists have found that the problem of monitoring inputs (such as labor effort) or outputs (such as quality of service) yields incentives to substitute bureaucratic controls for decentralized, market-like mechanisms. Popkin (1981) has recently applied this literature to the analysis of the nature of organizations arising from the production and marketing of different kinds of crops in Southeast Asia, and his work deserves close attention.

Not only should the research agenda be marked by the application of rational choice analysis to the origins of institutions; but also it could be marked by the systematic investigation of the ethical properties of institutions. A critical subject in contemporary economic research--and one studied as well by contemporary moral philosophers, such as Rawls (1971)--is the normative content of social decision procedures. Arrow's theorem, mentioned above, represents a seminal contribution to this research. Other investigators (Groves and Ledyard, 1977; Tideman, 1977) have examined the possibility of devising social systems for choosing optimal levels of public goods. Still others (Luce and Raiffa, 1975, Chapter 6) have designed procedures for resolving conflicts of interest in ways which the contesting parties would regard as fair. Works in anthropology, such as those of Colson (1974), suggest that there is much to be gained from regarding "traditional orders" as institutional frameworks which have been intentionally innovated and chosen. And there has long been a tradition in anthropology of interpreting "traditional societies" as institutionalized forms of a moral order. Another area, then, wherein anthropology and economics could interact to their mutual benefit would be in the investigation of the ways in which institutions can be structured so as to preserve ethical properties in the choices made by human societies.

CONCLUSION

The major message of this paper is that development economics is seriously, indeed fundamentally, flawed. While it provides a normative framework for evaluating the performance of developing areas, it provides little basis for studying the way in which people behave or choices get made in developing areas. This criticism does not originate from an external vantage point; rather, it originates from within the economic paradigm. Development economics has failed to pay attention to much that has been proven and learned in contemporary economics.

I have also argued, however, that portions of the apparatus of this field can and should be preserved. The assumption of maximizing behavior and the use of equilibrium analysis should, with suitable modifications, be retained as essential tools for positive analysis. These tools have been applied to the study of politics, regulation, and administration. They should be applied by anthropologists to the analysis of choice and allocation in other non-market settings. In particular, through the study of the nature and performance of social institutions commonly investigated in anthropology, they can be used to open up new lines of positive and ethical analysis--lines of inquiry that have briefly been sketched in the concluding portions of this paper.

Acknowledgement

The work on this paper was supported by NSF grant number SOC 77-08573Al, entitled: Research on the political economy of rural Africa.

Notes

[1] A valuable book in the Krueger-Bhagwati series is J. Clark Leith (1974).

[2] See, for example, Carl Gotsch and Gilbert Brown (1980).

[3] See, for example, the discussion in Scott Pearson and Dirck Stryker (1980) and Robert H. Bates (1981).

[4] See, for example, the critique by J. Heyer (1976).

[5] See the articles by L. J. Lau and P. A. Yotopoulous (1971). See also the important application of linear programming models of production contained in C. H. Gotsch (1975).

[6] In development economics, the locus classicus is P. Dasgupta, A. Sen, and S. Marglin (1972).

[7] A useful collection of essays on dynamics is contained in J. E. Stiglitz and H. Uzawa, eds., (1969). See also in G. C. Harcourt (1972).

[8] See, for example, the studies of Hans Ruthenberg (1976) and J. A. Roumassett (1976).

[9] See, for example, S. Marglin (1963); N. Beck (1980); T. Page (1979); and B. Barry (1977).

[10] A useful summary is contained in M. P. Todaro (1977).

[11] See, for example, the contributions in T. W. Schultz (1978).

[12] An excellent discussion of "rational ignorance" is contained in the second part of Anthony Downs (1957). For somewhat more technical introductory treatment, see Herman

Chernoff and Lincoln Moses (1967). See also the references listed in the chapter by Ortiz.

[13] For a highly accessible introduction, see also Dennis C. Mueller (1979).

[14] The best general discussion of this problem remains Mancur Olson (1977).

[15] The best overview of this work is contained in William H. Riker and Peter C. Ordeshook (1973).

[16] K. Arrow (1963). See also the more accessible discussion in A. K. Sen (1970) and the highly accessible "Vickery Proof" outlined in Dennis Mueller (1979).

[17] In this section I draw extensively on R. H. Bates (1981).

[18] For a critique of the Downsian model, see Brian Barry (1970). The limitations of this model are explored in chapters 11 and 12 of Riker and Ordeshook (1973). For an attempt to examine the dynamic properties of models of electoral competition, see Gerald H. Kramer (1980).

[19] It should be noted that, by all accounts, the Nuer do translate physical pain and suffering and even death into cattle equivalents. See Evans-Pritchard, p. 127 and Howell, pp. 25-48.

[20] A useful overview is contained in Paul Joskow and Roger Noll (1981).

[21] Kenneth Arrow (1974), Armen A. Alchein (1965). See also R. H. Coase (1937).

References

ALCHIAN, Armen A. 1965. The basis of some recent advances in the theory of management of the firm. Journal of Industrial Economics 14:30-41.

ALLAN, William. 1965. The African husbandsman. New York: Barnes and Noble.

ARROW, K. 1963. Social choice and individual values. New York: Wiley.

_____. 1974. The limits of organization. New York: Norton.

BARROWS, Walter. 1976. Grassroots politics in an African state: integration and development in Sierra Leone. London: Africana Publishing Co.

BARRY, B. 1967. Political argument. London: Routledge and Kegan Paul.

_____. 1970. Sociologists, economists, and democracy. London: Collier-MacMillan.

_____. 1977. Justice between generations. In Law, morality and society. P. M. S. Hacker and J. Raz, eds. Oxford: Clarendon Press.

BATES, Robert. 1976. Rural responses to industrialization: a study of village Zambia. New Haven and London: Yale University Press.

_____. 1981. Markets and states in tropical Africa: the political basis of agricultural policies. Berkeley and Los Angeles: University of California Press.

_____. 1983. Essays on the political economy of rural Africa. Cambridge: Cambridge University Press.

BECK, N. 1980. Discounting, efficiency and intergenerational fairness. University of California, San Diego, Political Science Working Paper 80-13.

BERRY, Sara. 1975. Cocoa, custom and socio-economic change in rural western Nigeria. Oxford: Clarendon Press.

BOSERUP, Ester. 1965. Conditions of agricultural growth. Chicago: Aldine.

CHENERY, H., et al. 1974. Redistribution with growth. London: Oxford University Press.

CHERNOFF, Herman, and Lincoln Moses. 1967. Elementary decision theory. New York: John Wiley and Sons.

COASE, R. H. 1937. The nature of the firm. Economica 4:386-405.

COLSON, Elizabeth. 1974. Tradition and contract. Chicago: Aldine.

DASGUPTA, P., A. Sen, and S. Marglin. 1972. Guidelines for project evaluation. New York: United Nations.

DODGE, Doris J. 1977. Agricultural policy and performance in Zambia. Berkeley, Calif.: Institute of International Studies.

DOMAR, Evsey D. 1946. Capital expansion, rate of growth, and employment. Econometrica 4:137-147.

DOWNS, Anthony. 1957. An economic theory of democracy. New York: Harper and Row.

EPSTEIN, T. Scarlett. 1962. Economic development and social change in South India. Manchester: Manchester University Press.

EVANS-PRITCHARD, E. E. 1940. The Nuer. Oxford: Clarendon Press.

FERGUSON, Phyllis, and Ivor Wilks. 1970. Chiefs, constitutions, and the British in Northern Ghana. In West African chiefs: their changing status under colonial rule and independence. Michael Crowder and Obaro Ikime, eds. New York: Africana Publishing Co.

GEERTZ, Clifford. 1963. Agricultural involution. Berkeley and Los Angeles: University of California Press.

GOTSCH, Carl. 1975. Linear programming and agricultural policy: micro studies of the Pakistan Punjab. Food Research Institute Studies 14(1).

GOTSCH, Carl, and Gilbert Brown. 1980. Prices, taxes and subsidies in Pakistan agriculture 1960-1976. World Bank Staff Working Paper No. 387.

GOULET, D. 1971. The cruel choice: a new concept of development. New York: Atheneum.

GROVES, Theodore, and John Ledyard. 1977. Some limitations of demand revealing processes. Public Choice 29:107-114.

HARCOURT, G. C. 1972. Some Cambridge controversies in the theory of capital. Cambridge: Cambridge University Press.

HARROD, R. F. 1952. Towards a dynamic economics. London: MacMillan and Co.

HAYAMI, Yujiro, and Vernon Ruttan. 1971. Agricultural development: an international perspective. Baltimore and London: The Johns Hopkins Press.

HEYER, J. 1976. Introduction. In Agricultural development in Kenya. J. Heyer, J. K. Maitha, and W. M. Senga, eds. Nairobi: Oxford University Press.

HILL, Polly. 1963. The migrant cocoa-farmers of Southern Ghana. Cambridge: The University Press.

HOPCRAFT, Peter N. 1976. An evaluation of the Kenya dairy production improvement programme. Institute for Development Studies, University of Nairobi, Occasional Paper No. 20.

HOWELL, P. P. 1973. A manual of Nuer law. London: Oxford University Press.

JACOBS, Alan H. 1980. Pastoral Maasai and tropical rural development. In Agricultural development in Africa: issues of public policy. Robert Bates and Michael Lofchie, eds. New York: Praeger Publishers.

JONES, William O. 1975. Republic of Zambia, agricultural and rural sector survey. Washington, D.C.: World Bank.

JOSKOW, Paul, and Roger Noll. 1981. Theory and practice in public regulation: a current overview. In Studies in public regulation. Gary Fromm, ed. Cambridge: M.I.T. Press.

KRAMER, Gerald H. 1980. Electoral stability: a general analysis. Paper presented to the 1980

Annual Meeting of the American Political Science Association, Washington, D.C.

LAU, L. J., and P. A. Yotopoulous. 1971. A test for relative efficiency and application to Indian agriculture. American Economic Review 61:94-109.

LEITH, J. Clark. 1974. Foreign trade regimes and economic development: Ghana. A Special Conference Series on Foreign Trade Regimes and Economic Development, Volume II. New York: National Bureau of Economic Research, Columbia University.

LITTLE, I.M.D., T. Scitovsky, and M. Scott. 1970. Industry and trade in some developing countries. London: Oxford University Press.

LUCE, R. Duncan, and Howard Raiffa. 1957. Games and decisions. New York: John Wiley and Sons.

MARGLIN, S. 1963. The social rate of discount and the optimal rate of investment. Quarterly Journal of Economics 77:95-111.

MUELLER, Dennis C. 1979. Public choice. Cambridge: Cambridge University Press.

OLSON, Mancur. 1977. The logic of collective action: public goods and the theory of groups. Cambridge, Mass.: Harvard University Press.

PAGE, T. 1979. A Kantian perspective on the social rate of discount. California Institute of Technology, Caltech Social Science Working Paper 278.

PEARSON, Scott, and Dirck Stryker. 1981. Rice in West Africa: policy and economics. Stanford: Stanford University Press..

POPKIN, Samuel L. 1979. The rational peasant. Berkeley and Los Angeles: University of California Press.

_____. 1981. Public choice and rural development: free riders, lemons, and institutional design. In Public choice and rural development. Clifford Russell and Norman Nicholson, eds. Washington, D.C.: Resources for the Future.

POSNER, Richard. 1953. A theory of primitive society. Journal of Law and Economics 23:1-53.

QUIRK, James, and R. Saposnik. 1969. Introduction to general equilibrium theory and welfare economics. Homewood, Illinois: Richard D. Irwin.

RAWLS, John. 1971. A theory of justice. Cambridge, Mass.: Harvard University Press.

RIKER, William H., and Peter C. Ordeshook. 1973. An introduction to positive political theory. Englewood Cliffs, N.J.: Prentice-Hall.

ROSTOW, W. W. 1961. Stages of economic growth. Cambridge: The University Press.

RUTHENBERG, Hans. 1976. Farming systems in the tropics. London: Oxford University Press.

ROUMASSETT, J.A. 1976. Rice and risk: decision making among low income farmers. The Hague: North-Holland.

SCHULTZ, T. W. 1964. Transforming traditional agriculture. New Haven and London: Yale University Press.

_____, ed. 1978. Distortions in agricultural incentives. Bloomington and London: Indiana University Press.

SCHUMACHER, E. F. 1975. Small is beautiful: economics as if people mattered. New York: Harper and Row.

SEN, A. K. 1970. Collective choice and social welfare. San Francisco: Holden-Day, Inc.

STIGLITZ, J. E., and H. Uzawa, eds. 1972. Readings in the modern theory of economic growth. Cambridge and London: Cambridge University Press.

TIDEMAN, Nicholas T. 1977. Introduction. Public Choice 29:1-14.

TODARO, M. P. 1977. Economic development in the third world. London and New York: Longman.

XIII. ANTHROPOLOGICAL ECONOMIC AND DEVELOPMENT PLANNING

Richard F. Salisbury

Development planners, and indeed many anthropologists, like to visualize the planning process as making rational decisions about the achievement of long-term macrolevel objectives for society at large. Some of the objectives visualized by planners are: an increase in industrial output or per capita GNP, a reduction of national dependence on imported capital goods or on agricultural exports, an improvement of the transportation or educational system, etc. Politicians may verbalize these objectives, and, if they are in power, they may order these objectives to be used as guidelines by national planners. In reality, however, the planning process is not as rational or purposive as visualized by practitioners and by some anthropologists. Many individual projects are proposed separately and in response to either hypothetical theories or fortuitous practical pressures. The projects are then screened for how well they fit with the national objectives, or with the guidelines that the politicians have given to the planners. This chapter discusses one way in which anthropological economics could, if informed by more technical sophistication, improve the judgement of planners in screening projects, and increase the likelihood that the projects selected will achieve intended social objectives.[1]

Let us admit that there are many reasons why development objectives are not met. Ideologies of development may be unrealistic, and even irrelevant for the country. The objectives of planners and members of government may not be widely shared by the rest of the country, and may even be antagonistic to the interests of some sectors of the population. Projects may also fail because, despite an official acknowledgement that planning must be an integrated process, actual decisions on particular projects are often approved at the whim of government ministers, or for the sake of political patronage or payback. The projects that are brought to the attention of the planners, are often preselected (for example, by foreign advisers) so that none are really appropriate to national needs. But the reforms required to correct these slippages in rational planning are probably best studied and treated in other contexts than that of anthropological economics.

Economists are usually the most influential professionals in the pursuit of rationality in the planning process. They advise politicians how to convert social objectives into macrolevel planning guidelines; for example, economists may advise that in order to achieve local independence from foreign pressures, consumer demand should be restricted, local capital investment should be encouraged, and local education and research budgets should be increased. These macrolevel guidelines, if accepted, then form the guidelines for microlevel projects and determine, for example, what discount rates are used in calculating capital costs, the restrictions on foreign currency, the priority of employment generating policies, and the importance given to environmental and social impacts. After evaluating the projects, the economist ideally should range them according to desirability, using a single index, so that the politicians can then make a simple choice. This index, if an ideal one is feasible, should reflect an evaluation not only of all the factors that a business enterprise would consider in deciding the profitability of a project--materials, labor, rent, output, etc.--but also all the social costs and benefits that are likely to be incurred or to accrue to the whole community as a result of the project. The value of each factor, cost or benefit should not be its current price in the market--which is often distorted by subsidies, quotas, monopolies or market imperfections--but its real cost, phrased as the opportunity cost of not using the same resource for other purposes. The measure of value is termed a numeraire. Social cost-benefit analysis (CBA) is the process of constructing such an index, and perhaps the best known version of it is that enunciated by Little and Mirrlees (1974).

CBA takes into account important social considerations, in ways that a business profitability analysis does not as Barlett (1980) has shown. In this paper, I focus, in particular, on four social considerations: the subsidy distortions of prices, real labor costs, income equalization, and externalities. I show how CBA reduces social considerations to a single index, to provide a convenient way for a central government to decide which one of a number of projects to support. CBA is probably the best technique currently available for project evaluation despite its need for improvement.

The argument of this paper is not that such quantitative indices are inappropriate, but rather that their use by political decision makers places power in the hands of those who are familiar with CBA techniques. Typically these are central government economists. The anthropological economist with an awareness of the real social costs and benefits within the community or region where a project is to take place, if unable to communicate in terms of CBA, is cut off from the planning process. The anthropological economist familiar with the logic of single-index CBA can contribute to central decision making, and make it more responsive to small scale social processes. Trying to apply the CBA logic attunes the anthropological economist to an effective quantification of social variables, and to the specification, in economic terms, of those linkages in the local economy that otherwise would be considered by a CBA analyst as vague externalities. At a deeper level, the attempt to visualize changes resulting from a project as part of a social economy of a community or region that can be quantified would enable the anthropological economist to make an important contribution to anthropology. Rather than merely studying "systems of production, distribution and consumption," the anthropological economist would also be studying how societies allocate resources of all kinds, especially social resources. Practical contributions to central planning, ensuring adequate reflection of local viewpoints, are matched by theoretical gains in social understanding.

I. THE CASE STUDY

In true anthropological style this chapter is inductive, starting with an empirical study, and deriving generalizations from it. To simplify exposition, however, and to enable me to use a number of available ethnographic studies, I use a fictional case--approximating reality, but simplified and somewhat generalized. The case I consider is a project to enlarge a fish-processing plant in Outville, a part subsistence, isolated village on the rocky coast of Norland, about 600 miles north of the country's capital and major city of Bigtown. Features of the village match the features reported for other North Atlantic fishing communities analyzed by Barnes

(1954), Barth (1966), Brox (1963), Anderson and Wadel (1972), Matthews (1976), Paine (1978), and many others.

The anthropological analyses of fishing communities show how network processes are involved in recruiting boats' crews and in maintaining capital investment. These studies have also demonstrated the disruption of these processes with the advent of more expensive technology and the relevance of patronage and broker relations as the marketing of the fish steadily increases in importance in the overall economy. These studies show that the fishing decisions made by individuals are intimately linked to other features of these communities—to subsistence resources, employment for wives and children, social service and subsidy payments by the state, to opportunities as migrant laborers. They show the importance of kin and communication networks for the provision of local services and maintenance of local patriotism. Fishing decisions are also affected by the class structure of the communities where skilled government (or company) posts are usually filled by expatriates who are hired in the capital and spend only short periods of time in the fishing community; this skilled personnel is assigned the limited suburban-style housing, even though everyone in the community aspires to the same standard. The village of Outville shares all of the above characteristics.

The central government, faced by twenty local improvement projects demanded by members of the legislative assembly, and ranging from hydroelectricity to factory ships, requests a CBA of each project. This information allows the government to decide or justify a choice. The projects not only must have a positive social value—a balance of benefits over costs during its lifetime—but they must be ranked in terms of priority. Each project protagonist will argue that the project is profitable (or could be profitable with government subsidy), as a basis of pricing factors at market rates in dollars The CBA will modify the protagonists' "profitability analysis" based on dollars, by weighting social factors as they are added into the account, so that the eventual CBA will use "accounting dollars" as numeraire.

I now discuss some of the weighting procedures used by CBA to correct for four types of market price distortions: subsidy distortions of prices, real labor costs, income equalization, and externalities (or linkage effects of the project on other sectors of the economy, caused by the project, but external to it). For each type of distortion I then consider how an economic anthropologist could productively use the CBA line of thought, or could contribute with a better analysis.

A. Subsidy Distortion of Prices

The most obvious distortion of prices in Outville is that caused by the subsidized sea transport system. It makes manufactured imports cheaper in Outville than their real landed cost, while enabling higher prices to be paid for Outville exports than they would otherwise receive in an open market. A private Outville entrepreneur would estimate the price of imported machinery and building material for a fish plant at less than the real cost in CBA's accounting dollars, as the latter adds on the relevant subsidies. The fish plant that appears attractive (with subsidies) to the Outville fisherman, or to the anthropologist listening to local comment, may not appear so attractive to Norland as a whole, when it must pay the subsidies.

But once the economic anthropologist tries a CBA analysis of the project, and investigates the impact of transport subsidies, he becomes aware of the ramifications of the subsidy on local life, for example, the effect of subsidies on local wage scales, purchasing patterns, etc. For Outville these may constitute costs to the local economy (e.g., making imported food cheaper than local products), offsetting the direct benefits of the subsidy. The economic anthropologist might ask whether the cost of a sea transport service should not be counted instead as a fixed cost for Norland, as the cost of asserting sovereignty over the area. In that case only the marginal costs of shipping the machines to Outville should be included in the fish plant CBA. What seemed to be a simple issue rapidly becomes a question of the regional political economy: the CBA rule-of-thumb "correct subsidy distortions" conceals assumptions that are highly questionable. But to be able to question the assumptions one must be aware of the reasoning involved, and have the data to make alternative assumptions reasonable. The typical economic anthropologist lacks the awareness of

political economy, and the technical sophistication
needed to argue with the CBA.

B.   Real Labor Costs

     The CBA valuation of labor costs will certainly
differ greatly from the market prices used in the
profitability analysis of an Outville operation.
There is not an open market for unskilled labor in
Outville, as local people rarely work for wages.
During the fishing and hunting seasons unskilled work
is not wanted; even on days when weather makes fishing
impossible unpaid tasks like repairing gear are
preferred. During the winter, unemployment season,
there is little incentive to work for wages as those
eligible for unemployment insurance would lose
benefits. Whether wives and dependents are prepared
to take up paid casual labor depends more on household
relationships than on the wage rate offered.

     To assign a cost to the local unskilled labor for
the project the cost-benefit analyst argues that the
cost is what the rest of the economy must suffer
because of the new increment of demand for labor.
Given the overall underemployment in the area, the
outmigration in search of work, and the high transfer
of payments into the area, the CBA would say that the
project would merely employ labor that currently
produces nothing--that is, whose marginal product of
labor is zero--thus that the real cost of Outville
unskilled labor would be zero. The cost-benefit
analyst might even consider the marginal product of
labor as _negative_, and credit the project account
with an employment premium for absorbing each unit of
labor, thereby reducing the cost to Norland of welfare
payments to Outville unemployed. The cost-benefit
analyst alternatively might argue that the _marginal_
product of labor is the point when people switch from
preferring work to preferring leisure; the
cost-benefit analyst would then want to know the value
of the expected catch that tempts a fisherman to put
to sea and not opt to stay ashore in unfavorable
conditions. This figure, which might well approximate
the payments from unemployment insurance, would serve
as a measure of marginal product of labor.

     In any event the CBA is likely to value the cost
of unskilled labor for any Outville project at very
little. The project that receives most favorable CBA

reports for Outville is the one using most unskilled labor on simple tasks.

An economic anthropologist could clearly help the cost-benefit analyst by estimating a realistic and/or accurate figure for the marginal product of unskilled labor in Outville, though they rarely do so--largely because the theoretical significance of the figure is not obvious. Decades of anthropological study of occupational pluralism (Comitas, 1964) and of the informal sectors (Hart, 1972) has established that people who are nominally unemployed often produce substantial earnings from other activities, yet these studies have not eradicated the common CBA assumption that some underemployment implies a pool of people with nothing to do, and a zero marginal product of labor. Subsistence farmers or hunters (e.g., Salisbury, 1969; Salisbury, et al., 1972) have often been shown to produce at well above official scales of unskilled labor pay, and not to be available for paid employment at those rates.

The effect of welfare and unemployment benefits in altering the threshold between work and leisure is still a matter of controversy, despite major experiments with guaranteed incomes in New Jersey, Manitoba, and Quebec (LaRusic, 1979). In my own field experience, informants drawing welfare or unemployment benefits readily verbalize the points at which "it does not pay to work." Quantified folk models of such decisions, analyzed by economic anthropologists with technical expertise, could contribute to an important theoretical issue.

The marginal product of female labor may be different, as may be the marginal product of labor at different seasons; both evaluations call for investigation by economic anthropologists. True, a low cash wage for intermittent part-time work has often attracted female workers in other fishing communities, where households are temporarily short of cash. But the real cost of female labor is what would happen if employment in an enlarged fish plant drew them away from contributing indirectly to the self-employed fishing enterprise (cf. Stiles, 1972), or to such household tasks as education. Here the marginal product of women's labor in Outville is high. The marginal product of labor of everyone is higher during fishing season than in the winter, while the advent of a film crew in Outville is likely to produce unskilled laborers demanding exorbitant wage rates.

CBA figures for unskilled labor costs may underestimate real costs; they are also likely to treat all unskilled labor as undifferentiated, and thus to equally commend any type of labor-intensive plant. In fact, there are different costs for different types of unskilled labor (casual versus full time female, self-employed versus unemployed male); furthermore, the type of labor the plant will use dramatically alters the desirability of the plant for the community. Only figures collected by economic anthropologists can ensure that the desirability is reflected in a weighted CBA accounting.

The cost-benefit analyst also faces problems in assigning a cost to skilled labor in Outville. Most skilled workers in Outville are government employees from Bigtown. Their salaries are at Bigtown rates, plus hardship allowances, free holiday travel, subsidized housing, etc. The cost-benefit analyst, reckoning that additional skilled labor would have to come from Bigtown, might well consider that the real costs of such labor for the plant were the total of Bigtown rates plus the extra allowances. The CBA results would tend to favor a plant that used relatively little skilled labor. In the third world a related argument has been used to justify the concentration of skilled jobs into urban areas, namely that as it costs less to build a modern infrastructure of schools, sewage and soap operas in town, and as skilled workers demand these benefits, one can justify high market rates paid to urban workers that are evaluated as costing less. Either way the rural area is prevented from obtaining skilled people.

The economic anthropologist would make a different estimate after interviews with Outville emigrants who have acquired skills. Many say they would return home if skilled work were available there; they claim that they would not need special premiums to attract them. If what they say is true, and could be expressed quantitatively, the CBA would assign a lower cost to rural skilled labor, and so encourage a greater use of it in the Outville project.

Other qualitative anthropological research supports this suggestion, and could provide another means of calculating costs. Descriptive comments abound on the mechanical and calculating skills of fishermen, and on the traditional ways of passing on skills in fishing communities (cf. Anderson and Wadel, 1972). These skills are available locally and could be upgraded. If the operation of the plant were designed to absorb local people and then upgrade their skills, then the cost of its skilled labor would be that of unskilled labor, plus the costs of training, and of running the plant at lower efficiency during training. Almost certainly this cost would be less than the one calculated by following established CBA procedures.

The case of Outville brings out a development issue that is often begged by cost-benefit analysts: the relation of the project to the provision of social service in the community. What the immigrant skilled workers from Bigtown expect, and what the high CBA costs of their salaries reflect, is the cost of providing the sort of social services found in Bigtown. An anthropologist would argue that social services already exist in Outville, performing most of the same functions, though in a different style and form. There are interpersonal networks for care in time of sickness, educational facilities for training boats' crews, information channels to bring together crews and skippers, social control mechanisms to reduce crime and solve disputes through gossip, rather than through lawyers. Capital has been invested in these informal social services over generations. They need upgrading for the 1980s, but it is questionable whether destroying them and replacing them with bureaucratically organized services is more efficient, or economic. Building on local services, employing and training local people, and attaching the local service to the wider state system, rather than replacing it by a service staffed by skilled urbanites, would almost certainly imply lower imputed costs for rural skilled labor than are imputed in CBA. It would almost certainly result in externalities such as "improving the quality of rural life." Anthropological studies of the costs and benefits in the provision of rural service by different mechanisms are vitally needed. Their findings are of importance in planning the location of plants, the sort of labor force to be used, and the cost evaluations of rural skilled labor. My guess is that with this information in hand planners would then tend to stress the use of local skilled workers and the training of unskilled workers.

The CBA may even underestimate the real costs of employing nonlocal skilled workers.. Inter-ethnic conflicts in communities like Outville have been massively documented by Paine (1978), though Turner (1981) has shown how careful selection of imported skilled workers may mitigate such conflict. But increased conflict and careful selection represent "costs." The outmigration of ambitious young locals must also be considered as a cost, if jobs go to skilled outsiders and local personnel is not trained, leaving the community as a truncated social unit without local leadership (Salisbury, 1971). It is true that local training may lead to some loss of residents through a brain drain. But the indirect benefits to the local community when native sons and daughters effectively represent the local viewpoints (as "community brokers") at higher managerial levels in Bigtown should vastly outweigh this loss. Quantification of these effects by economic anthropologists is needed.

To sum up, superficially plausible CBA assumptions about real labor costs in Outville probably overestimate costs of skilled labor, and underestimate costs of unskilled labor. Anthropological studies are needed to quantify what the real costs are, both in Outville and elsewhere. CBA misevaluations would favor rural projects using low skill levels in large amounts, but making minimal use of higher levels of skill. Their evaluations would lead to rural underdevelopment through such projects. The anthropologist wishing to combat this tendency needs both the quantified data and the sophisticated arguments that CBA employs.

C.   Income Equalization

The CBA measures benefits in terms of the increase in socially desirable consumption--either the salaries going to the poorest people, or dollars to be allocated by government in desirable ways. It recognizes the desirability of income equalization when it includes increases in the incomes of high-paid employees in the total of benefits at only a fraction of the rates actually paid. Insofar as Outville is seen as a poor community by the planners in Bigtown, and few skilled workers are included in the project, almost all the salaries paid by the project will be heavily weighted as benefits in the CBA.

The economic anthropologist studying consumption patterns in Outville might well ask whether the increased salary payments will lead to socially desirable consumption. Modern consumerism has already been mentioned--TV, junk foods, stereos, joyriding on snowmobiles, etc. Without taking any moral stance towards these items, we know that few of these are produced in Norland, and that their import represents a major monetary leakage from Norland national accounts. Income so used, perhaps, should be weighted less than income to government. Some aspects of project expenditures, however, might even be more socially desirable than government income, hence their "cost" should be treated as a positive benefit. For example, if a project necessitates a local water system, or preventive medical checkups, or better food storage to improve local diets, these benefits should be heavily and positively weighted as they will reach most of the local population.

We are here approaching a fundamental issue: who decides what benefits are socially desirable? The central planner in Bigtown assumes a uniform national consensus on desirability; the anthropologist is aware of local divergences in preferences, and should seek to document these with studies of consumption patterns to ensure that consumption divergences are taken into account in evaluating benefits. Communities armed with such documentation are better able to weight decisions in terms of what is locally desirable.[2]

If universal standards for the evaluation of benefits are insisted upon, the universal availability of basic human services (housing, food, water and medical services) might be considered as meriting the highest weighting, and incremental incomes to the poorest might receive the next highest weighting. To argue for this the economic anthropologist needs to determine whether the community lacks basic human services.

D. Externalities

Two main types of externality are considered in CBA evaluations. Increased demand for inputs by the project may change the price of those inputs, upwards or downwards, for everyone in the society. So too the outputs of the project may change the prices of those outputs (usually downwards) for everyone, often permitting activities that were previously impossible. Increased costs to the rest of society, or benefits produced indirectly should be included in the project accounting. Thus for Outville the new fish plant with its demand for more regular shipping, or more mechanics to service the machinery might well result in cheaper transportation and cheaper repairs to fishing boats in Outville. The production of electricity by a larger imported generator for the plant might not only result in power sales by the project (a direct benefit), but might make feasible new industries that would bring an additional benefit to Outville.

Assigning a specific value to such externalities is extremely difficult, and this difficulty is second only to recognizing all of the relevant externalities. Little and Mirrlees (1974) are explicit on this difficulty, and urge that if no specific value can be assigned, then at least the externality should be mentioned qualitatively in the CBA report, so that the decision maker can take some account of it.

It is probably in this area that the anthropologist has the most contribution to make, since the discipline's strength is the analysis of interrelations between aspects of society that do not immediately appear connected. At the same time, it is also an area most involved in political argument. For example, Little and Mirrlees (1974) cite the debate over transnational corporations, and whether their advent creates positive or negative externalities. If the import of a new technology benefits the whole economy the externality for the project where the import takes place is positive. If the continuing nonlocal control has negative effects elsewhere, for example in purchasing or marketing policies, then the externalities are negative. Quantitative measures of the costs of these externalities are hard to come by, and should be a subject of research by anthropological economists. It is critical, however, that the anthropological economist should think clearly along CBA lines in order to formulate the elements to be quantified.

Out of the vast range of possible externalities that an Outville fish plant might have (many of which, it must be noted, would not have large effects), I take up only one for further discussion: the issue of economies of scale. Little and Mirrlees (1974) cite

this issue as the one most stressed by cost-benefit
analysts. Our earlier ethnographic description for
Outville has already indicated that according to CBA,
bigger transport needs would reduce shipping costs for
everyone, that bigger electric generators would reduce
electricity costs, that a bigger plant could process
the output of bigger boats. Many analysts can make a
case that bigger is better and cheaper.

The anthropological study of Outville does not
necessarily support this. We have already suggested
that subsidized shipping costs are not an unmixed
blessing for Outville. Consumerism and dependence on
imports, coupled with an underutilization of local
resources, are some consequences. Other consequences
already mentioned are: the possible distortions of
labor costs, and the negative effect of cheaper
shipping rates on local multiplier effects. While
cheaper electricity could benefit a large sector of
Outville's population, it would require an expensive
oil-fired generator; yet small hydroplants and wind
generators are the types that currently look like the
most effective and cheapest way to meet the relatively
small needs of isolated communities like Outville. The
installation of a large oil-generator would probably
halt the movement towards the use of such technology.

The costs of changing the size of boats, and
investing in a larger scale technology have been the
subject of much discussion by anthropologists (cf.
Anderson, 1972). The monetary costs have not been the
severest problem, as so far the costs commonly have
been met by government subsidy or loan programs.
Maintenance of the new technology, through appropriate
financing, skilled use, and knowledge of how best to
repair equipment, has been a problem that is still not
solved and constitutes a continuing cost. Another
equally serious problem is the transmission of
acquired technical and management skills to succeeding
generations. These problems had been largely solved
for the simpler technologies with routine provisions
for the repair or replacement of gear, the use of
rules of thumb based on generations of experience with
similar technology, and a social organization of
training fitted to village, family and social life.
Most acute have been the problems surrounding crew
recruitment for larger boats, as the extended family
has become too restricted a unit in numbers and in
skills for the regular manning and smooth operation of
a large vessel; furthermore, a fair division of the

returns from fishing among a crew of unrelated workers
has not yet been worked out. One may well question
whether larger boats would benefit Outville, when all
the costs outlined above are weighted against their
greater productivity.

Underlying the economies of scale argument for
Outville, however, is a critical assumption: namely,
that the improved fish plant would utilize the same
marketing arrangements used elsewhere in Norland for
shipping fish to an international market. Ships of
multinational fish marketing firms collect the
semiprocessed products from medium-size fish plants in
other parts of Norland; the products are then packaged
under the firm's label and are sold in the
international market. If the fish marketing firms
respond to the improved fish processing plant in
Outville by extending their run to this town, and if
by so doing, the firms manage to marginally increase
their output and sales, then indeed the new plant will
lead to some economies of scale. Most of the benefits
from the economies of scale, however, would accrue to
the marketing firms and the places like Bigtown where
further processing, packaging, marketing, advertising,
and financing are conducted. The CBA has to include
these benefits by examining the ramifications of the
existing marketing system. This examination,
unfortunately, means that the CBA closely resembles
the profitability analysis of a multinational fish
marketing firm, modified only to account for the
subsidies to Outville, and to the population sectors
in Outville that the planners consider need to receive
most of the benefits.

The possibility of a distinctive marketing
arrangement for Outville is unlikely to be considered
by a national planner. Yet the special marketing
position of Outville as a far northern village must be
considered because it affects the viability of
projects to increase output of processed sea products.
Outville's most valuable products (salmon, arctic
char, shrimp and scallops) are not available in
quantities that justify the use of large ships or the
factory-type processing that uses every element of the
catch, if only for fertilizer. The investment in a
larger factory will exert a pressure for more bulk
fishing of less valuable species, in order to keep the
plant operating at capacity. The high value Outville
products, for example smoked, or delicately packed
locally to meet gourmet standards, do not need a large

market; it is feasible to distribute them through direct arrangements by air. One international hotel or airline adopting Outville's products as its speciality would probably absorb the output of a fish plant similar in size to the presently existing plant. It may be more important to upgrade the product than to increase production levels. A small fish plant producing higher quality products would absorb more skilled local labor, and would make better use of existing fishing equipment and knowledge. Such a plant, furthermore, would make greater use of the existing social arrangements and so keep cost down and reduce the need for new social investment.

Economies of scale, in short, are easy to identify if one starts from a central planning office (or from the industry-wide perspective of a multinational firm) and one thinks big. The economies that would come from a project designed to make fuller use of diverse existing resources in a small community are harder to see, unless one is based in the community, as the anthropologist commonly is. Whether these local benefits do outweigh the benefits that the nation as a whole would otherwise receive from a large-scale operation is what a CBA needs to evaluate. But if no one designs and advocates a project that is specifically planned to suit local conditions, the centrally planned large-scale project is assumed to be better by default. It may even be the only type of project that comes to the attention of the central planning office. It is small wonder that people living in outlying communities have such negative views of central state planners.

II. THE ROLE OF THE ECONOMIC ANTHROPOLOGIST

Though this paper has treated only cost benefit analysis, the argument it has made might well be generalized beyond CBA to the total process of development planning. Basically, central plans are made using a language that is technical, and focusing on those aspects of behavior that the technical experts have been trained in, or in which they have acquired expertise. These aspects may not be those that are most significant at the local level, while the planners may be unaware of other more locally significant factors. The anthropologist who knows what is significant locally, and who is trained to consider the wider relevance of every aspect of a

413

social system may castigate the seeming insensitivity
and rigidity of the planner.

But there is no dialogue if the critique does not
use the language of the planner, as the latter simply
would ignore what the anthropologists say. I have
tried to show how CBA can incorporate social arguments
about relieving unemployment, equalizing incomes, or
making social services available. My argument is that
anthropologists could undoubtedly add to the list of
social factors needing inclusion, and will find the
experts ready to listen and incorporate the factors
when the anthropologists learn to use the language of
CBA. The anthropologist who does so will find that a
CBA can, in return, teach valuable lessons in thinking
about social economy. Economic anthropology as a
discipline needs the rigor of quantitative thinking.

The economic anthropologist who is prepared to
take CBA seriously, and to learn enough of its
language to express anthropological ideas when dealing
with specific local situations, can make contributions
at three main levels. As a fieldworker, the
anthropologist can collect the data to make CBA
quantification more accurate. My examples of skilled
wage labor costs, or of consumption standards in
Outville provide cases where the cost-benefit analyst
would be ready to use more accurate local figures than
those provided by national surveys, if such figures
were made available. An appreciation of what figures
are significant for planning purposes is essential.

At the second level the economic anthropologist
who can make a CBA of the project's impact on the
local economy, rather than on the national economy, is
well situated to assist the community in reacting to a
project proposal. The phenomena we have restated in
CBA terms in this paper have all been reported
ethnographically for fishing communities--occupational
pluralism of fisherman, informal structures for the
transmission of skill, ethnicity problems with
immigrant skilled workers, etc--but planners are
likely to be unaware of such literature. When the
argument is presented to planners in cultural
terms--for example, "fishermen do not like wage labor
as it prevents them from going hunting when they want
to"--planners may ridicule the argument as being a
"naive wish to preserve traditional ways." By
contrast, the same issue presented in terms of the
calculus of part subsistence workers choosing

self-employment as giving a higher marginal product of labor is likely to be heeded. Not only may the particular project be evaluated appropriately, but the cost-benefit analyst may accept the more general improvement in the use of CBA techniques. The dialogue could be as fruitful as that between economists such as Theodore Schultz (1964) and anthropologists who study peasant agriculturalists. It could refine the rationality of the planning process, and at the same time deepen the anthropological insight.

At a deeper level the informed anthropological economist may become the protagonist of alternatives to existing plans or planning methods. In the case presented the inbuilt technological assumptions on which project planning (and the CBA analysis) was based were indeed questionable, but only because the implications of the alternative technology were not spelled out with a rigor equal to that used by the original planners. The relevance of a rural project to patterns of internal migration, and to problems of class relations between skilled urbanites and rural unskilled labor may be taken as unavoidable by the planners (and indeed by the politicians in power), when national development really requires that inequalities be reduced rather than that the status quo be perpetuated. The anthropological economist who can formulate the alternative action in the same language as the planners, and can make the arguments that will move the alternative through the planning process, is much more effective than the critic who merely complains of the existing system.

III.   PLANNING AND ANTHROPOLOGICAL ECONOMICS

Though the argument so far has been about the contribution that the anthropological economist can and should make to development planning by helping the economists, whom Belshaw (1976) has called "sorcerer's apprentices," to realize their promises, there are major benefits that the anthropologist himself could gain from a closer involvement with planners.

Intrinsic to the present paper is the definition of economics as the study of the allocation of scarce means to alternative ends, and the recognition that those scarce means and alternative ends include social elements of all types, and not merely the material prerequisites of society. Economists have recognized some of the social elements that need to be considered, within their existing CBA studies. It is embarrassing to record that there are still anthropologists who would confine their economic analyses to the study of production, distribution and consumption. The study of social planning makes this blinkered view untenable.

For those concerned with social planning, but critical of economics as being too concerned with mundane detail, exposure to CBA thinking is an important corrective. There are choices to be made; it is rare for one option to be all good and the others all bad. Some calculus of costs and benefits is needed--some recognition of both the advantages and the disadvantages of any project--but in any situation a decision must be made and a way of selecting the best option available must be found. The logic of a social analysis that tries to be systematic and tries to quantify factors, needs to be grafted on to the ideas of the abstract social thinker, if the ideas are to have any relation to reality.

The anthropologist involved in the study of the small community who argues for its distinctiveness and who possibly is somewhat blind to the interdependence between that community and the wider national and world society, would profit from an involvement with national planners. There is clearly a disjunction between what happens in national capitals, and the reality of small community life. Though the disjunction is partly due to the explicit pressure from interest groups, it is also the result of ignorance on the part of planners of the situation in outlying areas. In trying to bridge the gap, while defending the interests of the small community, the anthropological economist is brought up sharply against questions of how far the local interest is identical to the national interest. The central planner constantly justifies his work as a search for rationality and the national interest; he is open to correction on facts and data, but the anthropological economist must constantly review his own material from the national perspective if his arguments are to prevail in discussion with the planner. The vaunted holism of the anthropologist, studying systems and their interrelations at all levels, is nowhere so challenged as when it is confronted with the need to defend local interests in the terms of the political economy used by central planners.

Acknowledgements

I wish to acknowledge the stimulating discussions with the Labrador Inuit Association, Peter Usher, Randy Sweetenham, Tony Williamson and Ignatius LaRusic. My indebtedness to earlier discussions with Geoff Stiles, Claude Bariteau, Bob Schneider, Raoul Anderson, Jim Acheson, and Ottar Brox must be recorded. This paper was written while holding a Killam Foundation Senior Fellowship of the Canada Council. It forms part of a wider study of decentralized development processes, as they contrast with centralized ones.

Notes

[1] Other anthropological contributions are not discussed in the present article which is aimed at improving anthropological dialogue with economists. These contributions will be discussed in my forthcoming book Decentralized Development: Lessons of James Bay.

[2] I am indebted to my commentator, Catherine Bledsoe, for stressing the importance of these questions, which I had tended to underplay as "non-economic" in my earlier drafts.

References

ANDERSON, R, and C. Wadel, eds. 1972. North Atlantic fishermen. St. John's: Memorial University Press.

BARLETT, P. F. 1980. Cost-benefit: a test of alternative methodologies. In Agricultural decision making. P. Barlett, ed. New York: Academic Press.

BARNES, J. A. 1954. Class and committees in a Norwegian island parish. Human Relations 7:39-58.

BARTH, F. 1966. Models of social organization. Royal Anthropological Institute, Occasional Paper 23.

BELSHAW, C. S. 1976. The sorcerer's apprentice. New York: Pergamon Press.

417

R. SALISBURY

BROX, O. 1963. Three types of North Norwegian entrepreneurship. In The role of the entrepreneur in Northern Norway. F. Barth, ed. Bergen University.

COMITAS. L. 1964. Occupational multiplicity in Jamaica. In Proceedings of AES Spring Meeting, 1963. V. Garfield and E. Friedl, eds.

HART, K. 1972. Employment, incomes and equality: increasing productive employment in Kenya. Geneva: International Labor Organization.

LARUSIC, I. 1979. The income security programme of the James Bay Cree. Montreal: McGill University P.A.D. Monograph 13.

LITTLE, I. M. D., and J. A. Mirrlees. 1974. Project appraisal and planning for developing countries. London: Heinemann.

MATHEWS, R. 1976. There's no better place than here. Toronto: Peter Martin Associates.

PAINE, R., ed. 1978. The white Arctic. St. John's: Memorial University Press.

SALISBURY, R. F. 1969. Vunamami: economic transformation in a traditional society. Berkeley: University of California Press.

_____. 1971. Problems of the Gazelle Peninsula, August 1971. Port Moresby, Government Printer.

SALISBURY, R. F., F. Filion, F. Rawji, and D. A. Stewart. 1972. Development and James Bay. Montreal: McGill University P.A.D. Monograph 7.

SCHULTZ, T. W. 1964. Transforming traditional agriculture. New Haven: Yale University Press.

STILES, R. G. 1972. Fishermen, wives and radio: aspects of communication in a Newfoundland fishing community. In North Atlantic fishermen. R. Andersen and C. Wadel, eds.. St. John's: Memorial University Press.

TURNER, R. 1981. God's power stations: social effects of a power station on a small Scottish seaside town.   Paper delivered at the meetings of the Society for Applied Anthropology, Edinburgh, April 1981.

NOTES ON CONTRIBUTORS

BATES, ROBERT H. (Ph.D., M.I.T., 1969) Professor of Political Science, California Institute of Technology. He has published a number of books and essays on rural development and development policies in Africa.

BENNETT, JOHN. (Ph.D., Chicago, 1946) Professor of Anthropology, Washington University, St. Louis, Missouri. His research interests have focused on resource management, American farmers, ecological adaptation of human populations and development. He has published a number of books on these subjects.

BERDAN, FRANCES F. (Ph.D., Texas, 1975) Professor of Anthropology, California State College, San Bernardino. Her research interests are on the Aztecs, central Mexican codices and Nahuatl language documentation in Colonial Mexico.

BLANTON, RICHARD E. (Ph.D., Michigan, 1970) Associate Professor of Anthropology, Purdue University. An archaeologist, who has worked on the evolution of prehispanic civilizations in the valley of Mexico and Oaxaca as well as in the central and southern highlands of Mexico.

CARRASCO, PEDRO. (Ph.D., Columbia, 1953) Professor of Anthropology, State University of New York, Stony Brook. An ethnohistorian, whose research interests have been focused on ancient Mexico and Tibet.

DALTON, GEORGE. (Ph.D., Oregon, 1959) He holds a joint appointment as Professor in the Departments of Anthropology and Economics, Northwestern University. He has published a number of books on development and economic anthropology.

GROSS, DANIEL. (Ph.D., Columbia University, 1970) Professor of Anthropology at Hunter College and the Graduate School of the City University of New York. His writings deal with social and ecological change, technological change, nutrition, traditional religion and local level politics.

HART, KEITH. (Ph.D., Cambridge, 1969) Visiting Associate Professor, University of Chicago, Anthropology Department. He has published extensively on political economy and development.

KANEL, DON. (Ph.D., University of Wisconsin) Professor of Economics in the Department of Agricultural Economics and the Land Tenure Center, University of Wisconsin. His research interests are on development issues and institutional economics. He has been a development consultant in Asia, Africa and Latin America.

KÖCKE, JASPER. (Ph.D., Northwestern University, 1980) His interests are in economic anthropology and the anthropology of economic development. He is presently working for the United Nations in Honduras on economic development.

LEES, SUSAN. (Ph.D., Michigan, 1970) Professor of Anthropology, Hunter College and the Graduate School of the City University of New York. Her research interests are in socio-political aspects of irrigated agriculture and ecology.

MAYHEW, ANNE. (Ph.D., University of Texas, Austin, 1966) Professor of Economics, University of Tennessee. Her research interests are on farm protest in the U.S., the history of American business cycles and the relation between culture and economic history.

NEALE, WALTER C. (Ph.D. University of London, 1953) Professor of Economics, University of Tennessee. His current research interests are change and development in rural India and problems of the western welfare state.

ORTIZ, SUTTI. (Ph.D., University of London, 1963) Associate Professor of Anthropology, Boston University. She has written on marketing systems, decision analysis and frontier expansion in Colombia's Amazonia.

SALISBURY, RICHARD. (Ph.D., Australia National University, 1957) Professor of Anthropology, McGill University. His research interests have ranged from economic organization of New Guinea highlanders to problems of rural development in

Canada. He has written a number of books in both subjects.

SMITH, CAROL. (Ph.D., Stanford, 1972) Associate Professor of Anthropology, Duke University. Her research interests have focused on marketing and regional analysis in Guatemala and Ecuador.

AUTHOR INDEX

SUBJECT INDEX